CORNISH STUDIES

Second Series

TWENTY

GW00671679

INSTITUTE OF CORNISH STUDIES

Cornish Studies (second series) exists to reflect current research conducted internationally in the inter-disciplinary field of Cornish Studies. It is edited by Professor Philip Payton, Director of the Institute of Cornish Studies at the University of Exeter, Cornwall Campus, and is published by University of Exeter Press. The opinions expressed in *Cornish Studies* are those of individual authors and are not necessarily those of the editor or publisher. The support of Cornwall Council is gratefully acknowledged.

CORNISH STUDIES

Second Series

TWENTY

Essays in Honour of
Bernard Deacon

edited by
Philip Payton

UNIVERSITY
of
EXETER
PRESS

First published in 2012 by
University of Exeter Press
Reed Hall, Streatham Drive
Exeter EX4 4QR
UK

www.exeterpress.co.uk

British Library Cataloguing in Publication Data
A catalogue record for this book is available from the British Library.

ISBN 978 0 85989 874 4

Typeset in Adobe Caslon
by Carnegie Book Production, Lancaster

Printed in Great Britain by Short Run Press Ltd, Exeter

MIX
Paper from
responsible sources
FSC® C014540

Contents

Notes on contributors

John Ault is a postgraduate student at the Institute of Cornish Studies, University of Exeter, where he is working on a PhD thesis on electoral behaviour in Cornwall, with particular reference to the Liberal Democrats. He is Chairman of the Electoral Reform Society.

Emma Bennett read English & History at the University of Exeter, Cornwall Campus, graduating in 2011. Her specialist study of the novels of Cornish-Australian children's author, Rosanne Hawke, formed the subject of her final-year interdisciplinary dissertation.

Allen Buckley holds an MPhil on Cornish adits (underground drainage tunnels) from the Camborne School of Mines, now part of the University of Exeter in Cornwall, and has worked underground at South Crofty as well being the mine's official historian. Recent books include *The Story of Mining in Cornwall* (2007) and *Dolcoath Mine: A History* (2010).

Merv Davey has recently been awarded a PhD for his thesis on folk tradition in Cornwall, completed at the Institute of Cornish Studies, University of Exeter, and is a well-known Cornish folk practitioner as well as writer and scholar. Among his several publications is (with Alison and Jowdy Davey) *Scoot Dances, Troyls, Furrys and Tea Treats: The Cornish Dance Tradition* (2009).

Gemma Goodman holds a PhD from the University of Warwick for her thesis on modern Cornish literature. She teaches undergraduates on the Academic Writing Programme at the University of Warwick, and has written widely on Cornish subjects. Her essay 'Seeing the Clay Country: The Novels of Jack Clemo' appeared in *Cornish Studies: Seventeen* in 2009.

Cheryl Hayden graduated from the University of Exeter in 2002 with an MA in Cornish Studies, and subsequently (2008) completed an MA in Creative Writing at the Queensland University of Technology. Following several years in journalism, she has completed two novels, one of which is shortly to be published in Cornwall.

Ronald M. James is State Historic Preservation Officer for the State of Nevada, United States of America, and Adjunct Assistant Professor at the University of Nevada, Reno, where he teaches folklore and history. He has written widely on the history and folklore of the Western mining frontier of North America, especially with reference to the Cornish. In 1981–82 he was the International Telephone and Telegraph Fellow in the Department of Irish Folklore at University College Dublin.

Neil Kennedy is a postgraduate student at the Institute of Cornish Studies, University of Exeter, where he is completing his PhD on the uses and applications of Cornish cultures. He speaks Cornish and is currently involved in work with the Cornish Language Partnership. He has taught in Breton-medium secondary schools, and was formerly lecturer in visual culture at University College Falmouth.

Alan M. Kent is a Lecturer in Literature at the Open University and Visiting Lecturer in Celtic Studies at the University of La Coruña in Galicia. He has written extensively on the literary and cultural history of Cornwall, and is also a prize-winning poet, novelist and dramatist. Recent books include *The Theatre of Cornwall: Space, Place, Performance* (2010) and *Celtic Cornwall: Nation, Tradition, Invention* (2012).

Sharon Lowenna is an independent scholar and Associate of the Institute of Cornish Studies. She holds an MA in Criticism and Theory from the University of Exeter, and has written on a diverse range of Cornish topics, including Daphne du Maurier and Henry Jenner. She was formerly Senior Lecturer in Cultural Studies at University College Falmouth.

Philip Payton is Professor of Cornish & Australian Studies at the University of Exeter, Cornwall Campus, where he is also Director of the Institute of Cornish Studies. Recent books include *John Betjeman and Cornwall: 'The Celebrated Cornish Nationalist'* (2010) and *Regional Australia and the Great War: 'The Boys from Old Kio'* (2012).

Garry Tregidga is Assistant Director of the Institute of Cornish Studies, University of Exeter, where he also directs the Cornish Audio Visual Archive and edits the magazine *Cornish Story*. He has written extensively on Cornish political history. Recent books include *Memory, Place and Identity: The Cultural Landscape of Cornwall* (2012) and (co-edited with Marion Gibson and Shelley Trower) *Myth, Mysticism and Celtic Nationalism* (2012).

Lesley Trotter is a freelance writer and archivist, and is currently a postgraduate student at the Institute of Cornish Studies, University of Exeter, where she is working on her PhD on nineteenth-century emigration from Cornwall as experienced by those wives who remained at home. She holds an MA in Cornish Studies from the Institute of Cornish Studies.

Introduction

As well as being the twentieth volume in the annual series *Cornish Studies*, this book is also distinguished by its status as *Essays in Honour of Bernard Deacon*. As the short article of appreciation that precedes this collection makes plain, Bernard Deacon has been one of the chief architects of what we have called 'New Cornish Studies', the comparative multidisciplinary and interdisciplinary movement that first stirred in the late 1980s and has developed apace thereafter, attempting to locate study of Cornwall and the Cornish within the mainstream of contemporary academic debate. Both learning from and contributing to such debate, New Cornish Studies has ranged across history, geography, social science, socio-linguistics, literature, cultural studies, and other fields, embracing new techniques and methods and theories. In this volume, each of the articles reveals to a greater or lesser degree the influence of New Cornish Studies, and all reflect the profound effect of Bernard Deacon himself upon those who engage in serious Cornish Studies today. Friends, colleagues, collaborators, students – undergraduate as well as postgraduate – and those who have read and profited from his many contributions, along with the many who have heard him speak at conferences and seminars, unite in acknowledging their debt to Bernard's work. This collection, then, includes contributions from a cross-section of such individuals, only a tiny proportion of those who have been influenced by Bernard but representative, perhaps, of the areas of inquiry that have benefitted from his interventions over the last couple of decades.

Following the editor's appreciation of Bernard Deacon, Alan M. Kent in his contribution acknowledges Deacon's central role in 'theorising' Cornish Studies in recent years. Kent makes an impassioned call for the New Cornish Studies that Deacon has so successfully pioneered elsewhere to penetrate what he (Kent) sees as the last bastion of reactionary resistance – medieval studies. Applauding the role of New Cornish Studies in stimulating innovative and exciting approaches to the early modern and later modern periods of Cornish history, he asks why it is that medievalists have been so reluctant to embrace the project, and urges them to take their cue from their more radical colleagues such as Sheila Delany and Bonnie Wheeler. Here Kent argues for the development of what he terms 'Celtic materialism' and, even more controversially, for the application of 'presentism' to our consideration of medieval Cornwall, the means of opening up that 'impenetrable' world to wider scrutiny.

Kent notes that one of those scholars of the early modern period influenced by New Cornish Studies is Cheryl Hayden, and in this volume Hayden returns to her specialist interest – the Prayer Book Rebellion of 1549 and its aftermath in Cornwall. She alights upon a hitherto little known late sixteenth-century document *The Present State of Cornwall and Devon, the two counties closest to Spain*, held in the Library of Congress' Rare Book and Special Collections division, and presents for the very first time a translation from the original Latin into modern English. The document was written by Tristram Winslade, the grandson of John Winslade, executed for his leading role in the 1549 Rebellion. Born in Devon *c*.1552, Tristram Winslade had begun his working life as a gentleman-servant in the household of Sir John Arundell of Lanherne, and was exposed to continuing anti-Reformation sentiment in Cornish society in the decades after the uprising. The document itself represents a secret 'plan', scoped by Winslade, which envisaged a Spanish invasion launched upon the death of Elizabeth, designed to restore England (and Cornwall) to Roman Catholicism. As Hayden points out, in the end Winslade's scheme was foiled by the simple fact that Elizabeth outlived the Spanish King. Yet it is for us an extraordinary insight into the state of Cornish (and Devon) affairs – and incidentally those of Wales, with which Cornwall is compared in Winslade's plan – some half a century after the traumatic upheaval of the Prayer Book Rebellion.

Sharon Lowenna, in her contribution, shifts the focus to the early eighteenth century, revisiting again those Cornish-language collectors, William Gwavas of Mount's Bay and Thomas Tonkin of Trevaunance, but this time viewing them through a Foucauldian prism, examining their social and ideological positionings by asking what *kinds* of texts they chose to address and which *specific* texts they selected for transcription of publication. This is exactly the type of materialist analysis advocated by Kent for the earlier medieval period, and this approach – with its emphasis on the significance of 'circumstantial context' – allows Lowenna to treat the well-worn narratives of the corpus of the Cornish language with a healthy scepticism. She does so with penetrating skill, offering a range of new insights and possibilities. But as she wisely concludes, in an observation that summarises the spirit of her inquiry but also stands as a broader characterisation of New Cornish Studies: 'No one analysis has the final word, no study should be regarded as unchallengeable. Scholarship is a process and not an achieved end, and questioning received wisdom is one of the ways in which scholarship progresses.'

A similarly critical edge, again born of New Cornish Studies, is observable in Neil Kennedy's article on 'Cornish Linguistic Landscape', in which he considers the current status of the Cornish language in relation to Cornwall Council's signage and other language policies. Employing the concept of 'linguistic landscape', developed with respect to territories where a 'minority' or 'regional' (subaltern) language co-exists with a 'majority' or 'national' (prevalent) language, Kennedy notes that if the subaltern language is clearly visible in public, private and commercial settings, then it is more likely to be taken seriously and to acquire an enhanced status. Applying this to Cornwall, he argues that the newly visible profile of the Cornish language may already be producing effects, with people in Cornwall more readily identifying with the language as they encounter it routinely in the various spheres of daily life. Yet this visibility is in itself contentious, as Kennedy acknowledges, linked often to tourism and heritage agendas that may be seen as controversial, and with signage and other policies dominated by the 'medievalist' assumptions of the language-revivalists who control the process. As Kennedy rightly observes, Bernard Deacon – 'a committed Cornish speaker' – is among those with serious reservations about this process. As Deacon has remarked, 'there was no widespread debate about the purpose of signage policies before it was hijacked by the revivalists'. The choice and deployment of particular linguistic forms – essentially, which Cornish? – is ideologically driven and inherently controversial, an indication that the 'linguistic landscape' of Cornwall is more profoundly complex than the casual observer might ever imagine. Kennedy himself concludes with wise words, conceding that signage work is just too important to be framed narrowly, requiring honest and careful reflection from all those who are involved in the process.

In similar vein, Merv Davey's discussion of 'speech communities' focuses on two competing interpretations of Cornish folk tradition and the implications of this competition for contemporary Cornish identity. 'Speech communities' here refers to groups of people who share common 'understandings' and have a shared 'language' which reinforces these understandings. The two competing 'speech communities' that Davey identifies are the Celto-Cornish movement (which sees folk tradition as integral to Cornwall's Celtic identity) and the British/English folk tradition, which sees Cornish tradition as merely part of a wider English tradition. Davey argues that the Celto-Cornish movement's engagement with folk song and dance was well established before the arrival of the English Folk Revival in the 1960s and 1970s. The movement sought to emphasize Cornwall's Celticity by establishing a folk tradition distinct from that of England and inviting comparison with those of Brittany, Wales and the other Celtic countries. The English Folk Revival, by contrast, arrived with preconceived ideas of the 'authentic' and the 'appropriate', finding itself at odds with the pre-existing Celto-Cornish movement and precipitating a power struggle of sorts. Although the more ideologically powerful of the two competing 'speech communities', with a vast reservoir of 'authority' upon which to draw, the English Folk Revivalists may yet be eclipsed – Davey argues – by the consolidating presence of the Celto-Cornish movement which refuses to accept uncritically the 'common sense' approach of its opponents. In that way, Cornwall has become something of a battleground for competing folk performance, a contest with wider implications for how contemporary Cornish identity is negotiated and understood.

From another perspective, folk tradition has also become increasingly important in the consideration of modern Cornwall. Until recently the preserve of antiquarian interest, which rarely considered the comparative context, Cornish folklore studies have only of late established themselves firmly within the realms of academic debate – continuing to note the richness and distinctiveness of Cornish tradition but placing it clearly within its wider European setting. Ronald M. James has been a leading proponent of this work. In his article in this collection he focuses on the widely-distributed story, common in Europe but also attested in Cornish folklore collections, which dwells on the fate of two young lovers who become separated. The man dies but his beloved does not receive the news – until she is visited by a night-time spectre who invites her to join him on his horse. Together, they gallop over the landscape but, as morning breaks, the young woman realises that she is riding with the spectral corpse of her lover. In most variants of the tale, she manages to escape, although sometimes dies shortly after. James investigates the origins of this story, moving on to William Bottrell's first volume of Cornish folklore, published in 1870, which has the most developed Cornish form of the tale – 'Nancy Trenoweth, The Fair Daughter of the Miller of Alsia'. He sets the story it in its international context and considers other Cornish variants, such as that recorded by Hunt, and Irish cognates. He concludes that, far from being a pale imitation of material from elsewhere, the Cornish versions point to a 'fully developed, thriving oral tradition [in] … Cornwall', one which we are only now beginning to appreciate and understand, and which requires extensive further research if its full complexity and significance is to be grasped and celebrated.

The 'figure in the landscape' features in a different sense in Gemma Goodman's discussion of rural geographies and literature in Cornwall. Comparing the impact of New Cornish Studies to the apparently near universal Cornish solidarity in confronting the (now defeated) 'pasty tax', she singles out Bernard Deacon's seminal call for practitioners within the field to take 'greater account of the internal diversity of the geography of Cornishness', together with his insistence that 'in order to explain aspects of historical and contemporary Cornwall, we have to be aware of processes simultaneously operating at a number of different scales'. In responding to

Deacon's cue, Goodman draws upon the methodology of Feminist Geography to inform her discussion of difference, nuance and complexity within Cornwall. She selects three literary texts which allow analysis of the figure in the landscape – Salome Hocking's *Norah Lang* (1886), Emma Smith's *A Cornish Waif's Story* (1954), and Charles Lee's *Cynthia in the West* (1900) – and show how regimes of gender and class collide and metamorphose in a dynamic rural context, where there are 'complementary and overlapping' as well as competing 'Cornwalls' in which space is socially constructed and inhabited.

This discussion of different 'Cornwalls' is given an international dimension in Emma Bennett's article on Cornish-Australian identity and the novels of Rosanne Hawke, the noted author of children's books in Australia. As Bennett observes, Rosanne Hawke has consciously adopted the hybrid identity 'Cornish-Australian', allowing her to explore her personal identity in the context of emigration from Cornwall and the establishment of Cornish copper-mining communities in South Australia in the nineteenth century. An advocate of 'multicultural' Australia, Rosanne Hawke also argues that it is vitally important for others – especially young people – to make sense of their identities by understanding their own ethnic and cultural origins. Such an understanding, insists Hawke, brings self-knowledge and well-being as well as tolerance of others whose backgrounds may be different. These beliefs, as Emma Bennett makes plain, underpin Rosanne Hawke's work. She discusses several key novels – *Zenna Dare* (2002), *Across the Creek* (2004), *Wolfchild* (2003), *The Last Virgin in Year Ten* (2006), *Sailmaker* (2002) – each of which reveal Hawke's motivations as well as employing a wealth of Cornish motifs to give substance to her characters and plots. As Bennett concludes, Rosanne Hawke in her novels demonstrates a serious use of children's literature for an exploration of Cornish identity through Australian eyes. But, equally important, not least for the children for whom they are intended, they are good reads: 'most of all, her books deliver stories'.

The general theme of emigration is also addressed by Lesley Trotter who, in responding to calls from Bernard Deacon for a more quantitative approach to the study of the phenomenon, deals with the hitherto neglected issue of 'Husband Abroad' – the impact on the sending communities in Cornwall of widespread male emigration. As Trotter remarks, many Cornish husbands and wives often spent years apart, in effect living separate lives in an era of uncertain communications and difficult long-distance journeys. In her article in this volume, she attempts to discover the scale of spousal separation associated with emigration, to try to quantify its incidence and distribution across Cornwall. Census Enumerators Books (CEBs) are the primary source for this investigation, and Trotter discusses their strengths and weaknesses before analysing their data to produce comparative tables for census years from 1841 to 1891. Her findings are revealing. Despite emigration being a Cornwall-wide phenomenon, the non-mining areas – especially in East Cornwall – hardly feature in the elucidation of spousal separation. Perhaps this represents the tendencies for whole families to emigrate together from such districts, in contrast to the typical roving miner who left his family at home, but maybe the CEBs do not tell the whole story. Trotter suspects that the numbers of husbands specifically recorded as being abroad may be only a fraction of the true numbers, a suspicion given substance by a detailed examination of Gwennap parish. At the 1871 census 350 Gwennap men were away but only 57 of these were specifically recorded as being abroad. But despite such limitations, the data, although underrepresenting the scale of spousal separation, reveals the high correlation between such separation and the geographical distribution of the Cornish mining industry – even to the extent of mirroring Bernard Deacon's historical geography of Cornish mining, with the industry's growing concentration over time in the Camborne-Illogan district.

The characteristics of the Cornish mining industry are also the concern of Allen Buckley. He notes that, despite the literature devoted to major and usually fatal accidents in Cornish mines (of which studies Cyril Noall's *Cornish Mine Disasters* [1989] is the most significant), there has been no significant analysis of the whole range of accidental injuries suffered by Cornish miners. Instead, our understanding of Cornish mine accidents has been coloured by the portrayal of dramatic and catastrophic events, presenting a distorted picture of the hazards and dangers encountered underground. In his article, therefore, Allen Buckley offers a corrective, and presents a detailed comparative account of accidents of all types sustained at two Cornish mines – South Crofty and Geevor – in the period 1900 to 1950. His analysis indicates not only the range of injuries but also the variety of underground environments – shafts, stopes, winzes and so on – where they might be sustained and the actual causes, from rock falls to dynamite explosions. Perhaps surprisingly, Buckley discovers that a relatively high proportion of accidents were not serious, with large numbers of trapped fingers, bruised ribs, crushed toes, and various cuts and grazes. Also of note is the high number of teenagers working underground in the period 1900 to 1950, and the higher than average propensity for them to sustain injury. Yet there were relatively few serious accidents, and by starting young in the mines an individual would 'pick it up' as he went along, the lack of formal health and safety training compensated for by learning 'on the job' under the watchful eyes of shiftbosses and mine captains.

The first half of the twentieth century is also the focus of Garry Tregidga and John Ault, who in twin articles investigate the distinctive qualities of Cornish politics – especially Liberalism – in that period. Garry Tregidga is concerned principally with the career of Isaac Foot, who went on to become Minister of Mines in the National Government in 1931–32 and a Privy Councillor in 1937, his sensational by-election victory as an Independent Liberal in Bodmin in the March 1922 by-election having caught UK-wide attention. But despite this significant place in British politics, argues Tregidga, it is important to consider Isaac Foot in his specifically Cornish context. Here Foot is a paradoxical figure – a Plymothian who was to fare disastrously when he stood in a by-election in Plymouth Sutton in 1919, and yet who was able to forge a close relationship with Cornish Nonconformity and became entwined in a Cornish identity that he was able to project as a personal political asset. His reputation as a committed Methodist, his skill as an orator, and the support lent by Arthur Quiller-Couch, all played well with his Cornish audiences, especially in the chapels of the Liskeard and Callington districts where he preached regularly. Nonetheless, his opponents made much of the fact that he was not Cornish-born (although his wife was of Cornish parentage), and when he stood in Bodmin in the 1910 general election he was defeated by just forty-one votes – by the Unionist candidate, Sir Reginald Pole-Carew, local landowner and self-proclaimed Cornishman. But Foot's near miss had long-term consequences. He had established his credibility in Cornwall, and was recognised as a serious contender by opponents and supporters alike. Eventually, he assumed the leadership of Cornish Liberalism, his experiences in 1910 laying the ground work for the events of the inter-war period – including the victory at the Bodmin by-election in 1922.

John Ault, in his article, considers the Cornish by-elections of the inter-war period, assessing to what extent they were 'microcosms of rebellion' – or at least expressions of Cornish independence during what, to early twenty-first-century eyes, appears a period of bewildering political complexity. He begins with Isaac Foot's famous victory as an Independent Liberal in Bodmin in 1922, in which the electorate rejected the Lloyd George Coaltiton. As before, Foot won the public support of Sir Arthur Quiller-Couch but, deploying his radical credentials and Cornish sympathies, he was also able to appeal to the Labour Party locally. Thereafter, in the United Kingdom as a whole, there was a rapid switch of support from the Liberals to the Labour Party – the so-called 'age of alignment' – but Cornwall told a different story. In the 1928 by-election in St Ives, Hilda Runciman won the seat for the Liberals, holding it for her husband Walter (then still MP for Swansea) until he could take it in his own right. A few years later, in 1932, Sir Richard Acland was chosen to represent the Liberals in North Cornwall, and despite the existence of the National Government the Conservatives decided to put up an opponent. Yet by distancing himself from the National Government, Acland proved able to win support from across the political spectrum, from disaffected Tories to enthusiastic socialists, duly topping the poll. Subsequently, in the St Ives by-election of 1937 (which Isaac Foot narrowly failed to win) and in the 1939 North Cornwall by-election (which the electorate used as an opportunity to voice its hostility to Chamberlain's appeasement policy), Cornish voters continued to exhibit the 'rebellious' behaviour that they often allowed themselves, especially in the turbulent inter-war period.

Philip Payton,
Director, Institute of Cornish Studies,
University of Exeter, Cornwall Campus

I

Bernard Deacon

Philip Payton

The publication of the twentieth volume in any annual series is a cause for celebration and reflection. But the appearance of *Cornish Studies: Twenty* in 2012 in the wake of Dr Bernard Deacon's recent retirement from the Institute of Cornish Studies provides a timely opportunity to consider his ground-breaking contributions to the field of Cornish Studies over many years. As noted in the Introduction, this book contains articles by individuals who in one way or another have been influenced by Bernard Deacon – as colleague, collaborator, student, friend, or admirer of his work. It also reveals, in various ways, the influence that Bernard has had upon Cornish Studies itself, especially as expressed through the pages of this and earlier volumes in the series.

Born in Launceston (or Lanson, as he would have it) in 1949, Bernard Deacon hailed from a North Cornwall family – both parents came from villages in the locality, his father a shop worker before the Second World War, his mother in service as a domestic. In 1952 the Deacon family moved to Liskeard, where Bernard and his two younger brothers grew up. He attended the local Grammar School – the first of his family to do so – and achieved another family 'first' when he went to university. He graduated from the University of Exeter with a BA (Hons) in Economic History in 1970, followed swiftly by an MA in Modern Social History from Lancaster in 1971. As Bernard admits, he was part of the 1960s socially mobile working class whose exposure to higher education had a radicalising effect. Turning 'sharply leftwards', as he later explained it, Bernard found himself building upon and modifying his family's traditional Liberal-Methodist political roots. His views were also influenced by his experiences in the world of work, on the shop-floor of a factory and at the petrol pumps, the latter in Liverpool where he encountered Ulster Loyalism for the first time.

Acquiring a PGCE in the Midlands, Bernard then drifted (as he describes

it) to London, surviving for a time as a teacher in a boys' comprehensive
school in Wandsworth before landing the post of Lecturer in History at
Carshalton College of Further Education. But the pull of Cornwall was too
strong. Tiring of suburban life and anxious to join the Cornish movement, he
returned home in 1976, working part-time in further education and teaching
liberal studies and communication skills to welders, motor mechanics and
other vocational students – as he insists, he was not unlike the character
Wilt in Tom Sharpe's satirical novels! Bernard became heavily involved in
Mebyon Kernow in the late 1970s, and taught himself Cornish. He was
part of the group that in 1978–82 produced *An Weryn*, a radical nationalist
small magazine, and in the early 1980s organised a co-operative bookshop
in Redruth. He managed the shop for a time, before it went under. By now
living in the area, Bernard became a Redruth Town Councillor in the late
1980s.

In Bernard began working for the Open University in 1983, teaching social
science courses (general and political studies) and later history. He also began
teaching local history courses for the Workers' Educational Association and
for the University of Exeter's then Extra-Mural Department in Truro, which
rekindled his enthusiasm for Cornwall's past. His commitment to Cornwall's
present and future was evidenced in his campaigning against the then
County Council's infamous Structure Plan, which blithely pinned its hopes
on population-led economic growth, leading to massive in-migration and the
enduring high house price/low wage economy nexus that was to characterise
Cornwall for subsequent decades. His opposition to the Structure Plan
culminated in the widely acclaimed and influential *Cornwall at the Crossroads*,
co-written with Andrew George and Ronald Perry and published in 1988
by the Cornish Social and Economic Research Group (CoSERG), of which
Bernard was a founder member.

In the early 1990s Bernard married Penny, and (among many other things)
he taught their daughter Merryn to speak Cornish. Following her father's
upwardly mobile trajectory, Merryn would later go on to study at Oxford,
and despite his anti-elitist views Bernard would admit to a sneaking pride
in the family narrative 'of leaving elementary school at 14 to Oxford in two
generations' – a sentiment of which fellow Cornish scholar A. L. Rowse
would have heartily approved! By now a familiar and established figure in
the Cornish academic community, in 1997 Bernard joined the permanent
staff of the University of Exeter's Department of Lifelong Learning (as
the Extra Mural Department had eventually become). From 2001 he was
shared jointly on a 50/50 basis between Lifelong Learning and the Institute
of Cornish Studies, with which he had had links since its foundation in
the early 1970s, and in 2004 moved full-time to the Institute. As Director
of the Institute's MA in Cornish Studies, Bernard pioneered one of the

earliest on-line flexible distance-learning programmes at the University of Exeter, with students drawn from across the UK, America and Australia. Subsequently, with the development of the University of Exeter's Cornwall Campus at Tremough, he helped design undergraduate programmes in the humanities and social sciences, and contributed Cornish Studies modules to a variety of undergraduate courses. In 2010 he was appointed Director of Education (Cornwall) for History, a post he held until his retirement in September 2011.

Since his retirement, Bernard has been Honorary University Fellow at the Institute of Cornish Studies, and remains as active as ever – even to the extent of being spotted occasionally cycling around the lanes in the vicinity of Redruth, trying to avoid the excessive traffic. He still speaks (Modern) Cornish to his daughter Merryn but, having represented the Institute on the Cornish Language Partnership and helped to broker the Single Written Form of the language, he now counts himself thoroughly disillusioned with the Cornish language revival and has no interest at all in revived medieval Cornish (in its several competing forms). He is a trustee of the Royal Cornwall Museum in Truro, where he is also Honorary Courtney Librarian (in succession to Professor Charles Thomas), building on the close links developed between the Institute and the Museum when in 2007 Bernard led a successful bid to the Arts & Humanities Research Council for funding to develop a Knowledge Transfer project between the two institutions. He continues to write, with several completed articles already in the publication pipeline, and is working on projects as varied as a book on *Cornish Surnames* and a volume designed to critique Cornwall Council's latest version of the population-led growth strategy.

In his continuing work, Bernard draws upon more than three decades of research in Cornish Studies. His PhD thesis, 'The Reformulation of Territorial Identity: Cornwall in the Late Eighteenth and Nineteenth Centuries', completed at the Open University in 2001, reflects the mature consideration of material collected and perused over many years, benefiting from the accumulated wisdom and telling insights that often elude the more junior doctoral candidate at the beginning of his or her career. As his Bibliography (pp. 262–66) indicates, Bernard Deacon has been publishing since the early 1980s, and there have been few years since when something of his has not appeared in an academic journal or other scholarly volume. Among several books, his *Cornwall: A Concise History* – published by University of Wales Press in 2007 – stands out as a work of immense learning, a significant contribution to our understanding of Cornish history that brings together in grand synthesis all the fruits of the New Cornish Studies of which he has been so passionate an advocate and practitioner.

Like other devotees of New Cornish Studies, Bernard has readily admitted the norms and assumptions that have driven the project, his reflexive attitude informing the development of the theoretical perspectives that he has consistently brought to bear. Again, particular contributions stand out – each of them in editions of the annual series *Cornish Studies*, which has emerged over the years as the principal forum for the discussion of such ideas. 'Proto-industrialization and Potatoes: a revised narrative for nineteenth-century Cornwall', which appeared in 1997, was one of the first of such contributions and has heavily influenced the way in which we now routinely imagine Cornish history in that period. Similarly influential have been 'In Search of the Missing "Turn": the spatial dimension and Cornish Studies' (2000), 'Cornish Studies: new discipline or rhetorical space?' (2002), and 'From "Cornish Studies" to "Critical Cornish Studies": reflections on methodology' (2005). Together with various other milestone contributions from Bernard's pen, these articles represent major innovations in the way in which we think about, write and teach Cornish Studies today.

To Bernard Deacon's immense scholarly achievement should be added his personal qualities as friend and colleague. Sometimes misunderstood as a tendency not to suffer fools gladly, his wry wit and occasionally scathing observations unfailingly drill to the core of complex issues, encouraging others to pursue rigour in their own work and spotting flaws in what might at first appear sound analyses. His peers have benefited enormously from his demands for high standards, as have his undergraduate and postgraduate students. An amusing and insightful lecturer, Bernard has won many admiring followers, his courses invariably among the most popular on offer, his teaching style clear, crisp and engaging. As personal tutor, he has taken immense efforts to help students develop their potential and to grow intellectually. Essays, dissertations and other work have been marked promptly with painstaking care, and, once students have mastered the not inconsiderable task of deciphering Bernard's handwriting, his comments have always proved invaluable.

In this volume, we salute Bernard Deacon and his incomparable contribution to Cornish Studies. But even as we say farewell, it is gratifying and comforting for us to acknowledge that his work continues unabated – as Honorary University Fellow at the Institute of Cornish Studies, in the Royal Cornwall Museum, and in Cornish life generally where his sharp eye and penetrating questioning will continue to keep Cornwall's planners and policymakers on their toes. Long may he continue to work for the cause of Cornwall.

2

Mending the gap in the Medieval, Modern and Post-modern in New Cornish Studies:

'Celtic' materialism and the potential of presentism

Alan M. Kent

Introduction: Theorising Deacon

Of Bernard Deacon's considerable contribution to New Cornish Studies, it is his development of 'theory' which may well be the most lasting.[1] Although, before Deacon, a number of observers were attempting to map Cornish culture in a theorised way, comparing Cornwall to other Celtic territories,[2] it is Deacon's work which has helped to define and shape the field. Previously, Cornish Studies had been relatively unconcerned with aspects of 'cultural theory'. But Deacon was part of a new generation of Cornish scholars anxious to engage with wider academic debates. Often controversial and usually aiming to stimulate debate about the direction and purpose of Cornish Studies, Deacon's work thus fulfilled a vital function within Cornish Studies.[3] Broadly sociological, but rooted in social and economic history, his contributions have at times also bordered on the stoical and ethical (perhaps the next important stage of fully determining 'Cornish identity' along philosophical lines).[4] In many articles in the series *Cornish Studies*, Deacon has articulated an awareness of the medieval, the modern and the post-modern, which in the course of this essay we shall re-visit.

Refreshingly, Deacon's vision has never been parochial or narrow but reflects wider trends in contemporary scholarship – particularly within social science, but also within language, socio-linguistics, emigration and transnational studies, and cultural studies.[5] Such an imagining of theory in its widest sense has culminated in a range of important publications; among them, *Mebyon Kernow and Cornish Nationalism* (2003) (with Dick Cole and Garry Tregidga), *The Cornish Family: The Roots of our Future* (2004) (with Sharron Schwartz and David Holman), and his balanced yet provocative *Cornwall: A Concise History* (2007).[6] The point about these works is that all of them have, in some way, been influenced by Deacon's development of 'theory', which he has applied in their pages.

Mending the gap

One core element of this 'theory' that Deacon has articulated on a number of occasions is both the disparity and the relationship between the modern and post-modern in Cornish Studies; but also, perhaps more tellingly, the gap that exists between these two areas and the medieval. This is a view also recently expressed by Philip Payton in the 'Introduction' to *Cornish Studies: Nineteen*. Payton argues that one of the achievements of New Cornish Studies has been the shedding of 'antiquarian local history', although paradoxically he acknowledges its importance of the origins of the field. He also argues that Cornish Studies – of the kind advocated by Deacon – places Cornwall and the Cornish 'alongside that of other territories, nations and regions'. Most importantly, however, he notes the fact that while successfully recruiting historians and scholars from other disciplines, New Cornish Studies has 'generally failed to draw historians from the medieval period'.[7] Taking historians as meaning those from the economic, political and cultural fields, then this is an interesting interstice between what is hoped for and the reality on the ground.

This is a point I made in my review of *Cornish Studies: Nineteen* in *An Baner Kernewek*, where I noted that '[the medieval period] is a loaded field in which it is hard to break down monolithic and medievalist perspectives'.[8] Tellingly, Payton argues that this is changing, and certainly R. E. Stanfield's re-assessment of the career of Avery Cornburgh (d.1487) does offer a new perspective on the social politics of that period.[9] And yet, within the second series of *Cornish Studies*, relatively few articles have dealt directly with the medieval era. Out of nineteen editions, each containing an average of (say) twelve articles, making a total of some 228 articles over nineteen years, only 12 of these have fully focused on medieval Cornwall. Many of those directly dealing with the medieval period either focus on Cornish theatre or on other Cornish-language texts,[10] already 'traditional fare' for twentieth-century 'revivalist' Cornish Studies. However, in 2002 Allen Buckley offered (as we shall see below) a more reflexive consideration of the processes of writing medieval history.[11]

As Payton realises, there is a dichotomy within the field that needs addressing. It is one I have also considered in my own studies of the medieval period,[12] and which can sometimes prove controversial.[13] A recent high-profile review of my own work argued that my analysis of the medieval was too political. Partly, this is the metropolitan centre's view of the subaltern voice from Cornwall, but it is also related to the limitations of some medievalists. The achievement of New Cornish Studies over the last twenty years has radically altered the face of scholarship about Cornwall. But not only that: it has given the matter of Cornwall a new kind of credibility within the academy and in the 'centre', and has proved that scholars from a wide range of disciplines can contribute to a body of knowledge that deconstructs received wisdom and re-examines familiar subject-matter from different perspectives. Yet, in viewing work on medieval Cornwall, Payton has identified a nascent gap between what is desired and the reality of recent scholarship. Crucially, medieval scholars have generally failed to re-appraise their field in line with the innovative approaches to the modern period adopted by writers such as Perry and Tregidga,[14] or to the post-modern, such as that undertaken by Deacon and Howlett.[15] Indeed, it is clear that New Cornish Studies has only reached back as far as the early modern period (for example, in the work of Stoyle and Hayden[16]) and has on the whole failed to bring on board scholarship (beyond the Cornish language and medieval theatre) about the medieval period.

The medieval in Cornish Studies

If there is little current work on the medieval period within Cornish Studies, then perhaps we need to consider where it was completed in the past. Many publications during the nineteenth century dealt with medieval Cornwall.[17] These were generally completed in the field of antiquarian studies, but with a growing sense of scholarship and historical accuracy. Obviously archaeological investigations were also being completed into the medieval material past, alongside textual and historical inquiry. Much of this was being written up in articles for the learned publications of the period, notably the *Journal of the Royal Institution of Cornwall* (a publication which in the early twenty-first century still reflects its original medievalist agenda),[18] and in the early twentieth century in *Old Cornwall: The Journal of the Federation of the Old Cornwall Societies*.[19]

There is not the space here to examine all of the texts published. But some of the more influential works include Thomas Taylor's *The Celtic*

Christianity of Cornwall (1916), L. E. Elliot-Binns' *Medieval Cornwall* (1955) and John Hatcher's *Rural Economy and Society in the Duchy of Cornwall 1300–1500* (1970).[20] Some works on historical documentation have also been significant: P. L. Hull's *The Caption of Seisin of the Duchy of Cornwall, 1337* springs to mind here.[21] Charles Henderson and A. L. Rowse were significant commentators on the period in various publications (although Rowse was more comfortable writing about the Tudor period).[22] Extensive research into the medieval centuries has also been conducted by James Whetter, a scholar, who – as leader of the Cornish Nationalist Party – certainly shows political commitment.[23] Whetter's work, unlike that of some other medieval historians, has kept a firm eye on the wider implications for Cornish culture and identity.

It was in the first series of *Cornish Studies* (in its then guise as the in-house journal of the Institute of Cornish Studies), however, that much scholarship on the medieval period was completed. Under the visionary editorship of Charles Thomas, a number of articles explored this period of history in new and dynamic ways.[24] Yet, with the exception of one or two contributions,[25] the focus remained somewhat narrow.[26] Although such micro-studies in the long term might contribute to macro-arguments about cultural, economic and political history, they generally lacked the 'political commitment' characteristic of later Cornish Studies and – despite Thomas' lead in placing the field within an academic wider environment – did not engage with 'theory'.[27] Indeed, it was often ignored or sidelined.

More recently, the political commitment of observers such as John Angarrack and Jim Pengelly has prompted them to revisit medieval Cornwall, reviewing Stannary Law, the Duchy of Cornwall, and the 'assimilationist' project of the English nation-state.[28] At once both radical and populist, the observations of Angarrack in particular have fired renewed interest in the period. Community histories have also proved fruitful areas of research, often showing remarkable continuities up to the present day, and uncovering much micro knowledge while also contributing to a wider agenda of understanding Cornish identity.[29] So too has continuing work in the 'tradition' of language, literature and theatre studies.[30] The medieval period has also been re-evaluated by more recent observers – among them Payton, Deacon, Kent, and Peters – locating this age within a wider consideration of Cornish history, and demonstrating a political commitment lacking in earlier generations of writers.[31] Yet there is also a number of individual scholars and writers who, although writing consistently on Cornish matter and who are part of mainstream academia, seem distant from the general project of New Cornish Studies. Among the respected names we might include here are Nicholas Orme, Oliver J. Padel, Joanna Mattingly and Ian Arthurson.[32] Very often of course, as in the writing of all histories, it is the key moments in

Cornish history – for example, the events of 1497 and 1549 – which become touchstones as to how particular scholarship perceives medieval and Tudor Cornwall. There is, as one might expect, a wide range of perceived notions about these culturally symbolic dates, ranging from conceptualisation of the 'Anglo-Cornish wars' to perfunctory discussion of a 'minor rebellion in the West Country'.[33] As Walter Benjamin thoughtfully observes in his essay 'Theses on the Philosophy of History', 'who ever has emerged victorious participates to this day in the triumphal procession in which the present rulers step over those who are lying prostrate'.[34]

By necessity, the above survey has had to be brief but it does bring us to Allen Buckley's 2002 article. Buckley – a mining historian who has written prolifically on the early industry in Cornwall[35] – argues that one problem with the writing of medieval history is that it is 'sufficiently remote from us for it to have acquired a rose-coloured and romantic aspect', and that this 'affords people and society of that time the appearance of being fundamentally different from us and from out society'.[36] While true in some respects, some observers on medieval history would disagree with this conceptualisation. Ackroyd, for example, writing about English history, argues that human society in the medieval age had the very same concerns as our own, and that fundamentally the same processes occured.[37] We might also argue that this notion of 'remoteness' and 'difference' actually helps sustain the myth of medieval scholarship – that somehow those who deal with the medieval are 'more academic' and 'more learned' because they deal with this 'difference'.

Buckley also notes the problems of defining where and when the medieval period begins and ends, and the difficulties caused by the spread of documentation and texts in a wide variety of repositories, often outside of Cornwall.[38] He provides a survey of the prominent observers and scholars, similar to that given above, but also notes that within this body of scholarship there is 'not merely heterogeneity in subject matter, for there are also wide differences in approach and aims'.[39] We must concur with this, and it may be this lack of heterogeneity in approach that is restricting the full incorporation of the medieval into present Cornish scholarship. Perceptively, Buckley also observes that recent better cataloguing of resources (at for example, the Cornish Records Office) should open up the field, as will the increasing digitisation of material.[40]

Interestingly, Buckley cites Harold Fox and Oliver Padel's book on *The Cornish Lands of the Arundells of Lanherne, Fourteenth to Seventeenth Centuries* as an example of where astute medieval scholarship can benefit the wider understanding of Cornish history.[41] He likewise singles out Maryanne Kowaleski's article 'The Expansion of the South-Western Fisheries in Late Medieval England' and Ronald Waldron's essay in the *Journal of the Royal Institution of Cornwall* on the scholar and translator John Trevisa as representative examples of contemporary medieval scholarship.[42] While these are all valid investigations, Buckley is forced to conclude that future research 'lies in more cross-analysis, linking the often overly specialized, discrete studies with other topics and themes'.[43] Likewise, using examples from the work of Joanna Mattingly, he rightly argues for more 'holistic' work,[44] drawing once more on the ideas of Bernard Deacon.[45] According to Buckley, Deacon is arguing 'the need for comparative work to set Cornish Studies into a European, Celtic and Anglo-Cornish context', using his examination of the influx of Bretons into Cornwall in the late medieval period as his example.[46]

These opinions are, of course, entirely reasonable and, as we shall see, the kind of cross-analysis and holistic work argued for by Buckley – and the wider European, Celtic and Anglo-Cornish context proposed by Deacon – could be integrated, as argued below, into a wider 'Celtic' Materialist perspective or even incorporated into the boundaries of Presentist discourse. Before discussing this, however, we may wish to examine the wider and weighty problem of medieval paradigms as touched upon by both Buckley and Deacon.

How do you solve a problem like the medieval?

In much the same way that the fields of English Literature or Cornish Studies have a history, so too does Medieval Studies. The term 'Medieval Studies' was initially adopted by scholars in the opening decades of the twentieth century. G. G. Coulton's *Ten Medieval Studies* (1906) was one of the first texts to introduce a greater interdisciplinary aspect to the already established historical approach.[47] The usual foci for medievalists was upon disciplines such as archaeology, art history, architecture, history, literature and linguistics. We should note these subject areas because, even today, they remain the core base of medieval scholars. Although thanks to mass media, archaeology and art history have become more populist,[48] medieval literature and linguistics still remain the concern of the so-called 'expert'.[49] In Britain much of the thrust towards this interdisciplinary approach came from centres established in the University of Leeds (1967) and the University of York (1968) (York itself, of course, a centre of 'medieval life' and Mystery play drama). A rise of new institutes has followed in more recent years – among them, at the University of Bristol (1994) and also Bangor University (2005). Rarely though do Medieval Studies courses crop up in 'newer' universities, which might certainly be a problem for Cornwall, with one of the newest university set-ups in the United Kingdom. Celtic Studies (in its traditional form – with a focus on linguistics, textual study and folklore) is often also part of this interdisciplinary structure. This form of Celtic Studies has been critiqued as outmoded by a number of observers,[50] and yet the field still persists in 'less progressive' departments, conferences and journals.[51] Likewise, those coming to Medieval Studies from the more traditional Anglo-American literary focus would be likely to know of events such as the International Congress on Medieval Studies held at Kalamazoo, Michigan, in the USA, and the International Congress at the University of Leeds.[52] There is also a number of journals dedicated to reviewing and developing Medieval Studies.[53]

Against this background, we should consider where Cornish Medieval Studies fits into this wider activity. Although Buckley notes that research on medieval Cornwall is indeed being undertaken, it is generally completed outside of the forum of New Cornish Studies. Perhaps it is the very concept of 'New' that alienates such scholars, who might imagine that the field is only the concern of the modern and post-modern, and yet this is clearly not the case. One trend is clear: New Cornish Studies necessarily has a 'political commitment'. This rests upon changes apparent elsewhere in these islands, with the deconstruction of 'Britishness' and the recognition of Cornwall as a distinct component of the United Kingdom.[54] Yet it would appear that many of those medieval scholars notionally working in 'Cornish Studies' are sceptical about the political dimension of the project.[55] It is also implied by some medievalists that the medieval world is somehow a-political, and ought to be treated as such. To this observer at least, this seems wrong-headed, since there will always be a political dimension to project when a small, colonised territory is 'writing back' to the centre.[56] Indeed, without this agenda, Cornish Studies would surely lapse back into mere local history.

A second factor may be at work. There is the possibility of one up-man ship in Medieval Studies. It might be suggested that the scholarship here demands particular skills (the translation of impenetrable texts [perhaps in Latin, Cornish or Middle English], the dealing with difficult manuscripts, saints' lives and cults, and the cultural context of the time period), and thus requires particular scholars to undertake this difficult work. In this sense, medievalists may believe that they are offering 'true' and especially significant scholarship, valuable and insightful above and beyond that being offered by academics in modern and post-modern fields. Perhaps these are viewed by some medievalists as lightweight or even 'inauthentic'. There is certainly a perception that the medieval is necessarily outside the comprehension of scholars of later periods, a well-established myth within subjects such as Medieval History or Medieval English Literature and also particularly noticeable in mainstream and traditional Celtic Studies.[57] Cornwall, therefore, as I have argued elsewhere, faces double jeopardy here – not quite fitting into the realm of mainstream Literary, Historical or Cultural Studies, but also not fully embraced by medieval Celticists either.[58]

Finally 'theory' – with which we began this article – would seem alien to some medieval scholars. For them, 'theory' is something only to be applied in the modern and post-modern context. Some medieval scholars at least, believe this aspect of academia does not touch them because the medieval is distant and so sits 'separate' and 'unengaged'. It is this central problem with 'theory', and also how some more enlightened medievalists have engaged with it, that we shall turn to next.

Putting the materialist into the medieval

Not all medieval literary and cultural studies take the line of limited engagement with theory. One of the most influential works in terms of taking theory to the medieval is Sheila Delany's *Medieval Literary Politics: Shapes of Ideology* (1990).[59] Although now over twenty years old, Delany's text remains a benchmark for reinvigorating Medieval Studies because its starting point does not follow conventional medieval scholarship. Instead, Delany demonstrates that our view of medieval culture is pluralistic, contradictory, ideological, and that it is socially and politically mediated. This challenges the over-riding 'liberal' and often 'humanist' consensus (broadly the agenda of those scholars not contributing to New Cornish Studies) of what we may term Anglo-American medieval literary and cultural study.[60] Delany (drawing on the earlier theories of Janet Wolff[61]) considers the medieval 'text' as a piece of social production, and aims to examine the ways social meaning is created by medieval authors and modern critics. What Delany offers is, in effect, an alternative to what we may term 'conventional medievalism'. If there is an overt agenda to be handed to New Cornish Studies here, then it comes in the form of how medieval material should be examined. Undoing conventional ideologies about the period is clearly central to the vision – and this is where Cornish Studies can take its cue. Issues of gender, rebellion, religion, environment, sense of place, memory and imagination, and popular culture within the medieval, are all seen as vital areas of exploration. And if medievalist scholars in Cornwall wish to reinvigorate the field, they must surely do so with these suggested areas of investigation. At the same time, micro-specialist studies now seem much less relevant.

Although contributors to Helen Fulton's 2005 edited collection *Medieval Celtic Literature and Society* attempt to establish the links between cultural production and historical location, fifteen years on the ambition is nowhere near as radical as that offered by Delany.[62] Indeed, although the volume and its editor speak much about social context, the contributors to the collection only touch on this aspect, and most of the essays follow a fairly typical Anglo-American 'liberal humanist' line of close textual analysis. There is one Cornish contribution, from Oliver J. Padel, on 'Oral and literary culture in medieval Cornwall'.[63] Padel's article is an illuminating look at *Bewnans Ke* – with suggestions of possible sites for *Kelli wic* (one of King Arthur's supposed residences in Cornwall) and insightful allusions to Welsh connections. But there are two difficulties with this article. It dispenses with any political commitment, and there is little sense of the moment of production in materialist terms. The article follows the 'liberal humanist' line of criticism in medieval literature outlined above, and focuses on narrative, textual origin and influences, and on place-names and locales. The latter might have provided an opportunity to consider the wider cultural geography of the play but, unfortunately, such an approach is entirely absent. Thus the light that *Bewnans Ke* (and other texts) can shed on the cultural struggle between coloniser and colonised in medieval Cornwall is completely overlooked. This will disappoint practitioners of New Cornish Studies, with their interests in power relationships and issues of identity. Yet there will be some medievalists who will applaud this omission, because they do not subscribe to this view of Cornwall's cultural history. Moreover, as Helen Fulton's volume also indicates, medieval Celtic Studies has long been dominated by other Celtic territories – especially Wales and Ireland – with their specialist curricula, research and institutions, often leaving Cornwall in the margins.[64]

There is also the current agenda of the academy itself, where nowadays medieval studies are often deemed to be of limited impact and relevance. It is sometimes hard for research to demonstrate a wider engagement with the community when the matter seems obscure, ancient and remote. Thus, as Phelpstead, and Fimi have argued in their work on medievalism and the cultural impact of J. R. R. Tolkien, scholars must widen their engagement or risk becoming redundant.[65] A series of texts edited by Bonnie Wheeler, entitled 'The New Middle Ages' points the way forward, showing (among other things) how medieval studies might engage with Cornish Studies more readily. Wheeler's series is dedicated (much like Delane) to the 'pluri-disciplinary studies of medieval cultures'.[66] Amongst the titles which have already emerged are *The Postcolonial Middle Ages*, edited by Jeffrey Jerome Cohen, *The Persistence of Medievalism: Narrative Adventures in Contemporary Culture* by Angela Jane Weisl, and *Hybridity, Identity and Monstrosity in Medieval Britain: On Difficult Middles* by Jeffrey Jerome Cohen.[67] Wheeler's series ranges uncompromisingly across centuries connecting the medieval with the modern and the post-modern, often investigating subject-matter that is normally off the medievalist radar. Some eighty titles have now been developed in this series – again indicating a fruitful future direction for the medieval within Cornish Studies.

Indeed, one volume in the series – Alfred L. Siewers' *Strange Beauty: Eco-critical Approaches to Early Medieval Landscape* – mirrors two recent developments in research in Cornwall.[68] The recent study by Peter Dudley titled *Goon. bal, cliff and croft: the archaeology and landscape history of West Cornwall's rough ground* (2011) is, in its eco-critical approach, only a short step behind the kind of arguments articulated by Siewers.[69] Both writers examine the impact of the medieval landscape on culture, society and ecology. Siewers' work also matches a growing engagement with eco-criticism and sustainability in Cornish Studies, evidenced especially in articles in *Cornish Studies: Seventeen* (2009).[70] Here again, there is plenty of opportunity for medieval to meet modern.

The meeting ground between post-modern, modern and medieval may emerge in other ways. The Cornish Revival of the early twentieth century gazed upon the medieval in ways which today need further examination and deconstruction.[71] Similar to other pseudo-medieval movements and romantic nationalisms that emerged across Europe during the nineteenth century, the Cornish Revival incorporated the medieval into Cornwall in areas such as folklore, antiquarian studies and sometimes in art and literature. Additionally, the post-Pre-Raphaelite imagining of medieval Arthuriana in Tintagel in the 1920s and 1930s is a productive area of inquiry.[72] The way in which the medieval has been incorporated into the publishing and production of a revived Cornish literature should also be re-examined. In magazines such as *Delyow Derow* (*Oak Leaves*), innovative Cornish-language writers such as Richard Jenkin embraced a particular imagining of the Celtic medieval in their assertion of a new Cornish literature.[73] Much fiction in Cornish by contemporary writers such as Melville Bennetto and Ken George has also been preoccupied with the medieval and its interpretation.[74] The Cornish-language poets of the nineteenth and twentieth centuries too were concerned with writing in forms which drew directly on the medieval verse forms of the Middle-Cornish texts.[75] Contemporary magazines such as *An Gannas* have only recently altered their iconography to a more contemporary style, and yet many stories (often for Cornish language learners) have a medieval bent.[76]

These are all aspects of broadly what may be termed 'Neo-Medievalism' – a usage first popularized by the Italian medievalist Umberto Eco in his 1973 essay 'Dreaming in the Middle Ages'.[77] Although not fully defined, the term indicates the intersection between populist constructions and medieval history. Again, a productive area of investigation is the intersection between contemporary representation and past inspiration.[78] In this way, the medieval truly connects with the post-modern. There are numerous examples of this in Cornwall, from foodways (the tradition of medieval-style meadery restaurants), theatre (new conceptualisations and performances of the Mystery plays), music (the interest in ancient instrumentations and bagpipes), and the re-invention of St Piran (including the wish to re-open the buried oratory), to the heritage industry in general and what John Lowerson has termed 'Celtic tourism', the fascination with holy wells and other medieval locations.[79] In so many ways this echoes the modern literary and cultural writings of post-war observers such as Denys Val Baker, with his conceptualisation of Cornwall as the 'timeless land'.[80] The medieval materialist past truly connects with the present.

Celtic materialism: Grounding the Middle Ages

Encouraging current medievalists to contribute in a more engaged way to New Cornish Studies may not yet prove possible: they are a very conservative group.[81] However, two strategies offer themselves. Firstly, more scholars committed to New Cornish Studies might be encouraged (in the manner of Wheeler's 'The New Middle Ages' series) to engage with the medieval and not be deterred by its apparent impenetrability. Indeed, medieval studies desperately need exactly the kind of skills and approaches that such scholars can bring: the embrace of theory and the influence of critical movements such as post-colonialism, eco-criticism, and cultural geography. There are already some scholars in the field of Cornish Studies who are prepared to commit to this process, and these have not been afraid to grasp the nettle of modern critical discourse.

As I have suggested in successive publications, perhaps the most appropriate theory for dealing with cultural and literary production in Cornwall is that proposed initially by Alick West and Raymond Williams, but later shaped by Jonathan Dollimore and Alan Sinfield – cultural materialism.[82] The full theory emerged in the 1990s as a means of re-historicising literature and texts. Proponents of the theory rejected old-fashioned formalist and 'liberal humanist' criticism and earlier clumsy attempts to read literature in its historical context, and instead offered new ways of thinking about literature in relation to history and politics. If we are to regard medieval Cornwall as 'Celtic' (there seems no reason not to, since various critics and observers have viewed the territory in this way[83]), then we might conceive of medieval Cornwall through the sympathetic yet challenging lens of what I have termed 'Celtic' materialism. This Celtic materialism becomes, like its forerunner – cultural materialism – a way of understanding the implication of texts in Cornu-Celtic and wider Celtic history, distancing itself from the 'liberal humanist' notion of conventional medieval studies and asserting the texts' inherently political nature.

It is important to emphasise that this approach does not mean viewing medieval Cornwall as being complete, pure and uncorrupted by the processes of Anglicisation. That is not what Celtic materialism would argue. Indeed, what makes medieval Cornwall interesting is that it is a small territory exposed to and resistant of colonisation. Celtic materialism would thus criticise the idealised imaginings of Celtic-Catholic Cornwall observable in much Cornish Revivalist literature,[84] echoing the objections of Deacon and other contemporary observers.[85] Likewise, the diversity of medieval Cornwall would be recognised – subordinate cultures as well as the subaltern voice – and it is likely that competing interpretations of the period would emerge from such scrutiny. Indeed, mutually antagonistic views of the period would be accepted as an integral part of this critical perspective. In this sense, the self-protective safety zone of traditional medieval studies would be swept away as no longer fit for critical purpose.

The potential of presentism

Celtic materialism thus applied would open up for New Cornish Studies important new ways of understanding medieval Cornwall, significantly closing the gap between the medieval, the modern and the post-modern. Moreover, this process might be further assisted by the application of the related and controversial theory of 'presentism'.[86] Rooted in the economic criticism of cultural materialism, presentism argues that – in interrogation of cultural products, texts and historical documents – there is a never-ending dialogue between the past and present. If we acknowledge this, then we become aware of the present as a trigger for investigations of the past. Far from being condemned as 'historically inaccurate' or 'intrusive', a presentist perspective is thus a productive platform to link the present to the medieval. Proponents of this theory have an 'alternative' perspective of the rules of historical inquiry. Hugh Grady and Terence Hawkes, for example, use the theory of 'presentism' to re-consider Shakespeare and other Renaissance texts,[87] arguing that the scholar's situation in the present should not be seen as compromising or contaminating his or her view of the past – indeed, quite the opposite.[88]

Such a view could have a profound impact on New Cornish Studies. Medievalists often like to imagine that the canon of Middle Cornish literature (such as *Bewnans Kea*) is apolitical. But presentism would argue that such texts have travelled forward in time, and have become very precious within the collective cultural identity of Cornwall.[89] In this way, they can act as agents of change today, flowing back to the events of medieval Cornwall but influencing how we perceive them and modifying what they signify for us and other contemporary observers. Most medievalists would probably rather not recognise the 'aftermath' of the text, wishing to keep a 'pure' sense of its place in the historical continuum, but presentism argues that this is nigh-on impossible given where we are all on this continuum. For example, the current status of medieval Cornish-language texts within Cornish culture today is linked closely to their medieval moment of production.[90] Despite the passage of time, the texts still speak to us in the present.[91] This is vitally important and needs to be acknowledged, understood and acted upon.

Mending the gap: Stitching together past and present

This article began with a debate about minding and understanding the gap between the medieval, and the modern and post-modern in New Cornish Studies, in part inspired by the 'theory' suggested by Bernard Deacon over the past twenty years. The solutions proposed above are not perfect fits, and it may well take another twenty years of development for us to begin to truly synthesize these debates over Cornish history.

What is clear, however, is that many colonised territories like Cornwall have gone through very similar procedures of trying to deconstruct the medieval past.[92] As well as the general re-engagement with Cornish Studies required of the medieval historians, there is also a sense that Cornish Studies itself needs to offer opportunities to re-examine the medieval with new perspectives. Perhaps these will come when the micro-specialist studies evolve, and when old-fashioned formalist and 'liberal humanist' textual criticism is dropped. To use the phrase of one radical scholar, Kathleen Biddick, the trick is to create the 'shock of Medievalism'.[93] Likewise, it may be that, unlike the discipline of traditional Celtic Studies, Cornish Studies may well be able to offer alternative ways of investigating the medieval, which might mean a rejection of established models within that field. The work of Delany and Wheeler offers a possible way forward here, as does the embrace of 'Celtic materialism'.

Presentist readings may also offer a viable method of engaging with the difficulty of medieval texts and documents. It purports to look into the mirror of the medieval period and asks it to reflect back histories of modernist and post-modernist identities. Its heightened self-critical awareness may well be the kind of theoretical tool needed in order to mend the gap between New Cornish Studies and medieval studies. Clearly a denial of the importance of 'theory' when examining medieval history, literature or texts is no longer tenable. If the mediator of presentism opens vexed relationships in our critical examination of the medieval past, then these need embracing and exploring – not ignoring. Presentism could thus be one possible future for Cornish Studies.

Notes and references

1. B. Deacon, 'In Search of the Missing "Turn": The Spatial Dimension and Cornish Studies' in P. Payton (ed.), *Cornish Studies: Eight* (Exeter, 2000), pp. 213–30; B. Deacon, 'The New Cornish Studies: New Discipline or Rhetorically Defined Space?' in P. Payton (ed.), *Cornish Studies: Ten* (Exeter, 2002), pp. 24–43; B. Deacon, 'From "Cornish Studies" to "Critical Cornish Studies": Reflections on Methodology' in P. Payton (ed.), *Cornish Studies: Twelve* (Exeter, 2004), pp. 13–29.

2. See, for example, R. Lyon 'An Yeth Kernewek – Studhyans Cot' in C. Ó Lair (ed.), *For a Celtic Future: A tribute to Alan Heusaff* (Dublin, 1983), pp. 231–42; T. Saunders, 'Cornish – Symbol and Substance' in ibid., pp. 253–8, but also B. Deacon, 'The Electoral Impact of Cornish Nationalism' in ibid., pp. 243–57 and B. Deacon, 'Is Cornwall an Internal Colony?' in ibid., pp. 259–72. See also B. Deacon, A. George and R. Perry, *Cornwall at the Crossroads: Living Communities or Leisure Zone?* (Redruth, 1988).

3. See, for example, P. Payton and B. Deacon 'The Ideology of Language Revival' in P. Payton (ed.), *Cornwall Since the War: The Contemporary History of a European Region* (Redruth, 1983), pp. 271–90. See also responses to Deacon, for example, M. Williams. 'Discourse and Social Science in Cornish Studies – A Reply to Bernard Deacon' in P. Payton (ed.), *Cornish Studies: Thirteen* (Exeter, 2005), pp. 14–22.

4. B. Deacon, 'And Shall Trelawny Die? The Cornish Identity' in Payton, *Cornwall Since the War*, pp. 200–23.

5. See B. Deacon, 'Proto-industrialization and Potatoes: A Revised Narrative for Nineteenth-Century Cornwall' in P. Payton (ed.), *Cornish Studies: Five* (Exeter, 1997), pp. 60–84; B. Deacon, 'A Forgotten Migration Stream: The Cornish Movement to England and Wales in the Nineteenth Century' in P. Payton (ed.), *Cornish Studies: Six* (Exeter, 1998), pp. 96–117.

6. B. Deacon, D. Cole and G. Tregidga, *Mebyon Kernow and Cornish Nationalism* (Cardiff, 2003); B. Deacon, S. Schwartz and D. Holman, *The Cornish Family: The Roots of our Future* (Fowey, 2004); B. Deacon, *Cornwall: A Concise History* (Cardiff, 2007).

7. P. Payton (ed.), *Cornish Studies: Nineteen* (Exeter, 2011), p. 1.

8. A. M. Kent, 'Review of Cornish Studies: Nineteen' in *An Baner Kernewek / The Cornish Banner*, February 2012, pp. 36–7.

9. See R. E. Stansfield, 'A Duchy officer and a gentleman: The career connections of Avery Cornburgh (d.1487)' in Payton, *Cornish Studies: Nineteen*, pp. 9–35.

10. See, for example, P. Payton, '"… a concealed envy against the English": a Note on the aftermath of the 1497 Rebellions in Cornwall' in P. Payton (ed.), *Cornish Studies: One* (Exeter, 1993), pp. 4–13; J. Hall, 'Maxmilla, the Cornish Monetanist: The Final Scenes of *Origo Mundi*' in P. Payton (ed.), *Cornish Studies: Seven* (Exeter, 1999), pp. 165–92; B. Murdoch, 'Rex David, Bersabe and Syr Urry: A Comparative Approach to a Scene in the Cornish *Origo Mundi*' in Payton, *Cornish Studies: Twelve*, pp. 288–304; P. Manning, 'Staging the State and the Hypostasization of Violence in the Medieval Cornish Drama' in Payton, *Cornish Studies: Thirteen*, pp. 126–70; M. Spriggs, 'Additional Thoughts on the Medieval Cornish Bible' in P. Payton (ed.), *Cornish Studies: Fourteen* (Exeter, 2006), pp. 44–55; D. H. Frost, 'Glasney's Parish Clergy and the Tregear Manuscript'

in P. Payton (ed.), *Cornish Studies: Fifteen* (Exeter, 2007), pp. 27–90; E. Grigg, 'The Medieval Cornish Bible: More Evidence' in P. Payton (ed.), *Cornish Studies: Sixteen* (2008), pp. 19–25; E. Lavan, 'The Stage of the Nation in Medieval Cornwall' in P. Payton (ed.), *Cornish Studies: Eighteen* (Exeter, 2010), pp. 162–78.

11. A. Buckley, 'The Study of Medieval History in Cornwall' in Payton, *Cornish Studies: Ten*, pp. 90–104.

12. A. M. Kent, *The Theatre of Cornwall: Space. Place. Performance* (Bristol, 2010), pp. 149–329.

13. P. King, 'The Creation of Cornwall' in *The Times Literary Supplement*, 6 January 2012, pp. 12–13.

14. See R. Perry, 'The Making of Modern Cornwall 1800–2000: A Geo-Economic Perspective' in Payton, *Cornish Studies: Ten*, pp. 166–89; G. Tregidga, 'The Politics of the Celto-Cornish Revival, 1886–1939' in Payton *Cornish Studies: Five*, pp. 125–50.

15. Deacon, 'From "Cornish Studies" to "Critical Cornish Studies"'; J. Howlett, 'Putting the Kitsch into Kernow' in Payton, *Cornish Studies: Ten*, pp. 30–60.

16. M. Stoyle, *West Britons: Cornish Identities and the Early Modern British State* (Exeter, 2002); C. Hayden, '1549 – The Rebels Shout Back' in Payton, *Cornish Studies: Sixteen*, pp. 206–28.

17. See, for example. J. Whittaker, *Ancient Cathedral of Cornwall* (London, 1804); R. Polwhele, *The History of Cornwall* (London, 1806).

18. See, for example, C. North (ed.), *Journal of the Royal Institution of Cornwall* (1995); O. J. Padel (ed.), *Journal of the Royal Institution of Cornwall* (2011).

19. See *Old Cornwall: The Journal of the Federation of the Old Cornwall Societies*, Summer 1932.

20. T. Taylor, *The Celtic Christianity of Cornwall* (Felinfach, 1995 [1916]); L. E. Elliot-Binns, *Medieval Cornwall* (London, 1955); J. Hatcher's *Rural Economy and Society in the Duchy of Cornwall 1300–1500* (Cambridge, 1970).

21. P. L. Hull, *The Caption of Seisin of the Ducky of Cornwall, 1337* (Exeter, 1971).

22. C. Henderson, *The 109 Ancient Parishes of the Four Western Hundreds of Cornwall* [in *Journal of Royal Institution of Cornwall*] (Truro, 1955); C. Henderson, *Essays in Cornish History* (Truro, 1963); A. L. Rowse, *The Little Land of Cornwall* (Gloucester, 1986).

23. J. Whetter, *The History of Glasney College* (Padstow, 1988); J. Whetter, *The Bodrugans: A Study of a Cornish Knightly Family* (Gorran, 1995); J. Whetter, *Cornwall in the 13th Century: A Study in Social and Economic History* (Gorran, 1998).

24. C. Thomas (ed.), *Cornish Studies/Studhyansow Kernewek*, First Series, 1–15 (Redruth, 1973–1987).

25. A. Hawke, 'The Manuscripts of the Cornish Passion Poem' in Thomas (ed.), *Cornish Studies/Studhyansow Kernewek*, First Series, 9, pp. 23–8; K. George, 'How many People spoke Cornish traditionally?' in Thomas (ed.), *Cornish Studies/ Studhyansow Kernewek*, First Series, 14, pp. 67–70.

26. See for example, W. M. M. Picken, 'A Misdated Cornish Tax Account in the Book of Fees' in Thomas (ed.), *Cornish Studies/Studhyansow Kernewek*, First Series, 10, pp. 19–26; W. M. M. Picken, 'Cornish Place-Names and Fiefs in a Twelfth-Century Charter' in Thomas (ed.), *Cornish Studies/Studhyansow Kernewek*, First Series, 13, pp. 55–61; O. J. Padel. 'The Text of the Lanlawren Charter' in Thomas (ed.), *Cornish Studies/Studhyansow Kernewek*, First Series, 7, pp. 43–4.

27. An exception is M. F. Wakelin, 'Norse influence in Cornwall; A Survey of the Evidence' in Thomas (ed.), *Cornish Studies/Studhyansow Kernewek*, First Series, 4/5, pp. 41–9.

28. J. Angarrack, *Our Future is History: Identity, Law and the Cornish Question* (Bodmin, 2002); http://www.kernowtgg.com, accessed 10 March 2012. This website is called Tyr-Gwyr-Gweryn and is managed by J. Pengelly.

29. See, for example, J. Mills and P. Annear, *The Book of St Day: 'The Towne of Trynyte'* (Tiverton, 2003); A. M. Kent and D. L. J. Merrifield, *The Book of Probus: Cornwall's Garden Parish* (Tiverton, 2004).

30. J. A. Baker, *The Cornish Ordinalia: A Critical Study* (Cardiff, 1980); B. Murdoch, *Cornish Literature* (Woodbridge, 1993); Kent, op. cit (2010) Kent, *The Theatre of Cornwall*, A. M. Kent, *The Literature of Cornwall: Identity. Continuity, Difference 1000–2000* (Bristol, 2000); G. Thomas and N. Williams (eds and trans), *Bewnans Ke: The Life of St Kea –A Critical Edition with Translation* (Exeter, 2007).

31. P. Payton, *Cornwall* (Fowey, 1996); Deacon, *Cornwall*; Kent, *The Theatre of Cornwall*; C. Peters, *The Archaeology of Cornwall: The Foundations of our Society* (Fowey, 2005).

32. N. Orme (ed.), *Nicholas Roscarrock's Lives of the Saints: Cornwall and Devon* (Exeter, 1992); N. Orme, *The Saints of Cornwall* (Oxford, 2000); N. Orme, *Cornwall and the Cross: Christianity 500–1560* (Chichester, 2007); O. J. Padel (ed.), *W. M. M. Picken: A Medieval Cornish Miscellany* (Chichester, 2000); J. Mattingley, 'Stories in the Glass – Reconstructing the St Neot Pre-Reformation Glazing Scheme' in C. North (ed.), *Journal of the Royal Institution of Cornwall* (Truro, 2000), pp. 9–55. Arthurson mainly writes on the Late Medieval / Tudor Period. See I. Arthurson, *The Perkin Warbeck Conspiracy 1491–99* (Stroud, 1997). Contributors to N. Orme (ed.), *Unity and Variety: A History of the Church in Devon and Cornwall* (Exeter, 1991) also offer a particular view of the history of south-west England. One important exception in the work of Mattingly is 'The Helston Shoemakers' Guild and a Possible Connection to the 1549 Rebellion' in Payton (ed.), *Cornish Studies: Six*, pp. 23–45.

33. See, for example, the different approaches in A. L. Rowse, *Tudor Cornwall: Portrait of a Society* (Redruth, 1990 [1941]); Stoyle, *West Britons*; B. Webb, *An Anwan ha'n Gurun: An Sordyans Kernewek 1497 [The Anvil and the Crown: The Cornish Rebellion 1497]* (Cornwall, 1981); S. Parker (ed.) *Cornwall Marches On! [Keskerdh Kernow]* (Truro, 1998); N. Orme, *The Cap and the Sword: Exeter and the Rebellions of 1497* (Exeter, 1997).

34. Walter Benjamin 'Theses on the Philosophy of History' in H. Arendt (ed. and trans.), *Walter Benjamin: Illuminations* (London, 1992), pp. 245–55.

35. See, for example, A. Buckley, *The Story of Mining in Cornwall: A World of Payable Ground* (Fowey, 2007 [2005]), pp. 12–50; A. Buckley, *The Tudor Tin Industry: The Tinners and Tin Works of Penwith and Kerrier Stannary* (Camborne, 2009).

36. Buckley, 'The Study of Medieval History in Cornwall', p. 90.

37. P. Ackroyd, *The History of England: Volume 1 – Foundation* (London, 2011).

38. Buckley, 'The Study of Medieval History in Cornwall', pp. 91–2.

39. Ibid.

40. Ibid., pp. 92–3.

41. H. Fox and O. Padel, *The Cornish Lands of the Arundells of Lanherne, Fourteenth to Seventeenth Centuries* (Exeter, 2000).

42. M. Kowaleski, 'The Expansion of the South-Western Fisheries in Late Medieval England' in *Economic History Review* LIII, 3 (2000), pp. 429–54; R. Waldron, 'The Mind of John Trevisa' in *Journal of the Royal Institution of Cornwall* (2001), pp. 9–37.
43. Buckley, 'The Study of Medieval History in Cornwall', p. 99.
44. Ibid., p. 100.
45. B. Deacon, 'Researching the Medieval and Early Modern Periods' in *Cornish History Network Newsletter*, 12 (2001), pp. 8–11.
46. Ibid.
47. G. G. Coulton *Ten Medieval Studies* (Cambridge 2010 [1906]).
48. T. Taylor. *The Time Team Guide to the History of Britain* (London, 2010); W. Beckett, *Sister Wendy's Story of Painting: The Essential Guide to the History of Western Art* (London, 1994).
49. See L. Scanlon (ed.), *The Cambridge Companion to Medieval English Literature 1100–1500* (Cambridge, 2009).
50. See M. Chapman, *The Celts: The Construction of a Myth* (Basingstoke, 1992); A. Hale and P. Payton (eds), *New Directions in Celtic Studies* (Exeter, 2000); Kent, *The Theatre of Cornwall*, pp. 30–35.
51. For journals, see for example, J. F. Nagy (ed.), *Celtic Studies Association of North America Yearbook: The Individual in Celtic Literatures* (Dublin, 2001); P. Sims-Williams (ed.), *Cambrian Medieval Celtic Studies*, No. 34, Winter (1997).
52. http://www.wmich.edu/medievalcongress, accessed 12 March 2012; http://www.leeds.ac.uk/ims/imc/imc2012, accessed 12 March 2012.
53. These include *Journal of Medieval History*, *Journal of Medieval Military History*, *Speculum*, *Mediavalia*, *Comitatus*, *Viator* and *Tradito*.
54. A construct established in P. Payton, *The Making of Modern Cornwall: Historical Experience and the Persistence of 'Difference'* (Redruth, 1992).
55. O. J. Padel, has, in fact, been almost universally dismissive of the political dimension of contemporary Cornish Studies. This was reflected in the November 2010 series of three lectures he gave at the Royal Institution of Cornwall, Truro. In the third lecture, a debate was conducted between Padel and B. Deacon.
56. Views established in, for example. T. Eagleton, F. Jameson and E. Said, *Nationalism, Colonialism and Literature* (Minneapolis, 1990); J. Thieme, *Post-Colonial Con-texts: Writing Back to the Canon* (London, 2001).
57. This view is established in works such as M. Maclean, *The Literature of the Celts* (London, 1902) and J. E. C. Williams (ed.), *Literature in Celtic Countries* (Cardiff, 1971).
58. Kent, *The Theatre of Cornwall*.
59. S. Delany, *Medieval Literary Politics: Shapes of Ideology* (Manchester, 1990).
60. For background to this see J. Dixon, *A Schooling in English: Critical Episodes in the Struggle to Shape Literary and Cultural Studies* (Buckingham, 1991). For a critique of 'liberal humanism', see A. West, *Crisis and Criticism: Literary Essays* (London, 1975). 'Formalist' approaches (a scientific examination of literary style) are also part of this picture. See K. M. Newton (ed.), *Twentieth-Century Literary Criticism: A Reader* (Basingstoke, 1988), pp. 21–38.
61. J. Wolff, *The Social Production of Art* (Basingstoke, 1981).
62. H. Fulton (ed.), *Medieval Celtic Literature and Society* (Dublin, 2005).

63. O. J. Padel. 'Oral and literary culture in medieval Cornwall' in Fulton (ed.), *Medieval Celtic Literature and Society*, pp. 95–116.

64. See how this is enshrined, for example, in G. Carruthers and A. Rawes (eds) *English Romanticism and the Celtic World* (Cambridge, 2003); M. Williams, *Fiery Shapes: Celestial Portents and Astrology in Ireland and Wales 700–1700* (Oxford, 2010).

65. C. Phelpstead, *Tolkien and Wales: Language, Literature and Identity* (Cardiff, 2011); D. Fimi, *Tolkien, Race and Cultural History: From Fairies to Hobbits* (Basingstoke, 2010)

66. See for example, Alfred L. Siewers, *Strange Beauty: Eco-critical Approaches to Early Medieval Landscape* (New York, 2009), p. i. This is one of the many titles that Wheeler has developed as series editor.

67. J. J. Cohen (ed.), *The Postcolonial Middle Ages* (New York, 2001); A. J. Weisl, *The Persistence of Medievalism: Narrative Adventures in Contemporary Culture* (New York, 2003); J. J. Cohen *Hybridity, Identity and Monstrosity in Medieval Britain: On Difficult Middles* (New York, 2007).

68. Siewers, *Strange Beauty.*

69. P. Dudley, *Goon, Bal, Cliff and Croft: the archaeology and landscape history of West Cornwall's rough ground* (Truro, 2011). Contemporary archaeology in Cornwall is also starting to take notice of eco-critical angles. See several contributions to G. Kirkham and P. Herring (eds), *Cornish Archaeology* [*Hendhyscans Kernow*] (Truro, 2011).

70. See A. M. Kent, 'A Sustainable Literature? Ecocrticism, Environment and a New Eden in Cornwall's China Clay Mining Region' in P. Payton and S. Trower (eds), *Cornish Studies: Seventeen* (Exeter, 2009), pp. 51–79.

71. See the ideologies presented in D. R. Williams (ed.), *Henry and Katharine Jenner: A Celebration of Cornwall's Culture, Language and Identity* (London, 2004); P. W. Thomas and D. R. Williams (eds), *Setting Cornwall on its Feet: Robert Morton Nance 18730–1959* (London, 2007). See also M. Löffler, *A Book of Mad Celts: John Wickens and the Celtic Congress of Caernarfon 1904* (Landysul, 2000).

72. A useful article on this is C. Thomas, 'Hardy and Lyonnesse: Parallel Mythologies' in M. Hardie (ed.), *A Mere Interlude: Some Literary Visitors to Lyonnesse* (Penzance, 1992), pp. 13–26.

73. R. Jenkin (ed.), *Delyow Derow* [*Oak Leaves*], 1–15 (1988–1996).

74. M. Bennetto, *An Guran Wosek a Geltya* [*The Bloody Crown of Celtic Countries*] (Redruth, 1984); K. George, *Kellys* (Cornwall, 1993). The latter text is not entirely neo-medieval. There is a contemporary dimension to the narrative as well.

75. See examples in T. Saunders (ed. and trans.) *The Wheel: An Anthology of Modern Poetry in Cornish 1850–1980* (London, 1999).

76. See *An Gannas.*

77. See U. Eco 'Dreaming in the Middle Ages' (1973) in U. Eco, *Travels in Hyperreality* (New York, 1986), pp. 61–72.

78. A useful source here is E. A. Joy, M J. Seaman, K. Bell and M. K. Ramsey (eds), *Cultural Studies of the Modern Middle Ages* (New York, 2008).

79. See http:\\www.meaderyerestaurants.co.uk, accessed 12 March 2012; Kent, *The Theatre of Cornwall*, pp. 712–15; H. Woodhouse, *Cornish Bagpipes: Fact or Fiction?* (Redruth, 1994); J. Harasta, 'Arise St Piran – The Cult of Saints and the Redefining of Cornwall' in Payton and Trower (eds), *Cornish Studies: Seventeen*,

pp. 187–203; J. Lowerson, 'Celtic Tourism: Some Recent Magnets' in P. Payton (ed.), *Cornish Studies: Two* (Exeter, 1994), pp. 128–38.

80. See D. Val Baker, *The Timeless Land: The Creative Spirit in Cornwall* (Bath, 1973). Val Baker locates the origin of this creative spirit in ancient and medieval Cornwall.

81. See M. Bull, *Thinking Medieval: An Introduction to the Study of the Middle Ages* (Basingstoke, 2005).

82. See West, *Crisis and Criticism*; R. Williams, *Problems in Materialism and Culture: Selected Essays* (London, 1980); J. Dollimore and A. Sinfield (eds), *Political Shakespeare: New Essays on Cultural Materialism* (Manchester, 1985). See also A. M. Kent, *The Implication of Texts in History: The Rise, Development and Some Applications of Cultural Materialism*, M.Phil. diss. (Exeter, 1991), H. Dix, *After Raymond Williams: Cultural Materialism and the Break-Up of Britain* (Cardiff, 2008).

83. See a range of perspectives here in P. B. Ellis, *The Celtic Revolution: A Study in Anti-Imperialism* (Talybont, 1988 [1985]); S. James, *The Atlantic Celts: Ancient People or Modern Invention?* (London, 1999); Hale and Payton (eds), *New Directions in Celtic Studies*.

84. See H. Jenner, *A Handbook of the Cornish Language* (London, 1904); A. S. D. Smith, *The Story of the Cornish Language: Its Extinction and Revival* (Camborne, 1947).

85. See Payton and Deacon, 'The Ideology of Language Revival'; B. Deacon, 'Cornish of Klingon? The Standardization of the Cornish Language' in Payton (ed.), *Cornish Studies: Fourteen*, pp. 13–23; M. Everson, C. Weatherhill,. R. Chubb, B. Deacon and N. Williams, *Form and Content in Revived Cornish: Reviews and Essays in Criticism of Kernewek Kemmyn* (Westport, 2007).

86. See Q. Smith, *Language and Time: A Defence of Presentism* (Oxford, 1993); C. Bourne, *A Future for Presentism* (Oxford, 2009).

87. H. Grady and T. Hawkes (eds), *Presentist Shakespeares* (London, 2007).

88. Ibid., pp. 1–5.

89. Kent, *The Theatre of Cornwall*, pp. 699–841.

90. For their moment of production, see Bakere, *The Cornish Ordinalia*; Thomas and Williams (eds and trans), *Bewnans Ke: The Life of St Kea*.

91. New translations are important here. See, for example, Markham Harris, *The Cornish Ordinalia* (Washington D.C., 1969). A. M. Kent, *Ordinalia: The Cornish Mystery Play Cycle – A Verse Translation* (London, 2005).

92. See D. Walker, *Medieval Wales* (Cambridge, 1990); P. Lord, *Visual Cultures of Wales: Medieval Vision* (Cardiff, 2003); A. Breeze, *Medieval Welsh Literature* (Dublin, 1997); M. Richter, *Medieval Ireland* (London, 2005); Art Cogrove, *A New History of Ireland 1169–1534* (Oxford, 2008); S. J. D. Seymour, *Anglo-Irish Literature 1200–1582* (Cambridge, 2011).

93. K. Biddick, *The Shock of Medievalism* (Durham, North Carolina, 1998).

3

Tristram Winslade

The Desperate Heart
of a Catholic in exile

Cheryl Hayden

Introduction

The Elizabethan era is often described as an age of renaissance in which
England was pulled from the mire of medieval Catholicism into a triumphal
Protestant enlightenment which is still alive and loved today.[1] But how close,
in its later years, did one desperate Catholic exile come to undoing it all?
Is it conceivable that one man could ever have harnessed enough support to
rouse Celtic Cornwall and neighbouring Devon in a counter-reformation and
turn England back to Catholicism? As this article demonstrates, Tristram
Winslade tried, and he was not alone.

This article presents for the first time an English translation of a very
late sixteenth-century Latin document, held in the Library of Congress'
Rare Books and Special Collections division as part of the Hans Kraus Sir
Francis Drake Collection.[2] Titled *The Present State of Cornwall and Devon,
the two counties closest to Spain*, it was written by Tristram Winslade,[3] the
grandson of John Winslade, who was executed for his role as a leader of the
1549 Prayer Book Rebellion. According to the collection's catalogue, it was
written *c.*1595 and is a 'top secret' intelligence report for King Philip II of
Spain on the benefits to be had by invading England and converting it back
to Catholicism, and the best way of doing so.

The document places Winslade in the Spanish Netherlands, at the heart of
English exile resistance against Elizabeth's Protestant Reformation. It names
his supporters, both in Europe and in England, and, as Kraus' catalogue
remarks, 'heads would have rolled' if Elizabeth's Privy Council had known
what he and his friends were planning.

The document

The document was brought to my attention by a member of the Winslade family, who knew of my interest in the rebellion and its aftermath.[4] Its inclusion as one of sixty items in a collection devoted to the career of Sir Francis Drake is curious because Winslade mentions Drake only once, and then as a knight 'most ill-advisedly gilded' and as a robber, pirate and a thief [6].[5]

The dating, c.1595, appears to be correct, as Winslade expresses his frustration at Catholics having endured forty-five years of hardship for defending their faith [19]. There can be little doubt, given the role of the 1549 Prayer Book Rebellion in defining Winslade's life and the emphasis on it in the document, that this marks his starting point, bringing us to either 1594 or the first half of 1595. This theory is supported by the fact that the Spanish attack on Penzance, Mousehole and Newlyn in the summer of 1595 is not mentioned.

The Kraus catalogue gives its place of origin as Spain; however it also suggests that this document may be a transcript of an original and there are compelling reasons to support this. The first is Winslade's statement that he and his two co-conspirators were living in Belgium [8]. Other pieces of internal evidence are: the inconsistent spelling of Winslade's name; the clumsy attempts to avoid using the first person, for example, 'The third is the man who presents these matters, Tristram Winslade'[6] [8]; and, among several other linguistic oddities, some English place names and personal names (in addition to Winslade's) are very strangely mangled – as might be expected from the hand of a junior official in Brussels or even Madrid who had little or no acquaintance with England and the English.[7] Another is a notation on the Latin document, written in Italian [18]. Krause says this may indicate that the document was prepared 'for the use of the Papal court, as it is most unlikely that any such report would have been supplied to any other Italian authority'.[8] Finally, the document is not encrypted, and it is unthinkable that Winslade would have named his allies in Cornwall and Devon, especially considering his concerns about the need for security and stealth [9, 21]. The transcription and transport of this document must have been carried out in an exceptionally secure manner.

Here, then, we have a transcription of an unsolicited document addressed to the King of Spain, which advocates a new invasion of England and sets out precisely how and by whom it is to be carried out. It openly names high-standing citizens in Cornwall and the south-west counties of England who were ready to assist: Sir Francis Godolphin, Sir William Courtenay,[9] Thomas Denys, Baron Seymour, Sir George Trenchard, the former Bishop of Exeter, James Turberville, and several others less easily identified. Despite

Winslade's explicit denial that their actions would have been treason –
because the plan would only be activated upon the death of the Queen – it is
not difficult to imagine their plight had this document come to the attention
of the Privy Council. It is astonishing that no one found out until now.

Who was Tristram Winslade?

Tristram Winslade was born *c.*1552,[10] the son of William Winslade – landless
since the Prayer Book Rebellion – and Jane Babington of Ottery-St-Mary,
in Devonshire.[11] For a short time during his childhood he probably lived
with his parents in Devonshire, but at the age of ten years he began life as
a gentleman-servant in the household of Sir John Arundell at Lanherne in
Cornwall.[12] Here, he may have been in the company of other young men
left penniless by the rebellion, such as the sons of the rebel leader, Humphry
Arundell.[13]

By 1574, Winslade had entered the service of King Philip of Spain,[14]
although in what capacity is not clear because it is not certain that he left
Cornwall before the arrest of the seminary priest Father Cuthbert Mayne in
1576. It would appear that he travelled broadly in Europe,[15] and in August
1583 he entered the English College at Douai,[16] which had been established
by William Allen to educate well-born Catholic exiles and train priests for
'the English Mission'. At some point – perhaps in the first years of his service
– he must have had military training in Naples and Milan, as he served
with Sir William Stanley in Ireland and Flanders for a total of twenty-three
years.[17] In 1586, Winslade probably heard of the execution of his distant
cousin, Anthony Babington.[18]

Tristram Winslade next appears in 1588 aboard the *Nuestra Senora
del Rosario*, the first of the Armada ships to founder.[19] He was one of
numerous Englishmen sailing with the fleet under an arrangement between
King Philip and William Allen that should any of them be captured they
would claim that they had been forced aboard in order to be interpreters
after a successful invasion. Notwithstanding being listed on the Armada's
inventory as an Irishman,[20] Winslade was recognised as an Englishman,
arrested by Sir Francis Drake and taken up to London. He was racked by
Queen Elizabeth's master torturer, Sir Richard Topcliffe, but stuck to the
agreed story and in March 1590 the Privy Council ordered his release.[21]
Immediately, Winslade launched a legal quest to be named as the heir of
last earl of Devon,[22] but his plan either failed or was abandoned because by
1595 he was back in Brussels.

Religion in the late sixteenth century

In the sixteenth century, the way people prayed was of utmost importance to them and the Protestant Reformation had been cataclysmic. Beginning with Henry VIII's reforms, which made him head of the Church of England and enabled him to marry Anne Bolelyn, it was furthered under the reign of his son, Edward VI, with the introduction in 1549 of an English language prayer book. The Cornish, with their ethnicity and identity deeply imbedded in their language and a Celtic form of Catholicism,[23] had been early protestors against the Reformation, and when Latin and Cornish were removed from their church services they, along with the people of western Devonshire, protested *en masse.* Their attempted march to London quickly became open warfare and is known today as the Prayer Book Rebellion. It is well documented and was arguably the most dangerous threat, not just to the reign of Edward VI, but to the Reformation itself.[24] When Mary Tudor succeeded her half-brother in 1553, she and her Spanish husband, King Philip II of Spain, reversed the reformation. This did not last, as Mary died in 1558 and her half-sister, Elizabeth I, succeeded her, bringing with her a more moderate form of Protestantism and a toleration of Catholicism.

Elizabeth's toleration of Catholicism did not last and by 1583 it had been declared a form of treachery. Those true to the faith became victims of a campaign of persecution which included impossibly high fines for 'recusancy' (refusal to attend the State-sanctioned church), and arrest, imprisonment and torture for those who persisted in holding or attending Mass or who aided the growing number of priests being sent covertly into England from Europe. While most English Catholics were 'reconciled' and began attending the Church of England – often carrying out their Catholic rituals covertly – others chose exile. Tristram Winslade was among them, but rather than settle quietly he followed a family tradition of religious activism. His service as a soldier was directed at ridding England of a 'no religion' that had taken its 'profane and heretical rite ... from the stinking pit of the Calvinists' [5]. Having done that, he would be able to return home.

Anxiety in England

By the end of summer 1595, the Court of Elizabeth I was in a state of high anxiety following an attack by four Spanish ships on a number of villages on Cornwall's south coast. During the 1540s, fear of France had led Henry VIII to build a series of fortifications along this coastline, including Pendennis and St Mawes castles. Now, fear of Spain and the cost of defence led to increasing activity in the region, ranging from State-sanctioned piracy or 'privateering', which allowed people such as Sir Francis Drake to plunder Spanish ships for their treasure, to major constructions such as the fortification of St Mary's on the Scilly Islands. This project was being overseen by the Scillies' Governor, Sir Francis Godolphin, whose heart appears to have been with the Spanish cause.

Adding to the tension at Court was the Queen's refusal to name her successor, and in the latter part of his document, Winslade demonstrates his awareness of the factions being formed over the best way forward for England. With Mary Queen of Scots dead, and no alternative Catholic monarch for the English throne, factions also began to form among Catholics,[25] and those in England were living under an ever-increasing threat of persecution, torture and the most appalling of deaths. Their support of the Jesuit priests being sent over from Europe began to wane.[26]

Frustrations and factions in Europe

Winslade's circle of colleagues indicates that he was entrenched with those who were setting the agenda for the Catholicisation of England through the Council for the State of England in Brussels. His key co-conspirator, Gabriel Denys, had strong connections not only to the Council but also to the Catholic families of Devonshire. He had been an advisor to Don John of Austria (King Philip's brother) and, in 1595, was serving Father Holt, who was responsible for dispersing all money coming from England to support emigrants and exiles,[27] and one of two priests described as ruling 'all courses for England'.[28] Father Holt and Winslade's commander, Colonel William Stanley, were members of the Council for the State of England. Winslade's other local co-conspirator, Richard Bray, had connections in Cornwall – he was the son of a former Mayor of Bodmin, Henry Bray. Winslade seems, too, to have known Father Robert Parsons, another west-country Catholic, a leader of the Catholic Mission and among those most sought by the English network of spies. He seems confident of receiving Parsons' help [22].

Despite his connections, in 1595 Winslade was probably starving, and at the end of his document he lays bare his financial distress. It seems that this was the plight of many exiles and the situation had become so serious that it was the subject of much interest to Elizabeth's Council. For example, a Richard Williams, under examination in February 1595, revealed that he had served Stanley in Brussels for 20 crowns per month.[29] This compares to a report in the following month that the Brussels Jesuits were sending three bishops into the north of England on pensions of 4,000 crowns per annum (or approximately 330 crowns per month).[30]

The Winslade plan

It is tempting to believe that Winslade's plan led to the Second Armada of 1597. The English were receiving reports about the preparation of this Armada as early as 1596 and, according to Parsons, the King was determined to use 'all his force for the recovery of England from heresy' and install Cardinal Albert of Austria and his intended spouse, the Infanta of Spain, as joint rulers.[31] A report from Lisbon informed the Council that the fleet had comprised 100 vessels carrying 9,000 soldiers, bound for Falmouth or Plymouth 'at one of which places they have a friend in the captain of the castle'.[32] This fleet had come within sight of the Cornish coast, unopposed, when it was 'scattered' by a north-easterly, seriously damaged and forced to retreat.[33]

If this Armada was inspired by Winslade's plan, it was not faithful to its design. Winslade was insistent that an invasion should only occur 'on the death of the Queen' [5, 7, 8, 12, 17, 21], and he does not advocate assassination. Rather, his aim was to seize the throne while it was vacant and allow King Philip II to name Elizabeth's successor. Given that the Queen was still alive in 1597, the Second Armada raises an interesting set of questions. The first is, did the Spanish King simply take Winslade's plan and implement it to suit himself? If so, he placed Winslade's allies in Cornwall and Devon in a bind. Would they, had the Armada kept to its course and landed on the Cornish and Devon coasts, have remained faithful to the Queen, or would they have immediately implemented the Winslade plan? How would Sir William Courtenay, who had been sent back to Devonshire with 6,000 soldiers, respond? And how well would Sir George Trenchard, ordered back to Dorset to defend it, have guarded the narrow route through Sherbourne?[34]

The second is: did Winslade sail with this Second Armada? This is quite probable, as he made a return to Flanders in 1597 in the company of the Archduke,[35] presumably as part of an army, although it is not stated where they had been. His presence in an invasion force was not part of the plan he had offered the King. His distress at seeing his plan only partially implemented and end in total failure must have been considerable.

Another intriguing question is whether or not Winslade ever discussed the identity of a new Catholic monarch with Courtenay, whom he described as 'the most powerful and popular of all' [10]. Suffice it to note that Sir William Courtenay of Powderham was a direct descendant of Edward I and to wonder whether a return to the Plantagenet Kings may been considered as a satisfying solution to the issue of the monarch for the Catholics of England, and particularly to the Cornish who had perceived a significant erosion of their identity and autonomy under the Tudors.[36] Winslade's references to the Kings of Wessex and Henry Bolingbroke are intriguing when viewed in this light [3, 21].

Given the English spy networks that existed during this period, the security of Winslade's document must have been of utmost concern to everyone around him. Regardless of any threat from Spain, his allies in Cornwall and the south-west must have suffered acute anxiety over the health of the ageing Queen, never knowing when the vital news of her death would come and all the while leading 'loyal' lives, carrying out their duties and remaining undiscovered and untainted. The fact that they apparently did so demonstrates the ambiguity and stress of life as a Catholic-at-heart in Elizabethan England: English first, Catholic secretly second, and never countenancing the notion of a Spanish monarch. Had Winslade's document been discovered, could they have convinced the Privy Council of their loyalty?

Winslade's loyalty to the Spanish King was never in doubt and in 1597 the King ordered the granting of a pension, recognising that this 'well-born gentleman' had '... endured much suffering'.[37] In the end, the English Queen foiled Winslade's plan by out-living the Spanish King, who died in 1598. Winslade out-lived them both, and as suggested in his final paragraph, found another reason for living: the idea of founding a North American homeland for Catholic exiles.[38] Tristram Winslade died in 1605 and it was probably a testament to his dedication to the Catholic cause that he was buried in the chapel of the English College of Douai.

The translation by
Dr Judith Owen (University of Western Australia)
and Dr Michael Kelly

While every effort has been made to preserve the author's meaning throughout Winslade's rambling report (the syntax is often far from clear), this translation aims to turn its Latin into a plain English which retains the style and flavour of the original. Where the text has been so damaged as to be illegible, it has – wherever possible – been silently emended. And in order to prevent confusion, all names of people and places are presented in their standard modern form, and the punctuation has in places been changed to that of modern English.

Acknowledgements

The invaluable assistance of Judith Owen and Michael Kelly in providing the translation of the Winslade document is gratefully acknowledged. The accompanying map is reproduced courtesy of the Rare Books and Special Collections Division, Library of Congress.

Notes

1. A. L. Rowse, *The England of Elizabeth* (The Reprint Society, London, 1953). Rowse's prologue provides an eloquent description of Elizabethan England and its legacy.
2. T. Winslade, 'De praesenti statu Cornubiae et Devoniae quae duae Provinciae sunt Hispaniae proximores', unpublished manuscript 1595, Hans Kraus Sir Francis Drake Collection No 12, Rare Books and Special Collections Division, Library of Congress. http://www.loc.gov//rr/rarebook/catalog/drake/drake–8-invincible.html.
3. While the document is not signed, Winslade identifies himself as the author a number of times throughout it. In the document, his name is spelled as Tristan (which accords with the Spanish version used in *Tristan and Isolde*). In English documents, however, he appears as Tristram, and so I have referred to him as Tristram in this paper. His surname appears as Wideslade and Windeslade. I have used the usual English version – Winslade.
4. I wish thank Bruce Winslade for providing me with the digitized version of this document and for sharing his family research.
5. Notations in this style refer to the page numbers of the digitized version of Winslade's manuscript. (The original manuscript has different page numbering, possibly because of the size and orientation of the paper Winslade would have used. The digitized version appears to have been paginated to enable printing onto A4 paper.)
6. The translators have noted that periphrasis is employed on almost every possible occasion in order to avoid the first person that Winslade presumably used in his original.
7. For example, Perina instead of Penryn [9].
8. While the existence of the Italian notation may be significant, a translation of it suggests it to be a greeting from the Catholics of England.
9. Sir William Courtenay of Powderham
10. A. J. Loomie, *The Spanish Elizabethans: the English Exiles at the Court of Philip II* (New York, 1963), p. 263. Loomie tells us that in 1597 Winslade was 45 years old.
11. Visitations of the County of Devon 1564. The Babington pedigree shows that Jane Babington married a William Winslade. Also: J. Chynoweth, *Tudor Cornwall* (Oxford, 2002), p. 291.
12. A. L. Rowse, *The Expansion of Elizabethan England* (London, 1957), p. 43
13. Catholic Record Society – Miscellanea, Recusant Records Vol. 1 (taken from Cecil Papers 9/112). A list of people from Lanherne indicted for recusancy includes 'Trompeter Richardus Arundell' and 'Umpredi Arundell'. Richard and Humphry were the names of the sons of Prayer Book Rebellion leader Humphry Arundell.
14. Loomie, *The Spanish Elizabethans*, p. 263.
15. Rowse, *The Expansion of Elizabethan England*, p. 43
16. Second Douai Diary.
17. Loomie, *The Spanish Elizabethans*, p. 263
18. Anthony Babington's name has been given to the Babington Plot of 1586, which

aimed to assassinate Elizabeth I and install as monarch Mary Queen of Scots. He was executed in September 1586, the Queen of Scots in February 1587.

19. P. Martin, *Spanish Armada Prisoners*, Exeter Maritime Studies No. 1 (Exeter, 1998).

20. C. Knight, *The Penny Cyclopaedia of the Society for the Diffusion of Useful Knowledge* (1833), p. 350.

21. D. W. Rice, *The Life and Achievements of Sir John Popham, 1531–1607* (Madison, New Jersey, 2005), p. 177.

22. Chynoweth, *Tudor Cornwall*, pp. 302–5.

23. L. McClain, *Lest we be damned: Practical Innovation and Lived Experience Among Catholics in Protestant England, 1559–1662* (New York, 2004). McClain devotes a chapter to Celtic Catholicism in Cornwall.

24. J. Cornwall, *Revolt of the Peasantry 1549* (London, 1977). Other comprehensive accounts include F. Rose-Troup, *The western rebellion of 1549* (London, 1913).

25. A. L. Rowse, *Eminent Elizabethans* (London, 1983), p. 55.

26. Many texts are available on this subject. Among others, I have drawn on A. Hogge, *God's Secret Agents* (New York, 2005) and J. Cooper, *The Queen's Agent: Francis Walsingham at the Court of Elizabeth I* (London, 2011).

27. G. Panzano, H. Davy and J. Berington, *The collected works of Humphry Davy – Discourses delivered before the Royal Society – Elements of Agricultural Chemistry Part 1* (London, 1840), p. 52.

28. Calendar of State Papers, Elizabeth I, Domestic Series, 1595, Vol. CCLII – information gleaned from a document written by Father William Gifford to Throgmorton in Rome.

29. Calendar of State Papers, Vol. CCLII, 1 February 1595.

30. Ibid., March 1595.

31. Ibid., 24 February 1597.

32. Ibid., November 1597.

33. Peter Pierson, *Philip II of Spain* (London, 1975), p. 185.

34. Calendar of State Papers, 1595–97, Vol. CCLXIV, October 1597.

35. Loomie, *The Spanish Elizabethans*, p. 263

36. P. Payton *Cornwall – A History* (Fowey, 2004), p. 122.

37. Loomie, *The Spanish Elizabethans*, p. 263. Winslade's pension was 25 escudos or just over £6 per annum. On p. 248 Gabriel Denys' pensions are listed. They totalled four times that of Winslade.

38. D. Beers Quinn, *England and the Discovery of America* (London, 1974), p. 384.

On the Present Condition
of Cornwall and Devon,
the Two Counties nearest Spain

[1]¹ Cornwall is nearest Spain and has 17 towns, which are busy because of [   ]² and trade, and more than 200 parishes. Sixteen or seventeen thousand cavalry, at most, are enlisted, effective trained men for waging war on land; and at sea, [more than]³ three thousand sailors in addition to the nobles and all their attendants. In the general census of the whole county are found about 31 or 32 thousand fit for bearing arms from their eighteenth to their sixtieth year. Cornwall has a port called Falmouth, the equal of any English port, able to hold a thousand ships, even the largest. It also has another port called Mounts Bay, quite capable of receiving even large ships. This province abounds in fish and tin or white lead.

Devon lies next to Cornwall and has 33 towns or merchant centres, one incorporated city, and more than 400 parishes. From this province 34 or 35 thousand men are enlisted and trained in military service and more than two thousand in the navy, besides nobles and their whole retinues. The number of soldiers that Devon trains continuously in this manner exceeds 60 thousand men. The ports of this county are Plymouth and Dartmouth, able to hold a great many large ships.

[2] When the Queen prepares any expedition against Spain or the Indies, she brings down her warships to the port of Plymouth, and there equips them with sailors, arms, and other things necessary for an operation on land and sea, because from this bay toward Spain, just as from Spain toward this port of Devon, there is no danger from our waters. This province abounds

---

¹ As in the introduction, numbers shown in this style refer to the digitized pages of the original Latin manuscript.
² The manuscript is torn.
³ A probable reading (the manuscript is torn).

in woollen garments, which they call kerseys,[4] and the purest tin. It also supplies a great quantity of grain, meats, fish, butter, and of all the other things which are suitable for preserving a pleasant life.

Cornwall and Devon with their two adjoining counties (namely Somerset and Dorset) form a peninsula by means of two rivers; of these one is named the Wier[5] and flows north into the sea; the other is called the Stour and draws its source in a certain deer preserve which borders the Barony of Stourton, and releases itself into the sea to the south.

And the gap by which the heads of these rivers are divided, which extends four or five English miles,[6] is so fortified by marshes, ditches, earthworks and enclosures, and so suited by the nature and advantage of the site to undertake any form of fortification that these four counties, separated from the rest, can easily defend themselves against all the forces of the whole Kingdom. For though the rivers from their earliest spring to a distance of some furlongs[7] are not really deep, from this gap between their heads, which has just been mentioned, to their final outflow into the sea they cannot be crossed by cavalry, unless it makes its way to bridges, because of the thick and sticky mud. As soon as horses step into it, they immediately stick and sink and are swamped by the currents.

[3] This separation [of the four counties from the rest of England] was seriously considered in our lifetime by Thomas Denys,[8] a knight of great reputation and authority among the people of Devon. After the death of King Edward VI, Denys was in the favour of Queen Mary at the time when the Regent, the Duke of Northumberland, was working to substitute by public edict Jane, daughter of the Duke of Suffolk, who had been proclaimed through the entire kingdom in her [Mary's] place.[9] Today truly this quartet

---

4 A kersey was a jumper-like garment made of a woollen cloth known as kersey cloth.

5 This is probably the River Brue, whose source is near Brewham and only about 2km from Stourhead (that would be about 10 furlongs). Two guesses for the name 'Wier': first, the Brue was (and still is, via canal) connected to the Axe, which flows through the village of Weare, from which Winslade may have got the name; second, (perhaps more likely) the Brue was lined with weirs, as can still be seen on an Ordnance Survey map.

6 The reference to the English mile may be to differentiate between the English measurement of 1,760 yards and the Roman mile, in use across much of Europe, which was 1,617 yards.

7 The word in the document is stade, which is approximately 200 yards as opposed to the furlong's 220 yards.

8 Sir Thomas Denys was the Custos Rotulorum or Guardian of the Rolls (Pipe-Rolls) in Devon in the middle of the sixteenth century.

9 This is a reference to Lady Jane Grey, a cousin of King Edward VI who named her as his successor instead of his sister, Mary Tudor. Jane Grey was Queen of England

of counties, just as it is separated from the rest by the outpouring of waters through the kindness of nature, so too by the industry of men it is so fortified everywhere with such a density of enclosures, such an abundance of ramparts, and such a [quantity][10] of ditches, that if a proper army, however well trained, tried to [break through][11] them, to do this would seem to be impossible, or at least very difficult, unless some agreement [   ][12] on the matter had occurred. They are well trained in arms and the use of arms for their own defence against the Spanish; they are clever, industrious, and strong and quick of body; and the people of Devon and Cornwall are extremely experienced in naval affairs because of their frequent voyages over many years.

Indeed, so great is the courageous character of these peoples, or so especially conspicuous, that when our island had seven Kings, each of whom protected his wealth with arms, the Kings of Wessex (whose heptarchy was more or less bounded by the borders of these four counties) were so powerful that when all the rest were subdued by the warlike courage of their soldiers, they reduced all the regions of the whole of England into the Monarchy which now exists. Furthermore, the wealth of this kingdom alone was so great that one King of Wessex, Ine,[13] built at his own expense Wells Cathedral for his brother, the first bishop of that seat, and also two monasteries: one at Shaftesbury for his sister, the first abbess of the same convent, the other at Glastonbury for the Benedictine monks in honour of Saint Joseph of Arimathea, of the first group of apostles. And indeed, one heptarch left these three places so magnificently built and so richly endowed that of the rest of the Kings none can be found who built even one that ought to be compared with the least deserving of these three.

[4] Both the Monarch and most of the landlords continually harass and openly drain the common people in a wretched way with new censuses of tribute and taxes.[14] Though this occurs everywhere through all England,

---

for nine days before the Privy Council changed its mind about the succession and charged her with treason.

[10] The manuscript is torn here.

[11] The manuscript is torn here.

[12] The manuscript is torn here.

[13] King Ine of Wessex, r. 688–726, established the first church at Wells and the first stone church at Glastonbury Abbey, and whose sister, Cuthburh, was the first abbess of Wimborne Minster. Winslade may be confused about which abbey this is, as Shaftesbury was founded more than 150 years after Ine.

[14] Sense has been restored here by reading *novis* (new) for the odd but apparent *nonis* (nine).

it happens especially in Cornwall and Devon, because in those counties on account of their location and wealth, everything that is necessary and convenient for waging war against Spain is available. So with these ills oppressing their minds constantly, and with a weight greater by the day, the result is that the present condition of things troubles them greatly, especially the Cornish and Devonians, whose whole means of income on which they used to rely – namely cloth, tin, lead, fish, and the rest of the goods of their land, which were cheap at home because of their quantity but sold for more in foreign nations – could not take place, all commerce with other nations long since having ceased, so that all those whose means of livelihood consisted in exporting or importing goods were reduced to the greatest poverty. The majority of the people think that there is no other cause of this public disaster, and also of all the other evils by which they are beset, than that they have received a certain new – or, more accurately, no – form of religion, conceived by certain treacherous ministers and enacted by royal authority, after the rejection of the old and ancestral covenant which they usually called the Catholic religion. The strength and sinew of the commons in the whole kingdom of England is held in check. The Cornish alone, reluctantly bearing the unusually heavy yoke of King Henry VII and taking up arms against him, united in battle with Baron Audeley,[15] Flamank,[16] a nobleman of lesser rank, and a certain blacksmith[17] as the leaders of the war which was fought for a long time, with varying fighting and ambiguous fortune.

Again in our memory, the Cornish and the men of Devon took up arms with a popular army of the Catholic religion against the Dinasts,[18] who, while administering the Kingdom in the name of the ten-year-old Edward the Sixth, [5] rejected and openly destroyed the general wealth of the Kingdom and forced other profane and heretical rites dug out from the stinking pit of the Calvinists[19] onto all the churches of the whole of England, even against their will.[20] This battle alone made the power and the courage of the two counties very famous, because the Royal Army, even though it was put together from all the other counties of the Kingdom, would not

---

[15] Winslade is here describing the Cornish Rebellion of 1497, during the reign of Henry VII, which was protesting against heavy taxation being used to fund war against Scotland. The reference is to James Touchet, the seventh Baron Audley.

[16] Cornish lawyer, Thomas Flamank.

[17] Cornish blacksmith, Michael Joseph, commonly known as 'an Gof', the name of his trade.

[18] Rulers – the reference probably applies to King Edward's council and the Lord Protector, Edward Seymour.

[19] Followers of the Protestant theology of John Calvin.

[20] Winslade is describing the Prayer Book Rebellion of 1549.

have dared to advance into battle if the Burgundians and the Germans had not been accepted as allies. The prime leaders of the Catholic Army were Wide[sladu]s[21] and Arundell[22], who were considered to be among the more eminent in the Cornish nobility. Under their leadership, many – Bury, Smith, Coffin and others[23] – were leading even the noble ranks.[24] Winslade was the paternal grandfather of the one who wrote this report.

More examples of this kind, about the deeds undertaken by the English people are remembered among our historians, but from these two it is possible to judge how such a people could excel and strive for what it wants, and indeed with a willing spirit, against such great and so universal alienation of opinions from those who now have control everywhere in England, if some pious Prince should deign to take up their excellent cause and to offer favourable conditions to the people. These counties are very populous and are given with an amazing facility to repaying thanks to those who deserve well. They respect and admire nobility and are led by them for good or evil without discrimination, especially Cornwall and Devon, for the very reason that these regions are the most remote from the Court and the Monarch. And for this reason a few men of the prime nobility who are pleasing to the people are able to rouse a great upheaval in these regions. These two counties are today, of all the counties of England, the most hostile to the Monarch of the Spanish empire on account of their situation, ports, number of sailors, and other goods advantageous for naval and military uses. These regions are supplied with all these things in abundance, and, through the reconciliation of the opinions of those men who in their time were able to promote that undertaking vigorously, not only by their authority and advice, but also by joining forces, with a like ease they could be converted and summoned to promote the venture of the Catholic party. It is considered that this reconciliation can occur with ease, if His Royal Majesty thought it worth making preparation in this way, so that on the death of the Queen everything should be unhampered and in readiness.

---

[21] The manuscript is torn here. This damaged version of Winslade indicates only one of the ways in which his name is spelled in the Latin text.

[22] John Winslade and Humphry Arundell.

[23] A reference to three leaders of the Prayer Book Rebellion. John Bury, as leader of the Devonshiremen, became Humprhy Arundell's deputy and was tried and executed for treason, along with Arundell and Winslade. Robert Smith led the Cornish charge at the battle of Fenny Bridges and went on to live for another 20 years. Coffin (first name unknown) was a servant to Sir John Arundell of Lanherne.

[24] The manuscript is torn here; it is likely that a word has been lost.

[6] Humphrey Gilbert,[25] Francis Drake[26], knights ill-advisedly honoured, two of the Hawkins[27] and lots of others were from Devon. Grenville,[28] Lok,[29] Killigrew[30] and others were from Cornwall, much renowned for piracy and theft, not only in England, but anywhere in the world. Those robbers were hostile to all ranks of men (but mostly to those who were more eminent in rank and dignity) [and were noted] as much for their insolence and injuries committed in England, as because they were the principal agents when decisions were made about violating the peace and waging war on Spain. But noble men are not lacking in these same counties, more in number, greater in dignity, excelling much more in the strength and gratitude of the people, who will attend to exterminating those illegitimate shoots of the assassins, so that they do not make deeper roots in this land. If his Catholic Majesty wanted to ask some men for a test of faith, as far as it seems prudent to defend religiously the path we are labouring at, [there are two men who would be particularly suitable.]

An excellent man of the first of our nobility, Gabriel Denys, now lives in Brussels, the son of the renowned knight Thomas mentioned above. He has the closest connection, whether of blood or relatedness or at least of friendship with nearly all the illustrious families of any note of either county. And there are associates of his, relations and friends mostly all Catholic or Schismatics,[31] in other words, those more given to the Catholic party, although they do not walk along the right path. Many have for a long time conceived a serious hope that it will happen at some stage that, with his own people and everyone else groaning under the heavy heap of burdens, on a happier day the star of Gabriel will finally rise to assist them. For it is said that he is a prudent and mature man and suited to managing matters, of faithful service to the Catholic King, and that he has sailed for around forty years. They say that he was also very

---

[25] Sir Humphrey Gilbert, the half-brother of Sir Walter Raleigh, a noted sailor and explorer.

[26] Sir Francis Drake, renowned explorer and privateer (a practitioner of unofficially sanctioned piracy), and a favourite of the Queen.

[27] John and William Hawkins were renowned privateers.

[28] Sir Richard Grenville had been knighted in 1577 for having arrested Cuthbert Mayne in Cornwall, which effectively led to the wiping out of the great Catholic families in that county. Grenville was among those charged with interrogating Winslade after his arrest on the Spanish Armada.

[29] Michael Lok was a sea merchant whose story is notable for the losses he made by backing the exploits of Martin Frobisher.

[30] Sir John Killigrew was Governor of Pendennis Castle. Many of his family, including his wife, were renowned for privateering.

[31] The word 'Schismatic' was term used by Catholics to describe those among their number who only attended the reformed Church because they could not afford the heavy fines for failing to do so.

highly regarded by Prince John of Austria.[32] Indeed, these duties discharged by him thus far give confidence that his help in advancing these attempts of ours will, at the proper time, be extremely useful.

[7] The man who produces this account was born in Devon too, and he has both in that county and in Cornwall kinsmen, marriage relations and friends, who are great among their people both in name and in authority. There are, moreover, some hundreds of dependants who pay their annual rent in accordance with his Right of Lordship, because they recognise it to be diverted to him by hereditary right, just as [in the past] they knew all the other things, too, which were due in any way to his grandfather, John Winslade. Among these things, the whole of the society of Devonian leaders and several others not to be despised and even of importance – farmers and lesser folk, whose condition is now much worse than they frankly admit that it used to be – know that their lands are to be devolved on him by the same law. The restoration of their Lord [ie of Tristram himself], both to the house of his father and to all his patrimonial goods, they strenuously beg from God with continuous prayers.

So if the Catholic King decides that these two men, Gabriel and the writer, should be used as agents of His Majesty, and after having considered the importance of the matter proposed by them, places them as they may justly hope, and with whom they are to act in England, all those things likewise would be fulfilled by them which they will promise in the name of His Majesty.

They will carry out appropriate plans with the many powerful friends whom they have at home and through all parts of each county to promote the business undertaken by us, and who are placed so conveniently that when it is the right time (primarily at the death of the Queen) they should be ready with their troops to attack the ships, ports, castles, town, and to fortify the places that should seem to them the most suitable to their affairs, not only in these two counties, but also in Somerset and Dorset, if times allows and occasion offers, so that with their minds prepared, the four counties, joined in mind and in strength, should begin our undertaking.

On the death of the Queen, Godolphin,[33] having joined Harrison of Lifton[34] to himself, or with any other wise and faithful friend, will be able

---

32 Most likely a reference to Don Juan, the Spanish King's illegitimate son, who in 1578 raised an army of 3,000 Spanish veterans and marched them from Luxembourg towards Flanders, routing a Netherlands army en route.

33 Sir Francis Godolphin was Governor of the Scilly Islands.

34 This could be the Jesuit priest Father James Harrison, whom Winslade may have met in Newgate prison in 1588. (Catholic Record Society Vol. II. See also CRS Vol. V, pp. 162–63).

to lead the whole of Cornwall and govern it through his own decision. In Devon, Courtenay has all the yeomen and sailors at his pleasure. There are indeed yeomen of inferior position, nearly equal in wealth to the nobility, but less in dignity; the people, particularly in the country, do everything at their decision and leadership. You would correctly call them the Tribunes of the country people.[35] In the City of Exeter (which alone is fortified), Denys has citizens who will agree with all their hearts, if anything should be set in motion for the good of the State.

[8] Up until now our proposals, if they have been approved by his Royal Majesty – and the wisest Prince sees how important they are – [have been concerned with] the maintenance of the safety of his own Monarchy, for the destruction of the ever-increasing sects and the restoration of the Catholic religion, not only in England but also in other, neighbouring regions. It seems wholly clear that the Royal Legate,[36] who now lives in Belgium, as soon as he has received the order from His Majesty, will immediately and seriously take action and will promise and guarantee in the name of the King whatever seems advantageous for promoting and achieving the task.

And so that we may accomplish everything, namely that after the whole Kingdom has been shaken (as is very likely) by unplanned uprisings on the death of the Queen, and that everything regarding the successful performance of our undertaking should be found duly prepared, ready and correctly positioned, three noblemen born in Cornwall and Devon, who all now live in Belgium, are considered to be most suitable for taking control of this region.

The first of them is Gabriel Denys, the son of Thomas who planned the separation of the four counties as a service for Queen Mary. He [Gabriel] is the uncle of this outstanding knight Thomas Denys (who is still alive).[37] The second is Richard Bray, a Professor of Law, a man of known faith and piety, who was once a magistrate in Cornwall and in Devon. And in this duty he brought it about that among all the men of both counties he rendered himself not only well-known but also greatly loved.[38] The third is the man who presents these matters, Tristram Winslade.

As far as the disposition [of these three men] is concerned, it seems

---

[35] In Roman society, a Tribune of the people was a lesser magistrate.

[36] The Royal Legate was a representative of the King of Spain in Brussels.

[37] Sir Thomas Denys of Holcombe Rogus was the son of Sir Robert Denys (Gabriel's brother) and grandson of the Sir Thomas Denys mentioned earlier. He was born in 1559 and knighted in 1586.

[38] Richard Bray was very likely the son of Henry Bray, the former Mayor of Bodmin and a leader during the Prayer Book Rebellion. This may explain the affection in which he was held.

reasonable in our calculations that Gabriel, particularly because he is good at many languages, should linger in the Court at Brussels, where Father Baldwin[39] and he can not only continuously keep His Majesty's Legate informed about our negotiations and decide from the various daily success of the emerging matters in which direction they should go in the future, but can also equip the two remaining participants and look out for those very things that are necessary, or even convenient, to expedite their business with the help of the Legate.

[9] To this end it would be useful that Gabriel's knowledge be regarded as greater as far as payment of a stipend is concerned, which might cause him to distinguish himself better in his undertakings, and cause friends in England to embrace the same tasks more willingly when they see him so valued here. Bray has never served the Catholic King, and for that reason his cause is more favourable at home, and it seems that he could prepare the way in advance without difficulty, and, once established there, could achieve through friends (with some gold added to their prayers) that by a decree of the Senate[40] he can retire to his own house, where he can spend his life without worry with his wife, who is still alive, and under the care of a very powerful man who is extremely well disposed towards him. In his own country he is in the greatest favour among the greatest men. There is no one on whom Francis Godolphin would bestow more than on his friend Bray. He is held in the highest regard by Baron Seymour.[41] He is a very close friend of Courtenay and Denys. Borlack is his nephew by his sister. Polvil is a connection by marriage.[42]

So, established among his own people with security of this kind, he will be able, when occasion offers, to inform Francis Godolfin in Cornwall, and William Courtenay, Thomas Denys, Baron Seymour and others in Devon, to whom he has decided that the cause should be communicated, according to the character of the men, their situation and their favourable disposition,

---

39 Probably Father William Baldwin, who was actively involved in the Catholic Mission to England and may have lived in Brussels at the same time as Winslade.

40 Winslade may have used the word 'Senate' in order to clarify his meaning for the King of Spain. However, it may have been inserted by the transcriber of the document.

41 Probably Edward Seymour, first-born son of the 1st Duke of Somerset. However, this Edward was not his father's heir, as he sided with the Catholics. The heir to the Dukedom was the eldest son by the Duke's second wife.

42 Probably Borlase and Polwhele. Father William Polwhele was arrested in 1594 in connection with a plot to assassinate Queen Elizabeth. Borlase's activities at the time are unknown. The use of surnames only may indicate that Winslade expects the King of Spain to know who they are.

so that on the death of the Queen, having immediately armed, each with his own troops already and clandestinely conscripted, and with other equipment suitable for action as silently as possible, they may rise up in arms and occupy St Michael's Mount, Perina,[43] the Memorial of Saint Mawes,[44] and Launceston in Cornwall, Plymouth and Exeter in Devon, Ilchester in Somerset as well as Sherbourne in Dorset, which they should fortify sufficiently to cut the crossings between the two rivers, Stour and Wier.

Indeed they should declare that they are doing this for no other reason than for the good and security of the whole Kingdom. Firstly, [because] these four counties can be fortified in advance against the hostile attacks of all external forces, in case anyone should attempt to invade – something that could be justly feared in this state of affairs. Secondly, [because] it is thus assured that no disturbance can arise between the four which might, by want of moderation, lead to the depredation of fields and the plundering of towns (for by these actions, [10] the citizens would diminish their strength in a wretched way). Certainly if any one of those four counties recklessly joined the faction of any man not powerful enough or even not justly pretending to the throne, it would be to the certain destruction both of itself and of the whole Kingdom.

Finally, it should be understood that they [the four counties] have entered upon this course of action in order to strengthen and stabilise the future Prince – that is, whomever all the Ranks of the States in the general Committees of Parliament shall declare to be the rightful Heir of the Kingdom.

With these and other influences of this kind of effective reasoning, these men will easily win authority for themselves among the people: Godolphin in Cornwall, Courtenay in Devon, FitzJames[45] in Somerset and Waddam,[46] Trencer[47] or Turberville[48] in Dorset.

These things can also be communicated to certain people – those who seem to be most appropriate – in the two counties of Somerset and

---

[43] Probably Penryn, or, given the inclusion of St Michael's Mount and St Mawes in his list, Winslade could be referring to Pendennis Castle, which is close to Penryn and was built during the reign of Henry VIII. (Perina is evidence, perhaps, of a transcriber with poor English – no native of the West Country would have got Pendennis this wrong.)

[44] The village of St Mawes was named for Saint Maudez. Winslade may have been familiar with a chapel there, which was dedicated to the saint. The reference is probably to the fort of St Mawes Castle, built by Henry VIII to protect the River Fal, the harbour and the Carrick Roads anchorage.

[45] Either Sir Richard FitzJames or his son John (the latter was examined about his knowledge of the Babington Plot. Calendar of State Papers, 1590–1595 p. 100)

[46] Waddam's identity is unknown

[47] Most likely Sir George Trenchard of Dorset

[48] Former Bishop of Exeter, James Turberville.

Dorset. The same thing could no less usefully happen in Wales, so that the Welsh, too, when the time comes, may have everything and themselves in readiness.

It is to be definitely decided, even in the very beginning of the undertaking, which place each person of dignity or authority should be assigned, what thereafter is to be done, the task, and what awaits them and their men in the future, such as a perpetual Honorarium of Bravery. To carry off our cause well, it seems greatly to be of use that the leading part be assigned to Courtenay, because he is the most powerful and most popular of all, but, however, in such a way that he should undertake or set in motion nothing of great moment without the agreement of his coadjutors Denys and Baron Seymour. To these should be added likewise as advisor Gifford from Halesbury[49] and certain other Catholic men whose faith and prudence both in civil and military matters have been well recognised and well known.

[11] Of those present among all the Cornish (since the great Arundell and several others[50] are captive or absent) Godolphin would be greatly pleasing to the people, should he join the rest and present himself as coadjutor to Courtenay along with Denys and Seymour.

In Devon, Courtenay, Denys and Seymour are certainly the most powerful and by far the most pleasing to the people; everything is done in that county on their decision and authority. If the Cornish approach them, they will be well enough equipped in strength either to persuade the people of Somerset and Dorset – or certainly to compel them – to cross over to their side. For as often as Devon or Cornwall has taken up arms, or both counties at the same time, they have always had the people of Somerset and Dorset as allies. Never, however, have they ever armed themselves for a cause more just, nor have they attacked so clear an injustice with less risk and with greater security. If the grandfather of the author and Humphrey Arundell, when they took up arms against the heretic plagues who then held power in the name of the King, had stood fast in the Exeter siege and had occupied the other places mentioned by us above, it is indeed very likely that, if all that hill of perfidious people had been subdued, they would have restored the practice of the Catholic religion to all the churches of England.[51] Admittedly, at

---

49 This Gifford may have been related to the Jesuit William Gifford who was in Brussels c.1595.
50 Sir John Arundell of Lanherne was arrested with several others in 1576 for having harboured the Jesuit priest, Father Cuthbert Mayne. They included Sir Francis Tregian, whose home at Golden in Cornwall was Father Mayne's base. Arundell and Tregian were both imprisoned in London.
51 This is a further reference to the Prayer Book Rebellion of 1549, during the reign of Edward VI.

that time they had a King accepted by the whole people, on whose authority they approved huge troops not only of Englishmen but also of foreigners in order to overwhelm the Catholics by their numbers. For there were twenty thousand and more men trained in arms from Devon and Cornwall when they were besieging Exeter. But the men of Somerset, Dorset, Wilton and Hampton,[52] when messengers were sent to them, argued vehemently that, when the siege of the city had been lifted, they should hurry to London by forced marches in order to attack the enemy with joined strengths. So did the Welsh, who had armed thirty thousand men, binding their faith to them in a holy manner, that if they [the Cornish] hastened their journey, they [the Cornish] would meet them [the Welsh] with all their troops on Salisbury Plain, and would put the same fortune of war to the test with them. But when dissent arose among the people because of the caution of the leaders, who were trying to allay the dissident minds, [12] they [the Cornish] were left in the lurch. The royal army attacked seven or eight thousand of them in a wide field near the Sampford district of Devon.[53] However, when both sides had fought bitterly for the space of an entire day, and a very great carnage had been made of both factions, finally failing not with our spirits but in our bodies because of weariness, Victory was in the possession of the enemy.

But what we must do at the proper time, namely on the death of the Queen, is different by far – much more plausible, much easier both for persuading and for guaranteeing. Nothing here is done against the Monarch, nothing against the State, nothing against the power of the Sovereign, neither the one who is now, nor the one who will be in the line of succession. On the contrary, what we are now undertaking is the only plan for preserving the country. If it is saved in one piece and unshaken, that will not displease the people, but rather it will please them greatly that the Ranks of the Kingdom in the general Committees,[54] without the din of arms, with their own customary votes, choose and declare as King the one to whom they know to look by Divine and human Right. By this way of reasoning, it will be proper for Catholics and Schismatics to worship God by the Catholic rite to save their souls, as well as to enjoy temporal things – to their own comfort and that of their households. It is necessary to show some favour to the godless, the worldly, and the heretics, who know only earthly things, since the worldly things that they seek are useful, and in this condition of the State are better acquired, preserved and increased.

---

[52] Probably a reference to Wiltshire and Hampshire.

[53] Sampford Courtenay was the site of the last major battle of the Prayer Book Rebellion.

[54] This may be a reference to minor, more localized instruments or committees of government.

These four counties, as I have just said, separated from the rest, will easily be able to arm a hundred thousand strong men for battle on land, and to provide six thousand sailors at sea with arms and all the other gear that pertains to naval expeditions.

From this memorable example of the four Counties, since places of refuge are made for all those who want to join their faction, [13] the Catholics and the Schismatics will receive great consolation, all the others a great lesson as to how they ought to behave in this state of the times in order to gain the same security as they. The Welsh doubtless will join them, not only so that they may rejoice in this desired security with them and be able to return to the ancient rite of the Catholic religion, which nearly all the Welsh seek with their prayers, but also because of the unparalleled affection of love and those particular relationships that which exist between Wales, Devon and Cornwall from the daily trade in wares.

Since this authority to administer matters is already confirmed in Courtenay and the rest, or in others (for the business that, God willing, is undertaken is to be fulfilled), for us there is more help from the cause itself than from men. In Cornwall and Devon, Bray will make sure that he looks for some nobleman of faith and prudence, or several if that seems good, and with them Bray, or at least one of the priests, will immediately set out for Belgium, in the name of Courtenay and his coadjutors. Just before they return (and with them 40 or 50 military leaders well versed in military matters), they will have agreed with the Prince[55] by solemn oath about the amount and speed of the delivery of necessary assistance. In addition they will bring with them on their return books learnedly and piously written in our local language to train the people who are unacquainted with matters of faith, and about establishing the reformed rite. At the same time priests trained to persuade through doctrine and eloquence will be sent. The writer will accompany them and other men of our nation, whose efforts will be of some use in promoting our cause.

The Archduke[56] or His Majesty's Legate will promise with a solemn oath in the name of the King (if that business should be successful) that he will decorate Francis Godolphin, Thomas Denys and Seymour with the illustrious title of Baron, with its rights and prerogatives, and that he will assign to each of them the annual returns and profits which correspond fully to the titles conferred by him in England. To the leading men in Somerset and

---

55 This may be a reference to the Archduke, who was appointed by the King to govern the Netherlands on his behalf.

56 Winslade is probably referring to King Philip of Spain's nephew, Archduke Ernest of Austria, who was appointed Governor of the Netherlands in 1594. He died in Brussels in 1595.

Dorset, too, who help them [14] with their strenuous efforts he likewise will promise that he will repay them each according to the valour of his service. He will declare William Courtenay a Count of Devon. Tristram Winslade [the author] offers his approval of his [Courtenay's] election, as far as the title, estates and powers, on these conditions: that the Archduke or His Majesty's Legate in the King's name solemnly promises to Tristram in the same way as to the others that he will restore to him everything that his grandfather possessed and then lost on account of his steadfast defence of the Catholic religion;[on the condition] that he be allowed to exact and convert to his own use all the revenues which are called Arerages[57] seized by Mohun, Trelawney and the others,[58] from that time when Mohun, Trelawny and the others obtained his goods from the heretic-leading King. [On the condition] likewise that everything be restored to him that his father similarly lost because of the Catholic religion, everything to which he [Tristram's father] had a short time earlier been restored through the kindness of Queen Mary and the intervention of the Catholic King. All of this, however, immediately upon the death of Queen Mary, the cursed heretics usurped again.[59] [On the condition] likewise that he be admitted to all the possessions of Robert Winslade,[60] which have devolved on him by hereditary law, on the grounds that Robert died without male offspring. Reginald Mohun, indeed, took over the inheritance as the closest heir, denouncing John, William and Tristram Winslade[61] as guilty of *lèse majesté*[62] and the crime of Catholicism. And [on the condition] that the Areragias of these possessions be awarded to him, just as was earlier said about his grandfather's possessions. [On the condition] that all the possessions and the land of Wod at Nortauton[63] of the most vile and perverse heretic [Mohun] be returned to Tristram with all the profits

[57] A legal term for unpaid rents. Different spellings of the word soon appear.

[58] In 1590, Tristram Winslade mounted a legal case in the court of Chancery in which he claimed he was the rightful heir of Edward Courtenay, the last Early of Devon. (The case is described in detail by Chynoweth – referred to in the introduction to this translation.)

[59] A reference to the restoration of Buckland Brewer to William Winslade in 1558 and Elizabeth's decision to overturn its restoration in 1564.

[60] Robert Winslade was probably a member of the extended family; perhaps a cousin or uncle of the author's.

[61] Here Winslade refers to three generations of his family: his grandfather (John Winslade, the leader of the Prayer Book Rebellion, who was executed for treason in 1550), his father (William, the harper who became known as Sir Tristram), and himself, Tristram.

[62] The crime of treason.

[63] The name of this location is obscure. As W is not a normal Latin letter, it may be that this was a local place name given a Latin ending – wodus. Wod may be an ancient Celtic name.

therefrom, from the day he [Mohun] first usurped it. Indeed this, in the case of [the land of] Wod, so that the matter can be decided fairly and well on the order of the very next Bishop of Exeter, it will be entrusted to four men, two from the Church and two secular men, who will be able to judge and decide on the whole matter according to their conscience – but in such a way that this decision of theirs does not prejudice his [Tristram's] right to maintain all these possessions, both this [land of] Wod and whatever else, until it is established for certain by law that he does not have this right; until that time, he [the author] will be able to take possession with the agreement of Courtenay and the others who are in charge of affairs with him.

[15]

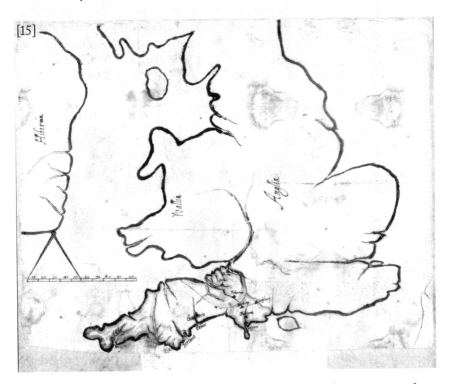

[16] [On the condition] that Courtenay does not exact Arraregiarum from Mohun, Trelawney or from anyone else of those who now possess land bordering on [those of] the last Count of Devon, until Mohun and the rest have fully satisfied Tristram for the unjust seizure of the lands and goods belonging to the family of Winslade. But if it is discovered that the means of those who now possess the Winslades' ancestral possessions are not sufficient to compensate for the injuries carried out over such a length of time, let it be conceded that the losses shall be made good from the possessions and goods of other heretics, but not [from those] of any Schismatic, even

though he [a Schismatic] may continue to occupy some part of them [the Winslades' ancestral lands], but only on the proviso that he is prepared to restore whatever he has unjustly occupied. If anyone should say that he did not seize goods of this kind but that he had bought them, let him meet with the seller [to discuss] recovery of his loss.

For this reason he [Tristram] freely agrees, or rather, vehemently desires, that overall command in Devon should be conferred on Courtney, and that Denys, Seymour and Godolphin should be honoured with the illustrious title and dignity of Barons, on the condition that the Catholic [Spanish] King be proclaimed as the Elector of the next King of England and the perpetual Protector of the whole Kingdom and nation. To fulfil this at the right time these four men will be able to combine the wealth and resources which they obtain by favour and authority from the whole populace in each of their territories. I dare to promise that once they have been restored to their own, they will as gentlemen assist in whatever may lead to the desired end, not only because they are all Catholics, or at least feel the same as Catholics on all matters, but also because they take into consideration their own safety and that of their households in the present circumstances, and because they [wish to] hand down to their descendants the wealth and honours received from their forebears, greatly increased by their own excellence and the generosity of the Prince. Indeed, the commons can easily be induced to embrace this business with open arms, partly because they are very attached to the four men mentioned, and to any other men of ancient nobility, particularly in this state of upheaval, and partly also because of the great hope that then will shine of recovering Peace, Friendship and Trade with Spain and Lusitania. Nothing more desirable than this could happen to them in this life.

[17] These are indeed the tasks that will fall to Bray as the designated agent, so that on the Prince's command he will try with pious zeal to manage these things according to his prudence and faith and to bring them to completion. Since he cannot succeed at his own expense, having long since been stripped of all his possession in England (where they would have been more than sufficient for his purposes), he entreats His Catholic Majesty to order that he should have the prospect of [being awarded] his necessary expenses.

The third agent is the author, determined from the occasions offered, wherever the business leads, to acquire material and instruments, [and to decide] with the help of Father Baldwin and the judgement of the agents, where they can be put to good use when the plan has been resolved. And it seem good to the author at least that being placed at Bordeaux in Gascony would be very helpful to him, in order to speculate and to do business, particularly because each year more than a thousand sailors flood into that city, indeed more than five hundred from Devon and Cornwall alone. On some occasion and pretext of trade, Bray will be able to instruct him from England with which men, in which business and for what reason he ought to deal confidently and without danger. He will also be able to inform him frequently about the state of his negotiations. And, being informed about the success of the affair, from Bordeaux he will be able with the same ease to instruct his men (to whom he looks) both in Spain and in Flanders in such minute detail that they will find out nearly every day how our affairs stand.

However, he undertakes to do this only on the condition that, hearing of the death of the Queen (if he is still alive and equipped with the things necessary for the task) he will immediately and without delay be sent to his ancestral counties of Devon and Cornwall with some leaders of war who are well experienced in military affairs. And to that end it is useful that it will be completely up to him to decide about himself, and on some change of circumstance either to remain in Bordeaux, to return to Belgium, or to convey himself without any limits of place or time to wherever it will seem more suitable if Father Baldwin's plans are also approved by the other two.

[18] [Scribbled in Italian by another hand] Respects to the Catholic King from the Catholics of England.[64]

Moreover, so that the agents can carry out their undertakings energetically and carry them through to a happy conclusion, it has to be completely agreed that to the Royal Legate living here in Belgium be attributed the free and full ability to pay each month's allowance from the annual salary which has been decided for these three agents, but in such a way that the taxmen are neither able to smell with the slightest suspicion what they are doing nor where they are.

The Royal Senators [the Privy Council in England] have for a long time now held in suspicion nearly all the men of the first rank in Devon and Cornwall and even the very people of both counties. For this reason they have deprived Courtenay in Devon and Godolphin in Cornwall of authority and have replaced them with Raleigh and Clifford, men of sworn allegiance, in order that they can attempt to bring it about that the inexperienced commons, [trusting] their false words and cunning machinations, may embrace them [Raleigh and Clifford] with willing minds. Once they have achieved this, harbours, cities, towns, fortifications, everything will be in their power.

Raleigh indeed, perceiving as something amazing that the whole people's sense of duty towards those who are of ancient nobility is such that they

---

[64] The translation of this largely illegible Italian notation is conjectural. It may also mean 'refer all matters regarding the English Catholics to the Catholic King'. The Kraus catalogue's idea that this is a second heading is incorrect; placed as it is in the Latin document, it bears no relation to the content.

cannot for any reason be torn away from them, acts in every way to reconcile the minds of both parties. Cecil and the rest who are of the Queen's private circle, Raleigh likewise and the others who hold high office in this state of affairs, are much anguished in their hearts when they consider the power of foreign enemies threatening their necks; when they see the minds of the Sectarians[65] so dissenting amongst themselves that they can in no way be composed; when they catch sight of a huge crowd of men, both of commons and of nobles, or rather even a large group and among them men who vehemently shrink away from the present system of administering the State, praying for and expecting reform. But this makes them [the Council] most confused, because in so great a ferment of confused minds, even though all clever men strain themselves, they do not know how to escape the difficulties of choosing a Prince, or even of establishing some form of State in which they can live forever with the splendour of dignity and wealth that they now have, and pass [these advantages] on to their descendants.

[19] In this confusion of opinion, it then occurred to them that it would be of advantage to resume friendly relations with the Spanish, to renew their old relationship with them, reasoning that they might thus securely enjoy the honours and the goods that they had gained, not only because they would thus be rendered safe from all retribution for injuries done to Spain, but also because the Catholic King would either take the hostile weapons of the French on his own shield or send them back against them. If safe against the French, they do not indeed heed the Scot much, whose hostile attack, if he sets anything in motion about the Kingdom, they will easily drive back with their own arms. In professing these notions, they seem to project some ambiguous and almost timid expression about 'freedom of conscience' or about 'I-know-not-what tolerance' to be conceded to Catholics. And indeed it is believable that they should wish to impose on the Christian leaders to think of some reconciliation by which Catholics are allowed to lead their lives with heretics, angels with demons, Christ with Baal, at least for the time being – their condition being that Christ should submit to the power and laws of Baal in all things. But may it not happen to us that, after forty-five years of enduring hardship in defence of the Catholic faith both at home and abroad, we should finally look for such a change of heart from the Pope and the Catholic leaders of the English Church. But if the plan proposed by us for reforming the State has those results that we deservedly ought to hope for from the very goodness of the cause, certainly the matter will be clearly

---

[65] This may be a reference to factions forming around the issue of the royal succession (as Elizabeth was refusing to name a successor) or it may be a reference to a push by some towards religious tolerance.

different. For, as is right, we place God the Best and the Greatest in first place as leader of his army, as arbiter of his cause. Then we make distinct orders of men – of Catholics, Schismatics and heretics. The Catholics, the true servants of God, are to be favoured by all means. The Schismatics are worthy of pity, for at heart they believe in God with us although they do not confess God aloud with us. God is to be begged to impart the spirit of courage to them so that what they piously believe at heart about justice they may bravely profess aloud about salvation. We place the heretics in the last position as being by far the most pernicious of all men that the earth bears. Nonetheless, we consider that all care should be taken to return them to sanity. But if they obstinately reject all continued care, it is thus to be decided about them, that they should not stand in the way of the pious attempts of Catholic men.

[20] Therefore these are the things proposed by us: to decide, as was said, about the distinct orders of men; to assign his place to each; to utterly eradicate all heretics (as far as we are able); to preserve the proper authority and dignity of Holy Mother Church undefiled; in England to restore ancestral morality, faith, honesty, innocence, and obedience to the Prince and to the magistrates.

Moreover all these things the writer considers to be much more achievable in this western region of England than in the other counties, because that body of four counties is to be united, not only politically, but also, as we hope, in piety. It is of such a kind, so suitable for receiving assistance from Spain conveniently, and, as occasion requires, even to help her; so well furnished with arms and ships, so strongly fortified against all who may try to invade from any direction, because of Wales, the sea, and its separation from the other counties. There is, therefore, no doubt there is no part of the whole Kingdom that is so greatly both able and willing to bring so many supports to promote the business of our cause.

Indeed, just as it will soon be declared by the common vote of all that the Catholic King is the Agonothetes[66] of this Sacred Army, that everything is to be done on his order, and finally that, once this business has been brought to success under the auspices of the divine Spirit, he is to be likewise named Perpetual Protector of the whole Kingdom and of the nation. We are suppliants to His Majesty, so that he himself may pledge his faith to us in return about all the things to be done that have been mentioned above by us, in so far as the titles and possessions or the annual return on them [for those] who answer to the splendour of the titles, and not only for the four

[66] The leader or general. In ancient Greece, the Agonothetes was the superintendent of the Sacred Games.

men touched on earlier by name, but also for as many others who are put forward for rewards and honours according to their own merit – those who have performed hard and outstanding service for the comfort and restoration of Catholics and for the overthrow and destruction of the opposing side, and for the complete eradication of heresies and errors.

[21] It will also have the greatest weight in demonstrating the glory of God, in strengthening the authority of [Catholic] churchmen, in reforming corrupt morals, in removing unjust laws and depraved habits from society, if those many Catholic men, whose faith, honesty and prudence have been well known and seen, he rewards with honours and defends with authority, and if to the individual Schismatics who have been raised to some positions of dignity he joins the individual Catholic men, whom he makes equal to them in dignity and authority. Magnates who are distinguished by excellent titles of honour should not be removed if they are found worthy of their places. But if they are not, it is much better for the State that both the honours and the rewards should fall to others who are more suitable to the duties.

It seems very advantageous to the honour of the Holy Spirit and an example to later generations that the deeds of these times be recorded in public registers, that they be placed among the monuments of the people to the perpetual memory of the undertaking.

In all this business, the appointed agents need authority, means, time, and clear instructions. They have to be cautious about to whom and how far they communicate anything secret – in this matter especially there is great need of prudence, because in daily use we risk the ruin of many. Henry Bolingbroke and Henry the Seventh clearly achieved all their business before the other side knew anything about it, offering us an example in this matter most worthy of imitation. Gabriel Denys would wish that some undertaking had already been made to hobble the pretensions of the King of Scotland. He urges even now that some plan be entered into by which the ships stationed at Ross may be captured immediately on the death of the Queen, and converted to our use. The author is rather versed in the matter of Scotland and he considers that he is able to somewhat excel in this business, if he should be instructed to act in the necessary matters. He will explain his reasons to the King's Legate, if it seems good. Furthermore, in this business of capturing the ships, he hopes that he will render useful assistance with the help of certain sailors who are from Cornwall and Devon and have at some time served the Queen. But this plan cannot be executed through them unless that business of the four counties has first been undertaken and the sailors still in [maritime] service. [22] Moreover, if these undertakings go well with divine help, the number even of the agents or negotiators will necessarily be increased; just as they are each bound by the authority of the Royal Legate to perform their duty, so it is fair that they should also anticipate rewards for their labours from him – just as the three agents mentioned above.

[These are matters for negotiation:][67] the conditions to be put by them [the negotiators] to the people in order to so win over and excite their minds that they may willingly agree to the proposals which they [the negotiators] support; the manner of reforming the State which will bring greater hope of peace and security; in addition, what other things in regard to the preparing and strengthening of men's minds may be brought to light for any reason, and will seem suitable in view of the times and changing circumstances. Father Parsons[68] will be able and willing to perform all these things, each at the proper time; and Father Baldwin and Gabriel Denys will stretch out a helping hand to him in this business.

If the things set forth here are accomplished in the order and manner advised by us: the Scots, the Danes, the French can be kept out of the Kingdom of England, or if they attempt to enter, they can easily be warded off; proper honour will again be shown to Christ; among the English, the Catholic King will leave to all his descendants the very sacred title 'Most August', which he received from his ancestors; Spain, Lusitania, both the East and West Indies will be made secure; there will be safe sea passage for everyone without an armed fleet; the Kingdoms of Ireland and Scotland will regain the Catholic religion; the Belgians will enjoy long-desired peace under the rule of their own Princes; a bridle will be placed on France; the heretics will be crest-fallen throughout Europe; the monstrous tyranny of the Turks will soon be at risk throughout their empire.[69]

This state of affairs, from what has been described, through the reconciliation of the parties in England, is without doubt most pleasing to God; it is of the least expense and has the least shedding of innocent blood; it is completely praiseworthy, popular and easy; it is not possible to think of another way more effective in reforming the state of England. For all the other ways that have been thought of up to now (apart from the reconciliation of the great part of the English people), [23] appear to be of enormous expense, bloody, uncertain, and totally useless at bringing about a good reformation. This very plan for reformation drawn up by us, your agents, the means and scope proposed in this whole business – all will restore glory

---

[67] It is not clear who the parties to such negotiations are to be as there is no form of introduction to the agenda that Winslade is putting forward. The word 'agents' suggests that Winslade may be referring to himself, Denys and Bray as the chief negotiators with parties in England and perhaps also Scotland.

[68] Father Robert Parsons was a leading figure among the Jesuits working in England.

[69] People across western Europe were very afraid of the Turks, Moors and other Islamic peoples. Attacks on the Cornish and Devonshire coast were not unknown and people were sometimes kidnapped and taken into slavery.

to the Divine Spirit, the restoration of the Christian State, and good and everlasting fame to His Catholic Majesty for an outstanding achievement. Everything is founded on religion, piety and reason. Whatever other and equally valid reasons [maybe advanced] by those who stand with us, [all agree] that in order to bring this business to a sound conclusion, there needs to be a great coming together of the men of the English race.[70]

The author will wait for a time pleasing to the Catholic King, if he should honour him and his proposals with a reply. And he trusts that there is a better outlook for him in the future than there has for many years until now. But if it is not to be, he will be His Majesty's suppliant (even if unwelcome) so that with his good blessing, he may enter into other ways of maintaining his life. For he [the King] has dealt with him so sparingly that for incurring the expenses of one whole year, barely the salary for even one month is obtained, and then only after much worry and prayers. The result of this is that he is permitted neither to remain here, because there is nothing for him to live off, nor to depart hence, unless he first settles the large debts that he has incurred here.

---

[70] The syntax of this sentence is exceptionally obscure.

4

William Gwavas and a Lost Cornish Vocabulary fragment at Trinity College Dublin

Sharon Lowenna

Introduction

The names of William Gwavas of Mount's Bay and Thomas Tonkin of Trevaunance are inextricably linked through their collaboration on the study and collection of the Cornish language in the early eighteenth century. There is, however, a need to differentiate between their respective circumstances, networks and motivations. Circumstantial context is not simply an optional supplement; rather it is essential to our understandings and interpretations of the texts. This Foucauldian approach helps to show how the survival, status and circulation of the choices they exerted still influence our perceptions today. The works of Tonkin and Gwavas are as a consequence not arbitrary, nor are their respective collection strategies. The texts themselves are affected (if not effected) by their respective social and ideological positioning. These factors arguably determine what *kinds* of texts each of them chose to address and which *specific* texts they selected for transcription or publication.

Tonkin knew Edward Lhuyd from his time at Oxford University[1] and helped to facilitate Lhuyd's access to some Celtic material through his 'gentlemen's network'. Their correspondence largely focuses on the costs and timescales Lhuyd estimated for him to acquire for Tonkin copies and translations of the known Middle Cornish texts. Tonkin obviously adopted the role of *commissioner* of texts from Lhuyd. Tonkin commonly deferred to Gwavas' superior knowledge of the Cornish language after Lhuyd's death, as his MS dedication (1736) to Gwavas (of the proposed *Archaeologia Cornu-Britannica*) makes explicit:

William Gwavas of Gwavas, In the County of Cornwall Esquire.
Dear Sir,
In dedicating the two following articles to you, viz.
Title VIII, A Collection of modern Cornish Pieces and, Title
IX, A Cornish Vocabulary I do but in a manner restore to you
what in a great measure belonged to you before, since 'tis what
you have, in the first of these, for the best and greatest part
supply'd me with out of your own store and compositions;
and as for the latter, viz. The Vocabulary, I must always acknowledge that without your kind assistance, I should never
have been able to have gone through with it, especially in the
Modern or Vulgar Cornish. It is therefore but common justice to lay before you these parts of the present undertaking, in
which you have so large a share, and to whom must be owing
their appearing, if not in perfection, at least without any great and
notorious errors.[2]

Tonkin was less interested in the vernacular Cornish around him, and
more concerned with his own conspicuous erudition for publication, in the
tradition of prestige antiquarian and parochial histories. By contrast, Gwavas
did not baulk at learning from older Cornish speakers. Robert Morton Nance
made the point that, whilst firmly of his time and privileged class, Gwavas
does not revile the old folks' ignorance, but says, 'they knew not how to write
it or rightly decide the words or sentences, yet gave the true pronunciation
and accent of the word'.[3] Gwavas himself said his knowledge of the language
came 'by some manuscripts & Collection, by oral Tradition & Conversing
with most of ye best persons that could discourse of ye speaking Cornish
Language including Mr John Keigwin of ye Mousehole & others. & 20 years
observations from my own'.[4] Gwavas was no less conventionally cultured or
educated than Tonkin. In his Commonplace Book,[5] Gwavas jotted down a
brief list of his philological and influences and sources which demonstrate his
familiarity with a wide range of canonic European writings on the philosophy
of language.[6] Gwavas' younger daughter Ann married Rev Thomas Carlyon,
who served as vicar of St Just-in-Roseland for more than fifty years. Ann
Carlyon inherited some of her father's personal papers which now form part
of the collection of documents relating to the Carlyon family of Tregrehan
(designated CN) at Cornwall Record Office. Amongst these are Gwavas'
book catalogue and valuation,[7] in his own hand, dated 1717. He signed this
in three languages:

Cornish – Wm Gwavas
als

Latine – Wilhelmus Cornubiens
als
Englished – William Winterly

Brick Court Middle Temple no. 4
a ground chamber on ye right hand

Penzance Cornwall May 5th 1716 In my studdy [*sic*] mentioned in this
Catalogue
ye totall value of ye books ...... comes now to £73:12:3

This catalogue firstly details his extensive law reference books, including those on tithes and the constitutional position of the Duchy of Cornwall. Several of these have a margin notes stating 'lost' or 'gone', and there are two margin notes saying 'bought of John Boson'. Then he lists the eclectic works he owned of philosophical, Classical, historical and Cornish interest, including Carew's *Survey of Cornwall* 'interleaving to binding'.[8]

Whilst Gwavas had his professional practice as a barrister, Tonkin had no focused profession or career as such. Tonkin played country squire, except for a brief period from 12 April 1714 until 5 January 1715 when his establishment and conservative credentials became explicit. He 'represented in parliament the borough of Helston. Alexander Pendarves ... was his colleague in parliament and his chief friend; they were Cornish squires of high tory repute'.[9] Tonkin's network from his spell at Oxford also included establishment and High Anglican figures such as Thomas Tanner (later Bishop of St Asaph) and Edmund Gibson (later Bishop of London). It is pertinent to remember that the politics of the English Civil Wars, the contested Divine Right of Kings, accession of William and Mary as constitutional monarchs, the Bill of Rights and Jacobite Risings of 1715 were still divisive issues in the early eighteenth century. Two texts in the Tonkin Bilbao MSS[10] exemplify how Tonkin and Gwavas differed politically. For publication in the proposed *Archaeologia Cornu-Britannica*, Gwavas sent Thomas Tonkin a copy of John Tonkin's Cornish verses in praise of William III.[11] Thomas Tonkin's final proposals for printing rejected Gwavas' selection, in favour of Keigwin's Cornish translation of King Charles I's[12] letter to his subjects of Cornwall. Robert Morton Nance's opinion is that John Keigwin 'merely chose the Letter of thanks as a convenient subject for an experiment in writing his own "restored" variety of Cornish' as Keigwin was far from being a staunch Stuart partisan. Nance suggests Keigwin believed Charles Stuart to be a 'roge' (rogue), but it appears this stemmed from a mis-reading of a partially damaged copy. The relevant word is not 'roge' but 'royal'. William Borlase quoted Keigwin's letter[13] to Gwavas in full:

To Wm Gwavas Esq at his chambers in the Temple, London
Sir. The Original of this being sent by Mr Hill of Trevennethick to
me. It was my promise to enterpret it in Cornish, and you have it as
a New Year's gift from me committing it to your approbation, not
doubting but you will conceal the weaknefs of it, if you dislike, or
communicate it to Cousin Nicholl &son and to Mr Anstis, if you
esteem well; the thanks come from a royal breast, and though it may
be kept a Monument to posterity in the English tongue, yet Cornish
men may not do amifs (to whom it is peculiar ...) to record their
meritts in their own.
　　Your well acquainted
　　John Keigwin

Henry Jenner's later description (1904) of John Tonkin's Williamite verses
could be said to be somewhat ideologically charged too:

Song on James II. and William of Orange, by
John Tonkin of St Just, a tailor, who appears to
have been a solitary Whig in a nation of Jacobites,
as with very few exceptions the Cornish certainly
were.[14]

In his description of the Borlase MSS,[15] Jenner repeated,

Another song ... more or less in praise of William of Orange and
in dispraise of James II ... He seems to have been a solitary Whig
in a nation of Jacobites, and I suspect him of being the 'gentleman
near the Lands End' who wrote a rather violent account, published at
the time, concerning the proclamation of James III at St. Columb by
James Paynter in 1715.

There were though many more than 'one solitary Whig' in Cornwall, however
much Jenner would have wished it otherwise. Whilst Jenner revered King
Charles I as divine saint and martyr, 155 men of St Just had put their names
to an opposing view in 1658:

Wee whose names are under written,
doe freely and voluntaryly engage
to be true and faithfull to his Highness the Lord
Protector Against forraigne invadors or dysturbers of
the peace of this Nation, as it is now setled under the
Comand of his highness, whensoever wee bee there

unto required of the defence of ye County, to the utmost
of our power, and hereunto have subscribed our hands the
first day of May, 1658.[16]

The 155 names include several Tonkins, a smattering of Usticks, and trio of
Drakes. Even as late as 1842, the then vicar of St Just felt strongly enough to
pronounce his divine judgement on these 155 supporters of Oliver Cromwell:

It is melancholy to reflect how many were these traitors to their King,
and on the miseries which the regicides entailed on themselves, their
families, and country.[17]

Nance said of John Keigwin that:

the Cornish-writing group of which he belonged seem to all have
been Whiggishly inclined. The absence of a single Jacobite rhyme in
so safe and secret a language and the treasuring by Gwavas of the very
anti-Jacobite verses of John Tonkin, of St Just, written in it, would
prove this, without Lhuyd's elegiacal ode in Cornish on the death of
William of Orange communicated to his Cornish friends.[18]

Keigwin's letter accompanying his Cornish translation of the King Charles
I letter displayed warmth and affection and also shows Keigwin's familiarity
with the Cornish network of those 'called to the Bar'. John Keigwin's letter
to Gwavas is suggested as variously dated 1693 or c.1707.[19] The later dating
is more feasible – if the earlier, Gwavas would have been just 17 years old.
What is clear however is that young Gwavas was establishing his Cornish
networks with the speech community of Mount's Bay and, through his
profession, the Middle Temple.

The Middle Temple and the letter to America

From the sixteenth century onwards, there was a strong tradition of Cornish
entrants to the Middle Temple specifically. For example, the 'Cornish family
of Carew had six representatives among the distinguished members alone'.[20]
During Gwavas' time at Middle Temple practice, his Cornish contemporaries
included Sir John Anstis and John Nicholls Esq of Trereife, as mentioned in
Keigwin's letter. Middle Temple members had also been prominent amongst
those investing in the New World colonies. Early emigrants were, of course,
subject to the laws of England despite lawyers and barristers being thin on
the ground.

Virginia drew few lawyers to its shore in the seventeenth century. Most of the councillors of state, members of the House of Burgesses, sheriffs, clerks of court, and justices of the peace on the Virginia county courts from 1634 to 1699 were nonlawyers. In other words, amateurs laid the foundations of the Old Dominion's courts, legislature, and laws.[21]

The educated and landed patriarchs of Virginia acted perforce as legal adjudicators, counsel and Justices of the Peace. It was therefore *de rigeur* for gentlemen to have law reference books in their private libraries[22] and doubtless expert legal opinion and case precedents were also sought from the Inns of Court in London. The Middle Temple was renowned above the other Inns for accepting pupillage candidates from America who then went on to practice law in the colonies.

> The claim that the Society of the Middle Temple took a leading part in the birth of the American nation through the number of members who were concerned in the settlement of Virginia has received general recognition ... One hundred and fifty (Americans) joined the Middle Temple and the stream of Americans reached its heights in the middle of the eighteenth century.[23]

In the latter half of the eighteenth century, the Colonists' arguments against Britain's rule were legal and constitutional: unsurprisingly, five members of the Middle Temple signed the original Declaration of Independence.[24] In Virginia, the College of William and Mary near Williamsburg was awarded its royal charter and land grant as early as 1693. Founded through the major charitable Brafferton bequest and other donations from England, 'the Colledge' prioritised Schools of Law, Divinity, Philosophy, Mathematics, and Grammar 'of ancient languages'.[25]

Drafted at the Middle Temple, William Gwavas' letter to America[26] has been something of a curiosity. Alan M. Kent notes its marked pantheistic tenor and suggests it could therefore have been ultimately intended for Native American recipients. That is a possibility as:

> language was added to the Royal Charter to list as one of the College's missions 'that the Christian faith may be propagated amongst the Western Indians, to the glory of Almighty God ... the College would keep soe many Indian children in Sicknesse and health, in Meat, drink, Washing, Lodgeing, Cloathes, Medicine, books and Education from the first beginning of Letters till they are ready to receive Orders and be thought Sufficient to be sent abroad to preach and Convert the Indians'.[27]

Should Gwavas' letter have reached that conjectured destination, all evidence would have been lost in a series of fires which destroyed the archives and library of the Colonial period. Kent also raises the valid possibility that Gwavas knew a 'learned gentleman' who may have shared his Cornish language interests, though the 'window of opportunity' for Cornish language transference was closing by the mid-1600s, given the westwards retreat of the language.[28] So, *could* Gwavas have known any emigrants who might conceivably have had some knowledge of the Cornish language as late as 1710? Gwavas certainly would have known *of* emigrants and returners to and from America. There were plenty of emigrants from West Penwith, where knowledge and use of the language persisted. Mount's Bay area Cornish who emigrated included, for example, one John Keigwin of Mousehole. He emigrated to Stonington, Connecticut, *c*.1695 and married Hannah Brown there on 10 October 1700.[29] There is evidence of a specific individual personally known to Gwavas. Sampson Trevethan was a bachelor in his thirties when he emigrated from Mount's Bay to Virginia *c*.1699 where he married Anne Church of Norfolk County, Virginia, in 1703.[30] They had two daughters, Mary and Ann. Trevethan was helped into employment by his older Cornish kinsman, Christopher Cocke of Helston. Cocke and his wife Grace (née Bolitho) had married at Wendron in 1673 and emigrated to Princess Anne County, Virginia, *c*.1675.[31] Cocke had become Clerk of the County and engaged Sampson Trevethan, on his arrival in America, as Surveyor and Customs supervisor of Lynnhaven Bay.[32] When Cocke died in 1716 he willed his chief mourner's ring to Trevethan. Sampson Trevethan in turn, as a sign of his high regard, willed a mourner's ring to William Gwavas. Trevethan was living in Princess Anne County at the time Gwavas wrote his letter to America, but he returned to Cornwall in 1714 and resided with his second wife (Katherine) at Lariggan, Penzance. Trevethan's will was proved in 1729:

> To be buried in the parish church of Madderne. Legatees: wife Katherine (including £400 due him on a mortgage by James Keigwyn, of Mousehole in said county) and after her death to his two daughters he left in Virginia, Mary and Ann Trevethan. To wife a messuage in Madderne called Shoals House.
> To (executors) William Gwavas Esq and Gregory Tregurtha, tanner, both of Penzance, all the rest of his estate, in trust to pay his debts, &c, and to pay his daughters Mary and Ann £200 each. All lands &c in Lynhaven parish, Va., to his two daughters.[33]

On Trevethan's death, William Gwavas declined to act as executor. It can be safely assumed that Gwavas' refusal was due to the discovery that

Trevethan's first wife Ann was still alive in Virginia, and that Trevethan's second marriage to Katherine was bigamous. There is also a later reference *c*.1750 to sustained Atlantic maritime links: a brigantine named the *Duke of Gloucester*, owned by a Charles Gwavas of Penzance.[34] Nor is Gwavas' letter to America the only evidence of migration of the Cornish language. A generation after Gwavas' death,

> Mr Barrington informed the Society, that Mr James Phillips, printer and bookseller, in George-yard, Lombard Street (London), hath lately told him, that John Nancarrow, junior, of Market Jew, who is not more than forty years of age, had learned the Cornish language from the country people during his youth, and can now converse in it.[35]

From Redruth, the Quaker anti-slavery campaigner James Phillips[36] was publisher of Pryce's *Mineralogia Cornubiensis*.[37] The John Nancarrow[38] referred to was one of the subscribers to the 1769 edition of Carew's *Survey of Cornwall*.[39] A Quaker, widower and mining engineer,[40] he emigrated to the Philadelphia area aged forty, in June 1774,[41] the same year as Thomas Paine,[42] the revolutionary author of *Common Sense*.[43] Nancarrow married Susanna Jones, of Philadelphia, and they had one son, also named John. Although a Quaker non-combatant, he embraced the Revolution's ideals, though his fortunes struggled as a result of the American War of Independence (1775–1783). John Nancarrow became a Pennsylvania abolitionist,[44] and was an active member of the American Philosophical Society of Philadelphia.[45] Both Nancarrow and Thomas Paine gave 'engineering witness' evidence in an intellectual property dispute over the invention of the first ever steamboat, which used modified steam-engine technology.[46] John Nancarrow signed the Philadelphia address to the Continental Congress in 1783,[47] met George Washington,[48] and there are letters extant between him and Thomas Jefferson.[49] Clearly an inventive and busy man, John Nancarrow[50] appears to have kept up correspondence with his Cornish and Quaker kith and kin.[51] In 1786, Nancarrow wrote a letter of condolence to Richard Phillips on the death of his father James – who was of course Daines Barrington's original informant.[52] Given this wealth of this kind of contextual evidence, spanning two centuries, it would perhaps be more surprising if Gwavas *hadn't* had the opportunity of contact with American Colonists.

The Gwavas Collection: Genesis I

The 'Gwavas Collection' is in the British Library, where it is designated BL Add. MSS 28554. Whilst the internet has become a valuable tool for

researchers, it is extremely common to find the wrong designation proliferated
ad infinitum – usually by copying verbatim from Henry Jenner's outdated
Handbook of the Cornish Language.[53] That is not to say that Jenner's citation
was incorrect. When he wrote the Handbook, he correctly referenced the old
British Museum designation which was the previous home of the Gwavas
Collection. There is another caveat for researchers – contemporary catalogues,
particularly on-line, can only ever be an *approximation* of manuscript contents
and details. They often involve the copying forward of previous catalogues,
complete with errors and omissions. In addition, catalogues are rarely updated
to take account of fresh scholarship in relation to dating, attribution and so
on. The 'Gwavas Collection' is no exception to this. Following Jenner, the
British Library current Manuscripts catalogue[54] dates BL Add. MSS 28554
as 1709–1736. This is misleading as it contains a wealth of material from
well outside of the stated date parameters. The contents span at least 100
years, not the narrow quarter-century implied. The collection is very varied:
parts of the New Testament, rhymes, proverbs, place names, a fragment
vocabulary by Gwavas (A–O), letters, songs, elegies and other material. It
seems unnecessary to repeat in detail the received wisdom that the collection
is a rich pageant of material by, amongst others, John Keigwin, the Bosons,
Gwavas himself, John Tonkin, and Rev. Henry Ustick. Yet, received wisdom
is exactly that and should remain open to critique. It would be nice if
attribution was a simple matter, but it involves complex issues of compounded
assumptions and historical opacity. Compare, for example, these descriptions
of versions of Genesis Chapter I:

Firstly, from Henry Jenner's Handbook:[55]

> Genesis i. Two versions, one by John Boson and
> one probably by John Keigwin. Both are in the
> Gwavas MS. One, Boson's, with his name to it,
> is in the Borlase MS. Boson's was printed by
> D. Gilbert ... There are many verbal variations from the Gwavas copies
> in the printed editions.

Secondly, from Oliver Padel[56] (on the 'Boson' Genesis I version)

> The first chapter of the Book of Genesis; Gwavas collection, f. 126,
> endorsed by Ustick 'Wrote by Mrs. Veale, the Eldest Daughter of Wm.
> Gwavas Esqire. She died Febry. 8th 1791'; Borlase MS, pp 160–162,
> endorsed by him 'The First Chapter of Genesis by the late Mr Boson of
> Newlyn. From his own Mss' ... It should be added that the attribution
> of our piece here to John Boson is not absolutely certain: Borlase simply
> calls the author 'the late Mr. Boson'.

Thirdly, the British Library current on-line catalogue:

> Two versions of the first chapter of Genesis, one in the hand of W. Gwavas and one in that of Mrs. Veale, his daughter. Printed by Davies Gilbert, one with the 'Creation', and the other with 'Mount Calvary'. ff 117, 126

Certainly one version is in Gwavas' hand. The second, according to its endorsement, is in the hand of his daughter Elizabeth Veale. It is worth noting that this 'Ustick Endorsement' is regarded as *de facto* evidence of her role as amenuensis. Yet these ambiguities around authorship and transcriber identity also detract from the fact that the Gwavas Collection contains a *third* fragment of Genesis 1 – unremarked and even uncatalogued. The fragment comprises verses 1–7 only, beginning 'En daladh Diw wrâs' It can be found in the Gwavas Collection at f. 127 (recto) – immediately following the full Genesis I version with the 'Ustick Endorsement'. The 'Gatley F' MSS (the Gatley Transcription) are housed at the Courtney Library, Royal Institution of Cornwall, and comprise, along with extraneous material in English, a full transcription in Gatley's hand of all the manuscripts in the Gwavas Collection. On cross-referencing the Gatley Transcription, I found that it too contains the uncatalogued Genesis fragment, including its own separate and anonymous (transverse) colophon, 'Part of ye 1st Ch. of Genesis in Cornish, from Mrs Veale of Trevaylor'. Clearly, this is a strong suggestion that Elizabeth Veale, née Gwavas, was not a mere female scribe in the history of the Cornish language. An attribution of original authorship to Elizabeth Veale should be hypothesised as the sole known contribution by a female to the Cornish of the extensive Gwavas Collection. Attribution is particularly complex where the authorship 'default assumption' is male, and is further problematised by the loss of female birth-name on marriage. This can obscure links and connections between individuals who had a degree of familiarity with vernacular Cornish. Robert Morton Nance mentions Ann Wallis, Mrs Berryman/Quick, Jane Barnicoat, Jane Cock and Jane Woolcock (both of Newlyn).[57] To these might be added more women with strong connections to Late Cornish, such as Florence Baynard,[58] Izabel Keigwin,[59] Anne Gwavas,[60] Mary Ustick[61] and Ann Carlyon.[62]

Ustick

Edward Lhuyd acknowledges the help of 'Mr. Eftwick of St. Yst' (Ewstick or Usticke of St Just).[63] Mr Ustick's collaboration with Lhuyd is mentioned where others are not, so one assumes that Ustick's contribution was authoritative and substantial – he is credited with copying the Cornish of William Rowe, from the manuscript in the possession of Mathew Rowe of Hendra. The Rev. Henry Ustick, Vicar of Breage, transcribed his Cornish collections, such as proverbs, and several pieces in the Gwavas Collection are attributed to him. As he married Mary, daughter of Dr Walter Borlase, thus Dr William Borlase was Ustick's uncle by marriage. It is perhaps unsurprising that they shared an antiquarian interest in the Cornish language. He and William Borlase went together to Scilly, searching out antiquities and ancient sites. Borlase would have been familiar with Ustick's handwriting through family correspondence and the exchange of sermons for contemplation so beloved of country clerics. There are though several inconsistencies regarding Ustick. Henry Jenner seemed to hold views which conflict with Borlase's appraisal of Ustick's competency in Cornish. Jenner says, in his descriptions of the *Borlase Manuscript* (my emphases):

4. The Ustick MSS: ... One Ms. of his, a copy of Boson's 'Nebbaz Gerriau dro tho Carnoack' ... (a few words about Cornish), only exists in a copy by Ustick, and, as Boson's writing was exceeding difficult to read, and *Ustick does not seem to have known much Cornish*, there are a good many passages in which a restored text is needed.[64]

Yet he quotes Borlase's observation:

16. Some compositions in the Cornish Language ...
'The first Chapter of Genesis in Cornish by the late Mr. Boson of Newlyn, from his own MSS.' ... and another note 'See the 3 Chr of Genesis and the 4 & part of the 2 Chr of St. Matthew *in good modern Cornish in Mr. Ustick's Cornish MS.*'.

Ustick says there that they are from the MS. of Matthew Rowe of Hendra, which I suppose is Hendra in Breage, of which parish Ustick was vicar.

Robert Morton Nance says of Ustick's transcription of *Nebbaz Gerriau*:

The MS. itself is unfortunately not Boson's original, but a transcript made by the Rev. Henry Ustick, Vicar of Breage, about fifty years later, and given by him to Dr. Borlase. That the transcriber knew little of Cornish is shown by his misreadings of common words'.[65]

Jenner is quite clear as to the source. In the same article, he introduces the *Borlase Manuscript* as:

> A collection relating to the Cornish language in the handwriting of
> Dr. William Borlase, rector of Ludgvan ... It bears on the outside
> an inscription, 'Mems of the Cornish Tongue. Natali Solo S. Lud (gvan),
> Jan 5, 1748.'
> The MSS. used by Borlase are the following:– The Ustick MSS. These
> were copies made by the Rev. Henry Ustick, vicar of Breage. They
> were lent to Borlase by Ustick's widow, and I am inclined to believe
> that he returned some of them to Mrs. Veale by mistake with the
> Gwavas collection.

I found Jenner's provenance of the *Ustick MSS* debatable as at that time the
Rev. Henry Ustick had no widow – he was not dead.

Several questions arose from my scepticism. If Ustick's Cornish was
proficient enough to transcribe William Rowe's lengthy Genesis 3, St Matthew
4 and part of St Matthew 2, why was Ustick's Cornish thought mediocre
in transcribing Nicholas Boson's *Nebbaz Gerriau?* If Ustick's Cornish was so
deficient, why would Edward Lhuyd credit his assistance so highly, second
only to John Keigwin? These apparent contradictions may have a simple
explanation. The Rev. Henry Ustick, Vicar of Breage, cannot be Lhuyd's
collaborator as he was not born until more than a decade after Lhuyd's
death – we *must* be looking at two different Usticks. Lhuyd died in 1709.
Rev. Henry Ustick was born in 1720 and married Mary Borlase at Madron[66]
in July 1751. At the time of his marriage, he was 'clerk of St Berian'. William
Borlase at that time was 'in plurality' the Vicar of St Just as well as Rector of
Ludgvan: Henry Ustick became his curate at St Just from 1752–1755.[67] Rev.
Ustick then served as Vicar of Breage from 1755[68] until his death. Whether he
had a crisis of faith is not clear but, following a lengthy period of depression,
Rev. Henry Ustick took his own life by hanging in 1769.[69] It now begins to
makes sense that there are 'slippages' in titling 'Mr Usticke / Rev. Ustick',
in an era when correct forms of address were mandatory. The proverbs and
other short pieces in the Gwavas Collection are probably correctly attributed
to the Rev. Henry Ustick and date to *c.*1745–1768. The same might be true of
copies of Nicholas Boson's *Nebbaz Gerriau* and possibly Ustick's transcriptions
of *Archaeologia Cornu-Britannica, Passio Domini* and *Gwreans an Bys* in the
Bodleian Library.[70] The more competent transcriptions of William Rowe's
Cornish writings could be those of an earlier Usticke (Lhuyd's Mr Estwick
of St Just), and therefore a contemporary of Edward Lhuyd, William Rowe,
John Keigwin, James Jenkin and Nicholas Boson.

Borlase's *Antiquities, Historical and Monumental, of the County of Cornwall*
was first published in 1754. In its introduction to the Cornish Vocabulary,
Borlase cites as sources, 'A few MSS of the late Mr Boſon From the Rev
Mr Uſtick of St. Juſt'. Confusingly, Borlase then cites in the key to his

Vocabulary '*Bof. Bofon MS*' and '*Uf. Uftick MS*' as if they are *different* sources. The actual contents of the '*Ufstick MS*' of St Just may have been glaringly obvious to William Borlase in 1748, and may or may not have been restricted to transcripts by Rev Henry Ustick of Breage. Indeed, Borlase makes the same assumptions of 'obvious-ness' about another of his Vocabulary sources – the 'JT' *Tregere MS*. Matthew Spriggs correctly identifies this is not a reference to further 'now lost works of the sixteenth century John Tregear, translator of Bishop Bonner's homilies into Cornish. It seems more likely that it is Borlase's contemporary who is being acknowledged here'.[71] Jon Mills concludes that the small number of words Borlase attributes to the *J Tregere MS* are not found in the *Tregear Homilies*.[72] One possibility that fits the right time, location and church milieu is that Borlase's 'JT' is James Tregere, churchwarden of St Just at the time that the Great Bell was cast and inscribed, 'St Just bell cast at St Earth [*sic*], 1741, so bless King George. James Reynolds, James Tregere & Admiral Vernon, Ch Wardens.'[73] The *J Tregere MS* (now differentiated from the *Tregear Homilies*) must have included Cornish for Borlase to have trawled it for words. This now lost manuscript or manuscript collection may refer to Cornish writings and transcriptions *by* J Tregere, but could also refer to a collection *in his possession* in the 1740s but comprised of earlier works in the Cornish language. If James Tregere, churchwarden of St Just, was the one who loaned these to Borlase around 1748, this was close to the time that Rev Henry Ustick was preparing to be appointed Borlase's curate at St Just.

The same rationale applies to Borlase's use of an '*Uftick MS*', which could comprise earlier Cornish works that included Boson and Usticke/Ewstick of St Just. There is a high possibility of course that some earlier MSS passed to Rev Henry Ustick via an Ewstick/Usticke family relationship. This material could have included William Rowe's Cornish, and possibly more. It explains the perceived *qualitative* differences between texts previously misattributed to an erroneous and conflated 'Ustick' authorship. An earlier Usticke/Lhuyd's Estwick begins to establish additional links to Rowe Cornish manuscripts – and the possibility that the 'Ustick' transcriptions of Rowe's Genesis and St Matthew could have been undertaken much closer to William Rowe in time – not fifty or sixty years later. The conclusion must be drawn too that the *Ustick Endorsement* of *Boson's Genesis 1* in the Gwavas Collection is also dubious. It verifies correctly that the purported transcriber, Elizabeth Veale, died in 1791. It must therefore post-date 1791 – but Rev Henry Ustick died in 1769. How much real credence can be given to an endorsement of factual attribution made posthumously?

'The Papers of Edward Lhwyd' at Trinity College Dublin

When Edward Lhuyd died in 1709, his collections of books, manuscripts and papers initially lay impounded by the authorities of Balliol College, Oxford, to whom he was in debt.[74] It was decided that his valuable early printed books would be retained by Oxford but his manuscripts be sold in lieu. During a five year chaotic hiatus, some items had their ownership disputed, some were lent and not returned, and still others were lost and pilfered. There was sustained interest from Oxford colleges and wealthy collectors in purchasing them. One antiquarian who was keen to purchase was Cornishman 'John Anstis (1669–1744), a collector of manuscripts, some of which he had actually given to Lhuyd. Anstis withdrew from the competition, at an early stage, supposedly for the praiseworthy motive of facilitating University purchase.' However, in 1715, the majority of Lhuyd's papers and manuscripts passed into the private ownership of Sir Thomas Sebright for his library at Beechwood House in Hertfordshire. The Sebright heir, Sir John, was encouraged to donate all of Lhuyd's known Irish manuscripts and papers to Trinity College Dublin in 1782. A similar generous donation of Welsh, Breton and Cornish manuscripts was made by a subsequent Sebright heir in 1797, to his cousin Thomas Johnes. These augmented Johnes' valuable private library at Hafod until a huge fire destroyed much, but not all, of the collection in 1807. The same year, a substantial amount of Lhuyd material, from various sources, was auctioned at Sotheby including 'Mount Calvary, &c In Cornish & English, by John Keigwin' … which Mr Lhwyd received from Mr Anstis.[75] Following the auction dispersal, parts of this Lhuyd material were later destroyed in two more large fires. Through subsequent purchase and donation, some fortunately survive in the National Library of Wales. This sorry history probably means that not all Lhuyd material has been traced and accounted for.

Nevertheless, when I undertook a search in the 1921 *Catalogue of the Irish Manuscripts in the Library at Trinity College, Dublin*,[76] it revealed an unexpected reference to Cornish manuscript material – a fragment of a Latin-Cornish comparative vocabulary (O–Z).[77] This is not listed in the contemporary Trinity College on-line catalogue. I undertook a one-day inspection visit, in order to confirm if there was in fact unknown Cornish material somehow residing with the 1782 Sebright Irish MSS donation. Trinity College Dublin (TCD) MS 1392 is a five volume collection of mainly Irish language material within the much larger collection known as the 'Papers of Edward Lhwyd'. The Volume 3 Cornish component is manuscript on paper, measuring approximately 41 cms × 28 cms. There is a modern handwritten note (probably dating from 1960s–70s when pencilled pagination was undertaken) inside the front cover which reads: 'No 3 Two copies of a fragment of a comparative vocabulary of the languages of Great Britain & Ireland. Beginning about p. 102, of the printed work'.

Cross-checking reveals the 'printed work' referred to is Lhuyd's *Archaeologia Britannia* of 1707. TCD 1392 Volume 3 comprises two fragment vocabularies, both containing Late Cornish words, but organised differently. For ease, I shall call these 3a and 3b. The 3b MS is the more scant in quality and content, is less well executed and is more biased towards a comparative glossary – Latin-Brythonic languages. It starts from <N>. As I did not expect to find *two* vocabulary fragments, I decided to prioritise my limited time scrutinising MS 3a. The TCD 1392 (3a) manuscript is clearly a working document – an undated draft and in swift handwriting rather than 'Sunday best' for circulation or publication. The handwriting is quite small and ample space is left between entries to allow for further additions. It comprises 27 folios (recto and verso) of Latin–Cornish vocabulary entries, from <Ob> to the end of entries for <Z>. Each page has approximately 20–25 word entries, in single or double column form. A sizeable minority of entries is accompanied by <Ar> Amorican comparators and occasional French equivalents. It is evident though that its primary focus is on the *Cornish* content. Neither 3a nor 3b are in Lhuyd's hand. Indeed, some entries are annotated <Lh>, indicating Lhuyd as their reference source, although the MSS do not entirely comply with Lhuyd's *Archaeologia Britannica* Cornish spelling or system of diacritics. Several entries are annotated with a dagger symbol (†); cross-referencing reveals all of these make reference to the Latin–Old Cornish *Vocabularium Cornicum*.[78] Whilst handwriting analysis is best undertaken by specialist inspection, I believe that both MSS 3a and 3b are in the hand of William Gwavas. This attribution to Gwavas is as a result of handwriting comparisons[79] with other extant MSS known to be in his hand – the Gwavas Collection (BL 28554),[80] Thomas Tonkin Bilbao MSS,[81] the William Gwavas Commonplace Book,[82] Gwavas Sermon Notes,[83] Catalogue of Books[84] and Gwavas' own annotated copy of Carew's *Survey of Cornwall*.[85]

In 1736, Thomas Tonkin wrote in his Dedication Addressed to Gwavas, for his proposed publication of *Archaeologia Cornu-Britannica*:

If there had been the least prospect left of recovering Mr. Lhuyd's papers, especially his Cornish Vocabulary (which he tells us in his Archaeologia pag. 253. he had by him ready for the press) I should have defer'd the publishing this yet for some time longer; but as I have long since given over my hopes of it, so I doubt the death of Sir Thomas Sebright (in whose hands, you know, all Mr. Lhuyds manuscript collections were) will put a full end to those, which you had so justly conceiv'd from

Sir Wm. Carew's late promises to you, and the fresh assurance of his assistance in procuring them for you, the heir being a minor of tender years, and the difficulties which attend such a state, from trustees, &c. not leaving you any probability of succeeding in it.[86]

Tonkin wanted to consult Lhuyd's manuscript Cornish Vocabulary – the *Geirlyer Kyrnŵeig*. It, however, had been purchased separately and was inaccessible in the private library of Shirburn Castle. There for more than 150 years, it was eventually obtained with a number of Welsh manuscripts by Sir John Williams for his Llanstephan Library. He later donated his library for the foundation of the National Library of Wales[87] where *Geirlyer Kyrnŵeig* is designated NLW MS Llanstephan 84.[88] The Dedication to Gwavas raises some interesting queries regarding their collaboration on the vocabulary for Tonkin's proposed *Archaeologia Cornu-Britannica*. If the TCD 1392 vocabularies were contemporary with Lhuyd and already with Lhuyd's Irish MSS in the Sebright Library, they would pre-date *Archaeologia Cornu-Britannica* by twenty years or more. Yet, in 1736, Gwavas may not have informed Tonkin that he had had previous access. This is a mystery, as it would help explain how the TCD 1392 vocabularies came to be with Lhuyd's Irish papers when they were donated to Trinity College Dublin. There is no known alternative provenance history by which they were acquired by Trinity College *after* the Sebright donation: it seems this unknown Cornish material has always been a component of the TCD 'Lhwyd's Papers'. Whitley Stokes was familiar with Lhuyd's Irish MSS at Trinity College, yet I can find no record of him noting the TCD 1392 Cornish material – though it is subsumed in the large Irish language collection. If TCD 1392 is contemporary with Lhuyd, it raises the possibility of closer links between Lhuyd and Gwavas than previously recognised. Lhuyd does not acknowledge either Tonkin or Gwavas in his preface to the Cornish Grammar of *Archaeologia Britannica*, though he may have gone on to acknowledge them had *Geirlyer Kyrnŵeig* been published before Lhuyd's death. There is a wealth of evidence of Lhuyd's direct contact with Thomas Tonkin – and John Keigwin certainly had connections to both Lhuyd and the young Gwavas. There is though that other potential link between Lhuyd and Gwavas, via John Anstis, who provided Lhuyd with much material. It was Anstis who had alerted Lhuyd to the Cottonian *Vocabularium Cornicum* which Lhuyd (or rather, William Jones) was then able to confirm as Old Cornish, and not Old Welsh as previously thought. This begs the question of *why* Anstis had strong suspicions that it was Cornish. Either Anstis himself had sufficient knowledge of Old Cornish to be able to differentiate it from Old Welsh, or someone else with that knowledge of Cornish had brought the misattribution to Anstis' attention.

This could of course have been John Keigwin. There is though another possibility that it could have been Gwavas given Anstis and Gwavas were both linked to the Middle Temple at the relevant time.

William Borlase, in his Preface to *Antiquities, Historical and Monumental* states:

> I had the favour of perufing all the MSS. relating to Etymology, which could be found in the Library of Sir Thomas Seabight [*sic*], Bart. Where the Literary Remains of Mr Lhuyd were thought to have been depofited. Among them I met with an imperfect English-Cornifh vocabulary; and in the other fcattered Memorandums, I found feveral Cornffh Words I had not seen before, which in the following Work are inferted.

The imperfect vocabulary Borlase saw cannot be TCD 1392 as it is Latin–Cornish and not English–Cornish. Much of Borlase's Vocabulary is derived from Lhuyd and uses, in the main, Lhuydian 'General Alphabet' spelling. Borlase's Vocabulary too uses the dagger symbol convention for words from the *Vocabularium Cornicum*. This dagger convention can thus be tracked consistently through *Archaeologia Britannica*, *Geirlyer Kyrnnẃeig*, TCD 1392 vocabulary fragment, *Archaeologia Cornu-Britannica MS*, *Borlase Vocabulary*, Pryce's published edition of *Archaeolgia Cornu-Britannica* through to Nance and Smith's 1938 *New Cornish–English Dictionary*. Borlase acknowledges William Gwavas as a source, but not specific texts. Doubtless, he used the Gwavas vocabulary fragment (A–O) in the Gwavas Collection.[89] By way of confirmation, in Borlase's Vocabulary all references to Gwavas as source stop abruptly at the letter <O>.[90] Tracking evidence of the incorporation of the TCD 1392 vocabulary fragments would be much more problematic as I have yet to find *any* references to or citations of them.

Concluding remarks

A conclusion might commonly be expected to summarise one's findings. Instead, my concluding remarks will be more speculative. Demonstrably, *TCD 1392* needs closer attention, particularly through palaeographic and language analyses. At the very least, copies of the TCD Vocabularies 3a and 3b ought to be made available to Cornish language researchers within Cornwall. Fortunately, there exists a full microfilm copy,[91] also in the Library at Trinity College Dublin. Ideally, Trinity College and/or the Government of the Republic of Ireland might be approached to donate copies to the Courtney Library and Cornish Studies Library, in much the same way as the Spanish state donated copies of the Tonkin Bilbao MSS. This would facilitate *TCD 1392* study alongside its contemporary material.

Helpful as an aid to provisional dating of *TCD 1392*, Robert Morton Nance characterises the Cornish of Gwavas' 1710 Letter to America as 'a mixture of Lhuyd's and older ways of writing'.[92] This description could equally apply to the Cornish of *TCD 1392* and implies a similar date. The handwriting too is characteristic of earlier Gwavas and would suggest a dating of the first quarter of the eighteenth century. Given the *TCD 1392* references to <Lh>, they probably post-date the 1707 publication of *Archaeologia Britannica*. The most similar comparisons of Gwavas' hand are the Gwavas *Sermon Notes* of 1717 and the Carew's *Survey of Cornwall* annotations of *c*.1710. I do not though rule out a dating before Lhuyd's death in 1709 – indeed there is a small number of one-word notes on the *TCD 1392* MS. that I believe may be in Edward Lhuyd's hand. This would give a much narrower window for dating – say, between the publication of *Archaeologia Britannica* in 1707 and the Sebright purchase in 1715. If this hypothesis can be confirmed, it is likely that the Gwavas *TCD 1392* vocabularies were used by Lhuyd to assist in his compilation of *Geirlyer Kyrnŵeig*. The most striking similarity is, like *TCD 1392*, Lhuyd's *Geirlyer Kyrnŵeig* does not use his 'General Alphabet'. The key questions for language specialists must include how much *TCD 1392* material might derive from the Cornish *speech community*, and are there any unknown words? There are grounds for optimism as the 1921 Catalogue short description of *TCD 1392* which references Lhuyd's *Archaeologia Britannica* suggests 'many words are given which are not there'. Also, it is wise to remember that the TCD 1392 vocabulary fragment (O–Z) is not a direct companion fit with the Gwavas Collection vocabulary (A–O). There is therefore always a possibility of more vocabulary fragments coming to light in the future.

The Gwavas Collection manuscripts in the British Library need to be re-appraised, with a fresh eye and open mind regarding conjectural dating and authorship. Of course, this is not simple: accessing original manuscripts, struggling to make out faded seventeenth- and eighteenth-century handwriting for comparisons and so on is onerous – an increase in the availability of high-quality digital imaging would help. In the meantime, I hope closer scrutiny of the Gwavas Collection will be eased by access to a complete microfilm copy of the entire collection, unearthed at the Cornish Studies Library in Redruth.[93] There must continue to be scope for speculative research, irrespective of immediate results or resolution; it is essential if future scholars are to follow up possible leads. Conjectural and provisional analyses do not mean unfounded or lacking rigour. For example, Andrew Hawke predicted in 1981 the existence of a then-unknown Thomas Tonkin MS, years before the Tonkin *Maker MSS* actually surfaced on a Totnes book stall.[94] In 1975 Oliver Padel addressed John Boson's letter to Gwavas (dated

5 April 1710) which includes Boson's appreciation of a communication from Gwavas explaining the ancient relationship of the Cornish language to Noah and the Tower of Babel.[95] Padel noted that, 'The section that Gwavas must have written concerning "the first man to speak Cornish" is not known.' It is thanks to Padel's lead that the complementary Gwavas writings have been located. They are in his unpublished *Essay on the Cornish Language* (drafted in English), tucked in the back of his copy of Carew's *Survey* at the Bodleian Library.

If conjecture means sometimes getting it wrong, then the alternative runs the risk of never getting it right. For example, I have a strong suspicion that there is a great deal of confusion between Thomas Tonkin Esq of Trevaunance and an earlier T. Tonkin from the St Just area, possibly himself related to John Tonkin of St Just. On this issue, Henry Jenner points to a 'T Tonkin (not the historian)'[96] and 'A Fisherman's Catch, given by Capt Noel [*sic*] Cator of St Agnes to T Tonkin. 1698'.[97] Given Hobson Matthews' assertion that Nowell Cator's rhyme came from the St Ives area,[98] not St Agnes, there are conjectural grounds for following this up. Indeed, it seems timely to re-focus on the configuration of a Cornish language 'St Just Posse',[99] individually active in the late 1600s in the St Just area, and probably responsible for more lost manuscript material than previously supposed. Those comprising an ad hoc *posse comitatis* would generally be of lesser landed and yeoman families, not necessarily gentry though possibly of minor branches. These kinds of literate and reliable men would have been required to make themselves available (individually or severally) for witnessing legal documents, wills, probate inventories and so on as well as undertaking minor local or parish responsibilities. Given the history of the assertive individualism and independence of St Just though, I would not rule out some with non-conformist sympathies. Certainly the contextual evidence suggests these St Just area individuals might include 'Whiggish' Williamites of Low Church sympathies, perhaps in lesser church and parish functionary roles such as churchwarden or constable. It was not uncommon for a church 'cleric', such as a vicar's curate or sidesman, to be described in parish registers as 'clerk' – there are descriptions extant of both Walter and William Borlase as 'clerk'. If the one reference to an earlier 'Rev' Usticke is to be believed, then it is entirely possible that 'Estwick' was the 'clerk' (cleric) of St Just who provided Lhuyd with the Cornish englyn. A conjectured 'St Just Posse' may well include, amongst others, Richard Angwin, T(homas) Tonkin, John Tonkin, William Rowe of Sancreed, John Reed (Joohan Landsend-man),[100] perhaps the maverick dissenter Joseph Sherwood[101] and the elusive 'Estwick of St Yst'.

My trajectory throughout this article has been to argue that scepticism towards well-worn narratives of the corpus of Cornish is healthy. No one analysis has the final word, no study should be regarded as unchallengeable. Scholarship is a process and not an achieved end, and questioning received wisdom is one of the ways in which scholarship progresses. Despite the best intentions, unintended errors and misunderstandings will no doubt creep into any study, including this one. However, it is by adopting the necessary critical distance to primary and secondary sources that those errors may be prevented from being repeated. This is particularly crucial in the study of Cornish language texts, in order to heighten the opportunities of rediscovering lost authors and even lost texts. If not, then we constrain ourselves to the habitual repetition of errors to be found in even our most revered and authoritative studies. It is as well to heed what, in 1711, William Gwavas aptly observed of an inaccuracy he noted:

> Carew not understanding of British Language mistook in writing it True, & Camden followed him, and Sams, and Bochartus followed Camden in ye Same Error. So it may be perceived that *Humanum est Errare*, and how one error – coming from a Learned Man – multiplies Even among ye most Learned.[102]

Acknowledgements

Bodelian Library, British Library, Cornish Studies Library, Cornwall Records Office. Courtney Library, Library of Trinity College Dublin, Peter Hayes, Ryan Air, Matthew Spriggs and, especially, Neil Kennedy for his encouragement and feedback on the draft.

Notes and references

1. P. B. Ellis, 'Thomas Tonkin', *Oxford Dictionary of National Biography* ed. H. C. G. Matthew (Oxford, 2004).
2. T. Thomas, 'Dedication to William Gwavas', Archaeologia Cornu-Britannica, *Bilbao MSS* (photocopy), Courtney Library, Royal Institution of Cornwall (1736). Also printed in *Cambrian Journal* (Tenby and London, 1861), p. 242. http://ia600301.us.archive.org/4/items/cambrianjournpt204cambuoft/cambrianjournpt-204cambuoft.pdf
3. R. M. Nance, 'Celtic Words in Cornish Dialect', *Annual Report of the Royal Cornwall Polytechnic Society* 1 (1917) p. 73. http://www.archive.org/stream/annualreport04royauoft#page/70/mode/2up, accessed 13 May 2011.
4. W. Gwavas, MSS notes in interleaving of his copy of Carew's 1602 edition of the *Survey of Cornwall*, Bodleian Corn. e 1 (*c*.1711).
5. W. Gwavas, *Commonplace Book*, '*Lyver Ve*', Courtney Library, Royal Institution

of Cornwall (*c*.1710). Note that the RIC Courtney Library currently designates manuscripts after their *donor*'s names. Gwavas' *Commonplace Book* is therefore known as one of the 'Gatley' MSS, after its donor. This can cause it to be confused with the 'Gatley Transcription' of the Gwavas Collection (BL Add. 28554) which is also at the Courtney Library. In order to assist researchers, Angela Broome at the Courtney Library has kindly allowed me to place a hard copy of the British Library extended catalogue listing for BL Add. 28554 with the 'Gatley Transcription' of it. I have included the caveat that folio numbering refers to the original BL Add. 28554 Gwavas Collection.

6. "Lhuyd's Archaeolog: Britt":
     "Davies Welsh Dictionary"
     "Camden's Remains";
     "Verstegan an Antiquity of Teutonic Languages"
     "Gasgoyne's Map of Cornwall"
     "Pezron, of ye Antiquity of a Nation, Gaulish, Englished "
     "Sammes Britan"
     "And Bochartus"
     "Strabo"
     "Sherringham"
     "Ninnus – i.e"
     "Lhuyd's fragments Brittainic" *(this refers to Humphrey Lhuyd)*
     "Leibnitz Leibnitius
     Etimologicon
     printed at Hannover Anno Dmi"

7. Cornwall Record Office, CRO CN/3460.

8. W. Gwavas, MSS notes in interleaving.

9. W. P. Courtney, 'Thomas Tonkin', *Dictionary of National Biography*, 1885–1900, Vol. 57 (London, 1900).

10. Thomas Tonkin, *Bilbao MSS*, Courtney Library, Royal Institution of Cornwall.

11. John Tonkin, *Kanna Kernuak*, Gwavas Collection, BL Add. 28554.

12. John Keigwin, King Charles I letter, Gwavas Collection, BL Add. 28554.

13. William Borlase, *Memorandums relating to the Cornish Tongue*, MS, Cornwall Record Office, CRO EN/2000 (1748).

14. H. Jenner, *A Handbook of the Cornish Language* (London, 1904), p. 36.

15. H. Jenner, 'Descriptions of Cornish Manuscripts – The Borlase Manuscript', *Journal of the Royal Institution of Cornwall* 19(2):60 (1913), pp. 162–76.

16. Rev. J. Buller, *A Statistical Account of the Parish of Saint Just in Penwith in the County of Cornwall* (Penzance, 1842), pp. 75–76.

17. Ibid.

18. R. M. Nance, RM, X 'John Keigwin's King Charles I's Letter', *Old Cornwall* 1: 4 (1842), p. 35.

19. Dating of 1693 given in J. Mills, 'Computer-assisted Lemmatisation of a Cornish Text Corpus for Lexicographical Purposes', unpublished PhD thesis, University of Exeter, 2002, p. 108; F. Jago, *The Ancient Language and the Dialect of Cornwall* (Truro, 1882), p. 25. Dating of *c*.1707 given in T. Chaudhri, 'Studies in the Consonantal System of Cornish', unpublished PhD thesis, Aberystwyth University 2007, p. 12. http://cadair.aber.ac.uk/dspace/bitstream/handle/2160/330/1_introduction. pdf?sequence=28; R. M. Nance, 'John Keigwin's Cornish Translation of King

Charles the First's Letter of Thanks to the Inhabitants of Cornwall', *Old Cornwall* 1:4 (1926), p. 35.

20. C. E. A. Bedwell, *Brief History of the Middle Temple* (London, 1909), p. 105. http://ia600304.us.archive.org/12/items/briefhistoryofmi00bedwuoft/briefhistoryofmi00bedwuoft_bw.pdf, accessed 6 May 2011.

21. W. M. Billings, 'Justices, Books, Laws, and Courts in Seventeenth-Century Virginia,' *Law Library Journal* 85 (1993).

22. B. C. Steiner, 'Law Libraries in Colonial Virginia', *The Green Bag* 9 (1897) p. 351. These included Cornishmen: In Lower Norfolk County, ... in 1697, Capt. Thomas Cocke of Princes Anne County owned "The Jure Maritimo" in quarto, "The Office of a Complete Attorney" in octavo, and "The Young Clerk's Guide", "The Compleat Justice", and "A Collection of the Laws of Virginia", in "twelves". These books are the indispensable ones and are found in several catalogues. Capt. Christopher Cocke, in 1716, seems to have had some of these very books, but he added to them others such as Lord "Cooke's" "Institutes", Swinburne on "Last Wills and Testaments", Shepherd's "Abridgement of the Common Law", "The Scrivener's Guide", the "Compleat Solicitor", the "Judge's Resolutions upon the Several Statutes of Bankrupts", and "A Catalogue of Law Books".

23. C. E. A. Bedwell, 'American Middle Templars', *The American Historical Review* 25:4 (July 1920), p. 680.

24. *The American Collection of the Middle Temple* http://www.middletemple.org.uk/library/the-american-collection.html, accessed 14 April 2011; see also The Rt Hon The Lord Judge, Lord Chief Justice Of England And Wales, 'No Taxation Without Representation: A British Perspective On Constitutional Arrangements', Broadmore, Colorado Springs, 28 August 2010. http://www.judiciary.gov.uk/NR/rdonlyres/C1C8212B-D1C9–4FE2–980F-FDDC7B623496/0/lcjspeechnotaxationwithoutrepresentation28082010.pdf, accessed 14 April 2011.

25. *The History of the College of William and Mary from its foundation, 1660, to 1874* (Richmond [Virginia], 1874), p. 46.

26. Gwavas Collection, BL Add. MSS 28554, British Library.

27. *The Indian School at William and Mary* [online] http://www.wm.edu/about/history/historiccampus/indianschool/index.php, accessed 14 April 2011.

28. A. M. Kent, '"Mozeying on down …":The Cornish Language in North America', in H. L. C. Tristram (ed.), *The Celtic Languages in Contact*, Papers from the Workshop within the Framework of the XIII International Congress of Celtic Studies, Bonn, 26–27 July 2007. http://opus.kobv.de/ubp/volltexte/2008/1927/pdf/193_216.pdf, accessed 6 May 2011.

29. John Keigwin (b. Mousehole, Cornwall 1642, d. 5 December 1736 Stonington, Connecticut). He married Hannah Brown (b. 5 December 1680, d. 3 March 1771) on 10 October 1700. John and Hannah had a son Lt. John Keigwin (b. 8 March 1703–4, d. 8 July 1775 Voluntown, Connecticut). Lt. John married Deborah Park 15 August 1728.

30. Sampson Trevethan, 1663–1726. Ann married Sampson Trevethan on 12 July 1703 at Princess Anne County, Virginia. It was Ann's second marriage, her first husband was Argall Thorowgood: J. F. Dorman and A. L. Jester (eds), *Adventurers of Purse and Person, Virginia 1607–1625, Volume Three, Families R–Z* (Thorowgood family) (fourth edition, Princeton, 1956).

31. Christopher Cock b. 14 December 1643 in Helston, Cornwall, d. 1716 in Prince

William, Virginia. Grace Bolitho b. 1655 in Wendron, Cornwall, d. 1720 in Virginia. Christopher Cock of Helston married Grace Bolitho of Wendron, 27 October 1673. The Trevethans, the Bolithoe and Cocke families are all intermarried and originated from Cornwall. In 1601 Katherine Trevethen married Walter Bolithoe at St. Anthonys, Cornwall while in 1630 William Trevethan married Emlena Cocke at Helston. In the late 1600s all three families are represented in the new settlement of Virginia, America. http://www.trevethan. net/America.htm, accessed 14 May 2011.

32. Letter from the Commissioners of the Customs, intimating that they had appointed Sampson Trevethan to be Surveyor of the Customs in Elizabeth River, read and entered: 'Sampson Trevethan, Surveyor at Elizabeth River in Virginia £45–0–0 pa' C. Headlam (ed.) 'America and West Indies: January 1703, 1–8' *Calendar of State Papers Colonial, America and West Indies*, 21, 1702–1703 (1913), pp. 91–109, British History Online, accessed 11 April 2011; W. A. Shaw (ed.) 'Declared Accounts, 1704–5: Customs', *Calendar of Treasury Books*, 20, 1705–1706 (1952), CCXLIX–CCCIII, British History Online, accessed 31 March 2011.

33. 'Notes From Princess Anne County', *The Virginia Magazine Of History And Biography, Published Quarterly by The Virginia Historical Society For The Year Ending 31 December 1920*, 28 (1920), p. 416 http://www.archive.org/stream/virginiamaga-zine28virg/virginiamagazine28virg_djvu.txt, accessed 14 April 2011.

34. W. Brown, 'Shipping in the Port of Annapolis 1748–1775', *Sea Power Monograph No. 1* (1963) http://mdhistory.net/msaref06/port_records/pdf/brown_vaughn.pdf, accessed 14 April 2011.

> Port of Entry Records for Annapolis 1748–1775
> Vessel: *Duke of Gloucester*
> Rig: Brigantine
> Tonnage: 60
> Stern: Square
> Built: Philadelphia, 1766
> Master: John Searle
> Owners: John Tearte and Charles Gwavas (Penzance)

A similar record for the *Ship Registers for the Port of Philadelphia 1726–1775*, explicitly states "both of Penzance" http://www.jstor.org/pss/20086110, accessed 14 April 2011.

35. D. Barrington, 'Some Additional Information Relative To The Continuance Of The Cornish Language'; *Archaeologia* 5 (1779). In a letter to John Lloyd, Esq, pp. 81–86, cited in C. Jeffery, 'John Nancarrow Junior', *Old Cornwall* 10:1 (1985) pp. 31–35.

36. Jeffery, 'John Nancarrow Junior'. The second wife of his father William was Catherine Phillips, a committed Quaker who undertook her own two and a half year mission to the American colonies 1753–1756. See Chapter IV, *Memoirs of the life of Catherine Phillips: to which are added some of her epistles*, edited and published by James Phillips (London, 1797).

37. W. Pryce, *Mineralogia Cornubiensis: A Treatise on Minerals, Mines and Mining* (London, 1778).

38 He was baptised at St Agnes in 1743. Father: John Nancarrow, Mother: Grace, née Polsue of Gorran. They lived in Sithney (1738), Helston (1741), Ludgvan (1746), Germoe and Marazion. John Snr was primarily employed in highly skilled

mine engineering, including at Great Work Main Lode. This information from 'The Nancarrows: A Forgotten Cornish Engineering Family', *Old Cornwall* 9:10, pp. 493–96.

39. R. Carew, *The Survey of Cornwall and an Epistle Concerning the Excellencies of the English Tongue* (London and Penzance, 1769 edition).

40. Jeffery, 'John Nancarrow Junior'.

41. Roberts, Grace (née Nancarrow) (1774), Extracts copied from diary of 1774; the writer's father spent day with his family at Marazion, then went to London to take ship for America where he died in 1801. Stephens Family papers, Cornwall Records Office MS CRO ST/67.

42 Thomas Paine arrived in America 30 November 1774.

43. T. Paine, *Common Sense* (Philadelphia, 1776).

44. He joined on 6 January 1794, see p. 57, *Centennial anniversary of the Pennsylvania Society, for Promoting the Abolition of Slavery, the relief of free Negroes unlawfully held in bondage, and for improving the condition of the African race* (Philadelphia, 1875) http://ia700108.us.archive.org/21/items/centennialannive00lcpenn/centennialannive00lcpenn.pdf, accessed 10 April 2011.

45. *Early Proceedings of the American Philosophical Society for the Promotion of Useful Knowledge 1744–1838* (Philadelphia, 1884), p. 220 http://ia600401.us.archive.org/31/items/earlyproceedings1884ameruoft/earlyproceedings1884ameruoft_bw.pdf, accessed 11 April 2011.

46. D. E. Turner, 'John Fitch: The Inventor of Steam Navigation', in *A Collection of Papers read before the Bucks County Historical Society*, Vol. 2 (Philadelphia, 1908), pp. 22–34.

47. This was an appeal by the City of Philadelphia to the Continental Congress of the Thirteen Colonies. It sought to re-instate Philadelphia as capital and meeting place of Congress following its relocation to Princeton during the Philadelphia and Lancaster army mutiny for pay arrears in June 1783. See also V. L. Collins, *The Continental Congress at Princeton* (Princeton, New Jersey, 1908).

48. W. S. Baker, *Washington after the Revolution*, (Philadelphia, 1908), pp. 86–87:
    "Philadelphia, August 4. (1787)—His Excellency General Washington attentive to every thing interesting to his country, yesterday [August 3] visited and examined the steel furnace belonging to Nancarrow and Matlack, lately rebuilt, in this city. It is much the largest and best constructed furnace in America, being charged with fourteen tons of iron at that time, converting into steel; and His Excellency was pleased to express his approbation of it."—*Pennsylvania Packet*.

49. *Thomas Jefferson Collection, 1773–1826*, Missouri Historical Society Archives, St Louis, Missouri: Folder 15, A0770:
    27 Dec 1792 John Nancarrow, a Quaker steel manufacturer, to Thomas Jefferson. Apologizes for not meeting with Jefferson when requested because he was busy meeting with farmers from out of town and states that "he knows from experience that one man cannot throw water 45 feet high." (2 pages)
    27 Dec 1792 John Nancarrow. Regarding drawing states, "This machine is simple, easily constructed & capable of raising water to any height provided the pumps are made in the Jack-head form." (2 pages)
    Drawing, ink on paper: Design of a machine to lift water. (1 page)

http://www.mohistory.org/files/archives_guides/JeffersonThomasCollection.pdf, accessed 18 April 2011.

G. Hunt (ed.), *Calendar of Applications and Recommendations for Office During the Presidency of George Washington* (Washington D.C., 1901), p. 132:

> Voight, Henry. Philadelphia, April 13, 1792. Applies for appointment as chief coiner in the Mint. He knows how to make all the machinery, having been for some years employed in the mint of Saxe-Gotha, Germany. During the war he manufactured guns and gunlocks for the Army: Philadelphia, April 13, 1792. Jno. Nancarrow recommends him.

J. F. Jenkin, *Thomas Jefferson's Germantown Letters, together with other papers relating to his stay in Germantown during the month of November 1793* (Philadelphia, 1906), pp. 124–25 http://ia600100.us.archive.org/7/items/jeffersonsgerman01jeff/ jeffersonsgerman01jeff.pdf, accessed 21 April 2011.

50. There were at least three John Nancarrows in the American colonies at the same time, including his own son who pre-deceased him at the age of thirty eight. Another John Nancarrow emigrated with his family from Plymouth (Devon), sent begging letters to Benjamin Franklin and may have lived in the Pittsburgh area, later relocating to Kentucky.

51. His daughter Grace, by his first wife Ann, may have visited him in Philadelphia according to C. Jeffery, 'John Nancarrow Junior'. See also Cornwall Records Office CRO ST/66 Letter to his daughter Eleanor Mary Richard, shopkeeper, of Marazion, dated 1774.

52. J. Nancarrow (6 February 1786) letter to Richard Phillips from Philadelphia, Photostat of 2 pp. *Condolences on the death of his father. The steam engine; probable significance in America.* From original in the Friends' Reference Library, London. http://amphilsoc.org/mole/view?docId=ead/Mss.Miscellaneous.Manuscripts-ead. xml, accessed 30 April 2011.

53. H. Jenner, *Handbook of the Cornish Language* (London, 1904). Andrew Hawke ('The Manuscripts of the Cornish Passion Poem', *Cornish Studies/Studhyansow Kernewek*, First Series 9 (1981)) warns how dated some of Jenner's material can be, and it is worth noting that the bulk of the historical section of his *Handbook* had already appeared in a paper he read to the British Archaeological Society at Penzance in 1876.

54 http://www.bl.uk/catalogues/manuscripts/HITS0001.ASP?VPath=html/15690. htm&Search=Add.+28554&Highlight=F, accessed 18 Dec 2010.

55. Jenner, *Handbook of the Cornish Language*, p. 42.

56. O. Padel, *The Writings of the Boson Family* (Redruth, 1975), p. 51.

57. R. M. Nance, 'When Was Cornish Last Spoken Traditionally' (reprint) *Journal of the Royal Institution of Cornwall*, New Series, Vol. 8 Part 1 (1973).

58. She married William Rowe 25 June 1685 in St. Just in Penwith.

59. Daughter of John Keigwin. The Keigwin copy of the *Ordinalia MSS*, National Library of Wales Peniarth 428, has her name on the first folio (Mills, 'Computer-assisted Lemmatisation', p. 89).

60. Mother of William Gwavas. His father died when Gwavas was young. It is possible that his mother encouraged Cornish language interests. She clearly did not discourage his interest.

61. Mary Ustick was niece to William Borlase. She married Rev Henry Ustick (who became Vicar of Breage in 1755).

62. Ann Carlyon, daughter of W. Gwavas, sister of Elizabeth Veale. Ann married Thomas Carlyon.

63. E. Lhuyd, 'Introduction to Cornish Grammar', *Archaeologia Britannica* (Oxford: printed at the Theatre for the Author, 1707).

64. H. Jenner, 'Descriptions of Cornish Manuscripts – The Borlase Manuscript', *Journal of the Royal Institution of Cornwall* 29(2):60 (1913), pp. 162–76. The Borlase MSS are now Cornwall Records Office, Enys Collection CRO EN/2000.

65. R. M. Nance, 'Nicholas Boson's "Nebbaz Gerriau dro tho Carnoack"' *Journal of the Royal Institution of Cornwall* 23(2) (1930), p. 327.

66. T. Taylor (ed.), *Cornwall Parish Registers. Marriages Vol. XII, 1674–1812, Madron with Penzance* (London, 1900). http://www.archive.org/stream/cornwallparishre12phil/cornwallparishre12phil_djvu.txt, accessed 3 May 2011.

67. P. A. S. Pool, *Walter Borlase* (Redruth, 1986).

68. H. R. Coulthard, *The Story of an Ancient Parish: Breage with Germoe* (Camborne, 1913), pp. 83–85.

69. Coulthard, *The Story of an Ancient Parish*.

70. These lesser known (but sizeable) collections of Rev H. Ustick are now designated Bodleian Corn. c 1 and Bodleian Corn. n 3. Matthew Spriggs makes the correct attributions to Rev Henry Ustick, Vicar of Breage, in 'William Scawen (1600–1689) – A Neglected Cornish Patriot and Father of the Cornish Language Revival' (in P. Payton, *Cornish Studies: Thirteen* (Exeter, 2005)). The first page of Corn. c 1 has a different signature, in an apparently older hand. Andrew Hawke ('The Manuscripts of the Cornish Passion Poem') identifies the initial as 'W' though I believe it to read 'Rev. M. Usticke'. Following the transcription of Keigwin's *Creation of the World*, the Corn. c 3 MS includes (f. 123) the observation:
    The greatest part of which Translation you have above but as the old Gentleman had left out many whole verses, & in many other places too, had quite Altered and Mistaken the Sense this has been carefully reviewed & amended so that I may safely say that the present translation. As well as the true Cornish Original, may be entirely depended upon as faithful and Just.

71. M. Spriggs, 'Additional Thoughts on the Medieval 'Cornish Bible', in P. Payton (ed.), *Cornish Studies: Fourteen* (Exeter, 2006), p. 52.

72. Mills, 'Computer-assisted Lemmatisation', p. 37; http://kar.kent.ac.uk/8301/1/thesis.pdf, accessed 9 May 2011.

73. Buller, *A Statistical Account of the Parish of Saint Just*, p. 23.

74. I am indebted here to the invaluable article by Eiluned Rees and Gwyn Walters, 'The Dispersion Of The Manuscripts Of Edward Lhuyd', *Welsh History Review* 7:2 (1974), pp. 148–78.

75. Ibid.

76. T. K. Abbott and E. J. Gwynn, *Catalogue of the Irish Manuscripts in the Library at Trinity College, Dublin* (Dublin, 1921).

77. Ibid., p. 260.

78. *Vocabularium Cornicum*, British Library, Cotton Vespasian A xiv.

79. Obtaining permissions for handwriting samples is extremely difficult, so I am very grateful to the relevant libraries for allowing me to have some small sample copies to take away for comparison. Copyright restrictions prevent the handwriting samples from being reproduced in this article.

80. Gwavas Collection, British Library BL Add. MSS 28554.

81. Tonkin, Thomas, *Bilbao MSS*, Courtney Library.

82. W. Gwavas, *Commonplace Book*, MSS, Courtney Library, (*c*.1710–1720).

83. W. Gwavas, *Sermon Notes*, MS. CRO CN/3435/11 (1717).

84. W. Gwavas, *Catalogue of Books*, MS. CRO CN/3460 (1717).

85. W. Gwavas, his own annotated copy of Carew's *Survey of Cornwall*, Bodleian MSS Corn. e 1 (*c*.1710–1720).

86. Reprinted in *Cambrian Journal* (Tenby, 1861), pp. 241–45. Included for publication was an accompanying letter from Prince Louis-Lucien Napoleon justifying his accusation of plagiarism against Pryce.

87. See National Library of Wales website, information on the Llanstephan Collection http://www.llgc.org.uk/index.php?id=llawysgrifaullanstephan, accessed 9 May 2011.

88. Llanstephan 84 is reproduced on-line, high resolution and page by page, by the National Library of Wales: http://digidol.llgc.org.uk/METS/LAN00001/physica l?div=0&subdiv=0&locale=en&mode=thumbnail, accessed 9 May 2011.

89. Gwavas Collection, British Library BL Add. MSS 28554.

90. After <O>, there is one instance where Gwavas is mentioned, but Lhuyd given as the source.

91. 'Papers of Edw. Lhwyd', TCD MS 1392, microfilm copy, Berkeley Multimedia ref no – WM II.55.

92. R. M. Nance, 'The Cornish Language in America', *Old Cornwall* 1 (1925).

93. Mistakenly catalogued as an 'Audio Book', the microfilm is currently stored in the furthest filing unit, to the left of the entrance, third drawer down. Its box is marked '*The Gwavas Collection*', *BL Add. MSS. 28554, BL Library Reference Division, Order SCH 67179*'. The microfilm copy is not of the best quality, though the MSS which are legible in the originals are (generally) legible in the microfilm copy. Ideally though, resources should be made available to digitise before the film deteriorates still further.

94. Hawke, 'The Manuscripts of the Cornish Passion Poem', p. 26.

95. Padel, *The Writings of the Boson Family*, p. 47.

96. Jenner, *Handbook of the Cornish Language*, p. 181.

97. Ibid., p. 38.

98. J. H. Matthews, *History of the Parishes of St Ives, Lelant, Towednack and Zennor* (1892, repub St Ives 2003), pp. 401–2.

99. 'posse comitatus'

100. W. Scawen, *Antiquities Cornu-Brittanick*, Thomas Tonkin MS. copy, British Library Add. MSS 33420, cited in Andrew Hawke, 'The Manuscripts of the Cornish Passion Poem', *Cornish Studies/Studhyansow Kernewek*, First Series 9 (1981), p. 23

101. See M. Spriggs, 'The Reverend Joseph Sherwood: Cornish Language Will o' the Wisp' in P. Payton (ed.), *Cornish Studies: Six* (Exeter, 1998).

102. W. Gwavas, his own annotated copy of Carew's *Survey of Cornwall*, Bodleian Corn. e 1 (*c*.1710–1720).

5

Cornish Linguistic Landscape

Neil Kennedy

Introduction

The aim here is to suggest some approaches to new ways in which Cornish is being used on signs by local government, businesses and individuals. Because these visual uses are collectively a very recent phenomenon, this consideration is necessarily speculative and inconclusive but the observations made are informed by participation in Cornwall Council's signage work and wider language activities. The peculiarity of Cornish as a revived language with few speakers makes it important to be cautious in applying experience from other places, yet much may be learnt from very different situations.

An important concept taken from studies elsewhere is that of 'linguistic landscape'. This has been developed in respect to territories where a 'minority' or 'regional' (subaltern) language co-exists with a 'majority' or 'national' (prevalent) language or where languages vie for space and the physical, political and social boundaries of groups and their languages are contestable.[1] The basic idea is that written language in the environment forms a textual landscape and is part of the visual setting within which languages are spoken, heard and seen. Consequently, it is also related to social, cultural, and economic concerns and contributes to how a language is viewed, literally and figuratively. A language that is clearly posted in public, private and commercial settings is likely to be taken seriously whilst its position in relation to other languages and the ways in which it is presented (e.g. colour, lettering styles, associated images) are discursive. Linguistic landscape emerged as a field primarily in work on French as a subaltern language in Canada where the 'language of public road signs, advertizing billboards, street names, place names, commercial shop signs, and public signs on government buildings combines to form the linguistic landscape of a given territory, region, or urban agglomeration'.[2]

Language is thus a further facet of the conventionally defined landscape which is the subject of multiple gazes, strongly linked to constructions of identity. Furthermore, there is much in the linkage between landscape and language that is amenable to commodification, making it a potential ingredient for branding and marketing in the cultural, heritage and tourism industries. In Cornwall, regional aid has coincided with an institutional 'distinctiveness agenda' supported by those who believe that, 'in an increasingly competitive world, there is a need to accentuate the Cornish brand, and use of the language on labels and in advertising can provide visual distinctiveness for Cornish products'.[3]

Cornwall Council signage policy

To set the scene, there is a primary layer of Cornish linguistic landscape in the form of place-names which features prominently in identity narratives. A second, neo-Cornish layer is under construction, mainly in the form of street-name signage, ostensibly aimed at furthering language revival. Despite widespread private uses, in naming houses, for example, the greatest additions to this new layer now come from public signage, so before considering some implications it is worth reminding ourselves of how this has come about. Cornwall Council's language policy (2009) includes plans to 'implement a system of bilingual signage with regard to street and place names for new and replacement signs'.[4] Signs are only replaced when damaged, worn-out, missing or entirely new but the work, begun in 2010, is being put into practice with such energy and speed that we may expect a high proportion of signs to be bilingual within a few years. To avoid added costs, the project uses the voluntary translators of a Cornish Signage Panel and signs have the same dimensions as monolingual ones. Although the Cornish appears in much smaller text below the English (the subtitles of linguistic landscape), this use goes beyond previous expectations and some revivalists told me of their amazement at finding bilingual signs near their homes. This is an outcome of the creation of MAGA – the Cornish Language Partnership – and the UK Government's signing of the Council of Europe's 'Charter for Regional or Minority Languages' in 2000/2001. The Government included Cornish under the terms of the charter after a seven-year campaign that built on strengthening support from councillors and officers, some of whom had attended Cornish classes, and it lead to a Council resolution: 'This Council sees the Cornish language as a vital part of contemporary culture and welcomes the work being done to promote its wider usage and status. This Council will, where appropriate, encourage the use of the language for the naming of streets.' (8 April 1997)

Considering the campaign helps to put signage in context. Firstly, it connected with a sense of marginalization and struggle within the Cornish Movement and the wider community and was lead by people who had also campaigned for jobs, notably and symbolically during the 'tin crisis' (1985–2000) and the Keskerdh Kernow march to London in 1997.[5] Its success was therefore felt as a hard-earned victory. Secondly, it united Cornish enthusiasts across the divides of the spelling disputes that hampered development in 1990, quickly gaining the participation of Andrew George, M.P. and Robin Teverson, M.E.P. It also mobilized affective alliances between linguistic minorities, so that some of their politicians and civil servants argued Cornwall's case within British and European institutions. The Government commissioned *An Independent Study of Cornish*,[6] then included Cornish under Part II of the Charter (2002). Cornwall Council created a Cornish Language Partnership and secured funding for staff.

Cornwall Council was not the first body to introduce bilingual signs, however. Some had been put up by individual towns in the 1980s and 1990s, notably Liskeard and Camborne, where spelling controversies were brought to the attention of the public. One or two councils, notably Newquay, had even put up welcome signs in the 1960s and 1970s. It was not until 1996, however, that Penwith District Council launched the first co-ordinated project to put up bilingual signs at the entrances to villages and towns.[7] Signs went up at Hayle, Lelant, Carbis Bay, St Ives, St Buryan and Mousehole and this would have extended to most of Penwith had the Cornish Language Board not objected to the spellings. The Cornish Sub-Committee of the European Bureau of Lesser-Used Languages later developed a policy, endorsed by Cornwall's erstwhile district councils (though not Scilly) and in 2006 Kerrier District Council produced ambitious plans to make 'new and replacement street signs' bilingual with 'no significant additional costs'. This was extended to Carrick and informs the current Cornwall-wide policy.[8]

Signage is at the centre of spelling controversies and differing attitudes to Cornishness[9] that make developing projects a burdensome task. Bernard Deacon considers that the current scheme extends 'the wrong turn adopted by inter-war revivalists'[10] by which he means that an emphasis on conservative Middle Cornish 'loses all relationship to the historic Cornish of the landscape'. The project is said to show 'no visible sympathy for our history or landscape' and to have 'ripped Cornish out of its historic territorial setting and made it much more difficult for people to relate the language to their heritage'. In failing to connect with popular tradition, it is said to represent 'a sadly wasted opportunity'. On the other hand, those involved consider re-spellings of early Cornish to be an appropriate recasting for modern use and consider the later forms of names to be 'corrupt'.[11]

Branding

For revivalists, neo-Cornish signs are an assertion of Cornishness, similar to other interventions in the landscape, such maintaining vernacular architecture, building Cornish hedges and flying St. Piran's flag. These practices are seen as defending distinctiveness against homogenizing trends that nationalists cast as Anglicization and which Celticists see as affecting 'the '"traditional" place-based sense of Celticness',[12] yet paradoxically they also contribute to commodifiable 'regional distinctiveness'[13] that may feed the demographic and cultural trends that erode difference. A possibility is that Cornish is undergoing a transformation from being the symbolic language of a militant Cornish Movement to being a safely depoliticized element of marketable difference. Some ways of foregrounding it as heritage may even reinforce economically unhelpful portrayals of Cornish people as 'traditional'[14] with the connotations of backwardness, remoteness and ineptitude that prevail in constructions of Celticity.[15] Some visual elements that accompany language activity, such as revived and invented folk traditions, music and dance and bardic ceremonies are also amenable to such representations and may be mediated through branding and advertizing for tourism.[16]

Emerging evidence[17] suggests that Cornish naming is attractive to visitors but it is not known whether this simply offers potential for correspondingly branded products and services or whether it will add to trends in second-home ownership, in-migration and a presumption against economic activities that clash with 'Lifestyle Cornwall' – that new permutation of tourism defined by 'high end', 'quality' and 'exclusive' leisure activities. Safely ethnic-looking signage may, ironically, become part of this package, appealing to affluent incomers and visitors at the expense of disadvantaged sections of the Cornish community. One or two commentators have begun to suggest that signs might contribute to 'selling Cornwall as a gigantic theme-park'[18] or hyper-real 'Kernowland'[19] but the inherent dangers have not dawned on most Cornish enthusiasts who are understandably pleased by the awareness and approval of visitors and the justification it provides for projects. If the suspicions are founded, they may be unwittingly collaborating with developers whilst believing that they are asserting Cornishness, but to be fair, it has become hard to frame schemes that use Cornish without recourse to the prevalent logic of commercialization. This, in combination with heritage discourses, has ousted nationalist arguments in language promotion so that revivalists employ commercial logic strategically, sometimes subscribing to it. Thus Mebyon Kernow councillor Dick Cole argues that Cornish signs are good for tourism and branding: 'Cornwall's uniqueness is its Celtic heritage and we have to promote that as a brand to attract more overseas visitors. These sorts of things are vitally important when trying to make an area stand out from the rest.'[20]

The oversight is that it appeals to UK visitors as well, with possible consequences for the property market, irrespective of any other applications. *Visit Cornwall* relays the revivalist message to inform potential visitors that, 'On exploration of Cornwall you will come across many unusual and distinctively Cornish place names which allude to our native language,'[21] also telling them that, 'the proliferation of the Cornish language adds yet another dimension to this exclusive haven beyond the border of the River Tamar.' This supports the observation from the Isle of Man that fostering 'national identity' is 'linked with commercial development and marketing the island as a distinct (and distinctive) entity'[22] and that 'it is reasonable to conclude that the linguistic landscape of the island is configured with not only its permanent population, but also visitors, in mind'.[23] Graham Busby makes similar points about signs in Penwith, comparing the appeal of Welsh road-signs to tourists.[24]

Academic approaches primarily consider linguistic landscape as a site of contestation where speech communities compete, often for wider social and economic concerns such as housing, access to jobs, political change and claims to territory. Linguistic landscape has therefore been related to 'ethnolinguistic vitality'[25] where the extent to which languages appear and the ways in which they do so indicate the vibrancy of the speech community and its status. The immediate difficulty in applying this perspective is that the nascent neo-Cornish speech community is tiny, producing a mismatch between the ambition and scale of signage projects and linguistic realities, belying the view that signs are for Cornish speakers. Increasing use of Cornish on signs is not matched by a widespread use of spoken Cornish so cannot be a straightforward indication of vitality. This kind of situation has already been referred to by Bourhis and Landry[26] who note that visible uses may be largely symbolic and may exaggerate or under-represent vitality producing 'discordance'. This may even involve deliberate falsification, motivated politically, commercially and by strategies for language revitalization. Thus signs may 'manipulate an individual's assessment of the status of languages and ... affect that individual's linguistic behaviour',[27] revealing the two-way relationship between visible use and socio-linguistic context.[28] Revivalists have sought inspiration from territories with large speech communities such as Wales and Ireland but the incongruity of these models in Cornwall is described as 'misguided' and 'self-deception'.[29] In order to reflect upon a better adapted approach, it may be useful to consider some motivations.

Place-names

Two connected ideas underpin Revivalism. Firstly, Cornish is held to be 'an outward and visible sign of nationality',[30] a fundamental part of aspiring to 'recognition' as a Celtic nation and achieving political and administrative changes, including those that led to regional aid when 'The existence of Cornish as an emblem of regional distinctiveness was an important factor in Cornwall being awarded Objective 1 status.'[31] Secondly, Cornish is thought to belong to Cornwall and be inseparable from the land and a cultural and geographical space. The revivalist, Ernest Retallack Hooper (Talek) wrote: 'Language is the audible and visible sign of a nationality and Cornish is an interesting language in itself; its range of expression is great. It belongs to Cornwall and nowhere else.'[32]

Then there are overlapping and competing romanticisms which, in looking both to the future and to the past, risk losing sight of the present. Some revivalists associate Cornish with familiar constructions of Celticity, imaginatively linking it to ancient sites such as Boscawen Ûn and Tintagel, rugged coastal and moorland scenery and neo-traditional cultural practices. Others partially or wholly reject this vision and instead, or as well, imagine Cornish as formerly spoken around the hearth and in the fields, harbours and mines – a suitable vehicle for protest.[33] These imaginings all bind Cornish to landscape and naming, going some way to explain a long-established emphasis on place-names. These, and derived surnames on shop signs and so on, were the only Cornish element of the linguistic landscape in the nineteenth and twentieth centuries and still represent an incontestably traditional foundation to which the neo-Cornish layer is being added. They are the language 'which is to be seen all around us on the sign-posts'[34] so that the landscape is the main interface with Cornish. In fact, traditional place-name signs, rather than new bilingual ones, are still the main Cornish component of linguistic landscape where they name, not just settlements, but the intimate details of the landscape (and seascape), such as rocks, fields, springs, woods, former mills and mines. They describe topography, vegetation and past activity whilst as simple names they conjure up familiar places and call to mind experiences and stories, even for those that do not know Cornish. Place-names are not always considered in work on linguistic landscape so it may be significant that a Cornish-speaking researcher, Davyth Hicks, should consider them as an important 'occurrence of text'[35] in discussing signage in Scotland. Hicks discusses some narrative functions, showing how names may prompt story-telling, connecting with folklore and mythology and giving rise to 'folk etymologies', but this may go deeper still, connecting with the inter-generational stories through which communities produce and reflect ideas of a shared identity.

Of course, most groups have sentimental reference to toponymy but what makes it especially poignant in Cornwall is that Cornish remains inscribed in the landscape, despite not being spoken outside revivalist scenes and widely considered dead. Through place-names, the landscape 'speaks in another language'[36] and as the most prominent feature of a Celtic heritage they have a heightened focus as living testimony, providing a continuous, if tenuous, tradition. Holding on to this has been a revivalist priority and the Old Cornwall Societies have 'recorders' charged with 'The collecting, recording and using of place-names, especially those of fields, lanes, earthworks, streams, pools, cliffs, rocks, fishing grounds, etc., with the old pronunciations.'[37] In keeping with this, Craig Weatherhill considers place-names to be 'historical monuments of equal importance to Cornish heritage as the stone circles, quoits and hill-forts'.[38] This compares with situations where languages have retreated to be spoken by a small proportion of a population in a reduced area, as Hicks identifies in discussing how place-names reveal past linguistic borders in Scotland.[39] In Brittany, where language shift is on-going, people may identify the former range of Breton from place-names, sometimes being motivated to learn it, but in Cornwall they have hitherto been the only generally visible and audible proof of the language's existence. Toponomy has long been symbolically charged, informing constructions of an ethnic identity since at least the mid-eighteenth century when the spoken language was no longer available for that purpose. This helps to explain established street names, such as nearly a hundred examples in Falmouth which include Cornish elements, like the easily recognizable and symbolic *tre* and *pen*.[40] Current discourses have a genealogy in eighteenth- and nineteenth-century antiquarianism when: 'the study which was intriguing Cornishmen, which was directly connected with the language, was the study of place names. With the death of the language ... Cornwall was left with a countless number of place names which, in the eyes of most people, were merely gibberish'.[41]

Recording place-names became part of 'a kind of duty in us Cornishmen to gather together the remains of our departed language'[42] and their sounds could not 'fail to affect a Cornish heart with that peculiar sort of pleasing melancholy which is excited by the portrait of a dear departed friend'.[43] Even those who were happy to see the language's demise could use it symbolically, as in Davies Gilbert's arrangement of place-names as verse:

Velandrukya Cracka Cudna,
Truzemenhall,
Chûn Crowzanwrah,
Bans Burnnhal Brane Bosfrancan,
Treeve Trewhidden Try Trembah ...[44]

With revivalist publications, more people could access these names so that Cornish became 'a visible sign of expressing Cornish nationhood'.[45] Combined aesthetic and nostalgic appeals to place-names throughout twentieth-century revivalism were said to 'stir the memory'[46] and had this repertoire not survived language shift the Cornish would surely have forgotten that their ancestors had ever spoken another language, the wider revival would not have happened and Cornwall would be very different, culturally, politically and socially. There would probably not be an ethnic dimension to regional distinctiveness, nor the cultural motivations and justifications for Objective One and dependent projects such as the Combined Universities of Cornwall campus at Tremough. In the event, reference to place-names has been a springboard for revival. Echoing Cornish writers, Henry Jenner observed that: 'The spoken language may be dead, but its ghost still haunts its old dwelling, the speech of West Cornish country folk is full of it and no one can talk about the country and its inhabitants in any sort of topographical detail without using a wealth of Cornish words.'[47]

Place-names thus stimulate the revival of Cornish which 'so recently ... was in use, that for Cornish people it is in a very real sense the language of our forefathers'[48] and learners often cite the wish to understand them as a motive. When UNESCO classed Cornish as extinct in its *Atlas of the World's Languages in Danger* (2009),[49] successful objectors cited place-names and earlier philological and antiquarian study as evidence of continuity with the revival[50] and achieved its reclassification as a 'language undergoing revitalization'. Place-names also furnish neo-Cornish with otherwise unattested words, filling 'lexical gaps'[51] and providing 'a language repository'.[52] For people with topographical family names, together with their relations and neighbours, their connections with place may be apparent so that identity is embedded geographically. This is seen in attention to locating names in family history research. At the Cornish Studies Library in Redruth I met a Tregonning who had visited Tregonning Hill and somebody who had traced her mother's surname to Spargo near Penryn. A Mr Woon wondered which place-name containing 'woon' might be the origin of his family and in Truro Tourist Information Office a Rosevear from Melbourne fruitlessly asked for directions. Place-names relate intertextually[53] to topography and narratives to recall the shared references upon which group identity depends and feature in seemingly redundant conversations that locate individuals within the group. For example, in a recent controversy surrounding Duchy of Cornwall mineral rights, local objectors quickly made humorous use of the apocryphal and well-known Talskiddy Treacle Mine, putting up signs.[54] Although not everybody pays place-names attention, enough people do for them to be important. At Truro Cattle Market, five farmers immediately understood the question 'What do you think about Cornish farm names?' and without prompting, linked them to being Cornish, the survival of their industry and the importance of passing on local knowledge.[55] In fact, their responses were more emphatic and articulate than those from neo-traditional musicians and carried a sense of beleaguerment and stubborn resistance.

The worry that place-names and their pronunciation will be lost results in complaints about radio and television presenters whose mispronunciation is said to show disrespect and arrogance. The issue regularly displaces the business of meetings for other purposes. Thus, at a discussion in the Royal Institution of Cornwall, a participant referred to the 'Lost Pronunciation of Heligan'[56] and I heard similar complaints in everyday settings – at a workshop in Cornwall College, from teenage mothers at Redruth, and in the waiting room of Devoran Surgery. There are concerns that distinctiveness is being erased as names are left off sign-posts and maps, misrepresented or lost to a weakened oral tradition, and the issue serves as a proxy for wider anxieties about the perceived erosion of identity. Cultural activists cite, amongst others, the iconic names Tol-Pedn-Penwith and Landewednack, both of which have disappeared from O.S. Maps. A researcher mentioned the misspelling of Colwyn as Coldwind and said 'My blood boils every time I drive past it.' Another saw this as wilful 'Anglo-centric thinking' where decision-makers 'slowly and quietly switch to English-sounding names, hoping nobody will notice'.[57] Specialists cite numerous minor place-names that have been replaced in recent decades. Weatherhill mentions 'Ventonegga, which bore that name for centuries, before it vanished to be replaced by Brook Cottage'.[58] Institutions are seen as 'removing centuries old place-names', sometimes claiming they are hard to say and remember. Locals still refer to Treliske Hospital, rejecting its renaming as The Royal Cornwall Hospital, and objections to the omission of Tremough from the CUC campus address are said to explain new signs (2011) showing Tremough in large lettering.[59]

Enhancing the linguistic landscape

These worries also give rise to the wish to revitalize the linguistic landscape with new names and motives for neo-Cornish signage have something akin to those of graffiti artists tagging their neighbourhoods, staking out territory and proclaiming their presence. Projects attempt to (re)claim physical and cultural territory and foresee the re-installation of spoken Cornish. The greater the perception of losing ground, the more the iconography of identity is posted and the more cultural retrieval and historiography are undertaken politically. Landscape is linked to the past as the setting for histories, collective struggle and experience. As David Lowenthal observes, 'The place of the past in any landscape is as much the product of present interest as of past history' and 'the survival of the past depends on our memory'.[60] Keeping names alive in the landscape is part of such a 'present interest' and in nationalist/revivalist narratives,[61] they demonstrate persistence, symbolizing the endurance and tenacity of the Cornish themselves and connecting them to bygone generations. This story has strengthened with the emergence of 'the new Cornish nativism'[62] where an embattled indigenous community is presented in language reminiscent of accounts of Native Americans.[63] Enhancing the linguistic landscape means recreating the imagined lost space of an authentic Cornwall, raising questions about which of several imagined periods and cultures represents a Cornish Utopia for those involved and how these differ between revivalists and other sections of the public.[64] The question 'When was Cornwall?'[65] thus relates to differing ideologies and identity discourses, including those that give rise to different attitudes to spelling and signage. As in more obviously colonial situations, recovering names is thought to challenge hegemonies and re-appropriate space, a reversal of the naming and mapping that exercise power under colonialism.[66] In alleging misuses of place-names by academics, John Angarrack draws analogies with Africa and India, discussing post-colonial re-naming as a process of de-Anglicization and citing 'moves to change Calcutta back to the Bengali Kalikata'. Cornwall is said to suffer a 'cultural blight' which it is 'failing to resist'.[67] From these standpoints, signage is not cosy heritage but rather visible evidence that 'the language is fighting back'.[68]

Contested naming in very different circumstances to those of Cornwall may share common points. Where languages have been replaced or are thought to be threatened, policies may be produced, as in Quebec where concerted efforts have markedly increased the number of French place-names displayed and where a 'Commission de toponymie' links them to maintaining the language.[69] Linguistic landscape may be transformed even more dramatically as I saw in Galicia where Galician[70] has re-emerged with the establishment of autonomous government[71] and linguistic policies (1987, 2007)[72] that assure use on public signs. Despite some opposition, a largely Galician linguistic landscape has been achieved with the hope that Galician will become 'a factor of social cohesion'.[73] In Scotland, Gaelic and Scots projects are similarly seen as reclaiming lost ground where: 'Naming a place is an act of ownership and possession. By reviving, using and even re-creating Gaelic and Scots names for places in Scotland we take back ownership of our country, we define it for ourselves.'[74]

Edward Said describes his feelings on seeing Arabic names in Palestine/Israel represented in the US Press with Hebrew instead of Arabic spellings,[75] obscuring the meanings and implying that the names are not Arabic. He asks 'How much trivial malice can we bear?'[76] This sense of erasure and cumulative small injuries is felt and voiced by some Cornish people, albeit in far less dramatic circumstances, and it extends to complaints about the naming of housing developments which are said to be unimaginative and insensitive: 'Instead of introducing a little creativity by using traditional Cornish names, developers, unimpeded by the authorities, make the simple choice of plumping for culturally intrusive, but safe and easy, Home County type names. In time, unless a stand is made, Cornish place-name diversity will die out and the Cornish will be able to recall nothing of their heritage.'[77] The Exeter-based Highways Agency is criticized for giving 'bland English names like Highgate Cross and Boxheater Junction' to junctions and roundabouts.[78] Weatherhill describes them as 'happily introducing meaningless English names all over the place', and adds Stopgate and Maiden Green.[79]

Territory is involved in forming identities, as recognized in Anthony Smith's definition of an ethnic group as one with a name and 'common ancestry myths and shared historical memories, elements of a shared culture, a link with a historic territory, and some measure of solidarity, at least among the elites'.[80] This understands that territory is not just a surface area delimited by borders, but also qualitatively conceived as familiar landscape upon which are written intragroup stories. For revivalists, nationalists and tourism operators alike, place-names mark Cornwall as a distinct territory and the Tamar, ever-present in Cornish imaginations, is repeatedly presented as a sharp linguistic frontier that confronts visitors with difference and Celticity:

> [C]rossing the River Tamar into Cornwall one's first impression is of the un-English place names. Names such as Mawgan-in-Pydar, Treryn, Porthgwarra, Lostwithiel, Landewednack, Kennack, Gwithian, Caerhays and Boconnoc. They are names which remind one of Wales or Brittany. It is not really surprising. Cornwall is not really England nor can the Cornish be classified as English.[81]

Weatherhill writes of 'the utter strangeness of the place names which assail the visitor to Cornwall from the moment the River Tamar is crossed and the familiar world of English place names is left behind'.[82] In keeping with this Ken George considers that neo-Cornish signs serve 'To show that Cornwall is a Celtic country distinct from England', and Julyan Holmes describes them as 'an immediate and unavoidable reminder of Cornwall's unique distinctiveness from English counties'. Similarly, Deacon argues that their main purpose should be 'to alert residents and visitors, Cornish and English, to the existence of the Cornish language and to the fact that Cornish is/was a separate language from English'.[83]

Signage often involves a 'hardening of space, a reinforcement of boundaries and distinctions, and the fortification of property, place or nation'[84] where the ambiguities of toponymy are ironed out. The Tamar, accentuated by place-names, is a metaphor for ways of thinking about Cornishness. Clearly defined boundaries are comfortingly reassuring, avoiding the need to grapple with ambiguous cultural realities but, as Chris Williams observes in Wales, 'the fully unified, completed, secure and coherent identity is a fantasy'.[85] All identities need imagined boundaries, whether special or not, but there is a danger of rejecting inconvenient uncertainties and hybridity to the detriment of inclusive, confident cultural dynamism. For example, the practice of translating very early English names in East Cornwall, suggests that the revivalist elite might resemble counterparts in Wales where, allegedly, 'most Welsh intellectuals (not only nationalists) have been reluctant to face up to the implications of Wales' "fuzzy borders" and its long experience of multicultural experiences, if not multiculturalism'.[86]

Signs have both informative and symbolic functions and the argument is made that they may work symbolically to increase spoken Cornish, giving rise in turn to a context for more informational functions. They are seen as advertisements to stimulate interest and are expected to 'create a positive change, increasing the perceived relevance of the language' and produce 'a marked increase in the numbers of people wishing to learn Cornish'.[87] They are thus expected to precede an expanded speech community. Some revivalists also see them as 'a huge visual aid' for learning.[88] These views relate to the suggestions that the value attributed to a language will determine the extent of its appearance and that, conversely, its value is influenced by visibility. Landry and Bourhis suggest that the 'presence of private and government signs written in the in-group language might have acted as a stimulus for promoting the use of one's own language in a broad range of domains'.[89]

Signs in the subaltern language are thought to encourage its use in more areas of daily life, the thinking being that 'the act of displaying a language, especially on official, central or local government signage, carries the important symbolic function of increasing its value and status',[90] mitigating stigmas and acceptance of language loss. Displaying functional information in neo-Cornish is seen as supporting future applications so when a supermarket put up such signs some revivalists thought them more significant than bilingual names at historic sites, such as Pendennis and Restormel Castles, where Cornish may be associated with redundant heritage as another relic. As there are few speakers to inform, this again raises the issue of 'discordance'. Supposedly informational signs are largely divorced from any such function so that their role remains symbolic and perhaps commercial; yet the importance that revivalists attach to them recognizes that where and how language is used may be as important as the number of signs. In Brittany, the former restriction of Breton to occasional signs at the entry to villages and at heritage sites, confirmed its image as defunct and folkloric, unfit for present-day use, whilst supposedly Celtic lettering emphasized these associations. Recent projects therefore affirm Breton as modern[91] and road signage has been extended to the whole area where the language survives traditionally, along with parts where it has not been spoken for generations.[92] Not all signs have the same implications for status and whilst this seems obvious, it may be ignored by enthusiasts in seeking visibility. As in the adage 'no publicity is bad publicity', they may consider any signs desirable, disregarding unhelpful connotations, including those that serve Cornwall's role as a leisure zone.

Pol Hodge suggests that signs may, 'give a bit of pride to people who live here',[93] so could Cornish people, who are nearly all non-speakers, draw benefits to morale from visual uses? Julyan Holmes thinks they could and that signs may communicate 'knowledge of their own unique and valuable heritage' and 'help to strengthen communal solidarity and bolster the confidence of those who are fed an image of themselves as a backward and inferior version of English'. Nev Meeks adds that: 'you can be more confident about yourself if you know who you are, where you have come from and that you are part of a culture that is real and respected. Connecting history, culture, language, people and place is important for social cohesion.'[94]

These perspectives connect to Bourdieu's notions of cultural, symbolic and social capital, all of which may be important for building resilient, cohesive communities.[95] They also relate to Diane Reay's 'emotional capital', a concept that recognizes the psychological dimensions of well-being that are encapsulated in individual and collective worth as feelings that need not correspond to economic wealth.[96] Through these frameworks, the concept of cultural vigour may be extended to the status attributed to groups and cultures. Notably, Landry and Bourhis discuss the 'symbolic functions' of linguistic landscape to hypothesize that 'the experience of the linguistic landscape by members of a language group may contribute to social psychological aspects of bilingual development'.[97] Adapting this to Cornwall, where bilingualism is rare, we might hypothesize that seeing Cornish in prestigious settings could contribute in ways that are not dependent on bilingualism but which involve enabling feelings that arise from perceived worth.

Yet for this to be the case, there would need to be symbolic identification with Cornish. Little is known about public sentiment but there may be a clue in the scale of the petition for a 'Cornish Assembly – Senedh Kernow' which in 2000–2001 achieved 50,000 valid signatures.[98] Although this need not indicate support for the language, its strength stems from the discursive context of the Cornish Movement and the campaign has a bilingual title and explicit references to Cornwall's 'unique culture, language and history'.[99] Further indications come from small-scale studies and anecdotes. In a piece of action research by Robert Reynolds in Saltash, 92 per cent of 'young people'[100] were aware of Cornish, 44 per cent even knew 'a word or two' and 78 per cent favoured learning, figures that compare favourably with Brittany where 49 per cent of fifteen to nineteen year olds think it worth promoting Breton.[101] At Cornwall College, a group of eighteen students told me they knew there were Cornish speakers, although some had not noticed bilingual signs.[102] When these were seen, most students welcomed them and expressed pride in Cornwall having 'its own language', despite not speaking it. Just a few thought them a 'waste of money'. A dozen or so retired people at an event in Camborne all recognized Cornish as having some, however vague, connection to them, but they also· affirmed that they did not understand a word, despite one of them saying 'Kernow bys Vyken' (Cornwall for ever) and another telling me Chynoweth meant 'new house'. One woman said: 'It's something we got, they [others] haven't got.' and another that, 'We should keep hold of it [Cornish] and not leave it go again.' Only one person suggested that Cornish was 'all a long time ago' and that 'there's more important things to spend money on these days'. In Bodmin, St Austell, Falmouth and Penzance, I asked locals and visitors about signs in a chain of café-restaurants. Several locals, including two staff members, echoed expressions of pride in 'Cornwall's own language' and several visitors thought them interesting.[103] A local couple had heard of spelling disagreements and wondered if the wording was 'proper Cornish' or 'all made-up' but even this did not prevent them from welcoming the signs. If these reactions are anything to go by, signs are often valued by locals and interest some visitors. Similar public reactions are reported by MAGA.

Conclusion

The value attributed to a language has implications for all who are distinguished as belonging to the traditionally associated group, not just those who speak it. Thus attitudes towards Welsh people, Welsh-speaking or not, is related to imaginings of Welshness which incorporate perceptions of the language. Is there then an emergent tendency to associate Cornish people with language? That has not been the case but perhaps the newly visible profile of Cornish is producing an effect. Demands for translation by businesses and individuals on moving to Cornwall may be early evidence,[104] demonstrating awareness outside Cornwall and suggesting that some outsiders expect the Cornish public to be pleased. This hints at Cornish acquiring prestige and value but the phenomenon is altogether too recent for us to be sure. If prestige has consequences for emotional capital, well-being and capacity, we may nevertheless speculate that such a trend might benefit people beyond revivalist spheres.

Like heritage projects, interventions in linguistic landscape may be primarily nationalistic or motivated by commercial interests that do not benefit everybody, but they may also be creative, celebratory, valorizing and challenging. In the Cornish case it is too early to be sure what is going on but not too late to reflect on policy and deal with conflicts of interest and dilemmas surrounding Cornwall's image. To summarize, signage has implications for Cornish identities generally, not just for language revivalists, and the non-commercial and symbolic roles, connected to narrative and heritage, may be more important to well-being than those related to commodification or revivalism, *per se*. Deacon, himself a committed Cornish speaker, considers that, 'there was no widespread debate about the purpose of signage policies before it was hijacked by the revivalists'. This understands linguistic landscape to have ramifications that are too important for signage work to be framed narrowly and points to the need for reflection.

Acknowledgements

Thanks to the past and present members and advisors of the Cornish Signage Panel, to Jenefer Lowe of MAGA and to Bernard Deacon and Sharon Lowenna.

Notes and references

1. e.g. R. Bourhis and R. Landry, 'Linguistic Landscape and Ethnolinguistic Vitality: An Empirical Study,' *Journal of Linguistic and Social Psychology* 16:1 (Santa Barbara, California, 1997), pp. 23–49; J. Cenoz and D. Gorter, 'Linguistic Landscape and Minority Languages', *International Journal of Multilingualism* 3:1 (London, 2006), pp. 67–80; D. Gorter and J. Cenoz, 'Knowledge about Language and Linguistic Landscape', in *The Encyclopedia of Language and Education*, Vol. 6, *Knowledge About Language* (2nd edition, Berlin, 2007), pp. 343–55.
2. Bourhis and Landry, 'Linguistic Landscape and Ethnolinguistic Vitality', p. 25.
3. C. Weatherhill, responses to research questionnaire.
4. http://www.magakernow.org.uk, accessed 14 September 2011.
5. S. Parker (ed.), *Cornwall Marches On? Keskerdh Kernow 500* (Truro, 1998).
6. K. MacKinnon, *An Independent Academic Study on Cornish* (Plymouth, 2000).
7. A collaboration with C. Weatherhill.
8. http://www.magakernow.org.uk, accessed 25 June 2011.
9. See, P. Payton, 'The Ideology of Language revival in Modern Cornwall' in R. Black et al. (eds), *Celtic Connections: Proceedings of the Tenth International Congress of Celtic Studies*, Vol. 1, *Language, Literature, History, Culture* (Edinburgh, 1999), pp. 395–424; P. Payton and B. Deacon, 'The Ideology of Language Revival' in P. Payton (ed.), *Cornwall Since the War* (Redruth, 1993).
10. B. Deacon, responses to a questionnaire.
11. A notion connected to prevalent linguistic purisms.
12. D. Harvey et al., *Celtic Geographies – Old Culture, New Times* (London, 2001).
13. A current theme in Cornwall Council spheres.
14. See, A. Hale, 'Creating a Cornish Brand: Discourses of Traditionality in Cornish Economic Regeneration Strategies' in U. Kockel (ed.) *Review of Culture and Economy* (Aldershot, 2002), pp. 164–74.

15. See discussion by A. Hale in P. Payton (ed.), *Cornish Studies: Four* (Exeter, 1996), pp. 158–70.

16. See, A. Hale, 'Representing the Cornish – Contesting heritage interpretation in Cornwall', *Tourist Studies* 1(2) (London, 2001), pp. 185–96.

17. E.g. Comments by M. Bell of Visit Cornwall at 'Cornish Culture – Good for Business' conference, Truro, 12 February 2011.

18. Anonymous responses to a questionnaire.

19. N. Kennedy and N. Kingcome, 'Disneyfication of Cornwall – Developing a Poldark Heritage Complex', *International Journal of Heritage Studies* 4:1 (Exeter, 1998).

20. D. Cole in *This is Cornwall*, http://www.thisiscornwall.co.uk, 12 November 2009.

21. http://www.visitcornwall.com/site/explore-cornwall/towns-and-villages, accessed 12 September 2011.

22. M. Sebba, 'Discourses in Transit' in A. Jaworski and C. Thurlow (eds), *Semiotic Landscapes: Language, Image, Space (Advances in Sociolinguistics)* (London, 2010), p. 63.

23. Ibid., p. 66.

24. G. Busby, 'Cultural Capital in Cornwall: Heritage and the Visitor', in P. Payton (ed.), *Cornish Studies: Sixteen* (Exeter, 2008), p. 150.

25. Bourhis and Landry, 'Linguistic Landscape and Ethnolinguistic Vitality'.

26. R. Bourhis and R. Landry, 'La loi 101 et l'aménagement du paysage linguistique au Québec', *Revue d'Aménagement Linguistique* Special Issue (Quebec, 2002), pp. 107–31.

27. G. Puzey, 'Planning the Linguistic Landscape: A Comparative Survey of the uses of Minority languages in the Road Signage of Norway, Scotland and Italy', MSc dissertation, University of Edinburgh, 2007. http://www.era.lib.ed.ac.uk/bitstream/1842/2118/1/2007PuzeyGDissertationMSc.pdf, accessed 5 April 2012.

28. See, Cenoz and Gorter, 'Linguistic Landscape and Minority Languages', pp. 67–68.

29. Responses to a questionnaire from researchers.

30. *Old Cornwall* 2:5 (1933), p. 29.

31. http://www.magakernow.org.uk, accessed 24 June 2011.

32. E. G. Retallack Hooper, in A. S. D. Smith, *Lessons in Spoken Cornish* (undated).

33. See, R. Gendall, *Carn* 57 (Peel, 1987) and *Carn* 63 (Peel, 1988).

34. R. Gendall, *Carn* 63.

35. D. Hicks, 'Scotland's Linguistic Landscape: The Lack of Policy and Planning with Scotland's Place-names and Signage' Paper given at World Congress on Language Politics, Barcelona (Edinburgh, 2002), also cited in G. Puzey, 'Planning the Linguistic Landscape', p. 10.

36. C. Berry, *Cornwall* (London, 1949), p. 95.

37. http://recorders.oldcornwall.org/, accessed 5 October 2011.

38. Responses to a questionnaire.

39. Hicks, 'Scotland's Linguistic Landscape', para. 20.

40. c.v. 'By Tre, Pol and Pen, You shall know the Cornishmen.' R. Carew, *Survey of Cornwall* (London, 1602; republished Redruth, 2000), p. 62.

41. P. Berresford Ellis, *The Cornish Language and its Literature* (London, 1974), p. 140.

42. W. Borlase, *Antiquities of Cornwall* (London, 1754) cited in P. Pool, *William Borlase* (Truro, 1986), p. 118.

43. *The Cornish Magazine*, anon. (1828) cited in B. Deacon, *Cornwall: A Concise History* (Cardiff, 2007), p. 14.
44. D. Gilbert, b. 1767, d. 1839, in M. Hawkey (ed.), *A Cornish Chorus* (London, 1948), p. 89.
45. Berresford Ellis, *The Cornish Language and its Literature*, p. 196.
46. C. Berry, *Cornwall*, p.95.
47. H. Jenner, 'Cornish Place-Names', *Journal of the Royal Institution of Cornwall* 17 (Truro, 1910–11), cited in Berresford Ellis, *The Cornish Language and its Literature*, p. 156.
48. R. Gendall, *Tavaz a Ragadazow* (Menheniot, 2000).
49. http://news.bbc.co.uk/2/hi/uk_news/england/cornwall/7900972.stm, accessed 12 September 2011.
50. See, MacKinnon, *An Independent Academic Study*, p. 7.
51. See, for example, O. J. Padel, *Cornish Place-Name Elements* (Nottingham, 1985).
52. Alistair Quinnell, MAGA conference, Lostwithiel, 1 October 2011.
53. As used by J. Kristeva: *Séméiôtiké: recherches pour une sémanalyse* (Paris, 1969).
54. http://www.bbc.co.uk/news/uk-england-cornwall–16962119, accessed 5 April 2012.
55. Interviews in August 2011.
56. A reference to the Lost Gardens of Heligan.
57. Remarks made during discussions of spelling.
58. Personal email.
59. Observations by staff and students.
60. D. Lowenthal, 'Past Time, Present Place: Landscape and Memory', *The Geographical Review* 65:1 (New York, January 1975), pp. 1–36. http://www.jstor.org/stable/213831, accessed 25 January 2011.
61. E.g. R. Lyon, *Cornish: The struggle for survival* (Nancegollan, 2001).
62. B. Deacon, 'Cornishness and Englishness: Nested Identities or Incompatible Ideologies?' *International Journal of Regional and Local Studies* 5:2 (2009), pp. 9–29.
63. E.g. J. Angarrack, *Breaking the chains* (Camborne, 1999) and J. Angarrack, *Scat t'Larrups. Resist and Survive* (Padstow, 2008).
64. Observations by Sharon Lowenna.
65. See, Gwyn A. Williams, *When was Wales?* (London, 1985).
66. The theme of B. Friel's *Translations* (London, 1981).
67. J. Angarrack, *Our Future is History. Identity, Law and the Cornish Question* (Padstow, 2002), pp. 55–59.
68. Remarks by Pol Hodge, MAGA education officer.
69. Charte de la langue française, 1977; Information from L'Office québécoise de la langue française.
70. The language was banned under the dictatorship.
71. Xunta de Galiza: http://www.xunta.es/portada, accessed 12 August 2011.
72. http://www.observatoriodalinguagalega.com, accessed 12 August 2011.
73. Comments by the president of the Xunta de Galiza, Alberto Núñez Feijóo, 25 July 2011.
74. Paul Kavanagh, newsnetscotland.com, accessed 3 September 2011.
75. Spellings used when these languages are represented in English texts.
76. E. Said, *After the Last Sky – Palestinian Lives* (New York, 1999), pp. 133–36.
77. J. Angarrack, *Our Future is History*, p. 59.

78. Ibid.
79. C. Weatherhil, responses to questions, 5 September 2011.
80. A. Smith, *Nationalism and Modernism* (London, 1998), pp. 159–65; Cited in B. Deacon, 'From ethnie to nation? The three moments of the modern Cornish identity' (unpublished paper, 2012).
81. Berresford-Ellis, *The Cornish Language and its Literature*, p. 1.
82. C. Weatherhill, *Cornish Place-Names and Language* (Wilmslow, 1996), p. 1.
83. George, Holmes, Deacon: Responses to questionnaires.
84. D. Mitchell, 'Cultural landscapes: the dialectical landscape – recent landscape research in human geography', *Progress in Human Geography* 26:3 (2002), pp. 381–89.
85. In J. Aaron and C. Williams (eds), *Postcolonial Wales* (Cardiff, 2005), p. 14.
86. Ibid.
87. C. Weatherhill, responses to a questionnaire.
88. Remarks by a revivalist.
89. Landry and Bourhis, (1997) op. cit., p.45.
90. A. Jaworski and C. Thurlow, *Semiotic Landscapes: Language, Image, Space*, (2010), p.10.
91. www.ofis-bzh.org/upload/ouvrage/fichier/350fichier.pdf, accessed 5 March 2012.
92. Information from Y. Madeg, place-name specialist at Offis ar Brezhoneg.
93. Responses to a questionnaire.
94. Responses to questionnaires. Nev Meeks chairs the Signage Panel.
95. P. Bourdieu, 'Les 3 états du capital culturel', in *Actes de recherche en sciences sociales*, vol. 30, pp. 3–6, (Paris, Novembre, 1979).
96. D. Reay, 'Gendering Bourdieu's concept of capitals? Emotional capital, women and social class' in L. Adkins and B. Skeggs (eds.), *Feminism after Bourdieu*, The Sociological Review, Vol. 52, Issue Supplement, (London, 2004), pp. 57–74; c.v. S. Charlesworth, *A Phenomenology of Working Class Experience*, (Cambridge, 2000).
97. Bourhis and Landry, 'Linguistic Landscape and Ethnolinguistic Vitality', p. 23.
98. http://www.cornishassembly.org/, accessed 8 September 2011.
99. Ibid.
100. Research involving the Livewire Youth Project, 2007 (unpublished).
101. F. Broudic, *Parler breton au XXIe siècle: Le nouveau sondage de TMO-Régions* (Brest, 2009), p. 152.
102. Conversations in April 2011.
103. Remarks included: 'really good', 'cool', 'fascinating', 'different', 'like going to Wales'.
104. Information from MAGA.

6

The Celto-Cornish Movement and the Folk Revival

Competing speech communities

Merv Davey

Introduction

This essay considers two groups of people in Cornwall with competing interpretations of Cornish folk tradition and the identity it represents. The first group is that of the home grown Celto-Cornish movement, which sees local folk tradition as part of Cornwall's Celtic heritage. The second is that of the British/English folk movement, which understands Cornish tradition as part of a wider English culture tradition and, therefore, sees no barrier to importing material from England to represent Cornwall. There are three concepts which underpin this discussion: understanding folk tradition as a process rather than stasis; recognising the significance of 'lore' in relationship to folk tradition and identity; and the notion of 'speech communities' as groups of people with a shared set of understandings and a shared language which reinforces these understandings.

The emergence of 'folk' as a genre of popular music and dance in the 1950s compromised long-held beliefs about the nature of folk tradition and the sanctity of its deep historic origins. Distinctions were drawn between the traditional, and the contemporary written in a style perceived as traditional. Organisations such as the International Folk Music Council replaced the term 'folk' with the 'traditional', 'roots' or 'ethnic' in order to try to accommodate this. In the latter part of the twentieth century popularly held beliefs about the nature of folk tradition were nevertheless subject to an almost terminal critique by writers such as Harker and Boyse.[1] In effect, they showed that what was accepted as common sense in folk tradition owed more to the ideas and beliefs of a small group of influential people than historical evidence.

This author has argued elsewhere that there is a case for separating 'folk' as a genre of popular music from 'folk tradition' as a social phenomenon.[2] This allows for folk tradition to be understood as a process that happens to a tune, a song, a dance or a custom, as it is performed, as it is communicated and as it is understood. Folk tradition is a process that involves both continuity and change in the structure of the material, the context of its performance and the meaning ascribed to it by those involved. Multiple factors govern this change, and the outcomes can seem chaotic and random. It is important to recognise that some are a reflexive response to wider social trends, and that some changes are the result of careful reflection on the part of the participants. A tradition is an abstract vehicle taking the form of music, a dance, a custom or a combination of all three, that travels through time carrying structures and meanings with it which are modified by, and exchanged for, the new. Thus it is not a question of whether a folk phenomenon is traditional or not but where it lies in the traditional process and the extent to which it is owned by a community rather than artistic or commercial interests.

Another dimension that helps us to understand folk tradition is where the performance is located in both a physical and a social sense. Hoerburger suggests that a tradition can be understood as having two existences.[3] When an event takes place at a certain time of year in a given place involving a wide section of the community, then this can be understood as an original location or existence. The Helston Furry Dance would be an example of this.[4] If this dance is then taken out of this context and used for social dance events or barn dances, then this can be understood as a new location or second existence. This does not make the dance any less traditional in the sense that there will continue to be forces that influence change in structure and significance but these forces might have a different emphasis. Likewise, a song can be understood as being performed in an original location when sung in the local pub on a Saturday night but in a new location when taken into a concert setting where a group of singers leads audience participation. The line between original and second locations will always be a fine one but what is interesting is that in the second location performers are likely to be much more self-conscious about what they are performing and why, especially when linked to the expression of identity such as Cornishness.

When folk tradition is considered as a process, the narratives that surround it and what people believe or wish to believe provide a social reality that competes with the interpretations of the past. Here it is lore – that is, what people understand and the beliefs they share – which is as important as any evidence provided by history. The Padstow Mummer's day provides a good example of this. Following parliamentary censure as a racist event the author undertook a study, subsequently published in *Cornish Studies: Fourteen*, and made the case that neither the historical origins nor current day practice of the tradition were intended to caricature or demean minority groups.[5] Historical research suggested that it evolved from a Cornish Guize Dance[6] tradition but contemporary lore surrounding the festival ranged from it being a fertility rite in the shortest days of winter to the pragmatic suggestion that it was just 'party time' and an excuse for fancy dress. A particularly interesting narrative saw it as a celebration to commemorate the rescue of slaves from a ship that visited Padstow. The people of the village blacked their faces to confuse the slavers and release the slaves. There is no historical evidence as yet to support such a narrative but it is belief that is important here not the evidence of history. If this is what is believed about the tradition then it counters the notion that the event is intended to demean minority groups; quite the reverse.

From a sociological perspective, beliefs and narratives can also be understood as part of the discursivity that defines a community. In his study of the relationship between language and power Fairclough uses the term 'speech communities' to describe groups of people who share ideological norms and reinforce their world view discursively through use of language.[7] Bernard Deacon draws upon Fairclough's thinking to develop an understanding of identity in Cornwall or, to be precise, identities in Cornwall. Deacon suggests that 'Both Cornwall and the Cornish people have been and are being discursively constructed in a number of often conflicting ways.'[8] The Celto-Cornish movement and the English Folk Revival can be understood as two speech communities with the potential for quite different constructions of identity around Cornish folk traditions. For Fairclough, the issue of power is important when examining speech communities. He suggests that a characteristic of a dominant speech community is the 'capacity to naturalize ideologies; i.e. win acceptance for them as non-ideological common sense'.[9] History may provide the opportunity for interpretations of a Cornish identity other than English but the ideology of a dominant speech community might make it appear common sense that Cornwall should be counted as part of England.

This essay looks first at the relationship between folk tradition and the Celtic world generally. The involvement of the Celto-Cornish movement with folk tradition in Cornwall is then explored together with the advent of the Folk Revival. The discussion that leads from this considers the way in which these two speech communities compete, both for space to perform in and for a sense of authenticity.

'Celtic Roots'

The introduction of the term 'folk' ('Volkslied' – 'folk song') is conventionally attributed to Johann Gottfried Herder (1744–1803),[10] a German Lutheran pastor working in Latvia. Despite Russian and German political and cultural domination, Herder found that the Latvians had retained their language and an identity as a distinct ethnic group. According to Francmanis, Herder 'equated this ethnic community's popular tradition with its suppressed national consciousness and came to believe that this oral tradition contained the essence, or soul, of the Latvian nation'.[11] This captured the imagination of the Romantic Movement and the counter-reaction to the urban, mechanised world of the Industrial Revolution. It also offered a sense of authenticity for the emergent nationalist ideologies in Europe who saw in folk tradition evidence of the ancient civilisations and culture from which their nations derived.

Authors within Celtic studies such as Ó'Giolláin,[12] McCann[13] and Wood[14] show that the Celtic world was part of this movement and that there was, and continues to be, a close symbiosis between folk tradition and Celtic identity. In Scotland this was represented initially by Macpherson's Poems of Ossian but evolved to become the modern package of bagpipes, kilts and tartans that we recognise today. The story is similar in Ireland, a good example being that of Bunting and his interweaving of the repertoire of the itinerant eighteenth-century Irish harpists with the Gaelic language. In Wales we have Morgannwg's Gorsedd and in Brittany, Villemarquè's collection of ballads, Barzaz Breizh. As history, these examples have been the subject of scrutiny and deconstruction from the outset but perhaps immortalised more recently in Hobsbawm and Ranger's seminal work *The Invention of Tradition*.[15] As lore, however, they are the expression of a community's aspirations and the creative way in which the process of tradition and the sense of identity feed off each other.

A strong link between folk traditions and Cornish identity appears throughout the nineteenth century. Cornwall's relationship with the Celtic world is frequently alluded to, from Gilbert's reference to the Helston Furry as 'a specimen of Celtick Music'[16] to the linguistic connections made by Sandys.[17] Courtney referred to the linguistic connections but also acknowledged Cornish Celticity, with comments such as 'Cornish people possess in a marked degree all the characteristics of the Celts'[18] and 'Like all other Celts, the Cornish are an imaginative and poetical people.'[19] Unlike the Celtic world elsewhere, this connection, initially at least, does not go as far as recognising the expression of nationality. Dundes suggests that one of the drives to authenticate national ideologies using folk traditions was a feeling of inferiority in relation to dominant cultures.[20] Deacon shows that far from having an inferiority complex in the first half of the nineteenth century the Cornish were constructing a confident, positive self-image and exported this globally on the strength of their industrial expertise.[21] Perhaps the Cornish did not need folk tradition to express their identity.

This situation changed dramatically with the decline of the mining industry in the latter half of the nineteenth century. For Payton, this marks the emergence of a new phase of centre/periphery relationships where Cornwall and the Cornish become remote and marginalised.[22] It is here that we begin to witness the beginnings of a symbiosis between folk tradition and Cornish identity as a distinct nationality, perhaps encouraged, as Dundes suggests, by this sense of marginalisation. Furthermore, Cornwall had a very rich seam of folk tradition to call upon. Deacon shows that the industrial landscape developed in a diffused rural pattern with 'the cottages of the miners distributed amongst the small fields, lanes and footpaths filling the spaces between mines and settlements'.[23] This left social structures and families relatively intact and provided for continuity of oral folk traditions. It also introduced new experiences and context with which to clothe and embellish the folklore of the past.

The Celto-Cornish movement and Folk Tradition

Henry Jenner (1848–1934) is a pivotal figure in the emergence of a Celto–Cornish identity. He positioned the language ready for revival and campaigned for recognition of Cornwall as a Celtic nation. Unlike his counterparts elsewhere in the Celtic world, he did not embrace the opportunities that folk tradition offered for the expression of Celticity in Cornwall. His presidential address to the Royal Polytechnic Society in September 1920 was ironically entitled 'The Renaissance of Merry England'.[24] He used this title as a device to make the point that Cornwall should not be seen as part of England. He then proceeded to extol the virtues of folk dances, songs and customs as a way of bringing all classes together in order to shield against social unrest or, to put it another way, to maintain the status quo of social structures that privileged certain groups. He did not, however, connect folk tradition with Celticity in Cornwall, as did his antiquarian predecessors or indeed his immediate contemporary, Baring-Gould. For example, in the preface to *Songs and Ballads of the West* Baring-Gould attributes differences in folk melodies in the West to Celtic influences[25] and supports this by tracing Welsh and Breton links in some of the material.

Bearing in mind his Celtic affiliations elsewhere, Jenner had an intriguing and paradoxical relationship with Lady Mary Trefusis and the Cornish branch of the English Folk Dance Society. He served on the organising committee and appears to have been quite supportive of the society.[26] It may be that Lady Mary Trefusis appealed to his class sensitivities. The Cornish branch of the English Folk Dance Society was nevertheless quite unrepresentative of, and unsympathetic to, folk dance in Cornwall. Their festivals and teaching in schools focused on the Morris dances of the Midlands and the sword dances of further north together with a smattering of country dances. This was despite the work of people like Courtney but a few decades before, and despite a continuing tradition in Cornwall which included Guize Dancing in St Ives, Scoot Dances (hard shoe/step dances) in North Cornwall, and the village or chapel Tea Treats that featured dances such as the serpent.[27] The Cornish branch elected to adhere strictly to the dances and style promoted by Cecil Sharp, the dominant figure in the English Folk movement. Sharp had devoted little time to collection in Cornwall, with short visits in 1913 and 1914[28] – and these took place after most of his work had been published. His interest in Cornish dance was limited to the 'Helston Furry' and 'Padstow May Day' customs.

Jenner's distance from folk tradition is illustrated by the material he contributed to Graves for the *Celtic Song Book*.[29] This was a project which had grown out of the Pan-Celtic movement, and one would have expected Jenner to take full advantage of the opportunity to promote the Cornish language. Yet he neither translated any songs nor included the ubiquitous 'Deliow Sevy' from the Gwavas manuscript of 1698[30] for this compilation. Instead he provided a selection of material from Baring-Gould's collection, including 'Widdicombe Fair', rather than an older version from Helston and also repeated the mistake of setting the words of the 'Hal An Tow'[31] to the quite different tune of the 'Helston Furry Dance'. It may be that Jenner had little contact with those actively involved in folk tradition, or simply that he was increasingly elderly and frail at the time. His age and frailty did not stop him from contributing some fairly nationalistic material in Cornish to Dunstan's *Cornish Song Book*[32] the following year, however, so it remains an enigma.

It fell to Jenner's successor, Robert Morton Nance (1873–1959), to fully embrace the potential of folk tradition for celebrating the sense of a distinctive Celtic identity in Cornwall. Although he is now recognised largely for his work on the Cornish language, his formative experiences lay with Cornish dialect and the customs through which it was expressed, in particular what he describes as 'guise-dance-drolls'.[33] In 1882 Jago identifies Guizing as Cornwall's equivalent of Morris Dancing,[34] and contemporaries such as Bottrell and Courtney fill in the detail with descriptions of the step dances, social dances, songs and plays associated with this tradition. It was Nance's adaptation of Bottrell's 'Duffy and the Devil' which inspired the formation of the first Old Cornwall Society in St Ives in 1920 and encouraged a grass roots culture of collecting folk material in order to rebuild a Cornish identity.[35] Nance himself was a practitioner and innovator when it came to folk tradition, rather than collector, and one is never quite clear from his manuscripts and publications what the provenance of his material is. He never claims that his material is more than inspired by tradition but cross-referencing suggests that some is from living tradition and some his own composition.

Nance may not have been the classic folk song and dance collector but the proliferation of Old Cornwall Societies resulted in a large volume of folk material being collected by other people. From the first publication to date there are some 151 folk phenomena recorded in the Societies' magazine *Old Cornwall*. It is difficult to compare like with like, but, to place this in context, leading nineteenth-century collector/folklorists such as Baring-Gould and Courtney recorded just seventy three and fifty items respectively.[36] Activists like Wallace, Watson, Miners and Thomas connected the Celto-Cornish movement firmly with folk tradition as a way of expressing identity.[37] Unlike the visiting folklorist or folksong collector, they were practitioners who recorded what they performed and recalled from their own experiences. When the American folksong collector James Madison Carpenter arrived in Cornwall with his wax-cylinder recording machine in 1931, they were a well-organised force and descended upon him with some enthusiasm. They provided him with songs in Cornish and introduced him to singing sessions in the coastal villages where he was notably the first person to record the 'Cadgwith Anthem'. There are some forty-one items from Cornwall in the Carpenter Collection.[38]

The singing sessions witnessed and recorded by Carpenter are part of the 'lore' of what it is 'to be Cornish', whether the hymns sung by the balmaidens (female mine workers) or the emigrant miner's improvised harmony of the 'Sweet Nightingale'.[39] There is a sense in which these take place in an original setting where people are adding to a repertoire and adapting songs reflexively according to what takes their fancy rather than reflecting on whether it is consistent with their tradition or not. These singing sessions have continued as a living tradition through to the present day. They provided a rich seam of material for Peter Kennedy when he visited Cornwall in the winter of 1956 and recorded sessions and singers at Cadgwith, Redruth, Malpas and Boscastle. The singing sessions at Cadgwith were much looked forward to by the fishing and gig rowing community when the present author first engaged with the tradition in the 1970s,[40] and the Bolitho archive[41] captures examples from throughout the 1980s and 1990s. In 2006 the An Daras project compiled a collection of 'pub songs' from singing sessions across Cornwall, which showed both continuity with the repertoire recorded by Carpenter and Kennedy and new material that was bedding in to the traditional process, such as 'Cornish Lads'.[42]

The Old Cornwall Societies were instrumental in regenerating interest in Guizing customs, including the St Ives Guizing and the 'Hal An Tow' as well as the midsummer tradition of 'Golowan' (with its bonfires) and the 'Crying The Neck' ceremonies at harvest time. This interest was focused on preserving traditional customs and presenting them as part of Cornwall's distinctive cultural heritage. Careful reflection took place on how this might be achieved. The 'Hal An Tow', for example, was but a memory recalled by older Helstonians by the 1930s.[43] The Old Cornwall Society researched and revived the tradition by cross-referencing these memories with written accounts and comparison with the 'Padstow Obby Oss'.

Dunstan (1857–1933) is an interesting figure from the Celto-Cornish folk revival, in that he was a professional music academic with a career in London but had started out as a tutor/student bandsman in the midst of the Tea Treat and regatta culture of mid Cornwall. When he retired to Cornwall, he reconnected with his musical roots and published two collections of songs and dances from both his own experiences and that of his Cornish contemporaries: The *Cornish Song Book* in 1929 and *Cornish Dialect and Folk Song* in 1932.[44] Both collections contain a wealth of material from folk tradition but the first coincided with the inaugural Cornish Gorseth and includes material that overtly expresses Celto-Cornish identity. These two publications inspired a series of subsequent collections which drew on material collected from oral folk tradition in Cornwall, including *Canow Kernow* (1966) edited by Gundry,[45] *Hengan* (1983) edited by Davey,[46] and arguably the proliferation of song and tune books that became available following the advent of desk-top publishing in the 1990s.

The Celtic Congress was first held in Cornwall in 1932, and whilst it was used primarily as a showcase for the Cornish language, traditional music and dance from Cornwall was included in the concert programme. The onset of war put the activities of the Celto-Cornish movement on hold but by 1949 it had increased its stake in folk tradition, with a Cornish and Celtic Dance School forming in Truro and an Inter-Celtic Festival in St Ives in 1949. The aspirations of the Celto-Cornish movement were articulated by Denys Val Baker when he described the 1949 festival in the *Cornish Review*:

The aim of the St Ives festival will be to recapture the national culture of the Celtic people; the preservation and teaching of Celtic languages; the popularisation of the music dances, games and industries of the Celt; and the promotion of greater unity between the Celtic nations. Competitions will be held in Celtic music, literature, languages, dancing, and game ... The festival culminates in an all-Celtic Ceilidhe, with teams of visiting dancers, and the famous Helston Furry Dancers are performing the traditional Cornish Dance.[47]

The dance school in Truro was organised by Helena Charles, a

Celto-Cornish activist and founder member of Mebyon Kernow.[48] Her family had been involved in the Helston Furry before the First World War and she was critical of Cecil Sharp's interpretation of the dance, maintaining that he had been influenced by the advice of Lady Rogers (of Exeter) as to what she felt would look nice rather than what actually took place.[49] In 1950 Charles was involved in the Celtic Congress held at Truro, and staged an excerpt from the Cornish mystery play, *Bewnans Meryasek*, at St Piran Round. She took the opportunity to incorporate folk dancing and rounded off the performance with a mixture of Cornish and Breton social dance. In doing so, she was setting the scene for a shared sense of identity through folk dance which would become associated with the Celto-Cornish movement.

The following decade saw the emergence of popular music festival culture: the Cambridge Folk Festival started in 1964, the Isle of Wight in 1968, and the iconic Woodstock took place in 1969 followed by Glastonbury in 1970. This wave of interest also encouraged the development of 'Celtic Festivals' with all the variety of definitions, national allegiances and identities that the term offers. The festivals that influenced the folk traditions of Cornwall, however, were those that were expressly Pan Celtic with an expectation of, and opportunity for, representation from Cornwall. The largest of these was the 'Festival Interceltique' held in Lorient, Brittany (1970), which had evolved from an earlier bagpipe festival. Also very influential on the Celto-Cornish movement was the Irish 'Pan-Celtic Festival' (1970) and the Manx 'Yn Chruinnaght' (1978).

The impact upon Cornwall was to provide an international platform for Cornish performers, and an expectation that performance would represent Cornwall's Celtic identity. Brenda Wootton became involved as early as 1970 and subsequently described this as the launch of her professional career. Although locally well known, her activity until this date had largely been limited to events at the Minack Theatre, and the folk club circuit. Brenda Wootton is easily identifiable because of an established professional career but there were other Cornish performers' groups on the Pan-Celtic circuit at the time, such as 'Tremenysy' led by Cornish language bard, Tony Snell. Although the focus of this essay is the impact upon folk tradition, it should be made clear that the Celtic festival culture was much wider than this in its interests, which ranged from popular music to choirs – albeit anchored in Celticity by language or context.

One figure from the Pan-Celtic movement of the 1970s who was particularly supportive of Cornwall's involvement in this festival culture was Con O'Connail, Chief Executive of the Irish 'Feile Pan Cheilteach'. Not only did he canvass for wider Cornish representation at the Irish festival, he visited Cornwall in 1977 to encourage the establishment of a similar event there. In 1978 Brenda Wootton led a strong Cornish representation to the Irish festival which included the resident group at the Falmouth Folk club, Kemysk (Cornish, 'mixture'). The group's success with 'Deliow Sevy' in winning the traditional singing competition helped raise the profile of Pan-Celtic activities. Furthermore, chaired by Brenda Wootton's husband John, a group was set up to organise a similar event in Cornwall. The initial festival was held in Perranporth in October 1978 under the name 'Kernow Pan Celtic' but metamorphosed to become 'Lowender Peran' the following year, and has remained an annual event to date. Whilst this was a new event with new people, it had a clear lineage that took it back through the Celto-Cornish movement in Cornwall, to the Pan-Celtic festivals organised by the Celtic Congress in 1932, 1949 and 1950 and ultimately the activities of the Old Cornwall Societies in the 1920s.

Celtic Festival Culture, the opportunity for travel and large audiences, also encouraged the formation of dance teams along the lines of organisations such as Breton 'Cercle Celtique' and the Welsh 'Dawnswyr Werin'. The pressure was on for them to research Cornish dance traditions in order to establish a repertoire that could be understood as representing a distinctive Cornish identity. In this they were fortunate in that antiquarian interest in the nineteenth century, and the Old Cornwall Society Movement from the 1920s, had already laid down the foundations for the music and dance that might be used for this. Cornish Scoot (step) dancing, which lends itself well to choreographic arrangement for display, continued within oral tradition well into this period with practitioners who were able to teach the formative dance groups.[50] The popularity of social dance within Celtic Festival culture encouraged recognition of Cornwall's own history of social dance. The term ceili (ceili in Irish Gaelic – ceilidh in Scottish Gaelic) was first used in relation to dance at a London Gaelic Society event in Bloomsbury Square in October 1897 but was not used extensively for set dance events until the 1930s.[51] The root meaning of ceilidh is simply a gathering, a social event. It is interesting to discover that Cornish dialect should have developed its own term for social dance, troyl, as early as 1885.[52] The term troyl comes from the Cornish for a reel, whirl or spiral,[53] a quite different etymology from the term ceilidh.

The importance here is that the pan-Celtic festival culture created (and creates) a dynamic cultural environment for traditional music and dance, particularly encouraged by its participative nature. This environment inspired two major collection projects: *Corollyn: Cornish Dances* (1992)[54] and *Racca: Cornish Tunes For Cornish Sessions* (1997).[55] These are further examples of the sequence of publications set in motion by Dunstan that continues today.[56] What we have in Cornwall throughout the twentieth century to the present is an evolving culture of folk tradition taking place in original locations that might be the town or village feast day or a singing session at a party or local pub. We also have the impact of the Celto-Cornish movement which is promoting the sense of Cornish identity around these traditions, directly supporting them in their original location or existence and also providing new locations for performance.

A measure of this impact is to look at the performers at a festival like 'Lowender Peran'. A list of Cornish performers for the thirty-year period since the start of the festival was included in the souvenir programme for 2008. This listed 123 groups and individuals, all of which will have been asked to provide a performance that celebrated some aspect of a distinctive Cornish identity in a Celtic context. A similar snapshot from a different perspective is provided by 'Kesson', a specialist website selling CDs by musicians who present their material as distinctively Cornish. In September 2010 they advertised a total of 85 albums representing the work of 60 different groups.[57]

The 'Folk Revival' and Cornwall

Conventionally, there are seen to be two revivals of interest in British/ English folk tradition, the first lead by Cecil Sharp at the beginning of the twentieth century, and the second spearheaded by A. L. (Bert) Lloyd and Ewan MacColl in the 1950s and 1960s. Atkinson points out, 'Whereas the first revival was predominantly the activity of a comparatively small number of enthusiasts, the second was (and is), relatively speaking, a mass cultural movement which has continued, changed, but unabated, for half a century or more.'[58] It was as a 'mass cultural movement' that the revival arrived in Cornwall. It was packaged with a set of values and language associated with a specific genre of music and dance, which provided a recognised identity for subscribers. In Fairclough's terminology it was a speech community, and a powerful one in terms of both its size and its strong associations with a wider English identity.

The values of the second folk revival were bound up in the fusion of the eclectic and counter-cultural sixties folk-song revival with the fairly rigid Edwardian orthodoxy of the English Folk Dance and Song Society.[59] There were some inconsistencies in how nationality, class, gender and oral folk tradition were perceived, and this fusion should have made for a very complex speech community, if indeed one could be identified at all. For example, as Boyse shows, the Edwardian folk revival sought to preserve the hegemonic social structures of the British Empire,[60] whereas the sixties revival of A. L. (Bert) Lloyd and Ewan MacColl made great play of the songs that witnessed the working-class struggle against that very same hegemony.[61] In practice, these inconsistencies are ignored or interpreted in such a way as to avoid conflict. Indeed, Atkinson shows that by drawing on songs from the established canon of traditional material known as the 'Child Ballads'[62] and mixing this with new material, the folk revival was able to capture a sense of authenticity for its repertoire and a connection with the earlier revivalists.[63]

The second folk revival was expressed through a variety of media, from the increasingly vernacular BBC radio and television to the burgeoning commercial music industry with its package of LPs, albums and promotional tours. The most celebrated representation of the revival has perhaps been the Sidmouth Folk Festival, which started in the mid-fifties as a summer camp for the English Folk Dance and Song Society but embraced the folk-song movement in the late sixties to become a major festival.[64] From Cornwall's perspective, the arrival of the Folk Revival was marked by the advent of two particular institutions, the 'Folk Club' and the 'Morris Side'.

Competing for authenticity in song

The concept of a 'Folk Club' owed much to MacColl's experience of working with the people's theatres of the 1930s and provided an informal art-house performance space for folk music. The typical club formula was/is to have regular house acts and a series of visiting guest performers. For all the communist aspirations of Lloyd and MacColl,[65] there is no evidence that the folk club was ever a working-class space. As a venue for a particular popular music genre it could be seen as classless but there is still a suggestion here of the intelligentsia using folk song to enter into the world of working-class life by proxy.

The Count House at Botallack hosted the first club in Cornwall in the early sixties, followed by 'The Pipers' at St Buryan and the 'Folk Cottage' at Mitchell. These clubs became associated with a number of folk performers who subsequently became well established, including Ralph McTell, Wizz Jones, Pete Berryman, Michael Chapman and Brenda Wootton.[66] Pete Berryman describes the folk scene in Cornwall as 'a series of circles or families with the immediate local family based around the clubs in St Buryan and Mitchell and a larger, overlapping, family involving performers on the wider British club circuit'.[67] He explained that there was no sense of Cornish identity within this community but there was a shared sense of belonging to a group of performers and patrons with an interest in exploring the musical opportunities offered by the folk/blues scene. The 'Bodmin Folk Club', formed in 1969, was affiliated to (and subsidised by) the English Folk Song and Dance Society, and had a reputation for a fairly orthodox approach as to what was traditional and suitable for folk club performance.

There is no sense that these clubs set great store by material from oral folk tradition in Cornwall, apart from an occasional audience participation item in an evening's programme. Wootton was one of the few Celto-Cornish performers to have been fully embraced by folk club culture, and that may be because she led the clubs concerned. Furthermore, she seems to have moved on from the folk club circuit by the time she was presenting as the voice of Celtic Cornwall. In 1975 Kennedy published his *Folk Songs of Britain and Ireland* using material collected during a series of recording expeditions in the 1950s and 1960s.[68] He defied the convention of his predecessors, refusing to group songs as Irish, Scottish or English and choosing instead categories of lyric subject such as love or occupational songs, while also including sections on distinct linguistic groups with songs in Gaelic, Channel Islands French, Welsh and Cornish. The latter was very much influenced by Inglis Gundry and his connection with the Celto-Cornish movement. Despite Kennedy's 'Folk Revival' credentials, his Cornish songs seem to have found very little currency within the repertoire of most folk clubs.

The 'Fal Folk Club' at the Dock and Railway in Falmouth was an exception, possibly the influence of two of the organisers, Des Duckham and Ron Williams, who were also active members of Mebyon Kernow.[69] The publicity surrounding the Pan Celtic success of Fal Folk Club's 'Kemysk' drew attention to the fault lines between the English Folk Revival and the Celto-Cornish movement. A correspondent for the *Falmouth Packet* newspaper maintained that 'Delyow Syvy' was the only Cornish folk song and that there was no other traditional music to be found in Cornwall.[70] The subsequent debate centred on whether songs collected in Cornwall should be seen as distinctively Cornish or as part of a wider British/English tradition. This altercation voiced the English Folk Revival 'common sense' that denied the existence of a distinct Cornish tradition within the canon of British/American folk music while at the same time celebrating an English one. According to Atkinson, however, the distinctiveness of an English tradition within this canon might also be denied on the same basis.[71]

The 1990s saw an escalation in the material, available both in print and audio formats, which presented Cornish music as a distinct tradition. This raised the profile of Cornish folk tradition, but as O'Connor points out, also encouraged criticism from the Folk Revival establishment:

Opposition to newly identified Cornish material was fostered by a few vociferous speakers, some well respected. Some were conservative: reflecting Bodmin Folk Club's old extra-Cornish agenda they mistrusted anyone outside the EFDSS [English Folk Dance and Song Society] or not subject to academic overview. Some believed that nothing more could possibly remain to be discovered, so anything new must be false. Some saw the overt celebration of Cornish culture as an invention to promote Cornish political consciousness ... Today some still retain a cynical view of material identifiably Cornish or those promoting it.[72]

There is a sense here in which the more powerful speech community of Folk Revival places a greater burden of evidence for material to be recognised as Cornish than it does for English tradition. The trajectory of 'I love my love'/'Ryb an Avon' provides a good example of this. In 1905 the Rev Quintrell sent George Gardiner, an academic folk-song collector, the music score for a tune he had collected from a Mrs Boaden of Cury near Helston.[73] Gardiner in turn sent this to a fellow collector, Lucy Broadwood, who found that the melody was a very good match to the lyrics of a song called 'I love my love' and drew the conclusion that this must be its original and correct title.[74] Anyone listening to the lyrics of 'Clementine' sung to the tune of the hymn 'Bread of Heaven' will realise that such a deduction is not well supported. But Gardiner and Broadwood did succeed in making a very beautiful tune widely accessible by associating it with the words of 'I Love My Love', and it reached a wide audience through Holst's military band arrangement.[75] It was subsequently reclaimed for Cornwall by Tony Snell, who wrote lyrics in Cornish for it and renamed it 'Ryb An Avon'. It can be seen that neither name has precedence of authenticity over the other. But what is interesting here is that 'I love my love' is identified as more authentic than 'Ryb An Avon' by English Folk Revivalists.

'Crowns' represent a new generation of bands which take their Cornishness for granted and use it as part of their performance. They are a four-piece band who come from Launceston but are currently based in London. They feature an 'a capella' singing style mixed with punk rock instrumentation and fuse their own compositions with traditional material. What makes this group especially interesting is that for all their punk rock presentation, their use of Cornish material provides a good example of the folk process. The inspiration for their repertoire is both reflexive in that it comes from the informal 'pub' singing sessions they grew up with and reflective in that they emulate the punk Celtic style of the Pogues and arrange their music accordingly. They are influenced by the wider social trend around them that increasingly recognises a distinct Cornish identity and share this with their audiences. Part of their badge of Cornishness is to be sponsored by a brewery (Skinners) which makes good use of a range of Cornish images from the St Pirans flag to characters from folklore such as Betty Stoggs for its publicity.

Competing for authenticity in dance

The first Morris side formed in Cornwall in 1971 from members of the Bodmin Folk Club and took the name Trigg.[76] The term 'side' is used by the English Folk Revival to describe a team of dancers typically, but not necessarily, six to eight people along with their accompanying musicians. The dance styles vary from the Morris traditions collected by Sharp in the English Home Counties and Midlands to clog dancing and Rapper Sword dancing in the north.[77] Trigg Morris drew their repertoire from the Cotswold dances noted down by Sharp and have remained an all-male side. This is significant in that the tradition of all-male sides for ritual or display dances is an English phenomenon not shared by the Celtic cultures and fiercely challenged by folk-dance researchers such as Georgina Boyse.[78] A number of other Morris teams have formed in Cornwall since the 1970s. In 2012 there were nine groups advertising themselves, three all-male Cotswold dance sides, one mixed, three Border Morris sides and two ladies' North-West clog teams.

In their introductions, and the background information provided about their dances, these sides sometimes cite references in the St Columb parish records as evidence of the provenance of Morris dancing in Cornwall. There are certainly references to Morris dancing in Cornwall in sixteenth-century records such as the Green Book of St Columb[79] and the household accounts of the Arundels at Lanherne,[80] but these are concerned with the purchase of materials and provide no description of the dance or detail of the custom involved. The term 'Morris'/'Morysc' is used in the records but there is no evidence to suggest that this has the same meaning as Morris in twenty-first-century England. The best guess is that these would be akin to the Morris dances described by Arbeau in sixteenth-century France,[81] a notion supported by the images of the sixteenth-century bench ends in Altarnon Church. These resemble the diagrams Arbeau uses to explain a sword dance called the 'Mattachins'. Another hint of what was meant by 'Morris' in Cornwall lies at the other end of the time spectrum in the form of the 'Hal An Tow' which was described as a Morris dance in 1797[82] but bears no relation to the choreography of the Morris dances of, say, the Cotswolds.

Whilst it is dangerous to form firm conclusions about the provenance of Morris dancing in Cornwall, based on the interpretation of parish and household accounts there remain clear sign posts to the possibility of quite different dance traditions in Cornwall. There is certainly no record of anything resembling the traditions of the English Home Counties and the Midlands. It is interesting, therefore, that the emphasis of Morris sides in Cornwall should be on the importation of dance traditions from England rather than exploring the possibilities offered by local Guize and Scoot Dance traditions. There was a well-documented Scoot Dance tradition in Boscastle at the time Trigg Morris was formed,[83] and a little local research would have provided dancers with steps and moves that could have been interpreted to create a distinctive style of dance. Similarly, the Guize dancing tradition still extant in St Ives, with its history of cross-dressing, might also have provided inspiration for the development of a dance tradition along the lines of the revival of Molly dancing in East Anglia described by Elaine Brandke.[84]

The arrival of English Morris dancing in Cornwall thus resulted in competition for cultural space with indigenous folk dancing. The speech community of the Folk Revival did not recognise a distinction between Cornish and English folk tradition, so that presenting Cotswold or Border Morris dances as 'authentic' folk tradition to represent Cornwall would not be seen as problematic. A practical outcome of this mindset, for example, would be that a twinning association wishing to organise an event representing their own local culture would be encouraged by this speech community to use a Morris side. For example, during the 1980s the Wadebridge Folk Festival, which was at that time largely run by members of Trigg Morris and The Bodmin Folk Club, worked closely with the town twinning association and used Morris teams as part of their exchange with Brittany.

The Cornish Dance groups that developed out of the Celto-Cornish movement challenged this authenticity by presenting the dances they performed within an historical context in Cornwall. The tension between these two speech communities was articulated in the correspondence pages of the magazine *Cornish Scene* in 1986.[85] Following a broad article on Cornish music which mentioned dances a letter was published challenging the authenticity of these dances and dismissing them as 'spurious' products of 'over-enthusiastic Cornishness'.[86] This prompted several letters defending their provenance and praising the groups involved. Whilst there was an inevitable descent into the semantics of authenticity, what is interesting is that Morris dancers in Cornwall were not subject to the same scrutiny as groups representing the Celto-Cornish movement. The speech community of English Folk Revival was the more powerful and therefore represented 'common sense' against which the claims of Cornishness were measured.

The mindset of the Folk Revival is also illustrated in a different way by the 'Canow Kerrier Project' undertaken by Somerset-based organisation Folk South West in the Redruth and Camborne areas in 1997.[87] The published aim of the project was to engage the local community and schools with the oral folk traditions of their area. Volunteers were recruited to research the material and develop presentation skills in order to work with children using a pack prepared by the project. The songs used for the pack were those from recognised collections, such as Sharps, identified as coming from the area. The dances, however, were introduced by a section entitled 'Notes on Teaching English Country Dance'.[88] This section started by explaining the terms 'country dancing', 'barn dancing' and 'ceilidh dancing' but made no mention of the Cornish equivalent 'troyl'. Similarly, dance steps were introduced as 'Rhythms within the British country dance tradition' but no mention was made of the steps associated with Cornish Furry dances.

Six dances were included in the pack, three generic dances and three sourced from but not credited to the Corollyn project.[89] Two of the generic dances were re-named *The Stithians Shuffle* and *The Camborne March*. Reference was made to 'increasing interest in re-establishing a repertoire of Cornish dances in recent years'[90] but neither the Corollyn project nor earlier work by the Old Cornwall Societies was actually cited, despite the project leader being provided with this information.[91] Cornish collections were not subject to any critique in the text, leading to the conclusion that they were excluded because they did not fit in with the project leader's mindset rather than dismissed because of any inadequacy. This conclusion is supported by the fact that six other folk-dance information and resource packs are mentioned in the text and in the bibliography but these are all either from the project leader's own publications or from the English Folk Dance and Song Society.

There is a sense here in which the suggestion of an identity in Cornish folk dance as Celtic, rather than English, is part of a much wider threat to the homogeneity of English folk dance. If Cornish traditions are not English then what about the North East with its Rapper Sword Dancing, Border Morris and its Welsh connections or Molly dancing in East Anglia, all of which contrast strongly with Cotswold traditions? Conversely how can traditions seen as quintessentially English by Sharp, such as the Morris and the Rapper Sword traditions, also appear in Wales,[92] Ireland[93] and the Isle of Man?[94] Is there in fact a distinctively English folk tradition? In 1936, Needham[95] analysed ceremonial folk dance in zones and proposed that they were related to the areas of the Dane-law, Old Saxon Kingdoms of Mercia and Wessex, and the Celtic areas of Wales and Cornwall. Whilst Needham's proposal of such a direct geographic link with the early kingdoms of Britain and nineteenth-century folk traditions have since been substantially revised,[96] it nevertheless shows that folk-dance traditions in England vary to such an extent that the notion of a homogenous folk culture is questioned. Despite the fact that the 'Englishness' of the six-point star Rapper Sword configuration[97] and the Padstow Obby Oss are contested, both are used extensively by the English Folk Dance and Song Society as icons of English folk tradition.

In 2012 there were eight groups providing Cornish dance displays drawing upon social dance and Scoot dancing traditions for their repertoire and a number of processional/street bands that merge with Guising tradition. These groups are in direct competition with the Morris sides for performance space at events such as the Royal Cornwall Show and the summer season of outdoor festivals. They include younger groups such as Kekezza and Kemysk (no connection with the long since disbanded Falmouth Folk Club Group) who, like Crowns, take their Cornishness for granted and draw upon contemporary social trends for their interpretation of tradition.

Conclusions

This essay argues that the Celto-Cornish movement and its links with folk song and dance were well established before the arrival of the English Folk Revival in the 1960s and 1970s. The movement had engaged reflexively and reflectively in folk music and dance in its original location and provided new locations for its performance. The agenda for the Celto-Cornish movement was that in order to assert its Celticity, Cornwall needed to establish a distinctive folk tradition from England, one recognised in the same way as that of Brittany, Wales, Scotland, Ireland and the Isle of Man. Furthermore, in the spirit of building Nance's 'New Cornwall',[98] it also promoted/promotes new folk dances and songs within a culture expressing sentiments of Cornish distinctiveness.

When the English Folk Revival arrived in Cornwall it came packaged with its own imaginary concerning what was authentic and appropriate in folk tradition, and this did not fit with the approach taken by the Celto-Cornish movement. This essay argues that the English Folk Revival had a stake in Cornwall being part of the English imaginary. For Cornwall to be Celtic rather than English challenged the notion of Cornwall's Englishness. This was especially problematic for folk dance, and Morris sides in particular, as they would have no authenticity as a traditional activity of Cornwall. They would become a dance activity *in* Cornwall, like Scottish Country Dancing or Line Dancing, rather than enjoying the authenticity of being a native tradition *of* Cornwall as part of England.

The Celto-Cornish movement and the English Folk Revival can therefore be understood as two speech communities that use folk material as currency but interpret it in different ways and use it to express identities that potentially conflict. The English Folk Revival is a powerful movement. It has a large number of people investing in its identity; it has commercial backing, a large media presence and recognition within the school curriculum dating from the time of Sharp and the early publications for schools. The implications for the Cornish are that the mindset of this more powerful speech community risks becoming 'common sense', despite the lack of any evidence to favour this position against any other. The outcome for Cornish cultural identity of such 'common sense' is that indigenous folk culture risks losing out in the competition for social and performance space. It may be, however, that the 'common sense' of the English Folk Revival speech community is replaced by an increasingly powerful Cornish one, as demonstrated by the example of Crowns, Kekezza, and Kemysk and their association with modern Cornish identity.

Notes and references

1. D. Harker, *Fakesong, the manufacture of British "Folksong" 1700 to the present day* (Milton Keynes, 1985): G. Boyes, *The imagined village: culture, ideology, and the English folk revival* (Manchester, 1993).
2. M. Davey, '"As is the manner and the custom: folk tradition and identity in Cornwall", Folk tradition and identity in Cornwall', unpublished PhD thesis, University of Exeter, 2011.
3. F. Hoerburger, 'Once Again: On the Concept of Folk Dance', *Journal of the International Folk Music Council* 30:I (1968), p. 31: See Also discussion in Davey '"As is the manner and the custom"', p. 27.
4. The Helston Furry is a processional dance lead that takes place annually on the 8 May. It is danced through the streets of Helston at key points during the day, it is led by the local brass bands and a large number of people are involved. A number of towns and villages in Cornwall have their own Furry Dance. The term Furry is thought to derive from the Cornish for fair – fer, thus it is a fair day dance.
5. M. Davey, 'Guizing: Ancient Traditions And Modern Sensitivities' in P. Payton (ed.), *Cornish Studies: Fourteen* (Exeter, 2006), pp. 229–44.
6. Guizing is a term used in Cornwall where a party of people disguise themselves by cross dressing, wearing veils, dressing 'mock posh' or simply by blacking up faces. The party then tour an area performing a mixture of songs and dances sometimes incorporated into a folk play.
7. N. Fairclough, 'Critical Discourse Analysis' in N. Fairclough (ed.), *The Critical Study of Language* (London and New York, 1995); see also N. Fairclough, 'Critical discourse analysis in transdisciplinary research', research paper University of Lancaster: www.ling.lancs.ac.uk/staff/norman/paper4.doc, accessed 23 April 2008.
8. B. Deacon, 'From "Cornish Studies" to "Critical Cornish Studies": Reflections on Methodology' in P. Payton (ed.), *Cornish Studies: Twelve* (Exeter, 2004), p. 27.
9. Fairclough, *The Critical Study of Language*, p. 27.
10. J. G. von Herder (ed.), *Volkslieder* (Leipzig, 1778), online version *Volkslieder* (Leipzig, 1840) http://www.archive.org/stream/volkslieder01falkgoog#page/n6/mode/2up, accessed 2 July 2006.
11. J. Francmanis, 'Folk song and the "folk": a relationship illuminated by Frank Kidson's Traditional Tunes' in I. Russel and D. Atkinson (eds), *Folk Song: Tradition, Revival, and Re-Creation* (Aberdeen, 2004), pp. 186–87.
12. D. Ó Glolláin, *Locating Irish folklore: tradition, modernity, identity* (Sterling, VA, 2000), p. 25, with reference to Macphersons' Poems of Ossian and Renan's 'La poésie des races celtiques'.
13. M. McCann, 'Music and Politics in Ireland: The Specificity of the Folk Revival in Belfast', *British Journal of Ethnomusicology* 4, Special Issue (1995), p. 55. http://www.jstor.org/stable/3060683, accessed 31 October 2009.

14. J. Wood, 'Perceptions of the Past in Welsh Folklore Studies', *Folklore* 108 (1997), pp. 93–102, p. 97, citing: P. Morgan 'Keeping the Legends Alive', in T. Curtis (ed.), *Wales: The Imagined Nation: Studies in Cultural and National Identity* (Bridgend, 1986.), pp. 17–42; and G. Bowen, 'Gorsedd y Beirdd – From Primrose Hill 1782 to Aberystwyth 1992', *Transactions of the Honourable Society of Cymmrodorion* (1992), pp. 115–30.

15. E. Hobsbawm and T. Ranger (eds), *The Invention of Tradition* (Cambridge,1983).

16. D. Gilbert, *Some Ancient Christmas Carols* (2nd edition, London, 1823), The Helston Forey – a Specimen of Celtick Music.

17. William Sandys writing as Uncle Jan Trennoodle.

18. M. A. Courtney, 'Cornish Folk-Lore. Part 2 (Continued)', *The Folk-Lore Journal* 5:2 (1887), p. 85.

19. M. A. Courtney and T. Quiller-Couch, *Glossary of Words in Use in Cornwall: West Cornwall by Miss M. A. Courtney, East Cornwall by Thomas Q. Couch* (London, 1880), Introduction, p. 12.

20. A. Dundes, 'Nationalistic Inferiority Complexes and the Fabrication of Fakelore: A Reconsideration of Ossian, the Kinder- und Hausmarchen, the Kalevala, and Paul Bunyan', *Journal of Folklore Research* 22:1 (1985), pp. 5–18.

21. B. Deacon, 'The Hollow Jarring of the Distant Steam Engines: Images of Cornwall between West Barbary and Delectable Duchy', in E. Westland (ed.), *Cornwall: The Cultural Construction of Place* (Penzance, 1997).

22. P. Payton, 'Paralysis and Revival: The reconstruction of Celtic-Catholic Cornwall 1880–1945' in Westland, *Cornwall*, pp. 25–39.

23. B. Deacon, *Cornwall: A Concise History* (Cardiff, 2007), p. 124.

24. H. Jenner, 'The Renaissance of Merry England: Presidential address, September 1920', *Journal of Royal Cornwall Polytechnic Society* ??volume number?? (Falmouth,1922), pp. 51–61.

25. S. Baring-Gould and H. Fleetwood Shepherd, *Songs and Ballads of the West: A Collection Made from the Mouths of the People* (London, 1891), pp. vii–xi.

26. Henry Jenner, MS box Courtney Library, Royal Institute of Cornwall, copies of posters and notifications of meetings relating to the Cornish Folk Dance society.

27. M. Davey, A. Davey and J. Davey. *Scoot Dances, Troyls, Furrys and Tea Treats: The Cornish Dance Tradition* (London, 2009), pp. 17–56.

28. C. J. Sharp, Transcription of notebook, Vaughan Williams Memorial Library, Cecil Sharp House, London, vol. 3, p. 104.

29. A. P. Graves, *The Celtic song book: being representative folk songs of the six Celtic nations* (London, 1928).

30. Gwavas Manuscript, 1698 (BL Add. MSS 28554) p. 135 item 9.

31. The Hal An Tow is a 'play' performed on the 8 May in Helston at various locations in the town and quite separately from the Furry Dance.

32. R. Dunstan (ed.), *The Cornish Song Book, Lyver Canow Kernewek* (London, 1929).

33. R. M. Nance, *The Cledry plays; drolls of old Cornwall for village acting and home reading* (Marazion, 1956).

34. F. W. P. Jago, *The Ancient Language and the Dialect of Cornwall* (Truro, 1882). Entry under Guise Dance: 'A kind of comical or Bal masque at Christmas. Polwhele calls it the guise or disguise dance, for so the Cornish pronounce guise (geeze). This dance answers to the mummers of Devon, and the Morrice dancers of Oxfordshire &c. In Celtic Cornish ges, means mockery, a jest.'

35. R. M. Nance, 'What We Stand For', *Old Cornwall* 1:1 (St Ives, 1925), pp. 3–45.
36. Davey, '"As is the manner and the custom"' – handle: http://hdl.handle.net/10036 /3377, pp. 335–39.
37. Bessie Wallace, William Watson, Tom Miners and Jim Thomas were major contributors to the early old Cornwall Society Magazines, providing articles on folk songs, guizing customs, story-telling and the Cornish language.
38. James Madison Carpenter Collection, Library of Congress, Washington DC, AFC 1972/001.
39. R. Bell, *Ballads and Songs of the Peasantry of England* (London, 1857). Although the melody was not in fact collected until much later by Baring-Gould from a 'mining gentleman of Truro', Bell maintains it was collected from the singing of Cornish miners in the lead mines of Germany in 1856.
40. M. Davey, *Hengan: Traditional folk songs, dances and broadside ballads collected in Cornwall* (Redruth, 1983).
41. Bolitho Archive, Federation of Old Cornwall Societies Sound Archive, Courtney Library, Royal Institution of Cornwall, Truro.
42. R. Bryant, "Cornish Lads", Cornwall Songwriters, *Cry of Tin*, CD (St Ervan, 2000), LYNG212CD.
43. S. Toy, *The History of Helston* (London, 1936), p. 375.
44. Dunstan (ed.), *The Cornish Song Book*; R. Dunstan, *Cornish Dialect and Folk Songs* (Truro, 1932).
45. I. Gundry, *Canow Kernow: Songs and dances from Cornwall* (St. Ives, 1966).
46. Davey, *Hengan*.
47. D. Val Baker, 'Editorial', *The Cornish Review*, First Series, 2 (Spring 1949), pp. 6–7.
48. Denys Val Baker, 'People', *The Cornish Review*, First Series, 8 (Winter 1951), p. 67.
49. H. Charles, "Drama in Cornwall" *The Cornish Review*, First Series, 8 (Winter 1951), pp. 51–56.
50. Davey et al., *Scoot Dances, Troyls, Furrys and Tea Treats*, Section One.
51. J. P. Cullaine, *Encyclopaedia of Ireland* (Dublin, 2003), p. 176.
52. Davey et al., *Scoot Dances, Troyls, Furrys and Tea Treats*, pp. 1, 19.
53. W. Borlase, *Antiquities, Historical and Monumental of Cornwall* (Oxford, 1758, second enlarged edition, 1769), p. 459.
54. A. Davey (ed.), *Corollyn: Cornish Dances* (Perranporth, 1992), book/CD/Video format.
55. F. Bennett, et al. (eds), *Racca: Cornish Tunes for Cornish Sessions* (Calstock, 1995, 2nd edition, 1997).
56. See N. Davey, Fooch (Wadebridge, 2002); An Daras Project (www.an-daras.com 2003–); M. O'Connor, Ylow Kernow series (Wadebridge, 2000–).
57. www.kesson.com, The Cornish Music Collaborative, accessed 30 October 2010.
58. D. Atkinson, 'Revival: Genuine or Spurious?' in Russel and Atkinson (eds), *Folk Song: Tradition, Revival, and Re-Creation*, p. 152.
59. The Folk Song Society formed in London in 1898, under Cecil Sharp's leadership this became the English Folk Song Society and eventually combined with the English Folk Dance society to become the English Folk Dance and Song Society – EFDSS.
60. G. Boyes, *The imagined village: culture, ideology, and the English folk revival* (Manchester; 1993), p. 24.

61. A. L. (Bert) Lloyd, *Folk Song in England* (London, 1967), pp. 39–148.
62. The Child Ballads are named after Francis Child, an American literary academic who published five volumes of English language folk ballads between 1857 and 1893 and acted as a cross reference for most subsequent folk song collectors.
63. D. Atkinson, 'The English Revival Canon: Child Ballads and the Invention of Tradition', *The Journal of American Folklore* 114:453 (2001), pp. 370–80.
64. D. Schofield, *The First Week In August – Fifty Years of the Sidmouth Festival* (Sidmouth, 2005).
65. Both Lloyd and MacColl were active members of the Communist Party and the Workers Music Association funded some of Lloyds work.
66. R. White, 'Interview with Martin Val Baker', *Art Cornwall*, November 2006. http://www.artcornwall.org/interview%20Martin%20Val%20Baker.htm, accessed 9 February 2010.
67. Pete Berryman, interview with author, St Blazey, 9 September 2010.
68. Peter Kennedy (ed.), *Folksongs of Britain and Ireland* (London, 1975).
69. The author was a regular performer at the club between 1975 and 1979 and a member of Kemysk. It was at a Mebyon Kernow meeting which he attended shortly after moving to Falmouth in 1975 that he met Des Duckham and Ron Williams and was encouraged to attend the Folk Club.
70. *Falmouth Packet*, correspondence, May–June 1978.
71. Russel and Atkinson (eds), *Folk Song: Tradition, Revival, and Re-Creation*.
72. M. O'Connor, *Ilow Kernow 4: Cornish instrumental tradition: The resource* (Wadebridge, 2009), p. 127.
73. George B. Gardiner Manuscripts, Vaughan Williams Memorial Library, Cecil Sharp House, Regents Park Road, London.
74. L. Broadwood, 'Maid of Bedlam', *Journal of the Folk Song Society* 2:7 (1905–1906), p. 93.
75. Gustav Holst, Second Suite in F for Military Band (Op. 28, No. 2), Movement 2, 'Song without words – I'll love my Love' composed 1911 (London,1984).
76. Trigg Morris, information sheet and venue list 2010. Although Pete Marlow explained that there had been a group in Falmouth called Kernow Morris which started before this, but had not become fully established (interviewed 19 April 2011).
77. A style of dance from the North East involving six dancers using a metal blade with a swivel handle on each end which is held by the dancers and results in the need for some fairly precise choreography.
78. G. Boyes, "The lady that is with you", in G. Boyes (ed.), *Step change: New views on traditional dance* (London, 2001).
79. T. C. Peter, 'The Green Book of St Columb', *Journal of Royal Institution of Cornwall* 19 supplement (Truro, 1912).
80. H. L. Douche, 'Household accounts at Lanherne', *Journal of Royal Institution of Cornwall*, New Series 1(11):1 (1953), pp. 28–29.
81. T. Arbeau, *Orchesography* (Langres, 1589), English translation by Mary Stewart Evans, additional notes by Mary Sutton (Toronto, 1967), p. 177. Describes a Morris dance from sixteenth-century France and discusses its probable origins in Rome or the Basque country.
82. Durgan, letter addressed to Editor, Sylvanus Urban, *Gentlemans Magazine and Historical Chronicle for the year MDCCXC*, p. 520

83. Davey et al., *Scoot Dances, Troyls, Furrys and Tea Treats*.
84. E. Bradtke, 'Molly Dancing: A Study of Discontinuity and Change' in Boyes (ed.), *Step change*, pp. 61–86.
85. I. Marshall, 'Recording Cornish Folk Songs', *Cornish Scene* 1:5 (February/March 1986), p. 49; 'Letters to the Editor', *Cornish Scene* 1:5 (April/May 1986); *Cornish Scene* 2:1 (June/July 1986); *Cornish Scene* 2:2 (August/Sept 1986).
86. J. Penlee, 'Letters to the Editor', *Cornish Scene* 1:5 (April/May 1986), p. 12.
87. E. Upton, *Canow Kerrier* (Montacute, 1997).
88. Upton, *Canow Kerrier*, p. 32.
89. Davey, *Corollyn*.
90. Upton, *Canow Kerrier*.
91. Correspondence with the author, 23 February 1997: Provided a comprehensive list of Cornish folk song and dance publications plus details of songs collected in the area.
92. L. Blake, 'The Morris in Wales', *Journal of the English Folk Dance and Song Society* 9:1 (December 1960), pp. 56–57.
93. A. Gailey, 'The Nature Of Tradition', *Folklore* 100:2 (1989), pp. 143–61, p. 155. http://links.jstor.org/sici?sici=0015–587X%281989%29100%3A2%3C143%3AT NOT%3E2.0.CO%3B2-M, accessed 25 January 2008.
94. M. Douglas, 'Manx Folk Dances: Their Notation and Revival', *Journal of the English Folk Dance and Song Society* 3:2 (1937), pp. 110–16: The White Boys, *Lowender Peran 2007*, Tower Films 2008, DVD format. The Manx 'White Boys' use 'Swords' similar to those of Rapper sides to form a six point star. The same star that is used by the English Folk Song and Dance society as a logo.
95. J. Needham, 'The Geographical Distribution of English Ceremonial Dance Traditions', *Journal of the English Folk Dance and Song Society* 3:1 (1936), pp. 1–45.
96. E. C. Cawte, A. Helm, R. J. Marriott and N. Peacock ,'A Geographical Index of the Ceremonial Dance in Great Britain: Part One', *Journal of the English Folk Dance and Song Society* 9:1 (December 1960), pp. ii, 1–41.
97. The final choreography of the Rapper Sword dances involves the dancers slotting the swords together so that they form a star that can be held aloft by a single dance.
98. R. M. Nance, 'Introduction: What we stand for', *Old Cornwall* 1:1 (St Ives, 1925), p. 3.

7

'The Spectral Bridegroom'

A study in Cornish Folklore

Ronald M. James

Introduction

A widely distributed story, common in Europe and represented in the early folklore collections from Cornwall, draws on an array of popular beliefs and motifs. The tale involves a young, devoted couple who are separated. The man dies, but his betrothed does not receive the news. The woman receives a night-time visit from his spectre, and he invites her to join him on his horse. They charge across the landscape, and near the end of their journey as dawn approaches, the woman realizes that she is riding with the animated corpse of her lover. In most variants, she is able to escape, but she often dies shortly after the incident.

Gottfried August Bürger (1747–1794) made this story famous with his 1773 poem, 'Lenore'. Within a decade after its publication, the German-language masterwork appeared in English translation, becoming an immediate sensation: it is credited with influencing Coleridge, Wordsworth, and other British poets of the new, Romantic era. Bürger's publication was so influential that folklorists often refer to the tale simply as 'The Lenore Legend'.[1]

'Lenore' was not, however, the only early, printed example of this story. 'The Suffolk Miracle' took up the legend in an English-language broadside printed as early as 1689.[2] Appearing with the subtitle 'Or a Relation of a Young Man who a Month after his Death appeared to his Sweetheart', this English ballad anticipated 'Lenore' both in the use of the oral tradition and in its popularity and influence. Other printed versions from the period include the ballads 'Nancy of Yarmouth', 'Sweet William's Ghost', and 'Fair Margaret and Sweet William'.[3] The similarity of these publications to 'Lenore' was a point of curiosity among the learned.

The Cornish legends

The early collectors of Cornish oral tradition include several variants of this well-known story. In fact, the ballads aside, what people refer to as 'English' examples are most often from Cornwall, which gives it disproportionate representation.[4] The most elaborate Cornish expression of the story appears in William Bottrell's first volume of folklore, published in 1870. Bottrell's three volumes provide an early benchmark in the study of Cornish folklore, and without his contribution it would not be easy to arrive at a satisfactory understanding of pre-industrial Cornish folklore.[5] Bottrell's books are remarkable in the way that they often include elaborate tellings of folktales and legends, far exceeding what is found in most contemporary collections. For example, Robert Hunt, who sometimes reworked Bottrell's material for his own books on Cornish folklore, often abridged stories, presumably intending to make them easier to read. Even the Brothers Grimm, the German scholars who inspired much of the nineteenth-century collection of European folklore, published folktales in shortened, simplified form. Bottrell, however, offers unique insight into how the droll tellers, the traditional bards of Cornwall, told their stories. And because he includes so much detail, it is possible to fit the Cornish examples of the Lenore legend into a larger context.

Bottrell's story of 'Nancy Trenoweth, The Fair Daughter of the Miller of Alsia' is extremely long and may be the most developed version of the story recorded, although this analysis does not purport to be comprehensive in its international examination.[6] Without providing all the extensive details, the story unfolds as follows: Hugh Lanyon, a farmer with a hereditary claim to the aristocracy, hires Nancy Trenoweth, the daughter of a prosperous miller. Frank, the farmer's son, falls in love with Nancy. When his parents tell him to marry, he declares his affection for Nancy. His father objects and exiles the girl. The miller, in turn, forbids his daughter from seeing Frank, but her mother, touched by Nancy's sadness, helps her arrange meetings with the young man.

Frank eventually decides to leave Cornwall for a life at sea. He and Nancy meet for one last time at a holy well, where:

> they exchanged many vows of eternal constancy, swore, by the sign of salvation that stood near the holy fount, to be ever true and constant; held a ring between them in the bubbling brook, near the source of the limpid stream, whilst they called on all the powers of heaven above and the earth beneath to witness their vows of eternal love, through life and in death. Then the ring was duly placed on the finger of the affianced bride, and a silver coin broken, of which each one kept a

severed part, with many other superstitious rites then known and practised by the love-strick youths.[7]

In short, the couple uses numerous magical means to bind themselves, calling on supernatural powers in ways that exceeded church-sanctioned marriage vows.

Distraught at his son's leaving, old Hugh Lanyon asks Nancy to return to the farm, but her father refuses to allow it. Ultimately, the entire parish takes sides, divided by the cause of the miller and of the farmer. To escape the situation and to remove herself during what turns out to be her pregnancy, Nancy goes to live with her grandmother, 'Old Joan of Alsia'. This woman was a respected healer because of her knowledge of folk medicine and spells. After giving birth, Nancy leaves her son with her parents and travels even farther away to work as a servant.

At some point during Frank's long absence, a bottle containing his name and that of his ship mates turns up on the Cornish coast, convincing Nancy that her lover remains alive. She repeatedly asks her grandmother to cast spells to determine his fate. The old woman is able to divine that he will return, but specifics about how that will occur are obscured to her.

Finally, Nancy and two other 'love-sick damsels' call on the 'Powers of Darkness' on All Hallows' Eve to reveal each of their true loves. She sees Frank surrounded by waves and dripping wet, apparently angry at her. She shrieks, and the vision vanishes. The next girl asks to see her true love, and she sees a coffin: the story notes that she died soon afterwards.

Late one night in March, rough waters drive Frank's ship onto the rocks of the Cornish coast, and his crew struggles to climb to the top of the cliff overlooking the ocean. He makes certain his sailors are safe before he ascends by rope. Frank arrives on land battered and bleeding. He asks to see Nancy before he dies, but word fails to reach her. The night after he is buried, Nancy goes outside to look at the ocean, which is calm in the moonlight.

Suddenly, Frank arrives on the horse that he had always ridden when he arranged to meet with her before sailing away. He tells her that she will be his bride before the morning, but when they touch, she says he is cold and damp. He answers that, 'We have plighted our vows and sworn to be married, alive or dead; shrink not from me in fear, sweetheart. Come, mount behind me, and let us away; – ere tomorrow night thou shalt be my bride'.

Nancy sits on the horse and puts her arm around her love, finding herself frozen in place as they rush across the landscape. At one point, the horse stops to drink and Nancy is able to see Frank reflected in the water by the light of the moon: he wears a burial shroud, and she realizes he is dead. As they near her home village, the sight of a blacksmith and his fire rouses Nancy. She calls out, and Frank grabs her gown. The smith uses a red-hot iron rod to slice through her dress, freeing her. But this leaves a bit of Nancy's garment with Frank, who rides into the churchyard and plunges into his grave. People find the scrape of Nancy's dress on Frank's grave the following day. They also discover that the horse has died. The blacksmith assists in returning Nancy to her parent's home. There, they tell Nancy of Frank's fate, and after requesting to hold her child one last time, she directs that he be raised by Frank's parents. Finally, she asks to be buried next to Frank, and she dies in peace.

At the end, Bottrell notes 'the old story-tellers are particular in stating ... that the piece of the woman's dress burned off in the spirit's grasp was found in Lanyon's grave when it was re-opened for Nancy's burial'.[8] Bottrell then offers a sequel, lengthening the tale even more, and with this device, he is able to explain how Frank suffered terribly when Nancy used magic to see him. This epilogue also furnishes the means for his fellow sailors to explain what had happened during their long journey: pirates had captured the men, but the Cornish adventurers overcame their captors and claimed the ship and wealth for themselves, at which point they returned to Cornwall.

The international context

The path-finding Finnish folklorist Antti Aarne and his American successor Stith Thompson categorized this story as a folktale, listing it as Tale Type 365, 'The Dead Bridegroom Carries off his Bride'. A version appears in Robert Hunt's nineteenth-century collection of Cornish folklore as 'The Spectral Bridegroom', a title that is a more poetic summation of the contents. The classification of the tradition as belonging to the realm of the folktale is problematic because in most recorded cases it appears that people told the story to be believed and it ended tragically, both hallmarks of legends. The English folklorist Katherine Briggs, for example, groups five variants of this story in her compendium of British legends, not in her collection of folktales. Perhaps because of the story's complexity and wide distribution, Aarne and Thompson mistook it for a folktale, that is, part of oral tradition told as fiction and typically with a happy ending. It is also likely that the story slid between legend and folktale, serving as an example of how folklore can defy rigid classifications.[9]

Regardless of the tale's place in the taxonomical schemes of folklorists, 'The Spectral Bridegroom' provides an opportunity to assess an aspect of the Cornish legacy that plays a disproportionate role in British folklore. Francis James Child (1825–1896) in his important collection, *The English and Scottish Popular Ballads*, includes a useful discussion of the European variants of this story. The legend is also well documented in Ireland where it inspired an elegant 1983 overview by Ríonach Uí Ógaín and Anne O'Connor, thus providing a means to consider how at least some variants compare. Other examples from Iceland and even as far away as eastern Europe complete the means to understand the distribution of this widespread aspect of oral tradition.[10]

The Cornish variants are particularly important because Child cites them as evidence of an indigenous folk tradition spanning from Britain to the continent. Bürger's 1773 masterwork, 'Lenore', was so popular that people quickly recognized British counterparts in the form of printed ballads predating Bürger's publication. This raised the question as to the source of Bürger's inspiration: either he had seen the published English ballads or there was a widespread folk tradition that had separately inspired both the ballads and the German poet. Because the Cornish variants shared motifs with the continental oral tradition but not with the English ballads, it was possible to conclude that Bürger drew on a German oral tradition without necessarily having knowledge of the printed English materials. Within the context of the diverse European examples of the story, it is also possible to determine what is uniquely Cornish and what the variants imply about Cornwall's place in the spectrum of European folklore.

The 'Lenore' poem and 'The Suffolk Miracle'

A careful examination of the various examples of the story demonstrates the basis of determining the influence between the oral tradition and the literary forms. 'Lenore' features William, a Prussian soldier who fought in one of the eighteenth-century wars of Frederick the Great, King of Prussia. With peace, others returned, but not William. Eventually, Lenore, William's sweetheart, gives up, asks for death, and forsakes God. Late one night, William arrives by horse and calls for Lenore to ride with him. As he is persuading her to mount his horse behind him, William repeats a rhyme: 'Look round thee, love, the moon shines clear, the dead ride swiftly, never fear, we'll reach our marriage bed'. She consents, and William repeats his rhyme with varying words, inspiring Lenore to protest, asking him why he names the dead.

A cock crows just as the couple reaches a churchyard, and William warns the rooster away. William points to a newly-dug grave and says that this is their marriage bed, at which point, his flesh drops away, leaving only his skeleton. Lenore falls, and dancing fiends from Hell tell us that this is her punishment for giving voice to her dissatisfaction with God. But they add that if Lenore were to repent and call on God while still alive, she could still be redeemed. Lenore does just that and the spectres vanish. With dawn, Lenore wakens to realize not only that the entire incident was a nightmare, but also that her true love has arrived, alive and ready to join her in terrestrial bliss.[11]

Bürger's poem exhibits many motifs that are consistent with European oral tradition. The idea that the incident was merely a dream is a literary invention, unique to the poem, but much of what remains is clearly echoed in folklore. The earlier English songs that appeared in popular broadsheets lacked the poetic gravitas of Bürger's 'Lenore', but their wide distribution made them more well known in Britain.

'The Suffolk Miracle', a popular home-grown ballad situated in East Anglia, features a farmer's daughter named Nancy and a young neighbour named Frank, who loved her. Her father sought to break up the liaison and exiled his daughter to her uncle's home, 'forty miles distant'. Frank subsequently dies of a broken heart, but Nancy is ignorant of what has transpired. After 'a month or more', Frank comes to Nancy at night, riding her father's horse, and asks her to come with him. As they ride, Frank complains of a headache, and Nancy binds his head with her handkerchief. He takes her to her father's house and then stables the horse. Nancy reports to her father, who realizes that Frank, now long-dead and buried, had been his daughter's escort that night. Her father goes to the stable and finds his horse covered in sweat. They subsequently unearth Frank's corpse and find Nancy's handkerchief around his head, even though his body has turned 'into mould'. When they reveal everything to Nancy, who had been kept in ignorance about what had happened, she dies of fright and grief. A final verse warns parents against trying to separate young lovers.

As with 'Lenore', motifs appear in 'The Suffolk Miracle' that are alternatively consistent and inconsistent with most variants from oral tradition. Because the literary device of a dream is not employed with the ballads, there is the motif of the handkerchief around Frank's head: this furnishes physical evidence within the story that the incident really occurred, a powerful device, common in many legends.[12] The ballad deviates from most oral variants in that the corpse makes no effort to take Nancy into the grave.

Understanding the Cornish variant

Against this backdrop, it is possible to consider the Cornish versions collected and published in the nineteenth century by Bottrell and Hunt. Bottrell's story of 'Nancy Trenoweth', described above, uses the same names – Nancy and Frank – as appear in 'The Suffolk Miracle'. That aside, there are significant differences. Hunt's version is an abridged adaptation of the story that Bottrell published in 1870, and so the example from Hunt can be discounted for the purposes of this analysis.[13]

Additional Cornish variants appear in the collections of Bottrell and Hunt: the former published 'A Legend of Pargwarra', which relates a story located at a place that the 'old folks also called ... "the Sweethearts' Cove", from a tradition of its having been the scene of a tragical love-story'.[14] Hunt provides a similar story, 'The Lovers of Porthangwartha', which differs sufficiently to suggest that the two early folklorists recorded distinct recitations of the same legend. Bottrell's story tells of a rich farmer whose daughter, again named Nancy, falls in love with one of the servants, a young man named William, who goes to sea during the summers. In winter, William entertains the household with stories of distant lands. Nancy's mother realizes that her daughter has fallen in love with William and tells her to find a better match. Nancy's father, however, is sympathetic and suggests that if William were to take a voyage where he could win a great deal of wealth, he could have Nancy's hand.

Nancy and William vow their commitment to one another, using a variety of magical means to bind themselves together. After three years, Nancy takes to walking the cliffs, searching for the ship that would return her beloved William. 'One moonlit winter's night,' Bottrell tells us, Nancy 'heard William's voice just under her window saying, "Sleepest thou, sweetheart, awaken and come hither, love; my boat awaits us in the cove, thou must come this night or never be my bride".' Nancy's Aunt Prudence hears William's words and also Nancy's response that she would come. Prudence looks outside to see William, 'dripping wet and deathly pale'. Nancy leaves with William, and Prudence dresses quickly and follows, but no matter how fast she runs, she cannot catch up with the young lovers who 'seemed to glide down the rocky pathway leading to Pargwarra as if borne on the wind'.

Finally, Prudence sees them in the cove on a large flat rock beside a boat. A fog rolls in, and although Prudence calls, there is no answer. When the mist clears for a moment, Prudence sees by the bright moonlight that 'the boat and the lovers had disappeared'. The next day, William's father goes to Nancy's parents, expecting to find his son, because the previous night, the young man appeared before him and told him he was going to collect his bride. That afternoon, a sailor comes to William's father and tells him that William had become the captain of a ship with rich cargo. He had wanted to take the ship's boat to shore at Pargwarra to visit Nancy and her parents, but he had fallen into the ocean and could not be retrieved. Bottrell concludes by writing 'all knew then that William's ghost had taken Nancy to a phantom boat, and a watery grave was the lovers' bridal-bed. Thus their rash vows of constancy, even in death, were fulfilled.'

At the end of 'A Legend of Pargwarra', Bottrell makes three observations that are useful in this context. First, he indicates that 'there are other versions of this story, that only vary from the above in details of little interest'. While it would have been, in fact, of great interest for this analysis to know of the various 'details', Bottrell is revealing that he had encountered an active tradition where the story was repeated. This was not, as so often happens in nineteenth-century collections, a scrap from a distant past, a mere remnant of a once-vibrant part of local folklore.

In addition, Bottrell makes two references to printed material. He indicates that the story was 'best known to me from fragments of a quaint old "copy of verses"'. He also notes that 'I have recently tried in vain to find anyone who knows the old "copy of verses", the argument of which I have for the most part followed.' Apparently, the collector is suggesting that his version of 'A Legend of Pargwarra' was adapted from his memory of a document that he had seen at one time, but could no longer find.

Bottrell then indicates that 'the fragments I recited, however, recalled to a few old folks a newer piece called the "Strains of Lovely Nancy", that used to be printed in a broadsheet and sung and sold by wandering ballad singers of the west, forty or fifty years ago; and from what I have heard of the latter one might conclude it to have been a modernized and an imperfect version of the ancient tragedy'. With this, he is suggesting that 'A Legend of Pargwarra' inspired publications in the early part of the nineteenth century, and it is easy to imagine that while the oral tradition manifested as printed lyrics to songs, the printed version, in turn, influenced the oral tradition.[15] With these three observations, Bottrell provides valuable insight into the nature of the tradition as he encountered it with his work in the mid-nineteenth century.

Hunt also published this story, recording it as 'The Lovers of Porthangwartha', which he notes with the following: 'This is said to mean the Lover's Cove.' Hunt provides far less detail – as is usually the case – than Bottrell, but the former does relay that 'A simple story, however, remains, the mere fragment, without doubt, of a longer and more ancient tale.'[16] A comparison of the two versions of this story, attached to the same cove, is instructive. It would be easy to imagine that Hunt had simply reworked Bottrell's example, abridging it, but this is clearly not the case. As was typical, Hunt summarizes a great deal that a skillful story-teller would have used to elaborate, but not all story-tellers are created equally, and it is possible that Hunt heard his version in its shortened form. More importantly, while his story deviates significantly from Bottrell's, the two share motifs that suggest they are part of the same body of oral tradition.

For example, both versions lack the motif of the horse ride. Because the young man in these two legends is lost at sea, there is no grave to share. And unlike the more terrestrial variants, the woman dies while in his company, apparently satisfied to begin her eternal voyage with him that night. In addition, the stories share the motif of the rock where they are last seen before disappearing into the ocean, and moonlight – an essential feature to allow the events to be seen – adds the same eerie quality to both tales. An older woman observes the couple as they disappear into the waves, and in each story she reports hearing singing, which Bottrell attributes to mermaids, 'whose wild unearthly strains were wont, before tempests, to be heard resounding'.

While the shared motifs point toward the common body of oral tradition that focused on the same location, differences indicate distinct sources. Hunt tells of finding the body of the young woman 'a day or two after in a neighboring cove'. He also relates that people eventually heard that the young man died far away on the night of the incident. For Bottrell, William's death also happened that night, but it occurred while intending to land near his home. In addition, Hunt's lovers pledge their eternal devotion 'under the light of the full moon', while Bottrell offers an elaborate description of a night-time ceremony including that they joined hands 'in a living spring' and 'broke a gold ring in two ... each one keeping a part. And to make their vows more binding they kindled, at dead of night, a fire on the Garrack Zans (holy rock), which then stood in Roskestal townplace, and joined their hands over the flame, called on all the powers of heaven and earth to witness their common oaths to each other living or dead.' For all the detail, Bottrell does not mention a full moon, but rather refers to the ceremony occurring in the dead of night.

In addition, the witness to the incident varies in each: in Bottrell's version, she is an aunt, and for Hunt she is 'an old crone'. Bottrell has the young man fetch his bride-to-be, coming to her window, while Hunt describes the woman descending to the cove and waiting for her bridegroom who eventually appears before the two seem 'to float off upon the waters'. The array of distinct motifs throughout suggests a separate telling of the story. This reinforces the idea that there were, as Bottrell described, other versions of this story.

Hunt provides a hint of yet another variant in the introduction to his third edition of Cornish folklore. He credits Bottrell with information about a ballad from oral tradition, giving just enough details to suggest it was probably a variant of Tale Type 365. Hunt's includes five verses of the ballad sung by 'an old blind man' named Uncle Anthony James. The snippet establishes that two young lovers are separated by the death of the man, and 'then follows a stormy kind of duet between the maiden and her lover's ghost, who tries to persuade the maid to accompany him to the world of the shadows'.[17] This is not enough to grasp much about the specific motifs included in this version, but it is further information about how popular and widespread the story was in Cornwall.

The English folklorist, Katherine Briggs, suggests that the Cornish legend, 'The Execution and Wedding', which she calls 'Yorkshire Jack', is another variant of Tale Type 365. This story, which Hunt preserves, may be related to this complex, but even if that is the case, it deviates considerably, featuring the woman's death at the gallows. She then returns with the Devil to find Jack aboard a ship and sweeps him away with a large wave to an eternity married to her in the company of Satan.[18]

The Irish variants

The survey of the Irish variants of the story by Uí Ógaín and O'Connor provides a useful means to examine the essential components of 'The Dead Bridegroom Carries off his Bride'. Following this approach, it is possible to have a basis for comparison. The two Irish folklorists see the story as typically progressing through the following:

Establishing the situation with the couple. The stories describe two young people who pledge themselves to marry, but the union is deemed unacceptable because of religion or a difference in social status.

The young man's death. The Irish folklorists indicate that although there are various ways that the young man dies, 'in all versions … the boy dies without the girl's knowledge'.[19]

The rendezvous. As pre-arranged, the young man arrives at night with a horse for an elopement; she sits behind him on the horse.

The various accessories that appear. In some versions, she carries a bundle of clothes.

The journey. The Irish folklorists point out that 'in all versions the boy and girl ride away on horseback'.[20]

The discovery of the spirit's true nature. This part of the story shows greater variation. Three Kerry versions have the girl asking the boy to spur the horse to ride more quickly, but he says he cannot, the reason being that he has no strength in his foot because he is dead. In one of the Kerry versions, it is not directly apparent that something is amiss until he jumps from the horse and widens the grave so they can both sleep there. Many of the versions feature the crowing of a cock, which the boy denies is occurring or is of importance, or he makes no reply. In each instance, she becomes uneasy because of his strange words. In two Galway versions, she sees by the moonlight that the horse only has three legs. Some examples describe her seeing a moonlit reflection in a stream, revealing that he wears a burial shroud or a death band, the fabric tied over the top of the head to keep a corpse's jaw from flopping open.

The escape. The Irish versions also exhibit considerable variation in the conclusion. The Kerry variants have the girl throwing herself off the horse as they pass a house or a forge. In tales from Kerry and Longford, she leaves her bundle of clothes, which appear shredded the next morning, scattered atop the boy's grave. In another version, she is able to escape into a house and bar the door. He persuades her to put her hand through the window, and he slices off the tops of her fingers, which are found in his grasp during his wake the next day. The Galway versions have a blacksmith who runs to help the girl, driving away the revenant with a piece of red-hot iron, which the smith sometimes uses to burn through the fabric in the dead man's clutch. The blacksmith is absent in the Kerry examples. Many versions describe the girl's subsequent ill health, and the County Longford example explains that she died three weeks after the incident.

The unique Cornish contribution

The kinship between the Cornish and Irish variants is evident, but differences are significant as well. Bottrell's more elaborate tale compares nicely with the Irish material, including as it does, the midnight ride, the recognition of the lover's true nature as seen in his moonlit reflection in water, and the girl's escape with the help of a blacksmith and his red-hot iron. These motifs are sufficient to demonstrate a genetic relationship between the Irish and Cornish material and at the same time, it is clear that these two bodies of similar tales could not have grown separately out of the ballad tradition, which did not employ shared motifs. Similarly, the poem 'Lenore' could not have inspired these traditions, as it also lacks the motifs that appear in both Irish and Cornish material.

While much links all of the variants regardless of the country of origin, the maritime career and death of the Cornish young man represents a significant divergence from the rest. This device would have been less at home in Ireland, but it is nicely adapted if not essential to Cornwall's sea-going economy. And of course, this way of life is taken to an extreme in the stories of Bottrell and Hunt, both of whom describe the couple walking to a cove and boarding a boat that takes them to a watery grave. Here, Cornish story-tellers have modified the tradition into something that is nearly a new species, lacking the horse and the terrestrial resting place.

The motif of the moonlight plays a central role in the array of international examples, but the Cornish variants featuring the flight to the ocean requires the lunar illumination to serve another function. In most examples, the moonlight provides the means by which the young woman discovers that her companion is dead. Many of the stories describe how she sees his reflection in water, illuminated by the full moon, revealing that he is wrapped in a shroud or as occurs sometimes in Ireland, that he wears the headband used to keep a corpse's jaw from opening. And as occurs in two Galway versions, the revealing vision is of the horse's lack of a fourth leg. In an Icelandic legend, the man's head pitches forward as the horse takes a jump, and with that, the woman is able to see the back of his skull shining in the moonlight.[21] But in these Cornish expressions of Tale Type 365, the woman does not survive the night, and so she cannot fill in the details of how moonlight helped her understand what was happening. The moon consequently serves to illuminate the incident so a third party can bear witness to the strange events. The motif of the full moon remains, but it is forced into a new role by the change in the story.

The motifs unique to Cornwall set its folklore apart from the rest. Under the influence of the maritime industry, which regularly sent its sons on far off expeditions, the lost lover could comfortably be expressed in this context. But the implication of this deviation made the horse an awkward remnant of an older story. These changes, combined with the insights of Bottrell and Hunt, make it clear that a vibrant indigenous Cornish tradition celebrated and modified a story with international distribution.

One further bit of information hints at an additional, provocative connection. Child writes that 'the ballads seem less original than the tales; that is, to have been made from the tales, as "The Suffolk Miracle" was'. Child further notes that 'reverting now to the English tales, we perceive that the Cornish is a very well-preserved specimen of the extensive cycle'. Child also cites a version from Brittany collected by M. Paul Sébillot, which Sébillot indicated in 1879 was similar to the poem 'Lenore'. Child suggests the variant from Brittany is much like 'The Suffolk Miracle', but as he notes 'This is the English ballad over again, almost word for word, with the difference that the lover dies at sea.'[22] This is insufficient to demonstrate a shared Cornwall-Brittany oral tradition, together influenced and adapted to the sea, but this tantalizing clue suggests one may have existed.

Legends of the dead

The story of 'The Spectral Bridegroom' draws on two ideas that are widespread throughout the world. The first is the belief that some dead people feel the need to walk among the living. The second is that supernatural beings, whether ghostly or other types, occasionally have love affairs with people, usually with a tragic result. Both these motifs are practically universal in oral tradition and in turn have inspired a great deal of literature. Because the boundary between folklore and the written word is porous, publications have influenced spoken traditions as much as the reverse is the case.

Tales of ghosts permeate literature and have done so for thousands of years, with examples in Homeric poetry, the Old Testament, continental medieval literature, and Icelandic sagas, again to offer only examples rather than a comprehensive overview. Counterparts in oral tradition are so universal as to suggest that this has been a constant in folklore even before the invention of writing. Although stories of hauntings are widespread, it is a generally accepted that most of the dead keep their repose in peace. And yet, some do not. The Finnish scholar Juha Pentijäinen considers a particular belief in the dead who trouble the living because they lack an acceptable status, and this concept applies nicely to the situation of 'The Spectral Bridegroom', an observation that Uí Ógaín and O'Connor made previously.[23] The Spectral Bridegroom cannot rest because of the intensity of the love he and his betrothed shared in life. In addition, many stories underscore the excessive nature of their secret vows and the fact that the lovers often employ magic to bind themselves together. There is an implicit warning here that one should not use supernatural means beyond Christian prayer in an attempt to affect outcomes.

Numerous examples of ill-fated, supernatural romances come to mind in European literature. These sorts of liaisons have inspired medieval stories of sexual encounters between elves and people, ballets featuring enticing swan-women, and modern teen novels and films with rakish vampires. The popularity of broadsheet ballads describing the Spectral Bridegroom draws on this same fascination with what happens when people cross the barrier that separates the natural from the supernatural, all in the name of love.

For what appears to be the earliest manifestation of this motif, one needs to reach back to eleventh-century Scandinavian literature. The medieval collection of verse, *The Poetic Edda*, includes the 'Second Lay of Helgi the Hunding-Slayer/Helgakviða Hundingsbana II'. This describes how Helgi, a dead hero, returns from the grave on a horse to beckon his beloved, Sigrún, for one last night of conjugal bliss. The document hints at the age of the motif, but it also suggests that initially, the story may have played out differently: Sigrún willingly enters Helgi's burial mound to lie with him. The poem subsequently relates that the heroine 'lived but a short while longer, for grief and sorrow'. With this, the medieval text returns to the conclusion found in its more recent counterpart.[24] This example suggests that for pre-Christian society, crossing the line into the supernatural – or at least in this case into the realm of the dead – for romance was heroic. Nineteenth-century expressions of the story generally assert that no living person would want to enter the grave, even when it is the last resting place of a lover.[25]

Conclusion

Bottrell, ever the intuitive folklorist, recognized the similarities shared by the broadsheet ballads and his collection. Without the comparative tools developed only a few decades later in the early twentieth century, he could not have known how his stories fit into a larger oral context shared with other parts of Europe.[26] Even with a quick look at sources from other countries, it is clear that the Cornish droll tellers did not borrow these stories from the broadsheet ballads. They may have taken some motifs or names from the published sources, but the Cornish story-tellers forged a new direction for the international, centuries-old tales. The longer Bottrell version hints at how elaborate the telling of this legend could be. His telling is full of motifs, which in their diversity define a unique, Cornish contribution to the spectrum of variants of the story. The Cornish versions were not the poor cousins of material from elsewhere, but instead, they were part of the fully developed, thriving oral tradition of Cornwall.

The Cornish innovation of the maritime career of the young man was taken so far as to cause the horse to disappear altogether, replaced with a boat. The drowning of the woman on the night of the incident required a different witness to the startling event, shifting the moonlight away from its original role of revealing the nature of the spectre to allowing a third party to observe the entire affair. The famed Swedish folklorist, Carl Wilhelm von Sydow, identified variants adapted to local circumstance as ecotypes, borrowing a concept from biology. As Tale Type 365, 'The Dead Bridegroom Carries off his Bride', diffused from one area to the next, Cornish story-tellers changed the tale to suit themselves and their listeners, and this is precisely what von Sydow predicted for oral tradition in general.[27]

Stith Thompson, who did so much to shape perspectives when it came to stories such as this one, wrote in 1977 that 'no comparative study of the relation of [Tale Type 365] to the ballad has been made which would indicate whether verse or prose would seem to be the original form'. He then indicated that the Baltic States had many representations of the story, whereas 'versions hardly appear in other parts of Europe'.[28] A comprehensive monograph might confirm his suspicion that the story originated in the East, but the analysis of the Irish material and this look at Cornish variants demonstrate that the tradition thrived in Western Europe as well. Because many motifs shared in the stories do not appear in the ballads, it is clear the legend descends, not from an oral borrowing from printed ballads, but rather from a tradition that predates and ultimately inspired the ballads themselves.

Two additional examples serve to underscore the need for this sort of research into Cornish folklore: as pointed out, Aarne and Thompson, in their standard index of European tale types, give a geographic summary of the distribution of 'The Dead Bridegroom Carries off his Bride', but they fail to mention any English – and by implication Cornish – variants, except those that appear in Child's compendium of English and Scottish ballads.[29] Similarly, Bo Almqvist, retired chairman of the Department of Irish Folklore at University College Dublin, has a remark pertinent to this discussion. The noted scholar of the Celtic and Scandinavian worlds observes about another story, this one shared by Celts and Germanic people, that 'the legend is unknown not only in French tradition but also among the P-Celts of Brittany and Wales'.[30] Almqvist knows his material and is clearly aware that the Cornish belong to the P-Celt side of the equation. In addition, he certainly knew of the work of Hunt and Bottrell when he wrote this particular article, but without proper cataloguing and analysis, the Cornish material drops out of sight. Almqvist's lacuna, through no fault of his own, is another example of the greater problem. It will be a lengthy process to bring traditional Cornish folklore into focus, to continue the work that Bottrell, Hunt, and others started. In spite of the difficulty of the challenge, if Cornwall's legacy is to be celebrated and properly understood, the task of working with the historic forms of its oral tradition must be undertaken.[31]

Notes and references

1. C. Thomas, *An Anthology of German Literature* (Boston, 1909), pp. 387–91.
2. 'The Suffolk Miracle' appeared in many forms, the earliest of which may date to 1689: F. J. Child, *The English and Scottish Popular Ballads*, Part 9 (Boston, 1894), p. 67 cites a broadsheet printed for W. Thackeray and T. Passenger, for which he furnishes the date 1689, adding in italics, '*The date added by Wood*'.
3. 'Sweet William's Ghost' is Scottish. T. Percy, *Reliques of Ancient English Poetry: Volume III* (London, 1775), pp. 120–24. Child, *The English and Scottish Popular Ballads*, includes several versions of each of the ballads. In 'Fair Margaret and Sweet William', the roles are reversed, removing the ballad a step further from the tradition discussed here.
4. K. M. Briggs, *Folk Tales of Britain: Legends* (London, 2011; reprinted with emendations from the 1971 original; page numbers refer to the 2011 edition) lists five variants of Tale Type 365 on page 34, but one of the variants is 'The Suffolk Miracle', the printed ballad, which occupies a different class. 'The Fair Maid of Clifton' is also a ballad, but this was collected from an oral source. The other three are purely legendary from oral tradition, and all are from Cornwall.
5. For an overview of the Cornish folklore collectors see R. M. James, 'Cornish Folklore: Context and Opportunity' in P. Payton (ed.), *Cornish Studies: Eighteen* (Exeter, 2011), pp. 121–40.
6. W. Bottrell, *Traditions of the Hearthside: Stories of West Cornwall* (Penzance, 1870), pp. 468–527.
7. Ibid., pp. 478–79.
8. Ibid., p. 508.

9. A. Aarne and S. Thompson, *The Types of the Folktale: A Classification and Bibliography* (Helsinki, 1987), p. 127. Briggs, *Folk Tales of Britain: Legends*, p. 34. S. S. Liljeblad, in his *Introduction to Folklore: Elementary Forms of Popular Tradition* (Pocatello, Idaho, 1965), p. 113, for example, refers to 'The Dead Bridegroom Carries off his Bride' as both a folktale and as a testimonial legend.

10. For a Japanese variant, see H. Ikeda, *A Type and Motif Index of Japanese Folk-Literature* (Helsinki, 1971), pp. 95–96, but there is some question as to whether this isolate is related to the European tradition. For the Irish material, see R. Uí Ógaín and A. O'Connor, '"Spor ar An gCois Is gan An Chos Ann": A Study of "The Dead Lover's Return" in Irish Tradition', *Béaloideas* 51 (1983), pp. 126–44. For an Icelandic variant, see J. Arnason, *Icelandic Legends*, translated by G. E. J. Powell and E. Magnússon (London, 1864), pp. 173–77. A Hungarian variant appears in W. H. Jones and L. L. Kropf, *The Folk-Tales of the Magyars* (London, 1889), pp. 278–82.

11. Thomas, *An Anthology of German Literature*, pp. 387–91.

12. Compare the modern urban legend, 'The Vanishing Hitchhiker', where the apparition frequently leaves a garment she borrows on her tombstone as proof that the story is real. J. H. Brunvand, *Too Good to be True: The Colossal Book of Urban Legends* (New York, 1999), pp. 231–34.

13. R. Hunt, *Popular Romances of the West of England* (London, 1903); page numbers here are from the 1903 printing of the third edition, which first appeared in 1881. Lacking access to the rare first edition, which was published in 1865, it is not possible to say at this time whether Hunt's version of 'The Spectral Bridegroom' appeared then, before Bottrell's 1870 publication. Hunt, however, used Bottrell's notes, and it appears from the nature of the details in the two versions that the tale passed from Bottrell to Hunt and not in the opposite direction, whether Hunt took it from a publication or from Bottrell's notes. Perhaps because it is abridged, Hunt's version (and not Bottrell's) appears in other collections and in online sources, even though the extensive details suggest Bottrell captures what was closer to the oral presentation.

14. William Bottrell, *Traditions of the Hearthside: Stories of West Cornwall* (Penzance, 1870), pp. 149–53.

15. Ibid., p. 153.

16. Hunt, *Popular Romances*, p. 247. Again, lacking the rare first edition, it is not possible to determine when Hunt first published this story.

17. Ibid., pp. 26–27. Hunt refers to a source as having provided this information, but given the context, it is certainly Bottrell.

18. Ibid., pp. 256–58. The frequently cited T. Deane and T. Shaw, *Folklore of Cornwall* (Totowa, New Jersey, 1975), pp. 81–82 and 108–109 discuss variants, summarizing stories found in Hunt and Bottrell. They consequently add nothing to this discussion.

19. Uí Ógaín and O'Connor, '"Spor ar An gCois Is gan An Chos Ann"', p. 132.

20. Ibid., p. 133.

21. Arnason, *Icelandic Legends*, 173–77.

22. Child, *The English and Scottish Popular Ballads*, p. 63–64. And see M. P. Sébillot's story 'Les Deux Fiancés', in *Littérature orale de la Haute-Bretagne* (Paris, 1881), pp. 197–99.

23. J. Pentijäinen, 'The Dead without Status', from R. Kvideland and H. K. Sehmsdorf

(eds), *Nordic Folklore: Recent Studies* (Bloomington, Indiana, 1989)pp. 128–34, originally appearing in *Temenos*, 1969; Uí Ógaín and O'Connor cite Pentijäinen in their article. See also J. Simpson, 'Repentant Soul or Walking Corpse? Debatable Apparitions in Medieval England', *Folklore* 114:3 (December 2003), pp. 389–402; and G. D. Keyworth, 'Was the Vampire of the Eighteenth Century a Unique Type of Undead-corpse?', *Folklore* 117:3 (December 2006), pp. 241–60.

24. L. M. Hollander, translated with introduction and explanatory notes, *The Poetic Edda* (Austin, 1962), pp. 190–202. Hollander remarks on the importance of this source in relation to the story of 'The Dead Bridegroom Carries off his Bride'.

25. Liljeblad, in his *Introduction to Folklore*, p. 113, also notes the importance of this medieval lay in the context of the legend of 'The Dead Bridegroom Carries off his Bride'. In communication with the author, *c.*1977, Liljeblad described how the pre-Christian motif was apparently different from its later Christian counterpart in that the woman willingly spent the night with the corpse, an act of devotion that would have violated Christian sensibilities.

26. Aarne published his German-language tale type index in 1910; Thompson translated and enlarged Aarne's work, publishing his first edition in 1929.

27. C. W. von Sydow, 'Geography and Folk-Tale Oicotypes', *Béaloideas* 4:3 (1934), pp. 344–55, reprinted in von Sydow's *Selected Papers on Folklore*, edited by Laurits Bødker (Copenhagen, 1948), pp. 44–59. The term 'ecotypes' also appears in the literature as 'oicotype' and 'oikotype'. For critiques, see E. E. Kiefer, *Albert Wesselski and Recent Folktale Theories* (New York, 1973), pp. 23–29; D. Hopkin, 'The Ecotype, Or a Modest Proposal to Reconnect Cultural and Social History', in M. Calaresu, F. de Vivo, and J.-P. Rubiés (eds), *Exploring Cultural History: Essays in Honour of Peter Burke* (Burlington, Vermont, 2012), pp. 31–54; T. Cochrane, 'The Concept of Ecotypes in American Folklore', *Journal of Folklore Research* 24:1 (January–April 1987), pp. 33–55; S. Thompson, *The Folktale* (Berkeley, California, 1977), pp. 440–41, 443.

28. Thompson, *The Folktale*, p. 41. Child, *The English and Scottish Popular Ballads*, p. 60, also maintained that there was a Slavic origin for the tale, and this may have influenced Thompson.

29. Aarne and Thompson, *The Types of the Folktale*, p. 127. The same is true of S. Thompson's *Motif-Index of Folk-Literature: Revised and Enlarged Edition* (Bloomington, Indiana, 1955), p. 420: under 'E215, The Dead Rider (Lenore)', the only British examples are drawn from Child or from Baughman's compendium of ballads: E. W. Baughman, *A Type and Motif Index of the Folktales of England and North America* (Bloomington, Indiana, 1966).

30. B. Almqvist, *Viking Ale: Studies on folklore contacts between the Northern and the Western Worlds* (Aberystwyth, Wales, 1991), p. 75.

31. This is not to dismiss the remarkable work of scholars such as Katherine Briggs and Jacqueline Simpson who have done so much to address a full range of British folklore. Briggs, *Folk Tales of Britain*, deserves credit for cataloguing a wide variety of British folklore, and this includes much, but not all, of the Cornish material, and too often Cornish folklore is grouped – and lost – under the term 'English'.

8

Rural Geographies

The figure in the landscape in literature of Cornwall

Gemma Goodman

Introduction

As I write this article the 2012 budget has just been announced, and is being digested across the United Kingdom. There is the potential for Cornwall's economy to be hit hard by a so-called 'pasty tax' – VAT added to hot take-away goods which would result in a 20 per cent rise in the cost of the Cornish staple. A campaign has begun to voice opposition to this tax. When *Cornish Studies: Twenty* appears, the full impact of this measure may be known, but right now it occasions a coming together, speaking with one voice, or at least more than one voice, as and for Cornwall. The series *Cornish Studies*, over the past twenty years, has been instrumental in speaking about, speaking as, and speaking for Cornwall, articulating the tenets of what has become known as 'New Cornish Studies'. As Philip Payton stressed in the introduction to *Cornish Studies: Sixteen* (2008), this New Cornish Studies should be recognized as 'an important reservoir of knowledge and specialist opinion on Cornwall's past, present and future' that could be used productively to inform the contemporary governance of Cornwall.[1] The political issues noted above seem to be just such a situation where this knowledge would be useful.

Significantly, Payton also stressed the role of New Cornish Studies in 'projecting' Cornwall's 'aspirations and distinctiveness', while also 'demonstrating its responsiveness to the nuances and subtleties of Cornwall's communities'.[2] This echoed Bernard Deacon's observations in *Cornish Studies: Six* (1998), where he pointed out that 'Cornish Studies as a discipline has produced relatively few studies of differences, for example of identity or class or gender, within Cornwall.' Deacon called for practitioners within the field to take 'greater account of the internal diversity of the geography of Cornishness', and argued that 'in order to explain aspects of historical and contemporary Cornwall, we have to be aware of processes simultaneously operating at a number of different scales'.[3] In *Cornish Studies: Eighteen*, over ten years later, Deacon rightly complained that 'a more nuanced comparative investigation of "Cornwalls" as opposed to Cornwall ... [and] comparative work on intra-Cornish difference has been slow to emerge'.[4]

It is not surprising, however, that a relatively new field of study based on Cornwall as its presiding concept has produced more studies on Cornwall as a whole rather than smaller divisions or multiple divisions of place. The field is contextualized by the political shift towards devolution that has led to the creation of a separate parliament in Scotland and assemblies in Wales and Northern Ireland. And within this positive devolutionary political climate, greater acceptance of heterogeneous nationalities and identities existing within, contributing to (and antagonistic to) Britishness has been possible. Cornwall and Cornish Studies have no doubt benefited from the devolutionary environment in which Britain now exists and operates. And it is understandable that, in building on this devolutionary imperative, the consequent emphasis on Cornwall as a territory that can be differentiated from England, rather than divided into smaller divisions of place (or multiple versions of place), becomes most important. While this should not preclude recognition of differences within Cornwall, Cornwall's current political position, without its own assembly but needing somehow, as Payton puts it, to enable 'the wresting of new powers away from the tight grip of central government, [and] the avoidance of losing existing powers to unelected "South West" bodies', leads naturally to the repeated demonstration of Cornwall's credentials, such as its claim to be considered, like Wales, as separate from England.[5]

Deacon has already pointed out the 'perilous tightrope between being alert to heterogeneity and deconstructing claims that may underlie the struggles of disempowered and voiceless groups'.[6] There is naturally concern that a shift in focus to internal differences will diminish, or even threaten, the concept of a cohesive Cornwall and the longstanding recognition of its difference from England. However, while Deacon understands the tightrope he is asking Cornish Studies practitioners to walk, he continues to argue that a mature Cornish Studies must be prepared to incorporate the possibility of multiple Cornwalls and to be aware of the nuances associated with this term. Perhaps an occurrence such as that with which this article opens – the already infamous 'pasty tax' – serves to remind us of both the difficulty and the need to do both things at the same time. As early as 1989 Stuart Hall signalled the complexity of this task, stating that we need:

> [T]o conceive of how a politics can be constructed which works with and through difference, which is able to build those forms of solidarity and identification which makes common struggle and resistance possible but without suppressing the real heterogeneity of interests and identities, and which can effectively draw the political boundary lines without which political contestation is impossible, without fixing those boundaries for eternity.[7]

Perhaps this is now one of the foremost tasks of New Cornish Studies – to discover and enable methodologies that allow for 'Cornwall' and 'Cornwalls' to co-exist simultaneously.

Methodologies from within the field of Feminist Geography provide theorisation of gender and place, and their intersection with class and race. Like New Cornish Studies, Feminist Geography is an inherently interdisciplinary field and can provide perspectives and approaches to enable the identification and discussion of difference, nuance and complexity within Cornwall, while seeing this in relation to Cornwall as a whole. This article makes use of such perspectives to analyse the figure in the landscape in three literary texts – Salome Hocking's *Norah Lang* (1886), Emma Smith's *A Cornish Waif's Story* (1954) and Charles Lee's *Cynthia in the West* (1900) – all of which are set in the 'long' nineteenth century.[8]

Among the early proponents of Feminist Geography were Gillian Rose, Doreen Massey and Linda Mcdowell, who each produced keys texts in the 1990s that significantly developed the theoretical sophistication of the emergent field.[9] In her vital study *Gender, Identity and Place*, McDowell states that '[t]he specific aim of feminist geography is to investigate, make visible and challenge the relationships between gendered divisions and spatial divisions, to uncover their mutual constitution and problematize their apparent naturalness'.[10] She stresses 'the importance of questions about place, about the location and positionality of the person making the claims and about how to listen and interpret voices from the margins that we too often ignore' and, significant too for this article, that 'bodies in space raise all sorts of questions about the place they occupy'.[11]

The field of Feminist Geography has developed considerably since the 1990s becoming concerned with, among other avenues of inquiry, spatiality and embodiment. The concept of place as a fixed entity was contested by academics such as Massey who argued for a fuller understanding of place 'as a fluid, historically specific and socially constructed process'. In more recent work, as *Feminist Geographies* identifies, Massey has gone on to argue for seeing place in terms of 'a progressive sense of place'. Place here is interpreted as 'the intersection of sets of social relations which are stretched over particular spaces'.[12] Similarly, as Gregory and Urry state, '[s]patial structure is now seen not merely as an arena in which social life unfolds, but rather as a medium through which social relations are produced and reproduced'.[13] Related to this are discussions concerning embodiment, the body and its relationship to its environment, and work by the philosopher Judith Butler has been crucial in theorising gender 'performativity'. Levis and Pile articulate the potential connections between the body, performativity and the surrounding environment. Summarising their work *Feminist Geographies* states that:

> Levis and Pile suggest what effects the emphasis on bodily performance may have on understandings of space and place. Instead of understanding space and place as a pre-existing location in which performances take place, they argue that performances themselves constitute spaces and places in ways which are at once material and cultural. In this way, spaces and places become dynamic and shifting articulations of social relations of meaning.[14]

The theorisation of space and place and the alternative perspectives and approaches emerging from the field of Feminist Geography can be effectively applied to an analysis of literary texts from within Cornish Studies, and can provide a route into a more nuanced analysis of the representations of Cornwall and Cornish identity. This is an inherently interdisciplinary process, bringing together literary studies, Cornish Studies and Feminist Geography. But, while they are each very much attuned with the interdisciplinary ethos, it is worth noting that how these fields work together and exactly how theorisation within Feminist Geography can be purposefully applied to literary texts in general, and to literary texts within a Cornish context, is an on-going process in its early stages, and in which this article aims to participate.

Finally, before dealing with the novels themselves, it is important to note that discussions of gender and space have more typically tended to focus on the city rather than rural contexts: see, for example, Linda Mcdowell's *Capital Culture: Gender at Work in the City* (1997) or Deborah Parsons' *Streetwalking the Metropolis: Women, the City and Modernity* (2000).[15] When rural contexts are the focus, it is more often studies of third world countries rather than British rurality.[16] Rural spaces offer equally productive contexts for exploring the intersections between gender, class, space and place but there remains what Barber et al. call 'a series of interlinked silences surrounding rurality'. They rightly establish the need to 'identify the changing articulations of gender and class in rural localities'.[17]

Visibility and invisibility: Salome Hocking's *Norah Lang*

Somewhat ironically, given the discussion above, this section begins with the city – as a point of contrast to the exploration of Hocking's novella *Norah Lang* that follows. Parsons considers that the 'city is habitually conceived as a male space, in which women are either repressed or disobedient marginal presences'.[18] The diaries of Hannah Cullwick give us a rare insight into the life of a nineteenth-century woman in service, and detail the experiences of a woman who is a marginal presence within the cityscape of London. Inside the home those in service were invisible in a number of ways. Firstly, they were closeted away in particular parts of the house – below stairs or in the attic. When at work in the parts of the home inhabited by the family, tasks were either carried out before the rooms were occupied by family and visitors, such as lighting the fires, or if in attendance on the household, there were strict codes of dress, behaviour and etiquette to ensure that servants blended into the background as much as possible. Here invisibility is achieved via ceaseless adherence to strict codes associated with the role within the home, which controls everything from dress and behaviour to bodily comportment and movement within the spaces of the household. The servant's marginality is maintained through the mores set down and upheld by Victorian society.

Crucially, however, when Hannah Cullwick steps outside the domain of the household in which she works, her invisibility is secured by transgressing societal convention and specifically gendered conventions. Hannah goes out into the cityscape begrimed from her work and as a consequence is unseen as she moves about London. As Liz Stanley explains:

> Hannah, who indeed described herself as 'not a woman' ... goes out alone to public houses late at night, walks through crowds of drunken men without fear, wanders at night across fields and waste ground, and all without molestation or harassment. It would be a mistake to see her as atypical in this. Hannah and the other women who lived lives like hers avoided at least some aspects of Victorian notions of femininity.[19]

The dirt masks her, unsexes her, and as a consequence affords her to move about the city unseen – a marginal presence. Hannah becomes invisible by subverting traditional representations of femininity.

While Hannah was able to achieve freedom within the cityscape through transgression of Victorian mores (and, as Stanley suggests, so too were many other women), their role in service was an acceptable form of employment. There were other roles which women undertook, however, which were seen as a transgression in themselves. Salome Hocking's novella *Norah Lang: The Mine Girl* charts the fortunes of a working-class woman who must earn money to support her family, most specifically her invalid sister who is neglected by their lazy stepmother. Norah works firstly as a balmaiden (female surface worker) at the local mine and then as a field labourer. While these forms of rural work were carried out by many women in Cornwall and beyond, they were not seen as an acceptable form of labour for women.

This belief needs to be understood in relation to the increasing saliency of separate spheres ideology which, as well as gendering the public space of work as masculine, more generally associated physical work with masculinity. Mine labouring was not domestic work and it did not take place within the private sphere of the home. There was concern that working alongside men, and at such physical manual labour, would morally corrupt these young female workers and make them unfit for their future domestic role within the family home. For example, Richard Ayton, upon visiting a colliery in 1813, believed that the women working there 'lose every quality that is graceful in women, and become a set of coarse, licentious wretches, scorning all kinds of restraint and yielding themselves up, with shameless audacity, to the most detestable sensuality'.[20] Ayton's comments refer to the pit brow lasses of the north of England but the balmaiden was characterized in exactly the same way.[21]

Similarly, Roger Ebbatson points out that women's field labour was discouraged, by the Agricultural Labourers' Union, for example, which, in any case, did not allow female membership.[22] Often, however, there was little choice when an income was desperately needed (and it is also not necessarily the case that women disliked this type of work). In *Norah Lang* the young protagonist is keenly aware 'that by being a mine girl she should fall in the estimation of a certain class of people', and when the St George Mine closes she feels she has no choice but to turn to field work.[23] The suggestion here is that this attitude towards the female worker comes not from her working-class community but from the upper classes, which fits with the origination and promotion of separate spheres ideology as well as the top-down regulation of women's work by government. Significantly, *Norah Lang*, as one of only a few known literary representations of the balmaiden, writes against this social attitude towards the female worker through its depiction of Norah at the moral centre of the text.

The narrative of both the balmaiden and the female field worker is, like Hannah Cullwick's, one of invisibility and visibility, but in very different ways. Historically, they are largely invisible due to the lack of records and personal accounts. Ebbatson argues that 'women field labourers possessed virtually no voice of their own' and this can equally be applied to balmaidens.[24] While more recent studies are starting to uncover these women's lives, there remains a lack of Hannah Cullwicks telling their own story, at least from what we know at the moment. However, while historically invisible, both balmaiden and field worker are, due to the outdoor nature of their work and the reasons discussed above, what Katrina Honeyman calls 'painfully visible'.[25] These women were transgressing the mores of femininity through the physicality of their work, which required unconventional movement of the body, swinging axes or hammers for example, and they did so in the open countryside where they could be seen easily. This was a far cry from the closeted nature of domestic work and the regimentation it exerted on the female body within controlled spaces.

In *Norah Lang*, Hocking emphasizes the visibility of Norah but in a way that counters rather than compounds the prevailing Victorian attitude to working women. It is in the turnip-picking scene that Norah is most visible as a female worker. The reader is told that: 'The biting east wind continued for a while week and as Norah stood out in the field each morning, taking up the turnips and scraping the earth from them, the wind seemed to chill the marrow in her bones.'[26] Firstly, note Hocking's use of the words 'stood out'. Norah stands out in the expanse of the field and her physicality is accentuated by the reference to her bones. She is connected to the landscape both by her actions – scraping the earth – and by the effect of the chilling wind, which is internalized, reaching the core of her body. There is a focus here on her embodiment, extant in the landscape, but also on the effect of that environment on the body. She is painfully visible here not in terms of unease with her visibility but rather due to the physical pain caused by exposure in a vast expanse of landscape.

We can compare this scene in Hocking's novel to that of Tess and Marion turnip-picking at Flintcomb-Ash in Thomas Hardy's *Tess of the D'Urbervilles*, which was published five years after *Norah Lang*. Like Hocking, Hardy does not take issue with the visibility of the female worker and makes her the central focus of the narrative. He stresses the bleak expanse of land and its exposed aspect, describing 'a stretch of a hundred odd acres ... on the highest ground of the farm'. Tess and Marion's insignificance is conveyed by depicting their diminutiveness within the vast panorama: they are portrayed as 'crawling over the surface ... like flies'. Yet they are still visible; Marion is 'the single fat thing on the soil'. Here once again the painful visibility is emphasized in terms of bodily pain through exposure to the unforgiving environment. These two women can only scuttle across the surface of the landscape, struggling to penetrate the earth to release the stubborn turnip but, just like Hocking's description of Norah, this environment penetrates their bodies: the rain 'sticking into them like glass splinters' and the cold which 'chilled the eyeballs of the twain, made their brows ache, penetrated to their skeletons, affecting the surface of the body less than its core'.[27] Embodiment is emphasized here by the heightened tangibility of the effects of the environment on the interior of the female human form.

In Hannah Cullwick's diaries and in Hocking's and Hardy's fictional representations of the female worker, we have a specific experience of landscape which is classed, gendered and historically contingent and so such a perspective can help us to understand and view space and place as fluid, multiple and socially constructed. The bodies of these women in space do, as Massey asserts, 'raise all sorts of questions about the place they occupy' because their presence, their movement and their role is always resisting or complying with socially produced codes and so a social context from which it is impossible to extricate oneself.[28]

Perambulation and pain: Emma Smith's *A Cornish Waif's Story*

In *A Cornish Waif's Story* Emma Smith is put to work within the Cornish landscape in a similarly punishing but very different way. Republished in 2010, this autobiography begins in the last decade of the nineteenth century and describes Emma's childhood in and out of the workhouse between stints at her grandparents' home in Redruth. When handed back to her mother in Plymouth she is sold summarily to an organ grinder and his wife, and condemned to traipse the Cornish roads. It is a life that we are hardly able to imagine such are the 'appalling adversities' that this young girl (real name Mabel Lewis) faces.[29] She is abused by her 'owner' Mr Pratt and is reliant on the mercy of pitying women she comes across on her travels to provide her with clothes and shoes. This sad and harrowing narrative is related with simplicity and acceptance of what she had to endure. In his introduction to the 2010 edition Simon Parker calls it 'perhaps the most authentic account of late-Victorian child abuse and suffering since Dickens' *A Walk in the Workhouse*'.[30] This is clearly, therefore, a narrative of a working-class life and Emma's experience of the landscape, like that of Hannah, Norah and Tess above, is tied to and constructed by her class position, the role she must perform within it, and the specific historical moment in which she exists.

Given the context of the discussion so far, it is perhaps astounding that Emma's form of employment was not similarly viewed with disgust and profound unease, yet the sole purpose for which she has been employed by the Pratts is to be visible at the points on the journey where they stop, outside houses and in towns, to play the hurdy-gurdy machine. She 'would run and pick up pennies that dropped from windows' and later sing well-known hymns and tunes alongside the organ.[31] The intention was to use the child to invite pity from the audience and so educe greater donations. This was not a gender specific role as Charlie, Emma's predecessor, had been made to do exactly the same before running away from the Pratts' 'employ', but an age specific occupation which could only be effective by playing on a combination of poverty and youth, and which suggested to donors an essential itinerancy out-of-doors which is contrasted with the secure home within which these penny droppers were ensconced.

Unsurprisingly, Emma's relationship to that perpetual exterior environment through which she vainly trudges is dominated and determined by the role she is forced to play. Significantly, as for Norah and for Tess and Marion, her connection to the surrounding environment is made and mediated by the effect which it has on the interiority of the body. For Emma this is most specifically the excruciating pain caused by walking, in just stockings or in ill-fitting shoes donated by pitying mother figures. There are repeated references to 'blistered heels' and the extent of the discomfort this causes, sometimes to the point of laming her.[32] She notes that 'particularly did I suffer from sticky ragged stockings which were never washed or mended. I would have to pull the toes down under the foot further and further in my efforts to get some covering for my heels, which all the time I was with the Pratts suffered from a succession of blisters'.[33] Mrs Pratt's only duty of care other than occasionally wiping her face is 'pricking blisters' and on one return journey from Mousehole to Penzance Emma is unable to walk any further and they must bed down in a farmer's barn.[34] Emma's connection with the landscape then is registered by movement through it and by the resulting effects of this movement which penetrates her body through her nervous system and tattoos itself on her skin.

Emma's endless trudge through the landscape is punctuated by rare moments when her pain is eased and her hunger satiated due to the charity of momentary acquaintances. On one occasion in St. Just a woman supplies her with shoes and clean stockings and Emma believes that 'how good those stockings felt on me nobody could appreciate unless they had been in similar circumstances'.[35] Later a farmer's wife asks to 'tend the poor soul's little feet'.[36] Moments of pure joy are primarily derived from proffered victuals – in Newlyn a sweet-shop owner hands Emma some Kruger's Whiskers (she explains to the reader that these are 'little shreds of cocoa-nut sweetened and coloured brown with chocolate'). These 'sweetmeat[s]' were once enjoyed by Emma in her grandmother's home and so the connection heightens the pleasure and her grateful wonderment at being given something she had 'desired most at that moment'.[37]

Somewhat surprisingly, when yet another tramp is in the offing Emma is able to suppress memories of 'blistered heels and the like' and look forward to 'cottage gardens, glasses of skimmed milk, slices of cake, raw turnips in the fields, animals and birds of the farmyard'.[38] While once again food seems to dominate her understanding of pleasure, there is also consideration here of the landscape through which she will be travelling. This seems understandable given the proportion of her formative years spent out-of-doors traversing the roads of Cornwall. There are snippets where Emma contemplates and relates to the landscape and seascape around her. For example, in expressing her love for St. Ives she comments that 'the waves would speak to me; they seemed full of messages', and again about a St. Just visit she remembers singing 'before the row of cottages so near to the beach, the lap lap, of the waves on the shingle would mingle with our voices as we sang the old hymns that these people loved'. She finds the landscape around her 'exhilarating'.[39]

Yet, crucially, such emphasis on her surroundings is rare in the course of her childhood reminiscences. Ultimately, pain always intercedes in her relationship with the space around her, thus determining the way in which it is produced and re-imagined through memory and fixing her in a reality which suppresses reverie. The moment of equanimity at St Just is only conceivable 'before the blisters got bad'. Later that day 'there would be a walk through the woods' where Emma is once again drawn to contemplate nature. She muses about 'the moon chasing clouds overhead; then the loud hoot of an owl, then another' and declares that 'all these things thrilled me' but the moment can only act as a fleeting escape as she tells us that '[t]hen Pratt would spoil it all – after which, all I would be conscious of were my sore feet and my misery'.[40] Here both physical and emotional pain takes over and the surrounding environment recedes.

It is a situation which Emma herself is aware of. At the point at which she runs away from her torturous life with the Pratts she comments 'I left the village behind; it looked very lonely under its mantle of snow, but I have no eye just then for beauty; I was too much concerned with my knawing appetite'.[41] There is a personification of the village here and an empathic connection with it through imagining its loneliness, but the ultimate barrier which severs that connection is the pain of hunger. When Emma is able to commune with her surrounding environment that experience is heightened due to its contract with the bleakness and misery of her everyday existence. But that moment of enjoyment is as transient as her position within the landscape.

Landscape, class and gender: Charles Lee's *Cynthia in the West*

While Emma's relationship to the Cornish landscape is mediated by pain and hardship, Charles Lee's novel *Cynthia in the West* depicts the lives of an artist colony whose very purpose is to muse upon that same landscape and capture it on canvas. Published in 1900 and set in the fictional seaside village of Tregurda, the novel explores the complex relationship between artists and locals. The story is told from the perspective of Robert Maurice who arrives in Tregurda to join a colony of London artists who have made it their home for the summer. There are a number of parallels that can be drawn between

Robert, a Londoner who, although not an artist himself, comes to join and socialize with an artist colony in Cornwall, and his author. Lee too spent time in St. Ives 'rubbing shoulders with men whose fame as artists is now secure: Stanhope Forbes, Frank Bramley, Walter Langley and "Lamorna" Birch'.[42] What Lee produces as a result of his own detailed observations is a novel in which landscape within a particular moment in Cornish history is a nexus of class and gender relations.

Like mining, the Cornish fishing industry met with its own crisis in the late nineteenth century, so that by the early twentieth century it was not operating on a scale large enough to warrant classification as a principal industry. However, its fall from grace was more gradual than the collapse of mining. Therefore, from the 1880s onwards, there evolves what Deacon suggests are two communities and two cultures: the middle-class artist community and the working-class fishing community, separate artistic and industrial cultures that are operating simultaneously, jostling within the same space.[43]

In Lee's novel these two groups and their innate distinctions are clearly defined. The locals make their living from the sea and so their fortunes are inextricably tied to it. The 'close-huddled' houses of the village are arranged 'amphitheatrically' around the sea, beach and harbour – the sites of their labour.[44] The artists are incomers, temporary settlers whose work is to create art inspired by the Cornish landscape. The majority of the group actually do very little and spend most of their time in repose, contemplating their work, or finding ways to justify diversions from it. There are two spaces in the novel where the two groups meet – the beach and the artists' studios (former fish cellars) – which are the separate sites of their separate industries. The denouement sees both groups putting aside previous differences and gathering together on the beach to witness the rescue of a painter and a fisherman, and in the artists' studios locals adapt to their change of function by posing as models. There is, therefore, some accommodation (sometimes for monetary gain) by the local population of the artists, and some are prepared to adapt to the changing times. Mr Blewett in particular makes himself indispensable to the artists by providing services such as cleaning brushes and stretching canvases, and his daughter Nelly poses for Mr Forester's painting.

However, despite the rather convenient happy ending, which ties up all loose ends by uniting both groups in the face of possible tragedy, much of the novel registers the impossibility of complete assimilation due to the distinct separateness of the two groups. This is reflected in the instinctive reactions on both sides when a scandal that breaks in the village divides them in support of two opposing women. Mrs Wilmington calls the locals 'savages' and a local man declares "tis time for 'em [the artists] to clear out and leave we in peace'.[45] There is a sense that under the surface of any interaction are these indelibly opposed positions.

Lee's novel documents this complex relationship by demonstrating that the inherent divisions between the two groups are derived from their class positions. At the centre of these overlapping cultures is landscape, and the divergent positions both within and in relationship to that landscape experienced by the two groups. For the artist colony, the position of Mrs Wilimington's home (she is the matriarch and conductor of their 'social orchestra' as Otto Trist puts it) is representative of their position in relation to the landscape.[46] The house sits aloof from the village. En-route to the house for another evening soirée, Jack Gibbs and Maurice 'left the village behind [as they] quitted the main road' to reach it.[47] The house is therefore separate from the rest of Tregurda, walled off from its surroundings and in such a way that it looks down upon the rest of the village. The colony assemble at the stone balustrade at the bottom of Mrs Wilmington's garden from which they can survey the village below and, for some of the group, this position matches their own sense of superiority over the local population. Maurice, for example, notes Mrs Wilmington's condescension towards the locals in her 'genial patronage of "our friends below"', and Jack Gibbs rages that the 'boorish ... rustics' have 'no notion of treating their betters with proper respect'.[48] The artists maintain a distanced or prospect view of both the landscape and its inhabitants.

Inside the precincts of Mrs Wilmington's home there is a distinct contrast to its surroundings – this is Mrs Wilmington's world and it is completely under her control. The garden is manicured, nature is made to fit its owner's design as 'holly bushes and yew, [are] clipped and tended into formal shapes of sphere and pyramid'.[49] This environment resists and refuses to adapt to the world beyond its boundaries. Otto Trist notes that women such as Mrs Wilmington 'don't seem to be able to adapt themselves to their environment. They carry their accustomed social atmosphere about with them.'[50] Mrs Wilmington steers her guests in socialisation and conversation as if she is conducting an orchestra and she does so within a world which she has created, transplanted from London drawing rooms, and which she controls.

We can connect the positioning and characterisation of the Wilmington abode with the relationship of the artist colony to their surrounding environment. The act of painting, like Mrs Wilmington's act of creating her insular world, requires an organisation, control and delimitation of the Cornish landscape. As Sara Mills comments, 'within Western culture, the pictorial tradition represented landscape as something to be confronted and as something exterior to oneself rather than as something that is the source of one's livelihood'.[51] Mills stresses the positioning of the artist in relation to landscape as one of confrontation, suggesting a requirement to dominate and therefore control that landscape through the act of painting.

For some members of the Tregurda artist colony the possibility of exercising such control is never in question. For example, the narrative perspective mocks Jack Gibbs' 'firm conviction that Nature's lovely secret could be stolen from her by means of the cunning devices of the Paris *ateliers*, or forcibly wrested with the help of the newest engines of warfare in the shape of easels of complicated mechanism'.[52] Again the language is one which suggests confrontation, the artist's tools are weapons in a battle with landscape in order to subdue it via its immuration on the canvas. Similarly, on a day out cycling in the Cornish countryside, the colony bid Mrs Wilmington to allow them to linger a little longer in order to 'wait for the effect' of a beautiful sunset across the sea. Maurice's response is that 'the phrase … was characteristic of the colony, magnificently conceiving Nature as a spectacle marshalled for their exclusive gratification'.[53] The narrative perspective, taking advantage of Maurice's degree of separation from the group as a non-artist, certainly does not accept their ability to exert such control and mocks their hubris.

Despite overtures of doing battle with or controlling the landscape, the artists are only ever ultimately observers of it, just as Maurice is only an observer of them. Significantly, the act of painting, that process by which they could become more intricately connected to their surroundings, almost always takes place behind the closed doors of their studios, cut off from a prospect of the very landscape they are supposed to be evoking through artistic endeavour. It is only Cynthia who chooses to paint whilst surrounded by her subject matter. Like Cynthia, Mrs Wilmington paints flowers but hers are only those 'arranged in a pretty bouquet in a Japanese vase on a polished table, with a Liberty cretonne for background'.[54] Her control of the spaces she inhabits and of the natural environment is extended here to her art, which begs the question as to why she came to Cornwall to paint at all!

The presumption of the colony members that they can control the environment around them through the production of art is contrasted with the experience of the local population. For the fishermen and their families, the unpredictability of the sea governs their lives. When a catch of pilchards is landed on the beach one evening the locals rejoice that 'there would be bread and fish in the children's mouths all the winter' because this had by no means been a certainty.[55] Living with the capriciousness of the sea over which they can exert no dominion is most vividly registered in the text via the fisherwoman's clock which, when her husband is at sea she imagines predicting 'Wife, widow; wife, widow – over and over again'.[56] They are fully aware that they live their lives at the mercy of their environment.

Crucially, one member of the artist colony recognizes and vocalizes the inherent differences between the two groups in relation to landscape. Forester is a fascinating character in Lee's novel because he is a local artist who has made it in London and so he has an understanding of and affinity with both the artists and the local fishermen. He is the only character to successfully exist within both cultures, as will be demonstrated a little later. Forester 'vehemently' defends the locals in the face of Mrs Wilmington's withering admonishment of them and their lack of aesthetics, affirming that '[t]hey have no time to sit and look at Nature. Their life is one long fight with her.' Mr Wilmington agrees and muses that '[a]rt does in a way set the artist outside nature. He is doomed to be a spectator. These people are a part of it; they are in the thick of the fight, and have no time to look about them and collect impressions.'[57] This is the fundamental difference between the locals and the artists in their relationship to landscape.

That relationship is mediated by both class and gender, and it is in the chapter entitled 'On the Beach' where the full complexity of this nexus is realized. On an evening when the London set are gathered at a Wilmington soirée, they are invited by local man Mr Blewett to witness the bringing in of a pilchard catch on the beach below. It is during this scene, while both tribes occupy the space of the beach, that they are most notably contrasted. The passivity of artists who are 'shepherded' onto a 'little eminence' by Mr Blewett, from which they view events, is countered by the activity of the local population. 'A stream of people' come and go from the village shop, carrying 'slabs of salt' in which the pilchards will be preserved. The onlookers witness the following: 'A boat was hauled up past them, a dozen men clinging about its sides. One in front had a rope from the stem over his shoulder, and was tugging with his face nearly to the ground.' Lee emphasizes both the number of men under task on the beach and the intensity of their labour, carried out with an acute sense of urgency. He explains that, 'men rested, panting, and were summoned to fresh exertions before breath returned to them'. Meanwhile:

> The pictorial possibilities of the scene were discussed amongst the group [of artists]. Such talk at such a time completed their isolation. … One man held his lantern high in the air, and the two parties surveyed each other curiously. The contrast – the essential contrast of Tregurda – flashed before one.[58]

The female observers, inappropriately dressed, 'shiver in their thin dresses' and 'vowed it interesting – very interesting, and picturesque, and interminable; and wasn't it time to be moving back?'[59] Their viewpoint remains a purely aesthetic one. They can only consider the pictorial quality of the scene of which they are idle observers, while the locals rejoice amidst their toil, for the catch guarantees food for their families over the winter. However, while the contrast is clear to the reader and the narrator, the only member of the colony to appraise their position is Robert. Robert is affected by contemplation of his own inactivity in relation to the fisherman:

> The thick darkness shut in the scene with its moving lights and figures; the insistent roar of the sea filled the air like a tangible presence; and somehow, in the darkness and uproar, the business of grievous muscular toil took majestic proportions in Maurice's eyes. The men loomed bigger, grew Titanic in their struggle for the few shining fish. He was ready to doubt the existence of a world beyond this world in brief, with its toilers and lookers on. They were adrift together on dark space. And it was hard to stand idle in the midst of violent exertion; he was angry with his weedy frame and underdeveloped muscles; he was man incomplete and degenerate; the desire obsessed him to tug at ropes, to feel his sinews crack, to taste the delicious pain of physical fatigue.[60]

Mrs Wilmington's assumption of her superiority over the locals is engrained, but Robert is made to feel inferior through his idleness but also, crucially, his physical deficiency which prevents him from being active in the same way as the fishermen. For Robert, masculinity is clearly still defined by physical strength, which the local men demonstrate, rather than the intellectual or artistic ability of the set to which he belongs.

The separation of the two groups on the beach is contravened, however, by Mr Forester who steps forward to help when an over-laden boat gets stuck in the sand. Forester has been part of Mrs Wilmington's social set that evening. But, as noted above, he is a local artist rather than a London artist or a local fisherman. His help is accepted by the fishermen, but they express genuine concern that he will ruin his fine clothes. He is local, but not like them, and his clothes distinguish him. After his effort his clothes do indeed sport a 'black, tarry line', and one fisherman comments: "'He's branded! ... You'm one of us – a proper Cornish fisherman, sure 'nough!'"[61] His clothing registers his masculine toil, and his masculinity is enhanced by the dirt. Despite their fineness, his clothes also identify him as a local man and make him accepted as such. In contrast, when socialite Jack Gibbs joins in, fired by Forester's foray into the scene, he is summarily rejected and 'gently but firmly pushed aside' for fear he will 'get hurted'.[62] For the local fishermen, the gender roles and class positions between each set are as clearly defined as they are for Mrs Wilmington. Jack Gibbs does not embody the masculinity required for the task at hand and so his intervention is rejected and, apart from Forester, the boundaries of the two groups, set in relation to landscape by social rules of class and gender, remain intact, more indelibly drawn even, after the coming together on the beach. Yet the significance of Forester's intermediary position should not be overlooked. Crucially, also, the space has been socially constructed through the jostling of these two separate cultures, which relate to landscape in so very different ways. As Massey has said, 'place here is interpreted as the intersection of sets of social relations which are stretched over particular spaces'.[63]

Concluding thoughts

This article has attempted to examine and provide a 'picture of rural space as dynamic and varied', and to adopt a perspective that enables a consideration of 'how regimes of gender and class intersect, change and ramify in the context of rurality'.[64] There are 'complementary and overlapping' as well as competing 'Cornwalls' put forward by these texts which are classed, gendered and historically contingent, and which impact on how space is socially constructed as well as the meaning or significance of bodies within that space.[65] Perspectives afforded by such areas of research as Feminist Geography suggest the full complexity of the multiple Cornwalls first identified by Deacon over ten years ago, as well as the nuanced relations between these concepts of place within a social, historical and cultural context, hinting at some of the possibilities ahead during the next twenty years of New Cornish Studies.

Notes and references

1. P. Payton, 'Introduction' to P. Payton (ed.), *Cornish Studies: Sixteen* (Exeter, 2008), pp. 1–17.
2. Ibid., p. 3.
3. B. Deacon, 'In Search of the Missing "Turn": The Spatial Dimension and Cornish Studies' in P. Payton (ed.), *Cornish Studies: Eight* (Exeter, 2000), pp. 213–30.
4. B. Deacon, 'Mining the Data: What Can a Quantitative Approach Tell us about the Micro-geography Nineteenth-century Cornish Mining?' in P. Payton (ed.), *Cornish Studies: Eighteen* (Exeter, 2010), pp. 15–32.
5 Ibid., p. 2.
6. B. Deacon, 'The New Cornish Studies: New Discipline or Rhetorically Defined Space?' in P. Payton (ed.), *Cornish Studies: Ten* (Exeter, 2002), pp. 24–43.
7. S. Hall, 'New Ethnicities' in D. Lodge and N. Wood (eds), *Modern Criticism and Theory* (3rd edition, Harlow, 2008), pp. 581–92.
8. S. Hocking, *Norah Lang: The Mine Girl* (London, [1886]); E. Smith, *A Cornish Waif's Story: An Autobiography* ([London], 1954; repr. St Agnes, 2010); C. Lee, *Cynthia in the West* (London, 1900).

9. Those texts are: G. Rose, *Feminism and Geography: The Limits of Geographical Knowledge* (Cambridge, 1993), D. Massey, *Space, Place and Gender* (Cambridge, 1994); L. McDowell, *Gender, Identity and Place: Understanding Feminist Geographies* (Cambridge, 1999).

10. Ibid., p. 12.

11. Ibid., pp. 24, 40.

12. Quoted in Women and Geography Study Group, *Feminist Geographies: Exploration in Diversity and Difference* (London, 1997), p. 8.

13. Quoted in S. Mills, *Gender and Colonial Space* (Manchester, 2005), p. 24.

14. Ibid., p. 196.

15. L. McDowell, *Capital Culture: Gender at Work in the City* (Oxford, 1997); D. Parsons, *Streetwalking the Metropolis: Women, the City and Modernity* (Oxford, 2000).

16. See, for example, the types of articles which appear in the journal *Gender, Place and Culture: A Journal of Feminist Geography*.

17. P. G. Barber, M. Marchand and J. Parpart, 'Series Editors' Preface' to B. Pini and B. Leach (ed.), *Reshaping Gender and Class in Rural Spaces* (Farnham, 2011), p. xv.

18. Ibid., p. 1.

19. L. Stanley, 'Introduction' to L. Stanley (ed.), *The Diaries of Hannah Cullwick, Victorian Maidservant* (London, 1984), p. 4.

20. Quoted in A. V. John, *By the Sweat of Their Brow: Women Workers at Victorian Coal Mines* (London: 1984), p. 31.

21. For reactions to the balmaiden see L. Mayers, *Balmaidens* (Penzance, 2004).

22. R. Ebbatson, 'Women in the Field'. This paper has not yet been published but is due to be included in a forthcoming collection entitled *Rural Geographies of Gender and Space: Britain 1840–1920* edited by C. Mathieson and G. Goodman.

23. Ibid., p. 13.

24. Ibid., n.p.

25. K. Honeyman, *Women, Gender and Industrialisation in England, 1700–1870* (London, 2000).

26. Ibid., p. 102.

27. T. Hardy, *Tess of the D'Urbervilles: A Pure Woman* (n.p, 1891; repr. London, 1978), pp. 360–61.

28. Ibid., p. 40.

29. Stated on back cover of this edition Smith, *A Cornish Waif's Story*.

30. S. Parker, 'Introduction (2010)' to Smith, *A Cornish Waif's Story*.

31. Ibid., p. 25.

32. Ibid., p. 69.

33. Ibid., pp. 34–35

34. Ibid., p. 80.

35. Ibid., p. 36.

36. Ibid., p. 80.

37. Ibid., p. 31.

38. Ibid., p. 69.

39. Ibid., pp. 73–74.

40. Ibid., p. 74.

41. Ibid., p. 94.

42. K. C. Phillipps, 'Introduction' to K. C. Phillipps (ed.), *The Cornish Journal of Charles Lee* (Padstow, 1995), p. xv.
43. B. Deacon, 'Imagining the Fishing: Artists and Fishermen in Late Nineteenth Century Cornwall', *Rural History* 12.2 (2001), pp. 159–78.
44. Ibid., p. 16.
45. Ibid., pp. 263–72.
46. Ibid., p. 39.
47. Ibid., p. 33.
48. Ibid., pp. 45 & 24.
49. Ibid., p. 52.
50. Ibid., p. 39.
51. Ibid., p. 73.
52. Ibid., pp. 136–37.
53. Ibid., p. 212.
54. Ibid., p. 31.
55. Ibid., p. 154.
56. Ibid., p. 126.
57. Ibid., pp. 118–19.
58. Ibid., pp. 154–58.
59. Ibid., p. 163.
60. Ibid., pp. 156–57.
61. Ibid., p. 162.
62. Ibid., p. 160.
63. Quoted in Women and Geography Study Group, *Feminist Geographies*, p. 8.
64. Barber, Marchand and Parpart, 'Series Editors' Preface', p. xv.
65. B. Deacon, 'From "Cornish Studies" to "Critical Cornish Studies": Reflections of Methodology' in P. Payton (ed.), *Cornish Studies: Twelve* (Exeter, 2004), pp. 12–29.

9

Cornish-Australian identity and the novels of Rosanne Hawke

Emma Bennett

Introduction

Walter McVitty has noted that 'There is more to Australia than "sun, sand and surf and Crocodile Dundee", as many tourists visiting the country have discovered.'[1] One of the numerous surprises for visitors 'down under' is the strong state of publishing and fiction in Australia, in particular the thriving world of children's literature. As Peter Hunt observed in 2001, a recent 'study by the Australia Council found that of all the books bought in Australia, 30 per cent were children's books, and 30 per cent of those were Australian'.[2] Likewise, over the last forty years, books from Australia – as well as New Zealand and Canada – have increased their visibility, appeal and influence in the children's literature markets of both the USA and UK, impressing their overseas audiences with world-class authors and high-quality production values, and stimulating strong academic and public awareness of their significance. Nationally and internationally, then, children's literature is an important sector of the Australian publishing industry.

Although, as Felicity Hughes has noted, children's literature is often seen as merely a branch of popular fiction, it is in reality a complex and multifaceted genre, often hard to categorize and pin down.[3] Indeed, as Hunt has added, 'one of the delights of children's literature is that it does not fit easily into any cultural or academic category'.[4] For example, many books written ostensibly for children and young people turn out to be also popular with not-so-young adults. Scholars of children's literature have long argued that a 'good book for children is a good book for people of any age', and

Hunt considers that 'children's literature is a remarkable area of writing ... enjoyed passionately by adults as well as children'.[5] However, this blurring of generational boundaries ensures that children's literature is an ideological minefield. As Hunt explains, children's literature engages powerfully and in subtly different ways with an extremely wide and complex readership across the generational spectrum: 'it absorbs, it possesses and it inspires'.[6]

Multiculturalism and Rosanne Hawke

As McVitty has emphasized, 'Australians in general are predisposed favourably towards books and reading',[7] and the inter-generational appeal of children's literature is as apparent in Australia as it is elsewhere. Like Australian fiction generally, children's literature in Australia reflects the 'Anglo-Celtic tradition' – the preoccupations of the wider English-speaking world – but it often exhibits a specifically Australian dimension. There are, as McVitty has explained, distinctively Australian books about 'definite Australian subjects', written by 'Australian born authors for Australian readers'.[8] Alongside the commonplace 'Anglo-Celtic' themes of children's literature – love, shipwrecks, kidnapping, growing up into the adult world, and so on – there is often a tightly bound 'Australian-ness' threaded through the stories of Australian children's fiction.

Historically, Australian children's fiction has often been situated in 'the bush', the rural setting providing that distinctive quality of 'Australian-ness'. Here, as Pemell argues, is 'an Australian landscape that is ... portrayed as either inherently idyllic and awaiting appropriation or inherently hostile and a prevalent threat'.[9] Although, over the past forty years or so, there has been a partial shift away from the 'bush' to more varied settings, the Australian rural landscape remains significant as a 'historical fact' – the 'bush' as quintessentially Australian – around which many children's stories continue to be woven. Australian literary critics have not been slow to recognize the cultural implications of such assumptions. Hunt has warned that 'literature [can be used] as a weapon of "assimilation"', a means by which a 'dominant' culture can speak to and thus subvert or absorb minority identities.[10]

Although assimilation was once the declared aim of Australian immigration policy, the emergence of a 'multicultural' Australia in the decades since the Second World War has led to a greater appreciation of the importance of cultural diversity in moulding contemporary 'Australian-ness'. This growing emphasis on diversity has been reflected in turn in the 'multicultural' themes found increasingly in Australian children's literature – not least in the novels of Rosanne Hawke. An important figure in the buoyant world of Australian children's literature, Rosanne Hawke has pioneered multicultural approaches in her writing for young people. Having worked as a teacher in Pakistan and the United Arab Emirates, for example, she has tackled themes relating to Islam. But her primary self-ascription is 'Cornish-Australian', and it is this hybrid personal identity that has influenced so much of her writing and is the subject of this article. In particular, this article focuses on five of Rosanne Hawke's principal novels – *Zenna Dare*, *Across the Creek*, *Wolfchild*, *The Last Virgin in Year Ten*, and *Sailmaker* – and seeks to investigate the ways she has used 'Cornwall', the 'Cornish' and 'Cornishness' to develop stories that often have decidedly Australian settings.

Rosanne Hawke as 'Cornish-Australian'

Rosanne Hawke is herself of Cornish descent, a fourth generation Cornish-Australian whose family came from the Camborne-Redruth area of Cornwall to work at the Burra Burra copper mine in South Australia in the 1850s, and it is apparent that she is extremely proud of this heritage. 'Hawke' is her married name, a surname common in Cornwall (and South Australia), but her maiden name was the even more resoundingly Cornish 'Trevilyon'. When she was initiated as a bard of the Cornish Gorsedd, Rosanne Hawke took the Cornish-language bardic name *Myrgh Trevelyan* (Daughter of Trevelyan). Today she lives and works near Kapunda – another of South Australia's early mining towns – 'in an old Cornish farmhouse', and writes and lectures on Kapunda's Cornish identity.[11]

To put Rosanne Hawke's own 'Cornish-Australian' identity in context, it is important to appreciate the extent of the Cornish Diaspora in Australia, particularly South Australia. As Oswald Pryor recalled: "'Wherever there's a hole in the ground," runs an old saying, "you'll find a Cousin Jack at the bottom of it, searching for metal."'[12] The discovery of copper at Kapunda in 1843–44 led to the opening of mines very much like the one at the centre of Rosanne's story *Across the Creek*. Copper was likewise discovered at Burra Burra in 1845 and precipitated a large-scale Cornish emigration to South Australia, including Rosanne Hawke's own forebears, and around those two mining towns – Kapunda and Burra Burra – grew communities which exhibited all the signs of a distinct Cornish identity.

Philip Payton writes that in the years between 1836 and 1840, 'some ten per cent of all applications for assisted passage [to South Australia] were lodged in Cornwall, establishing a pattern which by the end of the century had ensured that perhaps as much as ten per cent, maybe more, of South Australia's population (about 35,000 people) were of Cornish birth or direct descent'.[13] As well as their mining skills, the Cornish emigrants brought their culture and way of life with them, and formed tight-knit communities. South

Australia remained a major destination for Cornish emigrants for much of the middle and second half of the nineteenth century. Payton indicates that:

> for example, in the period 1846–50 Cornwall was of all British counties far and away the most important source of South Australian settlers. Some 4,775 persons left Cornwall for the colony during those years, the next most significant county being Middlesex with a mere 1,412 immigrants. Indeed, 25 per cent of all emigrants from the United Kingdom to South Australia in this period were from Cornwall, establishing a significant and enduring link between the two areas.[14]

By the 1860s the early mining towns had been eclipsed as destinations for the emigrant Cornish by the newly-discovered copper mines of Moonta and Wallaroo on South Australia's northern Yorke Peninsula, an area soon known affectionately as 'Australia's Little Cornwall'. It was here that the Cornish gave full expression to what Payton has 'dubbed the "myth of Cousin Jack", the Cornishman having gone down in mining lore world-wide as the hard rock miner *par excellence*'.[15] In the early twentieth century the Yorke Peninsula mines experienced a new era of prosperity, especially during the Great War when the demand for copper was high, but in the period 1900 to 1936 South Australia's Cornish community was progressively assimilated into the mainstream of the State's life. Unsurprisingly, assimilation occurred more easily in the non-mining areas, while northern Yorke Peninsula clung with greater tenacity to its own regional identity.[16] Nonetheless, many individuals scattered throughout South Australia remained conscious of their families' Cornish origins, and the influence of the State's Cornish heritage continued to be reflected in many aspects of South Australian life. Today, in the early twenty-first century, there remains a vibrant Cornish Association of South Australia and the State's biennial 'Kernewek Lowender' claims to be the largest Cornish festival in the world.

Rosanne Hawke is one of the many contemporary South-Australian-born who remember their Cornish heritage and identify as 'Cornish-Australian',[17] a trend that, as Payton has remarked, is 'consistent with the Post-War Australian search for "roots" and historical identity'.[18] As Rosanne Hawke has acknowledged, the Cornish, with their distinctive characteristics, provide a strong basis for many of her novels, a source of rich historical material around which her stories can be built as well as responding to her enthusiasm for multicultural diversity. Indeed, she admits that a recurring theme throughout her novels is a fundamental human need for 'identity', for an individual to know who she or he is, and where they come from. She insists that it is vital for the self-development of young people that they should have an understanding of their own cultural background. Her own experience, she explains, reflects this: '[it] has been fascinating for me to research [my Cornish roots] especially since I have written several novels ... which have as a basic part of their genesis my growing awareness of Cornish heritage. Exploring my Cornishness in my writing has been satisfying to my own sense of cultural identity.'[19]

Exploring cultural identity

This was a theme Rosanne Hawke developed in her PhD thesis at the University of Adelaide, completed in 2005. Here she reiterated her belief that it 'is important to know one's cultural background', arguing that 'this helps with self-identity development, especially for young people'. She had noticed, she said, 'a cultural void in some Anglo-Australian students in ... my writing classes',[20] and this had reinforced her conviction that individuals should be made aware of their roots. In this way, Rosanne Hawke has used her novels to encourage young people to research their heritage and ethnic backgrounds, insisting that 'those less sure of who they are, in their psychological or cultural development, are more likely to express prejudiced attitudes towards others'.[21] As she concludes: 'We need to know something of our roots. Feeling secure about who we are enables us to respect and value others. So it seems a beneficial exercise to explore our own cultural identity.'[22]

Here Rosanne Hawke has been aided by the recent upsurge in genealogy in Australia. Many enthusiasts, not surprisingly, have found Cornish branches in their family trees, especially in South Australia. Although the figures are in dispute, the general consensus is that approximately 10 per cent of the population of South Australia, and 3 per cent of Australia as a whole, has a significant Cornish heritage. Rosanne Hawke believes the percentages may be considerably higher, however, and argues that 'if at least twenty per cent of South Australian young people have some Cornish background (though most may be unaware of it) then it is important to address this issue'.[23] As she puts it, it is imperative that 'individuals can understand their background and foster Cornishness as a matter of emotional wellbeing as a result of knowing and embracing their ethnic background'.[24]

As Rosanne Hawke is aware, there is evidence that such understanding is indeed growing in Australia. Commenting on the growth of family history research, she notes that academic writer Cheryl Hayden 'suggests Australians are becoming more interested in their Cornish heritage, in search for "authentic" roots that can provide the comfort of identity amid the confusion of a post modern world'.[25] Rosanne Hawke is also aware of a certain post-modern angst in Cornwall itself, with an increasing assertion of Cornish identity in many areas of contemporary Cornish life, not least through the political nationalist party Mebyon Kernow.[26] She likewise echoes Alan M. Kent's assertion that, 'for its relatively small size, Cornwall has been imagined and written about perhaps more than any other equivalent territory within Western Europe'.[27] She agrees that 'Cornwall certainly has an atmosphere that has lured many even from across the seas – du Maurier and Denys Val Baker call this the "Spirit of Cornwall"'.[28]

The 'Spirit of Cornwall' is a notion that Rosanne Hawke draws upon in her novels, subtly blending the 'magic' of Cornwall as she sees it – standing stones and ancient myths and legends – with the modernity of contemporary Australia. In this way, Cornwall and the Cornish become an important reservoir for her story-telling – and for conveying her ideological message to young and not-so-young readers that knowledge and understanding of one's identity is critical in the modern (or post-modern) multicultural world. Yet she recognises that in claiming 'Cornish-Australian' identity she and others can have an advantage over those in Cornwall who would also claim a distinct 'non-English' ethnicity. In Cornwall, such claims are often contested, with an insistence that Cornwall 'is in England'. In Australia, by contrast, as she notes, there is 'no stigma involved in "coming out" as Cornish'.[29] But she also recognizes that such hybridities – 'Cornish-American', Cornish-Canadian', 'Cornish-New Zealander', even 'Scillonian' – come with their own internal dynamics, alongside those of class, gender, religion, language and so on, adding to their potential richness as devices for story-telling.

However, despite the growing consciousness of 'Cornish-Australian' identity, and of Cornwall and the Cornish as a reservoir for story-telling, Rosanne Hawke is concerned that there are very few Australian novels for children and young people that draw upon this Cornish heritage. Authors have the literary ability to merge the boundaries between the empirical evidence of history and the flexible canvas of imaginative literature, so why is it, she asks, that the rich potential of Cornish-Australian heritage is barely touched upon? As she puts it: 'When one considers the number of titles showing, for example, the Irish identity in Australia, there is still a shortage of children's literature showing Cornish identity.'[30] Indeed, given the volume and intensity of Cornish emigration to Australia (and other parts of the world) in the nineteenth century, she argues, the emigration experience became part of Cornish-Australian identity and 'being a migrant became part of Cornish ethnicity'.[31] Moreover, given that the Cornish played such a founding role in South Australia, both economically and culturally, 'it would be shameful to "lose" this Cornish heritage through lack of written resources to access it'.[32] She adds that 'there are many young people in Australia who do not realise their Cornish heritage', and she sees it as her duty to address this deficiency. Rosanne Hawke's novels, then, have become a vehicle for perpetuating and disseminating Cornish cultural identity within the wider context of multicultural Australia. As Philip Payton notes: 'To be "Cornish" in South Australia … [is] not to draw boundaries between peoples but rather to celebrate one aspect of a felicitous diversity.'[33]

The novels

In her novel *Zenna Dare*, Rosanne Hawke confronts the complex issue of assuming a Cornish/Celtic identity in modern-day Australia. To some extent, the story and its main protagonist, Jenefer, reflect Rosanne Hawke's own experiences. As she admits, in Australia, 'once they know their Cornish ancestry, some [people of Cornish descent] take up Kernewek language study; they might even write narratives, making sense of their Cornish experience and how it fits in with their Australian identity, as I have done in *Zenna Dare*'.[34] The character Jenefer, it turns out, is a mirror of Rosanne Hawke, and *Zenna Dare* is to that extent autobiographical in nature. In the book's 'prelims', before the story begins, Rosanne Hawke offers a well-chosen quotation that sums up her own position: 'Being Australian isn't about how long you've lived here or what your parents look like; it's about a sense of belonging to the land.'[35] With this telling quote from Jeanette Wormald, the Australian singer-songwriter, Rosanne Hawke sets the tone for the entire book: that no matter what the situation on the outside, or what is going on around you, it is what is *inside* that matters to your sense of identity.

Zenna Dare is set in South Australia – at Kapunda, where Rosanne Hawke herself resides. The story begins with the protagonist, a young girl called Jenefer Tremayne, feeling displaced and lost as her family move home from the city to what she expects is an isolated and desolate country town. But on arrival Jenefer is pleasantly surprised. 'I have to admit,' she exclaims, 'Kapunda isn't as dry and dusty and derelict as I imagined',[36] a reaction that reflects the sentiments of those new arrivals from Cornwall a century and a half before. Jenefer has not moved that far, yet to her the journey is almost as great – psychologically and metaphorically – as the voyage that those from Cornwall undertook in the nineteenth century.

It transpires, as her surname suggests, that Jenefer is of Cornish descent, and the relocation to Kapunda proves more fruitful than she had expected. The affinity between Jenefer and her ancestors who sailed from Cornwall is revealed in various ways; for example, their shared belief in magical creatures. On one occasion, Jenefer hears noises in the house during the night, and the next day she asks her sister: 'Can you get me your storybook. The one Aunty Joy gave you about Celtic fairies and myths?'[37] Jenefer seems a little frightened as she asks this question, demonstrating that although she appears mature, she is still a child – an 'innocence' much like that of many of the miners' families who left Cornwall for Kapunda in times past. Jenefer continues with her investigation, and 'Then suddenly I see it. The fairy miners – the knockers. Knockers! This is it, I just know it. These are the sprites of the mines.'[38] The knockers are stereotypically Cornish creatures, and in making her discovery Jenefer is unwittingly affirming her Cornish heritage and claiming further affinity.

This affinity becomes more complex when Jenefer finds an old stage photograph of 'Miss Zenna Dare', the stage name of a young singer, Gweniver Rundle, who came from Camborne in Cornwall. Jenefer is immediately curious as to what Cornwall is all about, setting her further on the road to self-discovery. Intriguingly, Rosanne Hawke feels that the theme of Jenefer encountering her Cornish identity has been underestimated by reviewers: 'Maybe this is because she discovers so much else: a belonging to a rural area, a family secret and a relationship with an indigenous boy when she'd never met an indigenous person before.'[39] Yet Jenefer's uncovering of her Cornish roots is central to discovering her true self.

Simply stated, Jenefer wishes she could possess a distinct ethnic background, to know who she really is, just like her new Aboriginal friend Caleb who has a strong sense of his own indigenous identity. In *Zenna Dare* it is Jenefer's father who provides the vital evidence that finally unlocks Jenefer's emerging identity. 'Jenefer, in reality Cornwall is a county of England,' he explains, 'but ethnically, the Cornish have always set themselves apart. You see, they were Celts – there before the English came ...' For Jenefer, the revelation is extraordinary, and immediately she sees parallels between the English subjugation of Cornwall and the much later appropriation of Aboriginal Australia. 'Incredible,' she cries, 'The English were invading even then? Wait until I tell Caleb.'[40]

After her father's revelation, everything falls into place for Jenefer. As Rosanne Hawke explains in her own her discussion of *Zenna Dare*, 'Even though Jenefer realises that Caleb is able to lay claim to being a first Australian, she now knows that she has something worthy too, and together they can embrace the Australian culture, in all its diversity, with confidence.'[41] *Zenna Dare* tells the story of Jenefer's hunt for identity, and the problems of 'being Cornish' in Australia. Eventually, Jenefer realises that she does 'belong', that she is a Cornish descendant but also an Australian, living on Australian soil with that crucial 'sense of belonging to the land'.

Across the Creek, also by Rosanne Hawke, is full of Celtic imagery and the use of Cornish legends to animate the storyline. The novel focuses on Aidan Curnow, the lead character, and his struggle with his Cornish heritage. To some extent, Aidan's experience echoes that of Jenefer Tremayne in *Zenna Dare*, in that they are both very resourceful. But whereas Jenefer researches her family history closely and discovers her hidden Cornish identity, Aidan already seems to be aware, even subconsciously at times, that he is Cornish. His surname, after all, means 'Cornwall' in the Cornish language. Aidan's essential Cornishness is demonstrated when he fights the 'dragaroo'. This dragaroo, as its name suggests, is a strange creature; part dragon and part kangaroo – part Celtic and part Australian. Its symbolic role in the novel is to probe the nature of Cornish culture in Australia, suggesting the blending of the two identities but also the formation of a very different beast. It cannot be a kangaroo, nor can it be a dragon; much like those Cornish-Australians – including Aidan, who symbolically confronts the dragaroo – who struggle with the notion of Cornishness in an Australian setting. The dragaroo can be seen as an indication of the sometimes uneasy relationship between the two cultures, of an assimilation that does not always work. As Rosanne Hawke puts it, 'Maybe it is better to be a dragon in a kangaroo's landscape, and learn the belonging that comes from being an Australian with a Cornish background, and not to deny what we are, as we become something new.'[42]

Across the Creek deploys Cornish folklore in a very Australian context, an abandoned copper mine – that most 'Cornish' of Australian environments. In the story, the main character, Aidan, heads down an abandoned mine shaft and ends up in a mythical world called Trevelia, where missing children live with a fairy. The original reason Aidan enters the mine, aside from being led astray by the piskie Raff, is to search for a girl called Janice Trengove who disappeared a year before. Even in her disappearance there is an allusion to Cornish and Celtic mythology, articulated by Josie, one of the characters in *Across the Creek*. 'But you said Janice "as been gone a year yesterd'y," Josie said. "That's a year-and-a-day. My mam always said a year-and-a-day was a magic time.'[43] In Celtic folklore there was a strong belief in the symbolism of a year and a day, possibly originating from the existence of a leap day once every four years. A leap day is an intercalary day, 29 February, inserted in a leap year; it has a mystical quality and has long been associated with superstitious belief. It is a phenomenon that fascinates Rosanne Hawke. In two of her novels she makes use of the idea of a year and a day: in the above mentioned 'magic time' in *Across the Creek*, and secondly in *Wolfchild* where the character Raw – drawing upon the traditional rights of common law – insists that 'Only by staying away for a year and a day can I gain my freedom.'[44]

Published before *Across the Creek* but after *Zenna Dare*, *Wolfchild* differs from the two books discussed above in that it is set in not only a different country but also a different time. Unlike the previous novels, *Wolfchild* is located not in Australia but in the 'lost land of Lyonesse', the name given by romantic writers to the bridge of land that was supposed once to have existed between western Cornwall and the present day Isles of Scilly. The story is laden with references to Celtic mythology and traditions, and is given a strong Cornish flavour through the use of Cornish personal names such as

Morwenna, Eselda and Cadan, and by reference to 'Kernow' for Cornwall and 'Kernewek' for the Cornish language. Interestingly, the book is published in Australia for Australian children, and yet is set entirely in a Cornish world in Britain. As Karen Brooks observes: 'The reader is drawn into the mythic and real world of the ninth century. The burgeoning Christian faith, blended with mystic paganism, is beautifully drawn and captures the essence of the austere world of Morwenna and her family.'[45] By setting the story in Cornwall, as opposed to Australia, Rosanne Hawke not only offers what is in effect a fantasised history lesson but also introduces young Australians to Cornwall itself, on the edge of Britain, half a world away. Here they become acquainted with a land beyond England and a culture that is not English – an important insight for Australian children, whether of Cornish descent or not.

This separate Cornish identity plays an important role in another of Rosanne Hawke's books, *The Last Virgin in Year Ten*. Published in 2006, the novel returns to Australia and features another young girl of Cornish descent, Caz. However, in stark comparison to Jenefer in *Zenna Dare*, Caz is not comfortable with her mixed identity. She struggles to come to terms with her Cornish heritage and, much like the dragaroo in *Across the Creek*, she does not feel that she fits into the Australian landscape. More generally, Caz is trying to make sense of her life, fighting popularity norms and peer pressure, and *The Last Virgin in Year Ten* highlights the awkward transition period that most children experience as they progress through their teenage years into adulthood. However, an underlying issue that seems to be making Caz's transition even more problematic is her inherited Cornishness.

Fortunately, Caz finds solace in her new friendship with the character Matthew Tallack, who has embraced *his* Cornish heritage enthusiastically. Throughout the story, he continually discusses King Arthur, the Holy Grail and Lyonnesse, and seems very knowledgeable. '"I have this book," he says, "that proves where Avalon is. It's in Cornwall ... sunk under the sea on the way out to the Scilly Isles".'[46] Eventually, Caz asks Matthew the inevitable question: 'How come the interest in all things Celtic?' The answer is revelatory: 'All dad's people were Cornish, Miners and – Yeah. Just like us.'[47] Caz, impressed by the explanation and feeling an increasing affinity with Matthew as they explore their mutual Cornish ancestry, reasons: 'It's not so weird. With the amount of migration from the UK that happened here in the nineteenth century, there's a 20 per cent chance (maybe more dad says) of meeting someone with a Cornish background.'[48] In this way, as her relationship with Matthew develops, Caz becomes increasingly proud of her Cornish-Australian identity, which in turn has a profound effect upon her as she rises to the challenge of transition to adulthood.

The final book to be addressed is Rosanne Hawke's *Sailmaker*. The protagonist, Joel, lives on Yorke Peninsula, and so already there is an inferred link to South Australia's Cornish migration and mining history. Yet the prevalent Cornish theme in the novel is the tale of Tom Bawcock, a famous Cornish story in which the titular character manages to lift a famine that has descended on the fishing village of Mousehole, venturing out bravely into the fearful storm and returning at length with a plentiful catch. That the story is drawn from Cornwall itself somehow serves to strengthen the Cornish heritage of Yorke Peninsula, and adds to the ways in which Cornish identity is explored in Rosanne Hawke's fiction. In *Sailmaker*, she draws on the tale of Tom Bawcock's eve to provide an explicitly Cornish comparison as the Yorke Peninsula villagers struggle to prevent their lighthouse island from being washed away in a storm. Indeed, the storm in *Sailmaker* is highly reminiscent of the ruggedness and wildness of a Cornish south-westerly: 'The wind's so strong we can't walk upright. Even in the dark I can see white, flying up on the side like whipped sugar being flung off a giant fairy-floss machine. There's no way he'll survive in a sea like this.'[49] Here the Cornish drama has been transferred to Australia, with Cornish-Australians the fitting inheritors of Tom Bawcock's hardy and courageous persona.

Cornish names

As we have seen, each of Rosanne Hawke's novels employs Cornishness in subtly different ways. But one consistent device that runs through all the books considered here is her choice of Cornish names for both characters and places. Aidan Curnow in *Across the Creek* has a surname clearly derived from Kernow, the Cornish word for Cornwall. Similarly, in the same story, the lost girl Janice Trengove and the mythical world of Trevalia are obviously of Cornish origin, both sporting the characteristic 'Tre-' prefix, echoing the old adage: 'by Tre, Pol and Pen shall ye know most Cornishmen'.[50] In *Sailmaker* incidental characters such as Trenwith and Mr Pengelly are given Cornish surnames. Their Cornishness is not made explicit in the text, but the mere fact of their names – which the inquisitive reader can investigate further if s/he so wishes – adds to the Cornish ambience of the story. Indeed, prodding her readers to find out more about distinctive Cornish names appears to be another of Rosanne Hawke's objectives. In *The Last Virgin in Year Ten*, for example, Caz muses on the surname (Prideaux) of a boy she likes. She explains that: 'Because their name has an "x" in it their mother thinks it's French.'[51] But later she adds that 'Dad reckons Prideaux is Cornish. A lot of the names around here are, because of the Miners coming out in the old days.'[52] Matthew Tallack, for instance, sports another typical Cornish surname, and has a passionate interest in his Celtic ancestry.

The prevalence of Cornish names is a device used by Rosanne Hawke to disclose the often hidden 'Cornishness' of people and places in modern Australia, assisting in the awakening of identity that she seeks. In *Zenna Dare* the very title is immediately redolent of the Cornish village of Zennor, signposting the book's Cornish theme. But Zenna Dare turns out to be the stage name of Gweniver Rundle, who travelled to Australia from Camborne in Cornwall. Rundle, inevitably, is yet another Cornish surname, and Gweniver is a Cornish form of 'Jenefer'. Significantly, Jenefer is also a Cornish spelling, and thus Jenefer Tremayne (in the same novel) is likewise the lucky inheritor of two Cornish names. As noted earlier, Rosanne Hawke's maiden name was Trevilyan. It is remarkably similar to the mythical land of Trevelia in *Across the Creek*, and highly reminiscent of Jenefer Tremayne (her *alter ego?*) in *Zenna Dare*. Here, in these novels, Rosanne Hawke is herself very close to planting her own Cornish-Australian identity in the Australian soil.

Conclusion

In all her books discussed above, Rosanne Hawke demonstrates a serious use of children's literature for an exploration of Cornish identity through Australian eyes. For the young target audience, the novels provide a strong foundation from which to begin their musing and perhaps research into the Cornish in Australia. Older readers may be similarly inspired, as perhaps will be other writers alighting upon her work. In time, maybe, children's fiction in Australia with a Cornish theme will come to rival the number of titles reflecting Irish-Australian identity.

Reading transforms readers, adults and children alike, in different ways. What readers encounter not only offers them information about actual events, people and things, but also proposes extensions, alternative views and versions of living. In writing her novels, Rosanne Hawke encourages her readers – be they children or adults – to discover their own identities and to know who they really are. She understands that people are always looking for meaning in their lives – from watching television programmes to looking through old family photographs – and here, she argues, Australian children's literature has an important part to play.

Children's literature gives of its best if it is approached with an open mind. It often seems that the most gifted authors of books for children are not like other writers: instead, in some essential way, they are child-like themselves. Rosanne Hawke's books offer so much to readers young and not-so-young: magical and amazing journeys, humour, mystery, Cornish legends, and historical as well as contemporary adventures set in Australia and in Cornwall. However, most of all, her books deliver stories. And regardless of genre, for what more can readers, both young and old, ask?

Acknowledgements

First of all I would like to express my sincere gratitude to Rosanne Hawke, for allowing me to explore her work and for answering my many questions. I would also like to thank the patient staff at the Cornish Studies Centre (Kresenn Kernow) in Redruth, Cornwall, without whom I would not have been able to conduct the background research for the dissertation on which this article is based. I also thank Andrew McNeillie for his valuable guidance. Finally, I am indebted to Philip Payton, who has inspired me, and without whom neither the research for my dissertation nor my University experience generally would have been as enjoyable and rewarding as they turned out to be.

Notes and references

1. W. McVitty, 'Publishing for Children in Australia: A Thriving Industry', *Children's Literature Association Quarterly* 15:4 (1990), p. 167.
2. P. Hunt, *An Introduction to Children's Literature* (Oxford, 1994), p. 153.
3. F. A. Hughes, 'Children's Literature: Theory and Practice', *English Literary History* (hereafter *ELH*) 45:3 (1978), p. 550.
4. P. Hunt, *Children's Literature* (Oxford, 2001), p. 1.
5. Hunt, *An Introduction to Children's Literature*, p. 1.
6. Ibid., p. 1.
7. McVitty, 'Publishing for Children in Australia,' p. 168.
8. Ibid., p. 168.
9. Cited in S. L. Beckett (ed.), *Reflections of Change: Children's Literature Since 1945* (London, 1997), p. 107.
10. Hunt, *An Introduction to Children's Literature*, p. 259.
11. R. Hawke, 'Kapunda Cousins' in Jan Lokan (ed.) *Cornish Communities in Australia: Cornish Association of South Australia Biennial Seminar* (Wallaroo, 2009), pp. 1–21 and p. 115; see also R. Hawke, 'Cornish Inventiveness in Rural South Australia' in Jan Lokan (ed.) *The Ingenious Cornish – Inventions, Enterprises, Exploits: Papers from the Biennial History Seminar, Cornish Association of South Australia* (Wallaroo, 2011), pp. 55–66.
12. O. Pryor, *Australia's Little Cornwall* (Adelaide, 1962), p. 13.
13. P. Payton, *Making Moonta: The Invention of Australia's Little Cornwall* (Exeter, 2007), p. 42.
14. P. Payton, 'Reforming Thirties and Hungry Forties: The Genesis of Cornwall's Emigration Trade' in P. Payton (ed.), *Cornish Studies: Four* (Exeter, 1996), p. 114.
15. S. Schwartz, 'The Making of a Myth: Cornish Miners in the New World in the Early Nineteenth Century' in P. Payton (ed.), *Cornish Studies: Nine* (Exeter, 2001), p. 106.
16. P. Payton, 'The Cornish in South Australia: Their Influence and Experience from Immigration to Assimilation, 1836–1936', unpublished PhD thesis, University of Adelaide, 1978, Vol. 1, p. ii.

17. http://www.rosannehawke.com/view.asp?a=1728&s=395, accessed 23 March 2011.
18. P. Payton, *The Cornish Miner in Australia: Cousin Jack Down Under* (Redruth: 1983), p. 211.
19. R. Hawke, 'Jack and Jen in Oz: Cornish Identity in Australian Children's Literature' in Pamela O'Neill (ed.), *Exile and Homecoming: Papers from the Fifth Australian Conference on Celtic Studies* (Sydney, 2005), p. 8.
20. R. Hawke, 'Jack and Jen in Oz: Cornish Identity in Australian Children's Literature and some Observations on the Genesis of Glanville Park,' unpublished PhD thesis, University of Adelaide, 2005, p. 9.
21. Ibid., p. 9.
22. Ibid., p. 10.
23. Ibid., p. 11.
24. Ibid., p. 16.
25. Cited in ibid., p. 21.
26. B. Deacon, 'And Shall Trelawny Die? The Cornish Identity' in Philip Payton (ed.), *Cornwall Since the War: The Contemporary History of a European Region* (Redruth, 1993), p. 200.
27. A. M. Kent, *The Literature of Cornwall: Continuity Identity Difference 1000–2000* (Bristol, 2000), p. 12.
28. Hawke, 'Jack and Jen in Oz', unpublished PhD thesis, p.21.
29. Ibid., p.156.
30. Hawke. 'Jack and Jen in Oz' in O'Neill (ed.), *Exile and Homecoming*, p.139.
31. Hawke. 'Jack and Jen in Oz', unpublished PhD thesis, p. 11.
32. Ibid., p. 11.
33. P. Payton, *The Cornish Overseas: A History of Cornwall's Great Emigration* (Fowey, 2005), p. 411.
34. Hawke, 'Jack and Jen in Oz' in O'Neill (ed.), *Exile and Homecoming*, p.125.
35. R. Hawke, *Zenna Dare* (Sydney, 2002), p. 7.
36. Ibid., p. 16.
37. Ibid., p. 25.
38. Ibid., p. 27.
39. Hawke, 'Jack and Jen in Oz' in O'Neill (ed.), *Exile and Homecoming*, p. 136.
40. Hawke, *Zenna Dare*, p. 59.
41. Hawke, 'Jack and Jen in Oz' in O'Neill (ed.), *Exile and Homecoming*, p. 136.
42. Ibid., p. 138.
43. R. Hawke, *Across the Creek* (Sydney, 2004), p. 64.
44. R. Hawke, *Wolfchild* (Sydney, 2003), p. 117.
45. K. Brooks, 'Wonderworlds', *Australian Book Review: Young Adult Fantasy* (2003) p. 61.
46. Rosanne Hawke, *The Last Virgin in Year Ten* (Sydney, 2006), p. 23.
47. Ibid., p. 31.
48. Ibid., p. 31.
49. Rosanne Hawke, *Sailmaker* (Sydney, 2002), p. 132.
50. Deacon, 'And Shall Trelawny Die?', p. 56.
51. Hawke, *The Last Virgin in Year Ten*, p. 10.
52. Ibid., p. 10.

10

'Husband Abroad'

Quantifying spousal separation associated with emigration in nineteenth-century Cornwall

Lesley Trotter

Introduction

Conversations about Cornish ancestors frequently turn, sooner or later, to a great grandmother or more distant female relative who found herself raising the family alone because her husband was working abroad. It is a notion that is quietly ingrained in Cornish folklore – but rarely appears when the Cornish emigration story is presented to a wider audience. On the otherwise comprehensive website of the Cornish Mining World Heritage Site, for example, despite a claim to be as much about the people as the mining landscapes, any mention of women is confined to a few short paragraphs on balmaidens.[1] Little attention is given to the consequences of emigration on the sending communities in Cornwall other than references to depopulation and the remittance culture in economic, rather than social, terms. That numerous husbands and wives spent often years apart leading separate lives at a time of uncertain communications and slow, long-distance travel does not feature in the story at all.

In many ways such an omission is understandable as this aspect of Cornish emigration has been largely neglected in the secondary literature available to those presenting the story to a wider audience. This neglect is currently being addressed by a research project designed to shed light on the experiences of the wives who remained in Cornwall while their husbands worked abroad. An integral part of that research is an attempt to establish the scale of spousal separation associated with emigration, and this article describes work undertaken to quantify the incidence and distribution of this phenomenon.

Contemporary sources suggest that at times throughout the nineteenth century, the number of wives who had been 'left behind'[2] in Cornwall reached very high levels. Writing about the collapse of the mining industry in the late 1860s, Rowe notes that of the estimated 11,400 unemployed men in the mining districts of West Cornwall, 'about two-thirds of them left the western counties, leaving nearly 20,000 dependents behind them'.[3] The dramatic impact at parish level during these hard times is illustrated by the example of Ludgvan where fifty families had been left behind by husbands and fathers seeking work elsewhere.[4] Similar reports emerged in the local press some years later, with a correspondent from Liskeard noting that in the summer of 1875 there were 'considerable' numbers of 'married widows' in the town and outlying districts whose husbands had deserted or half-deserted them.

These reports hint at the existence of a significant social problem but only provide isolated snapshots scattered across time and place giving no idea of the true scale or longevity of the phenomenon. Attempts to put a figure to the levels of spousal separation in individual parishes have produced further isolated snapshots. Past estimates for the number of wives with absent husbands include 4 per cent for Camborne, Redruth and St Just in 1851,[5] between 8 per cent and 26–35 per cent for the same parishes in 1871,[6] and 12.5 per cent for Lanner in 1891.[7] More recently an analysis of the census returns for Gwennap revealed that 9 per cent of husbands were absent in 1851; about 18 per cent in 1861; around 25 per cent in both 1871 and 1881; and just over 21 per cent in 1891.[8] However, all these figures are for the number of wives whose husbands are absent, but have not necessarily left Cornwall, let alone the UK.

The most striking indication of the numbers of wives 'left behind' appears in the Census Enumerators Books (CEBs) where those for the mining districts are littered with numerous references to 'Husband Abroad' or 'Wife of miner in America' (or in any one of a number of far-flung destinations). Researchers with an interest in Cornwall are fortunate in that transcriptions of all the Cornish CEBs are available in a digital format that facilitates comprehensive searches and queries.[9] This offered the opportunity to use specific references to husbands who were described as being abroad in the census to estimate the numbers of wives in each census year whose husbands had emigrated, and their distribution across Cornwall.

Enumerating the absent

It is important to consider how such details of absent husbands came to be recorded in the CEBs. There was no requirement on the part of the person completing the census household schedule to provide such information. However, the census enumerators were instructed to gather information that might account and explain for any temporary increase or decrease in the population of the area they covered. The CEBs, into which the enumerator had to copy all the household schedules he had collected, contained blank tables that had to be filled in so that the overall demographic figures could be adjusted to account for temporary fluctuations in the local population due to special events occurring at the time of the census. How these figures were used can be seen in the notes accompanying the published census reports. For example, in 1841 the populations of St Austell and Roche were boosted by a influx of people attending the annual feast.[10] A temporary increase in the population of Bodmin in 1871 was partly down to the militia being assembled there at the time of the census,[11] whilst on a much smaller scale the apparent 15 per cent decrease in the population of St Michael Carhayes was attributed to 'the temporary absence of the greater part of a large family'.[12]

The instructions as to how the enumerators were to complete these tables left significant room for interpretation. The 1841 enumerators were told:

If any temporary influx of persons into the District, or temporary departure of persons from it, shall have caused a considerable increase or decrease of the Population of the District at the time of the Enumeration, the Enumerator is requested to state in the Table below, the probable amount of such increase or decrease, the causes to which either may be ascribed, and the kind of persons thus added to or deducted from the ordinary Population. If there has been no considerable increase or decrease, the columns may be left blank.[13]

As no guidance was provided as to what constituted 'temporary' or 'considerable', there was wide scope for variation in how consistently or conscientiously these tables were completed. They can, nonetheless, provide precious nuggets of information – for example, the tables in all but one of the 1841 CEBs for the parish of Gwennap are blank; the exception being Enumeration District 16, covering part of Carharrack, where the enumerator recorded that 'Six miners, whose families reside in the district are labouring in America or the West Indies.'[14] There is no indication as to whether these are married men and examination of the returns themselves provide few clues as to which families were involved. Anne Blamey, who appears to be heading a household comprising of only herself and three children, and whose occupation entry notes 'Husband – a miner', is a likely candidate. There are several other households consisting of an adult woman and children but as the 1841 census does not include any indication of marital status, these women could simply be widows.

It is interesting to note that the 1841 CEBs also had a table, directly under the one described above, with separate columns for male and female, in which the enumerator was asked to 'State the number of Persons known to have emigrated from the District to the Colonies or to Foreign Countries since Dec 31, 1840.'[15] The fact that the Gwennap enumerator had chosen to record the six miners in the 'temporarily absent' as opposed to 'emigrated' table indicates that is was clearly understood that these men were planning to return to their families.

Sadly for researchers of migration, the emigration tables do not appear in later censuses, but those requiring the enumerator to record information of temporary absence remained a feature of every census up to 1891. In 1851 the instructions on how to fill in this table were a little less ambiguous, requiring the enumerator to 'Estimate the number of persons who were absent from the district on the night of March 30th, but who usually dwell in the district. [State the cause of the absence of so many of the inhabitants, whether it fishing or in other employment.]'.[16] This still left room for interpretation as to whether a miner who was working abroad for possibly years would be considered as 'usually dwelling' in the district.

In order to complete these tables the enumerator had to have made some additional notes as he gathered the household schedules from the residents in his district. The 1851 'Instructions to Enumerators' refers to the use of 'a Memorandum Book' for recording at which houses household schedules had been left, but such a book does not figure in the list of supplies that the enumerator should receive in order to complete his task.[17] Enumerators were issued with precise instructions as to how they should ensure that the household schedules they were collecting had been completed correctly, including 'asking all necessary questions' to ensure that the required information was provided. Presumably, this would have been the opportunity to enquire about absent husbands and note it either on the schedule or elsewhere.

By the 1861 census the system had been tightened up and enumerators were issued with a Memorandum Book containing clear instructions as to how to use it. Enumerators were told that before leaving each house, having ensured that the schedule they were collecting had been completed correctly, they were to 'inquire whether any persons, whose usual home in therein, are temporarily absent, and if so, make a note of the number in the proper column of this book, and state any general cause of their absence, as attending a fair, market, etc., fishing, gone abroad, etc.'[18] The book helpfully included a 'completed example' page with a sample entry for a household where some of the usual residents were 'Abroad'.[19] The Memorandum Books continued to be issued for later censuses but that for 1891 makes no reference to enquiring about usual residents who were temporarily abroad and no entry appears on the 'completed example' page.[20]

Clearly one of the aims of the censuses from 1841 to 1881 was to gather information as to the extent of, and reasons for, temporary absence from home. This seems the most likely explanation for the inclusion of information in the census returns on husbands being absent and abroad. This information usually appears in CEBs in the occupation column for the wife and occasionally as a marginal note. It is possible that some wives included this information on their household schedule, but given the general literacy levels and the use of the impersonal 'third person' phrasing it seems likely that the majority of this information was added by the enumerator noting down the responses to his enquiries about any absent residents, either on the individual schedule or in his Memorandum Book, and then including it in his transcription into the CEB. This is supported by the element of standardisation of these entries within each CEB, although not among enumerators generally, with different phrasing and abbreviations being adopted by different enumerators.

It is logical to suppose that having made these entries when copying the details from individual schedules into the CEB, the enumerator would have found it simple to use them in combination with the entries in his Memorandum Book to complete the 'temporarily absent' table in the CEB, and therefore these tables ought to provide useful quantitative evidence for the number of men, including husbands, who were temporarily working abroad.

However, as enumerators seem to have had difficulty in accurately filling in the preliminary tables in the CEB that summarised the numbers of persons and houses enumerated, with their figures often having to be corrected by the checking clerks,[21] it is questionable that they were any better at completing the 'temporarily absent' tables. An examination of these tables for the parish of Gwennap seems to confirm this. Whereas the 1841 table for one enumeration district in the parish refers to the six miners mentioned above, the only reference to a temporarily absent man in any of the 1851 tables covering the parish is the note: 'One only known to be absent – assistant engineer.' In contrast, previous research looking at the absence of husbands from Gwennap found that 132 husbands were not at home with their wives at the time of the 1851 census and seven husbands are specifically listed as being abroad.[22] It does not seem credible that none of these men, or any single men from the parish, were away from home temporarily.

The 'temporarily absent' tables in the 1861 census appear to have been filled in with more diligence, which may reflect the clear and detailed instructions included in the Memorandum Books supplied to the enumerators that year. In all 186 men from Gwennap are noted as being abroad temporarily, including '20 copper miners' from a single enumeration district.[23] This seems more consistent with the figure of 44 husbands identified in the census returns themselves as being abroad out of a total of 257 husbands absent from the parish.[24] A similarly high number of men (208) were recorded in the 1861 'temporarily absent' tables for the enumeration districts in neighbouring Redruth,[25] and this again is consistent with the 178 named wives specifically described as having husbands abroad in the census listings for that parish. The enumerators for Redruth have carefully noted in the 'temporarily absent' table for all but one of the enumeration districts that these men are 'in Australia, America & elsewhere seeking work'. Unfortunately the equivalent tables in the 1871 and 1881 censuses, for Gwennap at least, are far less informative and seem to have been used only to record the numbers of inhabitants away from home visiting friends and relations despite the fact that very high numbers of wives with absent husbands are recorded in the census returns for the parish in both years.[26]

Even if the tables had been completed accurately, the inclusion of any individual would depend on whether their working abroad should be counted as a temporary absence, which without any clear definitions would have been a largely subjective assessment influenced by phrasing of the question, the understanding of the person answering it, and the enumerator's interpretation of that answer. This leaves plenty of scope for inconsistency regarding the inclusion of absent husbands in these tables, regardless as to whether they were abroad or in the neighbouring parish. It should also be remembered that the men recorded as being temporarily absent or abroad would have included single as well as married men.

Although the 'temporarily absent' tables in the CEBs do not offer a particularly helpful source in quantifying the numbers of husbands that were abroad leaving their wives in Cornwall, an awareness of their existence and intent does provide a useful insight into why and how the numerous entries of 'Husband Abroad' and similar phrases came to be recorded in the census returns. These tables, and those summarising emigration in 1841, may also represent a previously under-utilised source of information regarding emigration at parish, and even sub-parish level.

Searching for the missing husbands

It would appear that, even if they were not very conscientious about recording it in the manner intended, the census enumerators were aware at some level of the desirability of gathering information about usual residents who were away at the time of the census, and this may explain the frequent references in the CEBs to the whereabouts of absent husbands. The availability of transcriptions of the CEBs for Cornwall in a searchable digital form, therefore, does provide a way of estimating the number of husbands abroad across Cornwall from 1851–1891. By searching the returns for key terms and their variants it was possible to generate a dataset that gives a breakdown of the incidence of references to husbands abroad by parish and census year.

A series of searches were carried out on the transcriptions for each census year to pick up and record all incidences of the variety of different ways in which it was indicated that a husband was working overseas. The initial search was made for the term 'Abroa*d' as this rarely seems to occur in any context other than referring to a husband. The less frequent references to sons or other family members were easily excluded where they occurred. The wildcard "*" was used because it became apparent that the misspelling/transcription error 'Abroard' was not uncommon. The next step was a search on the term 'Hus*', again because this would pick up all references to 'Husband' as well as where the enumerator had used the abbreviation 'Hus' or 'Husb'. A search was also made on the term 'Hsb' as this abbreviation had also been used. Where any of the variants of 'husband' appeared in conjunction with 'Abroad' the entry was excluded as it had already been counted in the earlier search. This rule of excluding any match that included a search term that had already been used was repeated at each search stage to avoid duplication.

The advantage of carrying out such split searches was that it was possible to pick up the wide range of ways in which an absent husband had been recorded. 'Abroa*d' returned matches not just of 'Husband abroad' but variations that didn't refer to 'husband' but occupational terms such as 'miner', 'mine agent', 'engineer', etc., or simply 'Head abroad'. Similarly, searches on 'husband' and its variants returned matches where specific destination countries were given, e.g. 'Husband in America'. It also picked up more unusual variations, such as 'husband gone foreign'. References to husbands 'absent', 'at sea', in service, hospital, asylum, prison and even 'transported' were noted but excluded from the analysis, as were references to 'sends money' and similar, although the latter examples may well have been husbands working abroad.

Searches were not made on any particular occupation, with one exception – gold miners – as it can reasonably be assumed that any absent husband described as such would have been abroad, even if other details of the entry did not make this clear. The search term used was 'gold' which returned results for 'gold diggers' and 'gold mine agents' as well the more frequent 'gold miner'. This search proved especially worthwhile as it revealed a significant number of husbands that would not have been included otherwise.

The final searches in the series were made for references to the most likely common named destinations, such as America, Australia, Mexico and Cuba. This did pick up a few additional husbands, described only by their occupations (e.g. labourer, mason, blacksmith, cabinet maker, as well as the more obvious, miner) or referred to variously as 'head in ...', or even by name as in the case of Johanna Langdon, 'Wife to L. Langdon in America'. Searches could have been made for numerous other possible destinations, but given that the search for the common destinations such as Australia and America (the latter also picked up references to South American destinations) returned few results that had not already been picked up by the 'husband' searches, it was felt that this would not be practical. It is regrettable that it was impracticable to search for Chile/Chili in particular (a search on Chil* returned an overwhelming number of matches to 'children'/'child's', etc.). Unfortunately the search facility did not allow for the search 'miner in' as this may have picked up the more obscure destinations, as well as avoiding the return of increasing numbers of overseas birthplaces as well as other irrelevant matches.

It is clear that not all references to husbands abroad will have been identified by these searches, given the huge variation in the way they are described in the census, but although some will have been missed, it seems likely that the methodology described here will have accounted for the vast majority of them. More comprehensive searches for references to husbands abroad were made in five civil parishes (Camborne, Gwennap, St Agnes, St Cleer and St Just in Penwith) that had been selected for more detailed analysis as part of a wider ongoing research project.[27] Therefore the figures for the numbers of husbands indicated as being abroad in the census returns can be given with a higher degree of confidence for these parishes.

The wives who were 'left behind' have frequently been described as having been 'deserted',[28] which begged the question as to whether the census returns could be used to shed any light on this perception. Therefore, the CEB transcriptions for Cornwall were also searched on the term 'desert*' to see what this might reveal. Where it is indicated that the errant husbands were abroad, these references have been included in the analysis.

Results

Combining the results of the above searches it has been possible to establish the scale and distribution of references to husbands abroad in all Cornish parishes for each of the census years 1851 to 1891. These are plotted in Figures 1 to 5, in which, for ease of illustration on this scale, parishes have been combined into registration sub-districts.

Figure 1.   1851 – Distribution of references to husbands being abroad
at the time of the census.

As Figure 1 shows the 1851 census for Cornwall contains relatively few
references (56) to husbands that are abroad. Individual cases are mentioned
in the returns for Poughill, Jacobstow and Week St Mary in north-east
Cornwall; St Pinnock, near Liskeard, and Newlyn East further to the west.
However, there is a clear cluster in the mining areas around Redruth with
twenty-four husbands listed in Redruth itself, a further seven in neighbouring
Gwennap, and three each in Kenwyn, St Agnes, Illogan and Gwinear. Two
husbands from each of Crowan, Wendron, Breage and Ludgvan were also
noted. Where the husband's actual whereabouts is given, it is invariably
America. At this date this could have referred to both the northern and
southern continents, and men from Redruth and Gwennap are specifically
described as being in Chile, Brazil and Peru. Another favoured destination
was Cuba, with more than half (13) of the absent husbands from Redruth
said to be there.

In 1861 the distribution of references to husbands abroad is still clustered
in the mining areas around Redruth (see Figure 2) but there has been
a dramatic increase in numbers with 492 being recorded, 178 being in
Redruth alone, far outstripping the numbers that appear in the returns for
the nearby parishes of Gwennap, Illogan, Camborne, which themselves have
significantly higher numbers (44, 43 and 36 respectively) than the majority

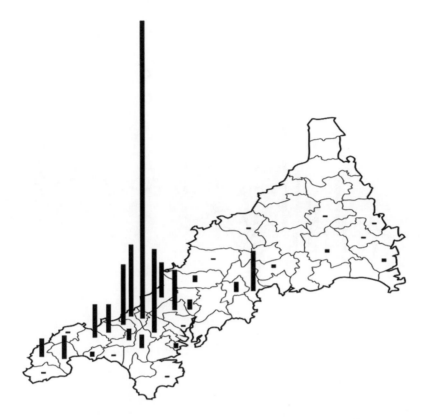

Figure 2.   1861 – There is a dramatic increase in the number of husbands recorded
as being abroad, clustered around Redruth in the central mining area.

of parishes. On the eastern fringe of this cluster sits Kenwyn (23) and St
Agnes (21), while more of the mining parishes further west are represented.
Other notable features of this distribution are what appears to be a secondary
cluster around St Austell, and the almost total absence of cases to the north
and west of Bodmin.

The 1871 census exhibits a similar pattern (Figure 3), but with generally
lower numbers (336) and a more even distribution across West Cornwall.
Numbers recorded in Redruth have fallen dramatically leaving Gwennap at
61 with the highest number of husbands abroad. In addition to the cluster in
the St Austell area, another has appeared in and around Liskeard. The decline
in the number of references to husbands abroad continues in the 1881 census
(273) (Figure 4), with a similar distribution covering the western parishes
with a focus on the Gwennap/Redruth/Kenwyn area, and a persistent cluster
around St Austell. References in the 1891 census are again fewer (178) and an

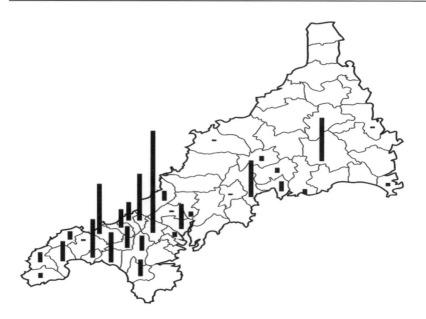

Figure 3.   1871 – Distribution remains focused on the central mining area with 'outposts' around St Austell and Liskeard.

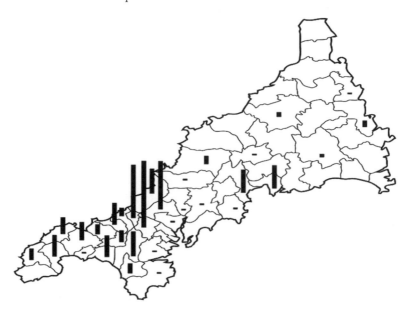

Figure 4.   1881 – The number of husbands recorded as being abroad has declined and distribution is more dispersed across Cornwall.

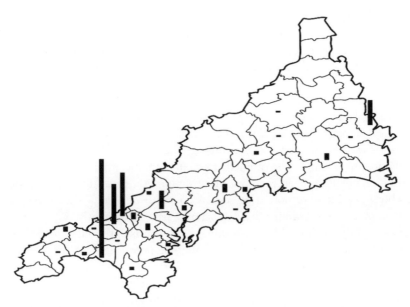

Figure 5. 1891 – Far fewer references to husbands abroad appear, with most cases found in the Camborne/Illogan, Breage and Kenwyn areas, as well as Stoke Climsland in the far east of Cornwall.

overall pattern more difficult to ascertain. Numbers are high in Camborne and Illogan, but far more cases appear in the returns for the parish of Breage (51) with more than average in neighbouring Germoe – and far to the east 14 husbands had left Stoke Climsland in the Tamar Valley.

As in 1851, where the husband's whereabouts are given in each of the later censuses in the majority of cases it is somewhere in the Americas (North or South). Comparatively few husbands are described as having gone to Australia, and most of these appear in the 1861 census, notably 30 from Redruth alone. Surprisingly little mention is made of Africa as a destination, although this migration stream was more important at the time of the 1891 census when far fewer references to absent husbands appear.

Meaningful data, or an artefact of enumeration?

Given that the intention, let alone the execution, of recording temporary absence abroad in the census seems to have been inconsistent throughout the nineteenth century, it is reasonable to question whether the results of this analysis represent a genuine distribution of cases or merely an artefact of the enumeration process. Undoubtedly there will have been anomalies in the recording from parish to parish, so comparison between individual neighbouring parishes may not be valid. In particular the lack of clear instructions to enumerators before 1861 and after 1891 means that the figures for those years should be viewed with less confidence than those for 1861–81. Nevertheless, it is clear that the overall distribution of cases across Cornwall is far from the random pattern that might be expected if the presence or absence of recorded cases were purely down to enumerator preference and diligence. Instead, there appears to be a remarkably close association between husbands working abroad and the mining districts.

Although it might be argued that the enumerators in the mining districts might have been more aware of emigration generally and therefore possibly more likely to note it, it seems too much of a coincidence that the enumerators in non-mining districts should have consistently not recorded husbands abroad while those in mining areas consistently did record them. What is more, not only does the distribution reflect that of the Cornish mining industry in general, with its concentration in West Cornwall and absence in north-east Cornwall, the more isolated clusters around St Austell, Liskeard and the Tamar Valley also reflect the localised mining activities in those areas.

It is also possible to detect a pattern in the change over time in the numbers and distribution of women with husbands working abroad. From a limited number of cases centred around Redruth and Gwennap in 1851, the phenomenon peaks in that area in 1861 whilst spreading across West Cornwall, gradually becoming more evenly distributed across the western mining parishes with outposts further east, before diminishing leaving only Camborne/Illogan and Breage with significant numbers of husbands listed as being abroad. Again, due to the possible inconsistencies in the approach to recording these absences in the different census years, caution is needed in interpreting this apparent pattern. However, it does resonate with our understanding of the rise and fall of the different mining districts across Cornwall, with as Bernard Deacon has summarised: 'copper rising in the west, shifting east and then collapsing, while tin production was distributed more widely, before becoming concentrated on the Camborne-Redruth area ... overlain by the more transient rise and fall of lead production'.[29]

Discussion

The quantitative analysis described here provides a baseline figure for the scale of the number of wives being 'left behind' in Cornwall. These are the husbands that we can be sure were abroad as the records are based on contemporary information elicited from the wives themselves. In total, the censuses from 1851 to 1891 contain 1,335 references to married men who are specifically stated as being abroad, with a spatial and temporal distribution that suggests a clear association with the mining industry. In a county that has numerous ports and a significant fishing industry one might expect the figures to reflect the distribution of the maritime trades, however these husbands are more usually recorded as being 'At Sea'. What is surprising, given the established extent of emigration from Cornwall as a whole, is that the non-mining areas, especially in eastern Cornwall, are barely represented. Even if there was a greater tendency for the Cornish from these more agricultural areas to emigrate together as families, one would expect at least some cases where the husband had gone on ahead, with the intent of sending for his wife and children once he had established some sort of home for them.

One explanation is that many more husbands had gone abroad than specifically indicated by the census returns, and the overall number of references certainly seems low in relation to the impression given by the contemporary press reports. Some husbands are recorded in the census as simply 'away', 'absent' or 'left' with no indication of where they had gone. In addition, some wives are described as 'being supported by' or 'receiving pay from' their husbands – a few unfortunate ones are noted as having been 'separated', 'deserted', 'discarded' or 'abandoned'. Any of these small groups could have included husbands abroad.

It is perhaps worth noting that all three of the husbands from north-east Cornwall recorded as being abroad in 1851, had in fact deserted their wives and gone to America. (The search for wives specifically recorded as having been deserted in the census returns produced very few references with incidences [usually single] in only twenty-four parishes scattered across Cornwall.)

The strongest reason to suspect that the numbers of husbands specifically recorded as being abroad are only a fraction of the true numbers comes from a recent detailed analysis of the census returns for the mining parish of Gwennap. At it peak in 1871 over 350 men were away,[30] yet the corresponding figure for husbands specifically recorded as being abroad at that census was 57. The whereabouts of the remaining 293 is unrecorded.[31] Some were undoubtedly in other parts of Cornwall or elsewhere in the UK, but given the scale of overseas emigration from the area, combined with individual cases where evidence from other sources has indicated the husband's whereabouts, it is very likely that a large percentage of these remaining husbands were also abroad.

Very rarely does the census provide any information as to how long the husband has been away, one notable exception being the miner husband of Jane Tonking from St Just in Penwith, who in 1871 was noted as having been in Australia for seventeen years. However, if, as suggested earlier, the notes made regarding husbands being abroad had been made to enable the enumerator to fill in the 'temporarily absent' table in the CEB, this would imply that the expectation was that these men planned to return at some point in the future, even if these plans were to change at a later date. This offers a possible explanation for the lack of references to husbands from the non-mining areas being abroad; it may be that wives had been 'left behind' in these parishes, but their husbands' absences were viewed differently, and therefore recorded differently, because they were intended to be permanent rather than temporary emigrations, with the expectation that the wives and families would follow them abroad.

For the men in the industrially developed Camborne-Redruth area the growing international market for skilled miners in the second half of the nineteenth century would have provided a particularly attractive opportunity for married men looking to improve their families' future prospects without necessarily abandoning their homeland forever. Being men who, on the whole, would have been slightly older, more experienced and with better developed industry networks, the married men would have been particularly well placed to secure this work. This provides a rationale for a distinctive trend for the temporary migration of married men from that area which would explain the findings of this study. Similar trends for temporary emigration have been identified in other centres of skilled industrial labour in the same period. Describing emigration from the industrial areas of Scotland at that time, Devine notes how 'Skilled and semi-skilled masons, granite workers and miners were able to exploit the shorter Atlantic crossings by steamship to spend the busy seasons working in America and then return to a more leisurely life in Scotland during the quieter months much more easily than low-paid common labourers.'[32] Parallels can be found here with the huge difference in the numbers of husbands abroad recorded between west and east Cornwall, with skilled workers in the mostly western mining industry better able to participate in the international market for skilled labour than their fellow Cornishmen from the predominantly agricultural areas to the east, and also, as in Scotland, more likely to return.

It seems possible, if not probable, that the phenomenon of married men working abroad reflects the changing fortunes of the different mining areas. The descriptions of distress associated with collapse of the industry in the mid-nineteenth century could lead to the assumption that these men were being forced to seek work abroad by the poor economic conditions in Cornwall. Indeed the 'temporarily absent' tables in the 1861 census for Redruth describe over 200 men as 'seeking work' abroad. However, Deacon's calculations of the overall value of mining production in Cornwall show that in the years leading up to the 1861 census the industry was at its peak,[33] and nowhere was production higher than in the Camborne-Redruth area from which the highest numbers of married men had left to work abroad. Certainly in 1861 it seems most unlikely that a lack of employment opportunities in the central mining district of Cornwall had caused these men to choose to leave their wives and children to find work in America and Australia.

Comparison with Scotland also offers an explanation here. Devine points out that the Scots from the industrial areas 'were not fleeing subsistence crises, or even, for the most part, escaping grinding poverty into "exile". Instead they were drawn by better wages (often three- to four-fold increases), opportunity, advancement and the search for "independence".'[34] Such possibilities would have been equally attractive to the couples in mining heartlands of West Cornwall willing to exchange a few years of separation for a better long-term future for the whole family.

The overall trend in mining production values shows a decline from 1862 onwards, but the years of recession in the mining industry (1865–67, 1877–79 and 1896–98) never coincided with a census year. With the exception of 1891, the few years preceding each census appear to have been ones of steady or improving prospects, therefore the censuses may be giving a more optimistic picture that possibly doesn't reflect the situation over the decade as a whole. The absences in the census may be subject to a time lag whereby the husbands abroad in 1871 and 1881 had actually left several years earlier during the more difficult times. This might possibly explain the more dispersed distribution of wives 'left behind' in those years, with married miners outside the dominant central mining district finding it harder to obtain more local work. As a result those who might otherwise have felt that separation from their wives and children was too high a price to pay for attempting to secure a better future may have had little choice, with 'need' replacing 'aspiration'.

Conclusion

Although they probably represent an underestimate of the scale of spousal separation associated with emigration, the results of this study of 'husbands abroad' in the nineteenth-century census returns pose an intriguing question. The numbers and distribution of these records, both spatially and temporally, suggest a clear correlation between records of spousal separation associated with emigration and the Cornish mining industry. However, is this because overwhelmingly more husbands from the mining parishes were abroad, or was the absence of these men being perceived differently from that of husbands from the more agricultural parishes? Either way, these findings would seem to indicate the existence of a distinctly different emigration culture within the mining areas, a culture characterised either by a greater propensity for husbands to travel abroad leaving wives and families behind, and/or an understanding that their emigration was intended (certainly initially) to be temporary.

In his assessment of the historical geography of Cornish mining in the second half of the nineteenth century, Deacon suggests that the history of mining in the Camborne-Illogan area 'differs significantly from the industry's experience in the rest of Cornwall'.[35] Is the concentration of numbers of married men from this central mining area recorded as working abroad simply a factor of the larger mining population in these parishes, or does it represent a social difference that reflects this different experience?

To answer this question fully would require detailed comparison of the emigration of married men from representative areas across Cornwall. However, the idea of high levels of temporary labour migration among miners throughout the nineteenth century is supported by the results of a previously reported study of miners' wives in Gwennap, which found that between 10–14 per cent of husbands who were absent in the 1851–71 censuses, and nearly 21 per cent of those absent in the 1881 census, were back with their wives in Cornwall ten years later, and that there was considerable evidence that many more had returned in the interim.[36]

It is logical to assume that, in general, married men with family responsibilities would have taken a more considered approach to the whole emigration question, than perhaps a single man eager to leave home and make his own way in the world. Those with wives and children would have felt a greater responsibility to provide for them in times of need, but were also more likely to engage in a project intended to improve the economic security and status of the family in the long term. Once abroad these men would also have more reason to return due to their emotional investment in wives and children, as well as possible economic investment in a house and smallholding. (Of course, escaping such ties and responsibilities may also have been why some men chose to go and not return!) Therefore the emigration decision-making process for married men is likely to have been different from that for single men, with marriage affecting how the men responded to changing circumstances and opportunities.

Memories of women in nineteenth-century Cornwall struggling to bring up families alone while their husbands were working abroad permeate the family histories of the Cornish all over the world, becoming part of the generalised folklore of the Cornish emigration. In indicating that the practice was primarily associated with, or took a different form in, the mining communities of mainly West Cornwall, this study provides a further evidence of intra-Cornwall difference. This would suggest that the impact of the, as yet unexplored, social and cultural consequences of this phenomenon would have had a variable effect on different communities across Cornwall, and illustrates the value, as Bernard Deacon has long argued, of Cornish Studies being applied at a meso-level between the very local and the county, of investigating 'Cornwalls' as opposed to simply Cornwall.[37]

Notes and references

1. http://www.cornish-mining.org.uk/delving-deeper/cornish-miner, accessed 16 March 2012.
2. 'Left behind' is a contested term, implying both a passive role for the women and backwardness in the sending community, but one that has commonly been adopted by anthropologists studying the phenomenon in modern migration studies. See C. S. Archambault, 'Women Left Behind? Migration, Spousal Separation, and the Autonomy of Rural Women in Ugweno, Tanzania', *Signs* 35 (2010), pp. 921–24.
3. J. Rowe, *Cornwall in the Age of Industrial Revolution* (St Austell, 1993), p. 322.
4. Ibid., p. 320.
5. M. Brayshay, *The Demography of Three West Cornwall Mining Communities 1851–1971: A Society in decline*, unpublished PhD thesis, University of Exeter, 1977, p. 349.
6. Ibid., p. 349; B. Deacon, *The Cornish Family* (Fowey, 2004), p. 43.
7. S. Schwartz and R. Parker, *Lanner: a Cornish Mining Parish* (Tiverton, 1998), p. 163.
8. L. Trotter, 'Desperate? Destitute? Deserted? Questioning perceptions of miners' wives in Cornwall during the great emigration, 1851–1891' in P. Payton (ed.), *Cornish Studies: Nineteen* (Exeter, 2011), p. 203.
9. These transcriptions are online at http://freepages.genealogy.rootsweb.ancestry.com/~kayhin/ukocp.html
10. Census of Great Britain, 1851, Population tables, I. Number of the inhabitants in 1801, 1811, 1821, 1831, 1841 and 1851. Vol. I. BPP 1852–53 LXXXV (1631), p. 61.
11. Census of England and Wales, 1871, Population tables. Area, houses, and inhabitants. Vol. II. Registration or Union Counties. BPP 1872 LXVI Pt [C.676-I], p. 243.
12. Ibid., p. 244.
13. Census of England and Wales, 1841, Census Enumerators Book (HO107/137 ED16 viewed on microfilm, Cornish Studies Library).
14. Ibid.
15. Ibid.
16. Census of England and Wales, 1851, Census Enumerators Book (HO107/1914 ED2q viewed on microfilm, Cornish Studies Library).
17. Census of Great Britain, 1851, Forms and instructions prepared under the direction of one of her Majesty's principal secretaries of state, for the use of persons employed in taking an account of population of Great Britain. BPP 1851 XLIII (1339), p. 33.
18. Census of Great Britain, 1861, Enumerator's Memorandum Book, p. i. Instructions

to the enumerator (content associated with 1861 census on www.histpop.org, accessed 15 March 2012).

19. Ibid., p. ii. Example as to the manner in which entries should made in this book (content associated with 1861 census on www.histpop.org, accessed 15 March 2012).

20. Census of Great Britain, 1891, Enumerator's Instruction and Memorandum Book, p. 5. Example of the manner in which entries should made in this book (content associated with 1891 census on www.histpop.org, accessed 15 March 2012)

21. E. Higgs, *Making Sense of the Census Revisited – Census Records for England and Wales 1801–1901* (London, 2005), p. 33.

22. L. Trotter, 'Desperate? Destitute? Deserted? Questioning perceptions of miners' wives in Cornwall during the Great Migration, 1851–1891', unpublished MA thesis, University of Exeter, 2010, p. 37.

23. Census of England and Wales, 1861, Census Enumerators Books, Gwennap (RG9/1576–1578 viewed on microfilm, Cornish Studies Library).

24. Trotter, 'Desperate? Destitute? Deserted?' thesis, p. 37.

25. Census of England and Wales, 1861, Census Enumerators Books, Redruth (RG9/1579–1580 viewed on microfilm, Cornish Studies Library).

26. Trotter, 'Desperate? Destitute? Deserted?' thesis, p. 37.

27. Current postgraduate being undertaken by the author, Institute of Cornish Studies, University of Exeter.

28. Trotter, 'Desperate? Destitute? Deserted?' thesis.

29. B. Deacon, 'Mining the Data: What can a quantitative approach tell us about the micro-geography of nineteenth-century Cornish mining?' in P. Payton (ed.), *Cornish Studies: Eighteen* (Exeter, 2010), p. 18.

30. Trotter, 'Desperate? Destitute? Deserted?' in Payton (ed.), *Cornish Studies: Nineteen*, p. 202.

31. Trotter, 'Desperate? Destitute? Deserted?' thesis, p. 37.

32. T. M. Devine, *To the Ends of the Earth: Scotland's Global Diaspora 1750–2010* (London, 2011), p. 145.

33. Deacon, 'Mining the Data', p. 22, Fig. 1.

34. Devine, *To the Ends of the Earth*, p. 144.

35. Deacon, 'Mining the Data', p. 30.

36. Trotter, 'Desperate? Destitute? Deserted?' in Payton (ed.), *Cornish Studies: Nineteen*, pp. 204–9.

37. Deacon, 'Mining the Data', p. 16.

II

Accidental injury in Cornish Mines, 1900–1950

Allen Buckley

Introduction

The miners' working environment is uniquely different from any other workplace. Conditions underground lead to injuries of a type which tend to be different from those suffered in factories, warehouses, shops, farms, shipyards, foundries or quarries. Their frequency is also greater than in those surface workplaces. Space is severely restricted, it is totally dark, the rock is sharp and sometimes contains poisonous minerals, the air is polluted, there is a lack of oxygen and the heat can be unbearable. Many parts of most mines can be extremely wet, so that miners often work in a constant deluge of cold, warm or very hot water. There are added hazards of rock falling unexpectedly and from ladders, which are slippery and sometimes poorly fixed. There are also dangers inherent in using explosives in these difficult conditions.

To the outsider, this whole working environment can appear hazardous or downright dangerous. Statistics appear to bear this out, with serious and fatal injuries far more common among miners than workers in other industries. However, this is to some extent a misconception, for the majority of miners complete many years of underground work without suffering a serious work injury. What he will almost certainly suffer will be several small injuries, which keep him away from work for relatively short periods of time.

Books and articles dealing with accidents in Cornish mines have tended to report on the major, serious and usually fatal accidents – the type reported in the press. Cyril Noall's excellent *Cornish Mine Disasters* (1989) is a case in point.[1] Peter Joseph's *Accidents in the St Just Mining District 1831–1914* (1999) also covers accidents reported in the press, which were serious and usually fatal.[2] Valuable as these works undoubtedly are, they can lead to a distorted

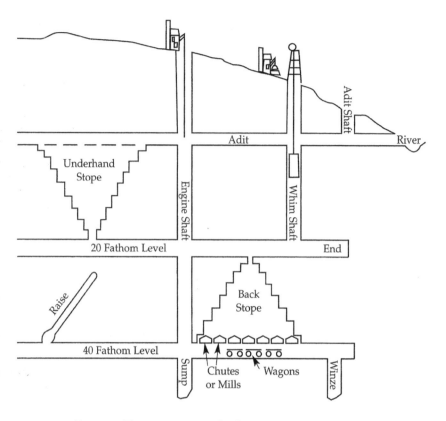

Figure 1. The arrangement of a Cornish mine underground

view of the hazards and dangers, which exist underground in Cornish metal mines. This study is different in that it intends to look closely at the whole range of accidental injuries suffered by Cornish miners during the first half of the twentieth century. We are fortunate in that there exists a complete accident record for South Crofty Mine for most of the twentieth century, and also extant are the accident records for Geevor Tin Mine for the years 1926 to 1946.[3]

The South Crofty records give information on most of the facts required to carry out detailed analysis. The names, addresses, ages, weekly wages and workplaces of the injured miners are given, as are the dates and times of the accidents. There is a brief description of each accident together with the injury sustained and the period of time off work. Also recorded is the amount of injury pay received by the injured man. The names of the supervisor (mine captain) and any person present at the time of the accident are also given. The Geevor records are only slightly less informative – they do not give the weekly wage of the injured party, nor the names of the supervisor and witnesses to the accident. The study covers the years 1900 to 1950 for South Crofty and 1926 to 1946 for Geevor.

The locations of the accidents will be examined together with the causes of the accidents. The length of time the injured were off work and how much injury pay they received, will also be analysed. Particular attention will be directed to the very young – the teenagers – and the relatively old, those over 50 years of age.

Accidents to teenagers

Particularly from the middle of the nineteenth century, legislation and social attitudes to employment, caused the ages at which miners started to work underground to increase. By 1900 it appears to have been accepted at such mines as South Crofty and Geevor, that boys should not start to work underground until they were at least 14 years of age. This is supported by the testimony of Martin Crothers, who began work underground at Carn Brea Mine in 1909, when he was 14 years old. He had spent the previous twelve months working on a farm, waiting to be old enough to go underground. In 1911, when Carn Brea temporarily closed, he went to work at South Crofty. At both mines he was employed 'beating the borer' (drilling) in stopes. The youngest miners found in South Crofty's accident books for the years 1900 to 1932 were 14 years of age. After this, 15 years was the age at which boys could work underground there, and although this was the case well into the 1940s, by the early 1930s it was far more normal for boys to wait until they were 16 before going underground.[4]

South Crofty

During the decades between 1900 and 1950 the average ages of South Crofty's teenage miners gradually increased. Between 1900 and 1919 there were six 14 year olds involved in accidents; in the 1920s there were four, and the last one recorded underground was in 1932. Fifteen year olds also decreased in number over the years. Before 1920 there were twenty-two injured underground, during the 1920s there were fourteen, in the 1930s there were nine and only four 15 year olds recorded in the 1940s. There was a similar picture for the 16 and 17 year olds, but in contrast, the number of 18 and 19 year olds remained high and gradually increased as a proportion of the total underground workforce.

Table A.   South Crofty: Ages of Injured Teenage Miners

	14 yrs	*15 yrs*	*16 yrs*	*17 yrs*	*18 yrs*	*19 yrs*
1900–09	0	1	5	6	13	9
1910–19	6	21	29	29	29	36
1920–29	4	14	20	27	49	26
1930–39	1	9	6	14	19	29
1940–49	0	4	3	10	43	43

Geevor

At Geevor, the records for the years 1926 to 1945 tell a slightly different story, although there are similarities. There were no 14 year olds recorded as being injured in those years, and by 1929 there were no 15 year olds either. In 1926 there were two 15 year olds injured, and in 1927 and 1928 only one in each year. Sixteen year olds were also declining, with only one injured in 1927, one in 1930 and no more until 1939, when there was one. War conditions and loss of skilled miners meant an increase in the 1940s, with two injured in 1940, and one each year from 1942 to 1944. There were three 17 year olds injured in 1926, two in 1927, four in 1935, one in 1942 and one in 1943. For the 18 and 19 year olds, however, there was a distinctly different patter, with young men being called up for military service and many being sent to the mines as 'Bevin Boys'. This policy, instituted by the wartime Minister of Labour, Ernest Bevin, saw thousands of youngsters sent to mines all over the country and Geevor was sent its share. In 1926 there were four 18 and 19 year olds injured, in 1927 there were three and only one 19 year old in the years 1928 and 1929. There were only four 18 and 19 year olds injured in the whole of the 1930s, but in the years 1940 to 1945 there was a significant upsurge in their numbers. In the years 1940 to 1942 there was only one injured, but in 1943, with the Bevin policy in operation this number jumped to twenty-eight. In 1944 there were nine, and in 1945 the number had dropped to three, because the original 'Bevin Boys' were by then in their twenties.

Table B.   Geevor: Ages of Injured Teenage Miners

	15 yrs	*16 yrs*	*17 yrs*	*18 yrs*	*19 yrs*
1926–29	4	1	5	3	6
1930–39	0	2	4	2	2
1940–45	0	5	2	14	27

South Crofty

It is impossible, from the data available, to give an accurate estimate of the proportion of teenagers in South Crofty's underground workforce for the years 1900–1949, as our figures are mostly based upon the accident records alone. This being the case, we cannot always be certain whether teenagers were more prone to accidental injury than older miners. However, we have a couple of 'snap shots', which offer some help in this regard. We do know the ages of individual miners at South Crofty in the years 1916 and 1926, which gives us some indication of such proportions. If we assume that the 1916 figures were fairly typical of the years 1910–19, we find that whereas 17.6 per cent of the workforce at that time were between the ages of 14 and 19, during the same period 25 per cent of those injured were teenagers. However, if we take the figures for the 1920s we have a totally different picture. During that decade teenagers appear to have made up 31 per cent of the miners, although they accounted for only 27.4 per cent of those injured.

Table C.   South Crofty: Ages of Miners in 1916 and 1926

1916	
16 yrs to 19 yrs	47 (Teenagers 17.6 per cent of the 267 miners)
20 yrs to 29 yrs	105
30 yrs to 39 yrs	61
40 yrs to 49 yrs	34
50 yrs to 59 yrs	16 (Over 50s 7.49 per cent of 267 miners)
60 yrs to 69 yrs	3
70 yrs to 79 yrs	1 (One 71 yr old)
	Total 267 miners (Average age of all miners 30yrs)
1926	
14 yrs to 19 yrs	57 (Teenagers 31 per cent of 183 miners)
20 yrs to 29 yrs	67
30 yrs to 39 yrs	42
40 yrs to 49 yrs	13
50 yrs to 59 yrs	2 (Over 50s 2.2 per cent of all miners)
60 yrs to 69 yrs	1
70 yrs to 79 yrs	1
	Total 183 miners (Average age of miners 26.2 yrs)

Table D.   South Crofty: Ages of Injured Miners

Decade	1900–09	1910–19	1920–29	1930–39	1940–49
14 yrs to 19 yrs	34	150	140	78	74
20 yrs to 29 yrs	66	248	180	203	209
30 yrs to 39 yrs	29	98	119	104	164
40 yrs to 49 yrs	23	58	57	22	66
50 yrs to 59 yrs	8	36	14	7	17
60 yrs to 69 yrs	0	7	3	1	8

1900–09   15–19 yr olds = 21.5 per cent of injured miners
1910–19   14–19 yr olds = 25 per cent of injured miners
1920–29   14–19 yr olds = 27.4 per cent of injured miners
1930–39   14–19 yr olds = 18.8 per cent of injured miners
1940–49   15–19 yr olds = 13.75 per cent of injured miners

We have no information on the ages of Geevor miners in general, and so cannot estimate the proportion of the total underground workforce that were teenagers. However, the records do show the ages of the injured miners there.

Table E.   Geevor: Ages of Injured Miners

	15–19 yrs	20–29 yrs	30–39 yrs	40–49 yrs	50–59 yrs	60–69 yrs
1926–29	19	17	30	10	5	1
1930–39	9	58	62	31	17	5
1940–45	48	113	84	33	23	2

Note: In 1940–45, 56 of the injured miners were 19 or 20 years old

Tasks teenagers carried out

What sort of tasks were these teenagers engaged in? Martin Crothers' testimony shows that he was engaged as a driller, in a stope, from the age of 14. Prior to the introduction of air-powered rock drills for such tasks, a stope might have anything from nine to eighteen miners working in it. They normally worked in groups of three men – one holding and turning the drill and the other two beating it into the rock. As most of the stoping was underhand stoping, these miners stood on the benches they drilled and beat the drill downwards for a depth of three of four feet. Usually the miners climbed into the stope from the level above and less often, they climbed up from the level below. Their tasks included carrying the 5–7lb hammers and drills into the stope and fetching the explosives (gunpowder or dynamite) prior to blasting. By the 1920s most stopes were worked with light-weight (about 50lb) rock drills, powered by compressed air. This meant only two men would be working where several more had previously been employed. The task was not made lighter for the miner however, as the drills and the necessary equipment had to be hauled up and down the stope, and the miners were expected to break a much larger tonnage of ore each shift. Another task carried out by these teenagers was crimping the detonators onto the end of the safety fuse. A proper crimper might be used, but where none was available, the miners crimped with their teeth – occasionally with disastrous results!

Examples of teenagers working as drillers are found throughout South Crofty's accident books for the whole period covered. In April 1909, Thomas James Keast (15) was injured when drilling. In November 1901, Charles Heard (16) was injured whilst drilling, and Joseph Thomas (16) was struck by a falling rock when drilling in a stope. In January 1936, Howard Mankee (15) had an accident whilst using a rock-drill machine in a stope. The proportion of teenagers working as drillers gradually fell as the century progressed. Teenagers were also engaged as trammers, skip fillers, assistant timbermen, track layers and pipe fitters. At Geevor the situation was similar, with most youngsters working in stopes as drilling assistants, until by the end of the 1930s the proportion tailed off. The 1940s saw most teenagers working on the level, with only three out of thirty-six accidents to them taking place in stopes. Undoubtedly, the influx of 'Bevin Boys' from non-mining backgrounds added to the trend for youngsters to work on lighter jobs.

Teenagers were not immune to more serious accidents at South Crofty. In July 1934, whilst working in an underhand stope, Jack Jervis (17) fell through a stope and was seriously injured. He was off work for six months and it was another twelve months before he could work underground again. In April 1937, Richard Trengove (16) was killed instantly, when he fell 60 feet in the stope where he was working. In September 1937, Charles Smith (19) was gassed by fumes from the explosives used in the previous shift. He died in the stope where he had been drilling. In January 1944, a 'Bevin Boy' called Douglas Couch (19) was killed when he fell through a stope. He was working as a trammer.

The work done by the 14, 15 and 16 year olds was typical of the general work of a miner at South Crofty and Geevor. There were no particular concessions to age and when they started underground they were more likely to be working in a stope or drive as a driller than they were to be working as a trammer or timberman. The records show that the same was true of older teenagers – 17, 18 and 19 year olds. What gradually changed some of these practices as the twentieth century progressed, was the tightening up

Table F.   South Crofty and Greevor: Fatal Accidents

Decade	Total Killed	Teenagers Killed
South Crofty		
1900–09	3	1
1910–19	10	2
1920–29	12	3
1930–39	7	2
1940–49	3	1
	Total 35	Total 9 (one 16, one 17, one 18 & six 19 yr olds)
Geevor		
1926–29	3	0
1930–39	1	0
1940–46	3	1 (16 years old)

of the employment methods of these mines and the introduction of new machinery, which necessitated a certain amount of training and skill. Before the Great War (1914–18) the 'tutwork' (piece work) contractors took on their own men and paid them. They were entered in the mine employment books and covered by the mine's insurance, but they were really employed by the contractors. After the War things changed and the mine captains took new men on and assigned them to their tasks. The use of powered rock drills, which were owned by the mine, meant the miners and their assistants had to be taught how to use them safely and efficiently.

Accidents to miners over 50 years of age

South Crofty

As noted in Table D, there was considerable variation in the number of older miners (over 50) involved in accidents at South Crofty between 1900 and 1950. The decades 1910–19 and 1940–49 showed sharp increases, with the former leaping from eight (1900–09) to forty-three (1910–19), and the latter going up from eight (1930–39) to twenty-five (1940–49). Both of these substantial increases might have been caused by older men making up a larger proportion of the face workers, due to a considerable number of young miners leaving for the armed forces during the two world wars. The number of men over the age of 50 working underground at South Crofty in 1916, as noted above, was twenty (7.49 per cent of the miners), whereas the number over 50 in 1926 had fallen to four (2.2 per cent of the miners).

We have noted that until the end of the 1930s there was little concession to age for youngsters starting underground. They were assigned the same tasks as adult miners. The same applied to miners over 50: if they were fit and willing to do the job, they did it. Some examples illustrate this. In October 1906, Thomas Harry (50) was injured whilst drilling; in March 1909, Alfred Roscholar (50) was injured when drilling into a hole which exploded; in August 1910, F. H. Uren (61) was injured when drilling; in October 1910, Henry Ayres (55) was injured when working in a stope; in July 1911, Thomas Ivey (56) was injured working as a driller in stope; in April 1912, James Hunking (57) was killed in a stope; and in July 1919, James Berryman (52) was injured when drilling on 245 fathom level.

Throughout the 1920s, 1930s and 1940s the same situation obtained, with miners who were well into their 60s continuing to carry out hard and wearing tasks of climbing into stopes, hauling up heavy gear and drilling holes for blasting. By the 1920s much of the drilling in stopes was by compressed-air-powered rock drills. By the 1930s hand drilling had all but disappeared at South Crofty. This did not make life easier for the miner. Hauling heavy machines, with their hoses, oil bottles and other gear up ladders into stopes was harder work than merely carrying drills and hammers up. What machines meant was that more holes could be drilled and more ground broken, using 2 men where several had previously been employed. The heavy 'bar-and-arm' machines had been used for main development (shaft sinking and tunnel driving) since the 1870s, whereas the lighter 'peg leg' stoping machines came into general use after the Great War. When Thomas Jenkin (63) was injured in a stope, in November 1944, he was using a light-weight machine.

However, the tendency for older miners to move to lighter work on the level continued throughout the period 1900–49. Thus, most accidents to men over 50 occurred on the level. Tramming, timberwork and general labouring were their normal tasks. In July 1909, Lewis Frankland (51) was injured whilst tramming; in November 1912, John Gregor (50) was injured tramming; and in October 1919, William Blight (53) was also injured when tramming.

Miners did not always remain in one job when working underground. Even older miners sometimes moved from lighter work on the level to harder work in a stope. In 1939, Thomas Jenkin was 58 when he was injured whilst tramming; he continued in that job until 1943, when he was 62, after which he went to work drilling in a stope. It is likely that he was returning to a job he had done when younger, as the mine was short of skilled drillers, due to the war. Older miners carried out all the normal underground tasks and because of their experience, they usually took the lead as stopers, developers and timbermen: building chutes, ladderways and support work. Many moved to such tasks as looking after the pumps, safety work and monitoring the drainage adits. They also became shift bosses and mine captains.

Geevor

At Geevor, in the period for which we have records, the situation was similar to that at South Crofty. A few examples demonstrate this: in July 1926, Isaac Newton (57) was injured whilst drilling with a heavy bar-and-arm machine on the level and two years later he was injured when drilling in a raise. Raise mining was the hardest of all underground work. In December 1932, when he was 63, he was injured whilst drilling in a stope. In March 1929, Richard Davey (62) was injured whilst drilling in a stope, and in August 1929, Richard George (51) was injured working in a stope. Also in the 1930s, James Nankervis (52), William Whitta (54), John Roberts (57), R. E. Ellis (58), William Rowe (56) and Robert Mathews (60) were all killed or seriously injured whilst carrying out the hardest tasks underground. Between 1940–45 the pattern continued, with several older miners injured in stopes, either drilling, barring down or carrying out safety work. Their ages ranged from 53 to 66 years old.

The records for Geevor are clear, during the 1920s, 1930s and 1940s, that men over the age of 50 regularly undertook all the tasks that younger miners did. As at South Crofty, there was no concession to age – if they were fit enough and willing, they did the job.

Locations and causes of accidents

Accidents underground could happen in shafts, stopes, winzes, raises or on the level (see Figure 1 above). An explanation of these terms is necessary, so that a proper understanding of the circumstances can be appreciated.

South Crofty

Shafts:
A shaft is a vertical or near vertical opening into a mine. Its depth can vary from as little as 100 metres to several hundred metres. Accidents in a shaft could be caused by rocks, timber or tools falling down the shaft and causing injury to men travelling in the shaft or working below. Men could fall from a gig or cage, or slip from a ladder in a shaft. Men sinking a shaft were also prone to have accidents when the stage upon which they were working fell away, or when rocks or even small stones fell onto them from a great height.

Examples from South Crofty illustrate the hazards attendant upon travelling in the shaft, carrying out maintenance in the shaft or sinking the shaft deeper. In September 1902, John Tonkin was injured whilst fixing a staging in Palmers Shaft. He slipped from the stage and fell 6 feet. In September 1903, J. H. Richards was greasing the main pump rod in Palmers Shaft, when he caught his fingers in the machinery. In February 1904, Phillip Roberts was loading a bucket in Robinsons Shaft when he jammed his thumb, causing serious injury. In March 1932, Ralph Opie fell from a moving skip in New Cooks Kitchen Shaft, and fell 36m to his death.

Shaft sinking was a job which seems to have been more dangerous than most, for a high proportion of serious and fatal accidents happened to shaft sinkers. During the first half of the twentieth century, both Robinsons and New Cooks Kitchen shafts were being sunk. In November 1913, Thomas Bawden was working with a group of miners sinking Robinsons Shaft, when a rock fell some 60m and struck him on the head, fracturing his skull. In March 1915, Thomas Sleeman was sinking New Cooks Shaft when he was struck by a piece of falling metal. In July 1916, Ernest Luke was sinking New Cooks Shaft when he was struck on the head by a small stone, causing 'concussion of the brain'.

Perhaps the most serious accident in the history of South Crofty also occurred to men sinking New Cooks Kitchen Shaft. On 12 December 1924, a group of miners were fixing timbers in the shaft, when the staging from which they worked collapsed, precipitating them to the bottom of the shaft. William James Mitchell, Harry Pendray and Frederick Richard Daniell were all killed. Three other men were seriously injured. Six months earlier, William Harris was killed by a premature explosion whilst engaged in sinking Robinsons Shaft.

The Level:
The level is the horizontal tunnel which is driven from the shaft at various intervals to gain access to the valuable lodes (mineralised veins). At South Crofty, in the late nineteenth and first half of the twentieth century, these levels were mostly driven from the shafts at intervals of 20 fathoms (120ft/36m), whereas at Geevor they were 100ft (30m) apart. At Crofty these tunnels were up to 7 feet square. Some older levels were only 6 feet high by 5 or 6 feet wide, and adit tunnels were usually only a couple of feet wide and about 6 feet high. By the 1960s these levels were 8 feet square and by the end of the century the norm was 9 or 10 feet. Rail track ran down the centre of these levels and the gauge at Crofty was 22 inches. For most of the first half of the twentieth century the wagons used for ore haulage were 10cwt and 16cwt and the trammers pushed them by hand. In the early 1940s small BEV locos were introduced and these pulled trains of one-ton wagons from the chutes or ore piles to the shafts. Also running along these levels were the main services of compressed air, in large pipes up to 10 inch diameter, and

water, in smaller pipes. At Crofty these pipes were fixed in the top corners of the levels. Thus, it can be readily appreciated, that even in tunnels which were 7 feet square, there was very little room. Where the ground was broken or potentially hazardous, timber supports would be inserted, further restricting the available working space. Where chutes were erected below stopes, to feed the ore into the wagons, more timbering was necessary, to protect the trammers and others on the level.

Most accidents on the level were to trammers loading ore into wagons from chutes (mills), or when conveying the ore to the shaft or ore pass for hoisting to surface. Rock could also fall from the back of a level and cause injury. Accidents to miners engaged in driving the tunnels on were also common. Premature explosions, rocks hitting miners when 'barring down' (bringing down loose rock) and accidents caused by drilling machines were not unusual.

Examples of accidents to men on the levels show a considerable variety. In June 1903, William Wearne (30), a stoper, was hit by a falling rock whilst walking along the 170fm level. In May 1904, Thomas Curry (40) caught his foot in the track on the 205fm level and a wagon ran over it. In February 1905, Martin Morrish (40) slipped whilst walking on the 170fm level and injured his side on the track. In August 1907, William Johns (19) trapped his finger when tipping a wagon into the ore pass. In November 1912, John Henry Gregor (50) was filling a wagon from a chute when a rock fell onto his foot. In March 1915, John Mills (20) was injured by a falling timber from a stull above the 170fm level. In January 1916, Richard Heather (32) injured his hand when a rock fell from the wagon he was pushing along the 225fm level. Also during the Great War, Samuel Kellow (40) was injured when he caught his hand in the rock-drill machine he was using on the 225fm level.

Stopes:

A large number, perhaps the majority, of serious and fatal accidents occurred in stopes. A stope is an excavation mined to remove the ore, usually from between two levels (see illustrations). At South Crofty and Geevor during the years covered by the accident books, the two types of stope operating were underhand stopes and back stopes. An underhand stope was so called because either it was worked below a level, or because it was working the lode by drilling down into benches formed in the stope. The broken ore was blasted down to the level beneath. These benches resembled large steps and the miners would drill the lowest step first and then move back up to the next step and so on. Normally, in the early twentieth century, three men would work on each bench, and if there were three groups working in a stope, at the end of the shift the three benches would all be fired. When compressed-air rock drills came into more general use in stopes, after the Great War, two men would normally work in a stope and drill many more holes to a greater depth than hitherto. This meant that benches were no longer 3 or 4 feet high, but up to 6 feet. With the wider use of drilling machines, there was a shift toward more back stoping, as these machines were more efficiently used drilling upward. An inherent danger with underhand stoping was that the miners, as they worked down from the level above, became farther and farther from the back, making it more difficult to bar down safely.

As noted above, the introduction of drilling machines into stoping, meant a general shift from underhand stoping to back stoping. Back stoping is also called shrinkage stoping, and here miners drilled upward into benches, which were like underhand benches but the other way round. They stood on the broken ore above the chutes located at the bottom of the stope. They were thus mining the back. Such stopes are called shrinkage (or shrink) stopes because it is necessary for trammers on the level below to regularly pull ore from the chutes to allow the miner space in which to work – shrinking the broken ore in the stope. Broken ore takes up much more room than unbroken rock. The dangers in such stopes tend to be from falling rock, and as these stopes were usually wider than underhand stopes, the hanging wall needed to be carefully checked to ensure there were no unexpected rock falls.

The causes of accidents in stopes were varied. Falling rocks were a common cause; stages erected in the stopes to work from could collapse, precipitating men considerable distances. The uneven nature of the broken ground in a stope, coupled with the great distances men could fall if they slipped, also led to serious injury. The hemp ropes, wire ropes, chains and ladders used to move up and down stopes could also slip or break, creating another all-to-common hazard. Sharp bits of wire could puncture the skin and cause poisoning. Rocks could roll off benches or piles above the workers, causing injury to men below.

A few examples serve to illustrate the type of accidents common in stopes. In May 1901, Fred Evans was seriously injured when he drilled into a hole with dynamite residue in it. In July 1901, William Caddy was working in a stope below the 225fm level, when he was struck by a falling rock. In April 1905, William John (18) was climbing up through a stope above the 225fm level when his hand slipped off the chain and he fell 42 feet. In the same month, Isaac Caddy (29) was preparing to descend a stope using a chain, when he slipped and fell 108 feet. In January 1913, Alfred Williams (18) was returning to his stope after blasting, when he fell through the stope due to some timbers having been damaged by the blast. To make the situation worse, his mate, Ernest Lawry (23), whilst attempting his rescue him, was injured when the rope he was using broke under his weight. In February 1916, Bernard Crump (25), working in a stope between the 225 and 245fm levels, was injured when a board he was standing on to drill, broke, and he fell 60 feet.

A significant proportion of all the fatal accidents at South Crofty, during the first half of the twentieth century, happened in stopes. Falls accounted for several of these fatalities, and there were several causes for these. In April 1912, James Hunkin (57) fell from a staging in a stope a distance of 12 feet and his consequent injuries proved fatal. The following month, Matthew Lamming (17) was killed when the board he was standing on slipped, and he fell 150 feet through the stope to the 205fm level. In February 1916, William Jefferey (36) was fixing stage timbers in a stope when they collapsed, causing him to fall 60 feet to his death. In April 1919, James Cock (30) went back into his stope to clear away loose rock, when he was hit by a small rock fall, causing him to fall to his death. In January 1920, William Oates (38) was climbing down through his underhand stope after blasting, when the chain he was using broke and he fell some distance, fracturing his skull and leading to his death. In June 1924, Thomas Jane (19) was killed by falling rock whilst underhand stoping above the 225fm level. In August 1925, Thomas Arthur (33) fell through his stope and a winze below it and was killed instantly. His fall was caused by a rock fall in the stope. In September 1929, William Care (39) was underhand stoping above the 245fm level, when his drill steel broke, causing him to fall some 60 feet to his death. Similar accidents killed Frank Bray in January 1934 and Richard Trengove in April 1937.

It will be noted how many of these falls were caused by falling rock, which either struck the miner or damaged the staging on which he stood. However, sometimes miners were killed by the rock fall itself. In June 1917, Sidney Williams (19) was struck by two rocks which fell from the side of the stope, pinning him to the side. It proved fatal. In September 1917, Leonard Judd (27) was killed in a stope under the 225fm level, when a rock rolled onto him.

Another less common cause of fatal accidents was due to premature or unexpected explosions. In November 1923, Albert Gregor (31) was charging a hole with dynamite, when 'by some means not known', it exploded, killing him instantly. It appears that some dynamite residue was left in the hole from a previous explosion. This type of accident was largely eradicated at South Crofty by insisting that miners do not drill into or close to the sockets left by the previous blast. In other Cornish mines this rule was often ignored.

Raises or Rises:
A raise or rise is a tunnel mined upward between levels. These could be mined all the way to the next level, or just high enough to start a stope. Box-hole raises were usually mined upwards for between 15 and 25 feet to link with a sub-level or intermediate level. These were mined at intervals beneath a back stope, and the distance between them depended, to some extent, on the strength of the ground. The sub-level would then become the stope, as benches were formed by drilling into the back. In order to maintain access as

the stope went higher above the level, a timber rearing or casing was erected up the side of the stope, into which a ladderway was installed. The rearing or casing acted like a fence to contain the broken ore on the stope side, and to ensure an open ladderway for access. The rearing and ladderway were extended continuously until the top of the stope was reached.

Accidents in raises could be due to rock fall or collapsing stages. Stages were for the miners to stand on whilst drilling. Rock falls could occur when the miners were climbing to the top of the raise after blasting. Stope chains were used for climbing the near-vertical raises, and men could slip off of them and fall. Not only could miners be injured by falling rock, but they could also be knocked off the chain and fall to the bottom of the raise. As the top of the raise could be 80 or 90 feet above the level, a miner would be seriously injured by such a fall. An added danger to the raise miner was due to barring down loose rock, as the man had nowhere to go if a large rock fell from above him.

In September 1901, Fred Cadwell (17) fell 14 feet down a raise above the 192fm level, when his stage collapsed. In September 1903, Edward Oates (17) fell down a raise and fractured his skull. In October 1901, John Gribble (21) injured his hand on his rock drill in a raise above the 225fm level. In May 1933, Cyril Lampshire (30) was climbing a ladder in a raise when the rope securing it broke, causing him to fall and injure himself. In August 1933, Philip Davies (17) fell 25 feet through a box-hole and was injured. In August 1933, William Mann (24) was killed by an explosion whilst working in a raise above the 110fm level in North Tincroft section of Crofty. Mann believed all the holes he had charged had exploded, but when returning to check the last hole went off and killed him.

Falling rock constituted the biggest threat to miners in raises as the following examples show. In August 1933, Reginald Prout (38) was hit by falling rock in a raise. In September 1934, Charles Kemp (26) was struck by falling rock in his raise. In October 1934, Stephen Harris (42) was injured by falling rock in his raise, and similar accidents injured William Buzza and Samuel Curtis in 1935.

Winzes or Winds:
Mining a winze could also be hazardous. Winzes were shafts sunk beneath a level either to the level below or to an intermediate level, a short distance down. Originally, winzes were used to evaluate and open up the ground by sinking onto the lode. Accidents to those working in winzes were mostly from men falling, rocks falling from kibbles or buckets, rocks falling from the sides of the winze or from accidents related to the windlass used to hoist the broken rock. There were also hazards due to drilling and use of explosives.

In May 1929, William Reed (31) was sinking a winze under the 245fm

Table G.   Locations of Accidents: South Crofty (1926–35)

	1926	1927	1928	1929	1930	1931	1932	1933	1934	1935
Levels	38	46	41	33	23	–	14	13	23	13
Stopes	14	21	24	31	20	–	23	14	19	17
Shafts	6	2	5	2	5	–	3	–	3	–
Shaft Stations	2	–	–	–	2	–	1	1	–	–
Winzes	–	1	1	3	–	–	1	–	–	–
Raises/Rises	3	5	1	1	1	–	2	4	4	2
Ladderways	–	2	4	–	–	–	1	1	–	–

Table H.   Causes of Accidents: South Crofty (1926–35)

	1926	1927	1928	1929	1930	1931	1932	1933	1934	1935
Falls	5	10	6	4	8	–	3	6	5	7
Rock Falls	10	22	13	22	8	–	7	7	13	10
Machining/ Drilling	8	7	12	11	5	–	11	6	7	6
Cuts:Fingers/ legs/arms	15	23	17	16	17	–	16	12	18	10
Wagons/ Chutes/Track	7	7	7	5	8	–	3	3	4	2
Dynamite Gas	1	1	–	–	–	–	–	–	–	–
Stages Collapsed	1	1	1	1	–	–	1	–	1	–
Gig/Cage/ Bucket/Barrow	–	2	–	2	–	–	–	–	–	–
Flying Scats	3	–	2	–	2	–	1	1	1	1
Ore Subsided in Stope	–	–	1	–	–	–	–	–	–	–
Dynamite Explosion	–	–	–	1	1	–	–	1	–	–
Miscellaneous	13	5	19	10	3	–	4	4	4	1

level, when a rock fell and injured him. In December 1929, S. W. Hole (23) injured his hand whilst hoisting a bucket from a winze. In the same month, Joseph Seymour (27) was injured by a rock, which fell from the side of the winze he was sinking. In May 1932, Stanley Curnow (26) was injured when the windlass he was using to hoist rock from below the Deep Adit, slipped, and he was struck in the face.

It is of interest to note, that at both South Crofty and Geevor, the most frequent cause of time off work for miners, was due to fingers, hands or feet being poisoned by mineral water. For example, at Crofty, during the months of September and October 1928, there were no fewer than nine men who went off work due to poisonous mineral water entering cuts and abrasions. The periods away ranged from 6 days to 62 days, with an average of 21 days. This relatively trivial reason for time off work caused a serious problem for the management of the mine, as it meant that a significant number of men were unavailable for work for long periods.

Geevor

Shafts:

The period covered by the Geevor accident records is far less than for South Crofty, but there are enough examples of accident types to demonstrate that the situation was similar in these two mines. Accidents in shafts were less common at Geevor than at Crofty, despite the fact that Geevor's Victory Shaft was being sunk throughout the period 1926–46. However, there was one accident recorded when sinking. In February 1937, George Thomas (35) was drilling with a machine at the bottom of Victory Shaft when the drill steel broke and cut his arm. More typical were the following examples. In May 1927, John Trewhella (32), a skip man, was hit by a falling object in the shaft. In August 1928, William Courtney (38) slipped from a ladder in the shaft and fell some distance. In May 1943, Reginald Monks (19) was excavating a reservoir in the side of Victory Shaft when he strained his wrist, lifting a rock. In February 1944, W. R. Stevens (36) was struck in the back by a falling drill steel in the shaft.

Accidents on shaft stations were more common. In August 1926, John Trewhella (31) suffered a crushed chest whilst putting a large rock in a skip. In August 1928, Joseph Webber (41) crushed his fingers when putting a wagon back on track on the shaft station. In April 1936, John Trewhella was again injured when loading a wagon into the cage for hoisting to surface. In August 1943, James Eddy (30) was injured whilst pushing a wagon onto the shaft station on No. 12 level. In February 1943, R. I. Jeans (26) was also injured when pushing a wagon onto the shaft station.

Accidents in pump stations were unusual, as the pumpmen rarely left the relatively safe environments of their workplaces. However, there were some recorded accidents there. In October 1937, Richard Jory (52), a pumpman, cut his finger whilst 'screwing a grease cap' on a pump. In January 1942, James Barnes (16), an apprentice fitter, damaged his hand whilst screwing a bolt.

Levels:

A large proportion of Geevor's accidents happened on the level. Many of these occurred when trammers were either loading ore from chutes into wagons, or when pushing the wagons along the level to the shaft or ore pass. Some examples illustrate this. In March 1926, George Alford (19) injured his finger when a rock fell from a chute. In May 1926, Joseph Webber (40) was also hit by a rock falling from a chute, as was Thomas Jelbert (40), in August 1928. In November 1929, Robert Maddern (34) caught his fingers between the chute and the wagon he was filling. In September 1934, William Addicoat (21) injured his hand when lifting a de-railed wagon back onto the track. In January 1936, Archie Williams (38) crushed his finger when he de-railed the wagon he was pushing.

In 1939, Geevor introduced its first electric locomotive underground, and the first recorded accident involving a loco occurred there in September of that year. Frederick Eade (37) lost control of the loco he was driving and it ran away, crushing him against a stationary wagon. His injuries were so severe that he did not return to work at the mine.

The variety of accidents on the level can be seen by the following examples. In August 1932, Nicholas James (31) was struck by a rock falling from the back of the level. In September 1933, Harold Hocking (30) slipped and injured his knee whilst walking along the level. In November 1933, Edwin Lawry (32) strained his chest and abdomen when carrying drill steels along the level. In October 1934, John Carter (33) was injured when a rock fell from the back of the level. In April 1935, John Roberts (57) was 'Timbering a man-hole in the level & fell down through a stope' to his death. In September 1935, William Whitta (54), a timberman, was struck on the head by a falling rock from the back of the level. He never returned to work.

Accidents also happened to miners driving the ends (extending the tunnels). In May 1930, Glamis Warren (16) was shovelling ore when a piece of spar entered his hand, which was poisoned by the mineral water. In September 1932, Thomas Eddy (52) was drilling in the end when a piece of rock hit him in the eye. In September 1935, John Williams (39) was drilling with a bar-and-arm machine when the drill steel broke and cut his hand. In April 1936, George Trathen (29) was 'charging a hole to blast' when he slipped and injured his hand. In January 1937, Richard Thomas (28) injured his finger when 'the drill broke in the machine'.

Less common accidents also occurred on the level. For example, in October 1929, Josiah Lawry (31) injured his face and eyes when an air tap burst, throwing grit into his face. In September 1935, Gerald Pender (17) suffered severe burns to his fingers when his acetylene (carbide) lamp exploded. This apparently happened at break time, when the lamp was being re-charged with carbide. In December 1935, James Rowe (41) fractured his patella when he 'jumped off top of wagon'. In January 1936, S. L. G. Edwards (33) was walking on the level when he fell into a winze and injured his head. In November 1937, W. J. Williams (42) stepped onto a plank with a nail sticking out of it and punctured his foot.

Stopes:

Undoubtedly, a stope was potentially a most dangerous workplace at Geevor, as it was at Crofty. Most of the mine's fatal accidents happened there. For example, in April 1927, Thomas Oates (35) was back stoping when the broken ore he was standing on subsided, causing him to be fatally injured. His mate, John Lawrence (39), was also killed. In May 1929, Alfred Hosken (46) was preparing to blast in a stope, when a rock fell on him and killed him. In December 1940, Gordon Lunn (16) was sampling the ore in a stope, when a rock fell and killed him. In September 1943, Thomas James (32) was working in a back stope, when the ore subsided and he was buried. He died of asphyxiation.

The above are examples of the most serious type of accidents in Geevor's stopes, but for the most part the accidents there were less so. For example, in January 1926, Edwin Bennetts (17) was struck on the head by a rock fall in a stope and was off for three weeks. In April 1926, James Olds (31) sprained his back whilst using a 'hammer jack' machine in a stope. In February 1927, Edward Johns (44) broke a finger when his drill steel broke. In July 1927, Thomas James (16) was drilling in a stope when he fell and cut his wrist. In March 1928, James Freestone's (19) thumb was struck by his mate's hammer when drilling in a stope. In March 1929, Frederick Osborne (37) was digging ore in a back stope, when the wall rock fell on him, trapping his hand, which had to be amputated.

Raises or Rises:

Due to the fact that Geevor often used a different method from South Crofty in extending its stopes upwards, the pattern of accidents when raising was also different. Whereas at Crofty, raises were normally mined prior to starting a stope, at Geevor the normal practice was to increase the height of a back stope as the work progressed, so that the raise was often formed by the miner merely raising a single 6- or 8-foot round at the top of the stope (see Figure 1). Box-holes, however, were mined in a similar way to those at Crofty. Vertical raises from one level to the next, 100 feet above, were less common at Geevor than at Crofty.

Some examples of the type of accidents to miners working in raises are as follows. In January 1926, John Sedgeman (35) was using a rock drill in a stope when the air came on unexpectedly, causing him to jam his finger. In the same month, George Angove (43) caught his hand on a nail in a piece

Table I.   Locations of Accidents: Geevor (1926–35)

	1926	1927	1928	1929	1930	1931	1932	1933	1934	1935
Levels	9	4	6	10	3	–	1	7	6	10
Stopes	12	13	9	10	8	–	4	4	8	16
Shafts	–	1	1	–	–	–	–	–	–	–
Shaft Stations	1	–	–	–	–	–	–	–	–	–
Ladderways	–	–	–	1	–	–	–	–	–	–
Winzes	1	–	1	–	–	–	1	–	–	–
Raises/Rises	2	–	1	–	–	–	–	–	–	–

Table J.   Causes of Accidents: Geevor (1926–35)

	1926	1927	1928	1929	1930	1931	1932	1933	1934	1935
Falls	–	3	2	3	–	–	–	–	–	2
Rock Falls	11	4	3	3	2	–	2	4	4	6
Machining/ Drilling	3	4	6	3	5	–	2	2	3	8
Hand Drilling	–	–	1	–	–	–	1	–	–	–
Chutes/ Wagons, etc.	7	3	2	9	2	–	1	3	5	5
Ore Subsidence	–	–	–	1	1	–	–	–	–	–
Slipped on Level	–	–	–	–	–	–	–	1	–	–
Shafts:Objects Falling	–	1	1	–	–	–	–	–	–	–
Miscellaneous	4	3	1	1	–	–	–	1	2	5

of timber in a raise. It went septic due to the minerals in the water. In July 1928, Isaac Newton (59) slipped on some wet timber in a raise and was injured when he fell to the bottom. In May 1936, Thomas Trembath (20) was hit by falling ground in a raise as he started to drill. In February 1944, W. J. Lawry (29) was working in a raise when the timber he stood on turned and he fell some distance.

Winzes:
Accidents in winzes at Geevor were similar to those at South Crofty. For example, in April 1926, Thomas Freestone (18) was hauling a bucket of ore

from a winze when he jammed his hand, which became septic from the minerals present. In February 1928, John Taylor (38) was struck on the head when a bucket used for hauling ore from a winze fell on his head. In May 1932, John Thomas May (19) was injured when the drill he was using to sink a winze slipped and cut his hand. In March 1936, Percy Banfield (27) was working at the bottom of a winze, when the haulage bucket fell and struck his head. In April 1936, Wilfred Fry (43) was struck by falling rock when sinking a winze. These examples were typical of the sort of accidents experienced by miners working in winzes in the first half of the twentieth century.

Time off work due to accidents

Analysis of the data on the periods of time off work due to accidents is very informative. It demonstrates quite clearly that most underground accidents were of a less serious nature. At South Crofty, for example, 14 per cent of injured were off for up to one week, 51 per cent for up to a fortnight, and 72 per cent for up to three weeks. At Geevor the figures were somewhat different, but still show that most accidents could not be classed as serious. There were 31 per cent off for up to one week, 54 per cent for up to a fortnight, and 69 per cent for up to three weeks. These figures are for the years 1926–35.

Table K.   Period Off Work Due to Injury: South Crofty (1926–35)

	1926	1927	1928	1929	1930	1931	1932	1933	1934	1935
<1 week	8	5	12	8	5	–	9	4	7	10
1–2 weeks	23	24	26	27	19	–	15	13	23	14
2–3 weeks	11	23	13	18	14	–	8	7	3	6
>3 weeks	18	24	24	17	12	–	2	3	2	9

Table L.   Period Off Work Due to Injury: Geevor (1926–35)

	1926	1927	1928	1929	1930	1931	1932	1933	1934	1935
<1 week	3	4	4	9	6	–	2	6	7	4
1–2 weeks	3	4	9	3	1	–	2	–	1	10
2–3 weeks	5	4	1	3	1	–	–	2	2	2
<3 weeks	14	4	2	6	3	–	2	3	2	9

Although these statistics tell us something, they do not represent the whole picture, for among those accidents which kept men off work for longer than three weeks, were several which were sufficiently serious to keep the miners off work for considerably longer periods. Of course, there were those accidents which were fatal and others where the men were so seriously injured that they failed to return to work at the mine.

Injury pay

The way in which injury pay was calculated varied over time, and it appears that several factors were involved when the amount to be paid was worked out. These factors also changed as the twentieth century progressed and, presumably, legislation and union activity began to influence the way such things were viewed. As with information on the accidents themselves, so with the factors taken into account when calculating the compensation, the data from the two mines varies. Although both mines give the ages of the injured parties, the periods of time off work and the payments made, only at South Crofty were the weekly wages given. This was a crucial factor when working out the injury pay at Crofty, and it must be assumed that it was also the case at Geevor.

South Crofty

Before we look at the situation in the period covered by this paper, 1900–49, it would be useful to examine the practice prior to that date. There are extant accident records for South Crofty for the last fifteen years of the nineteenth century, which helps us to appreciate how things changed at the turn of the century. The shortest period off work, for which injury pay was given in the years 1885–95, was three days, and payment for four days was regularly made. A few examples will inform us of the situation. In April 1887, James Jenkin, who was 'over 16', was off work for six days after injuring his hand. His weekly wage was £1 and he received 10s. (50p) injury pay. In the same month, James Mitchell, also 'over 16', was paid £1 for two weeks off work through injury. His weekly wage was also £1. In January 1888, Henry Sampson, 'over 16', was paid 7s. (35p) for four days off injured and his weekly wage was 21s. (£1.05). Thereafter, until the mine was temporarily suspended, in November 1895, there were six miners who received injury pay when off work for four days, and one surface worker who was paid for only three days injury. In all these cases their injury pay was 50 per cent of their normal weekly wage. As will be noted from the records, the situation changed with the advent of the twentieth century.

Between January 1900 and September 1907, there was no injury pay for the first sixteen days. After that date the line was drawn at ten days, until February 1908, when payment was (mostly) made after eight days. For the first few years injury pay continued to be normally half of the daily wage. Also, in the early years of the twentieth century, there appears to have been little or no distinction between the injury-pay rates of teenagers and old miners. Some examples serve to illustrate this. In June 1909, John Nancarrow (18) was off work injured for twelve days (two weeks) and was paid £1 injury pay. His weekly wage was £1. In April 1909, Hugh Rogers (42) was off for two weeks and was paid £2, which was his normal weekly wage. In August 1909, William Braizer (29) was off for two weeks and received 17s. 6d. injury pay, which was his normal weekly wage. In January 1910, William Sedgeman (18) was off for two weeks and was paid £1 compensation – his weekly wage. There are scores of identical examples from that time.

By July 1911, the rates had begun to vary somewhat, especially for youngsters. Discretion also began to play a part in the amount of injury pay awarded. One youngster was paid £1 for two weeks' injury, although his weekly rate was only 15s. Another was paid £1 when his rate was only 17s. a week, and yet another received the same amount when his weekly wage was 15s. 7½d. However, for the overwhelming majority of underground workers the rate remained at 50 per cent of their normal wage, until September 1917. After that date the rate was fixed for a time for miners off injured for two weeks, and earning over £2 a week, at £2 10s. Between September 1917 and December 1918, miners off work for a fortnight, and earning between £2 and £3 a week received £2 10s. injury pay. Miners earning less than £2 a week were paid at a lower rate.

This was followed by a period during which injury payments appeared to loose any identifiable pattern. By the end of 1919, however, standard rates for the better paid miners returned, with a fixed rate of £3 10s. for a fortnight off injured. During the 1920s, with economic times getting harder, injury pay was reduced. By 1925, a 20-year-old miner earning £2 10s. a week, was only paid £1 17s. 6d. for two weeks' injury. This situation continued throughout the inter-war years, so that as late as 1937, a 26-year-old miner, earning £2 2s. 6d. a week, only received £1 14s. 7d. injury pay after being off work for two weeks.

Once again, during those hard years, it was the youngsters who were slightly better off than their older colleagues. In 1927, Thomas Holding (15) was paid £1 2s. 6d. for a fortnight off injured, when his weekly wage was only £1. In 1932, William Jenkin (19) was paid £1 9s. injury pay for a fortnight off work when his weekly wage was only £1 7s. 6d. In 1936, Donald Stoddern (20) was paid £1 9s. 3d. for a fortnight injury pay when his weekly wage was only £1 8s. Compare this to the amount paid to Raymond Rogers (35) in 1934. He was given £2 2s. for a fortnight off work when his normal weekly wage was £2 16s. Also in 1934, Bill Williams (46) received £1 17s. 6d. injury pay for two weeks, when his normal pay was £2 10s. a week. There are dozens of examples of similarly low rates of injury pay during the 1920s and 1930s.

When the Second World War broke out, ending a long wage-related strike at South Crofty, the wage rates of miners increased dramatically. Commensurately, injury pay also increased considerably, but it never quite reached the standard 50 per cent achieved in the early years of the century. Despite this, the amount paid to the injured, for the most part, was related to normal earnings, although there were many eccentric variations, which are extremely difficult to understand. For example, there were various standard payments, which did not relate to either the ages of the miners or their weekly wages. In May 1942, Sam Isaacs (24) was paid £2 12s. 6d. compensation for a fortnight's injury. His wage was £3 3s. a week. In May 1943, Alfred Draper (19) was given the same amount for the same period, when his wage was £3 1s. 1d. a week. In March 1944, Bill Prisk (28) was paid the same amount for the same period and his weekly wage was £4 9s. 8d. In May 1944, William May (28) was paid the same amount for the same period off work and his wage was £4 7s. 2d. Several others, whose ages ranged from 19 to 32 years, and whose weekly wages were between £3 12s. and £4 19s. 3d., were also paid £2 12s. 6d. for a fortnight's injury pay. Another regular injury payment, which does not appear to be related to age or earnings was £3 7s. 6d. for a fortnight. Another large group was paid £3 for a fortnight's injury, despite earning between £3 14s. and £5 12s. 3d. a week. The only possible factor which might have contributed to these widely variant injury-pay rates, and which we have no way of determining, was length of service.

Geevor

Analysis of data for Geevor, between 1926 and 1946, is made more difficult due to the absence of the injured party's weekly wage. However, there were one or two trends in injury payments, which might help to inform us. There is a remarkable consistency in the injury pay received by miners off work for the same periods of time. If we take just those off work for twelve days (two weeks), we find that very frequently, they received the same amount of injury pay. Some examples illustrate this. In 1926, John Sedgeman (35) was off work injured for two weeks and received £3. In the same year, Stan Lee (22) was also off for two weeks and got the same payment. However, there were exceptions, for in 1932, Nicholas James (31) was paid £2 5s. 6d. for a fortnight's injury pay, and in 1934, William Harvey (24) was given £2 9s. 2d. for two weeks' injury. Thereafter, between 1935 and 1940, all injured miners bar one, who were off work for two weeks were paid a standard £2 5s. With the outbreak of War the injury payments vary and there is no discernible pattern.

At Geevor teenagers were treated differently than older men. Unlike at South Crofty, where teenagers were given relatively more injury pay than their older work mates, at Geevor they were generally paid less. However, as we do not know the weekly wages of the injured miners, it could be that they were paid at the same or at a better rate than their older colleagues. Some examples show the different amounts paid to youngsters. In 1926, Thomas James (15) was paid £1 9s. 6d. for a fortnight off injured. In 1927, William Wallis (17) was paid £1 13s. 6d. for a fortnight. In 1928, James Freestone (19) was paid £2 0s. 6d. for 2 weeks off injured. In 1928, Albert Richards (15) was given £1 1s. 6d. injury pay for a fortnight. It does seem likely that their injury pay was related to their wages.

Table M.   Geevor: Number of Miners Employed
and Number of Accidents

	Developers and Stopers	Other Underground Workers	Number of Accidents
1926	58	69	25
1927	87	81	18 (2 fatal)
1928	106	83	18
1929	109	97	21 (1 fatal)
1930	78	79	11
1931	0	7	0 (Mine Closed)
1932	32	34	6
1933	52	63	11
1934	87	86	14
1935	80	91	26 (1 fatal)
1936	78	104	27
1937	76	106	24
1938	107	103	33
1939	102	125	29
1940	98	118	21
1941	66	103	16 (2 fatal)
1942	73	110	39
1943	80	198	85 (1 fatal)
1944	77	168	79
1945	75	156	?
1946	52	102	?

What is apparent from Table M is the sharp increase of unskilled over skilled miners once the Second World War started. With the decline in the proportion of 'Developers & Stopers' (skilled miners) and the increase in the unskilled underground workers, the accident rate rose dramatically. Bevin Boys were to make up the largest part of this increase in unskilled workers, and they also, undoubtedly, were involved in the significant increase in the number of accidents.

Conclusions

A surprising fact, which emerges from this data, is the relatively high proportion of accidents which were not serious. Trapped fingers, bruised ribs and crushed toes were more common among miners working in dark and restricted places than to factory or shop workers, but they usually kept miners home for days rather than weeks. The effects of poisonous minerals on cuts and grazes also were common causes of time off work, but again, they mostly resulted in a few days off rather than longer periods.

The high number of teenagers working underground is also of interest, as is the significant proportion that were injured. Also, despite widely held beliefs to the contrary, there were many older miners working underground, with a significant proportion working at the 'rock face'. If we are surprised that 14 and 15 year olds were still employed underground for much of the twentieth century, we might also be amazed that men who had worked all their lives underground, were still carrying out the most arduous tasks well into their fifties and sixties, with occasional exceptional men remaining as development miners and stopers into their seventies.

The various ways that injury pay was calculated over the decades is also of great interest. It is hard to determine what motivated the mine management when deciding how compensation should be apportioned. The seeming generosity of the late nineteenth century was replaced by a more practical and apparently pragmatic approach to these payments. Hence, the way the period off work before payment was made, varied. First it increased and then settled back to a more generous approach. All this before the mines became unionised, during the Great War (1914–18). Thereafter, economic necessity reduced the amount paid to the injured, as the mines struggled to survive during the harsh inter-war years. The Second World War changed things again, out of necessity.

Safety: traditional risk assessment methods

An important area, which has not been examined, is that of risk assessment. Throughout the eighteenth and nineteenth centuries, a boy usually started underground with his father, older brother, uncle or family friend. Many youngsters were taken on by the tutworkers or tributers themselves and became the responsibility of these mining contractors. This situation gradually changed in the twentieth century, so that men were employed directly by the mine. Until the 1960s, the shiftboss to whom the newcomer was assigned, would put him with an experienced miner, on the level, to get him used to the dark, to the sudden loud explosions and to all the other potential dangers lurking in the mine. There was no period of 'induction', no formal training and no instructions on what to do or not to do. The new man had to 'pick it up' as he went along. The reason why there were relatively few serious accidents, despite the extremely hazardous environment, was that the success of 'risk assessment' was dependent upon the experience and good sense of the shiftbosses and skilled miners. They had all learned 'on the job', and were well aware of the potential hazards all around them. Intelligent and experienced miners were conscious of the dangers to themselves and their mates if they disregarded basic safety measures. They were guarded by the caution this understanding created. The best protection for these men and the men they were training was the experience of the miners in charge – the contractors and shiftbosses.

When a new workplace was planned, the mine captain and shiftboss would discuss what was involved and who should be asked to do the job. The miner chosen would be reckoned the most able to do the job. He would examine the ground at his new workplace and carry out his own 'risk assessment'. At each stage of the task, the miner would be assessing the potential dangers, the strength of the ground and the anticipated difficulties. His experience and caution were the best guarantees of his and his mates' safety. All these factors would be taken into account when the price per fathom was worked out between the miner and the mine captain.

Notes and references

1. Philip Payton (ed.), Cyril Noall's *Cornish Mine Disasters* (Redruth, 1989).
2. P. Joseph, *Accidents in the St Just Mining District 1831–1914* (Camborne, 1999).
3. These are in the private collection of the present author.
4. J. A. Buckley, *A History of South Crofty Mine* (Redruth, 1980), pp. 133–8, 141.

12

'A Shrewd Choice'

Isaac Foot and Cornish politics in the General Election of December 1910

Garry Tregidga

Introduction

In March 1922 Isaac Foot was elected to the House of Commons as an Independent Liberal following a sensational by-election victory over the Conservative-Liberal Coalition of David Lloyd George in the Cornish constituency of Bodmin.[1] As Stephen Koss wrote, the by-election 'launched what was surely the last of the great Nonconformist parliamentary careers'.[2] Although never becoming a cabinet member, Isaac Foot was to serve as Minister of Mines in the National government from 1931–32 and his political achievements were commemorated in 1937 when he became a Privy Councillor. But it was noticeable that there was also a strong Cornish dimension to the 1922 by-election. Although Westminster issues were prominent in the contest, there was local disenchantment over the perceived failure of the government to support Cornish tin mining after the war. An election song of the time included the words 'The Coalition would not help the Cornish miners poor' and was appropriately sung to the tune 'Trelawney'.[3] Similarly, newspaper reports claimed that the scenes at the declaration 'were Cornish of the Cornish; the enthusiasm of Nonconformist farmers, of earnest young preachers, of dark-eyed women and fiery Celtic youth had something religious about it. No such fervour could be seen elsewhere outside Wales.'[4] This article is intended as a preliminary study of the sometimes conflicting roles of Foot as a national politician and Cornish champion. After some initial reflections on Foot's career in a broader context it focuses on his initial entry into Cornish politics in 1910 when he first contested the Bodmin seat. Consideration is given to the politics of identity and the way in which deference, locality and radicalism shaped both the nature of the contest and subsequent developments.

Myth, tradition and place: Isaac Foot in context

It is important to consider Foot's career in a multi-level framework embracing both Cornish and British politics. In the first place the survival of the Liberal Party in Cornwall after the First World War has been a popular theme for historians and political scientists.[5] At Westminster the long-term decline of the party after its historic landslide in 1906 was to lead to its near extinction as an independent force by 1951. But west of the Tamar the Liberals were to enjoy notable victories in the 1920s and remained a credible alternative to both Labour and the Conservatives after the Second World War. By 1955, when the party's position was still precarious across Britain as a whole, there were signs of an early recovery in Cornwall. This was particularly the case in the eastern constituencies of Bodmin and North Cornwall. The party was able to demonstrate that it was still the main alternative to the Conservatives and both seats were to be recaptured by the Liberals in the more conducive climate of the 1960s. Significantly, this period covers the years of Foot's involvement in Cornish politics from the time when he first contested Bodmin in 1910 until his death in 1960. As a parliamentary candidate before the First World War he emerged as a leading figure at a time when the Liberals were still a party of government. His by-election victory at Bodmin in 1922 hastened the end of Lloyd George's coalition government with the Conservatives, while he played a prominent role in the regional Liberal landslides of 1923 and 1929.[6] Even after his retirement from active politics he was still influential. The Foot tradition arguably helped the party to survive as the second force in the rural areas of eastern Cornwall in the difficult years of the early 1950s and he continued to campaign for subsequent candidates like Stuart Roseveare and Peter Bessell. Foot's large home at Pencrebar, near Callington, described as the 'Mecca of Cornish Liberalism', was the venue for political rallies and provided a centre for the discussion of the anti-metropolitan policies associated with the party after the Second World War.[7]

Yet it is surprising that there is no major academic study of this pivotal figure in Cornish politics. Detailed studies have tended to be written by members of the Foot family so that the emphasis has been placed on sustaining the myth and memory of the founder of what was arguably one of the greatest political dynasties in Britain in the twentieth century. In 1980 Sarah Foot produced 'an account of my memories of my grandfather and reminiscences of others'. She emphasized that this was 'not a biography' and Michael Foot, her uncle, subsequently referred to it as 'a splendid celebration' that paved the way for further studies.[8] A detailed reference to Foot in the *Dictionary of Liberal Biography* in 1998 was similarly written by his third son John just a year before his own death.[9] Finally, in 2006 Michael Foot and his niece Alison Highet presented a volume that brought together a major collection of papers, letters, photographs and reminiscences. Although providing fascinating insight into his personal, political and religious life through empirical evidence, the book also highlighted the need for more detailed analysis and discussion of Isaac's cultural and political contribution. This is particularly the case in regard to the Cornish dimension of his career. Perhaps reflecting the Tamarside identity of a family uniquely based in both Plymouth and Callington there has been a tendency to use the words 'Westcountry' or 'Devon and Cornwall' to describe the spatial context in which Foot operated. Indeed, the book by Foot and Highet was even entitled *Isaac Foot: A Westcountry Boy – Apostle of England*. However, there needs to be a greater recognition of the complexities of spatial factors in relation to Foot. This was certainly the case in December 1910 since the clash of border identities between Cornwall and Plymouth featured prominently in the election campaign in Bodmin.

Foot's electoral performance also needs to be discussed in relation to the wider changes taking place in British politics. At one level the decline of the Liberals can be seen as an almost inevitable and sweeping process with the party losing seats on a fairly regular basis. From 400 seats in 1906 the Liberals had fallen to 272 by December 1910. The wartime split between Herbert Asquith and David Lloyd George resulted in just 36 Independent Liberals in the 1918 general election. Although the party was able to reunite and win 159 seats in 1923, its representation had fallen to 40 in 1924 and a mere 21 seats by 1935. But there was considerable diversity at the micro level where some candidates were more successful than others. One such example was Alec Glassey, Liberal MP for East Dorset in 1929, who was able to win in a three-cornered contest despite the party being in third place earlier in the decade.[10] At least the Liberals had been successful in East Dorset on a number of occasions before the First World War. In other areas of Britain the party was able to achieve a series of surprising victories in the 1920s in seats like Hereford, Oxford, Ashford and Tiverton that had rarely or never elected a Liberal before.[11] This fluidity in some areas of Britain challenges the assumption that the decline of the Liberals, at least on a local basis, was inevitable. Wales is a good example. Admittedly, the Liberals failed to retain their supremacy throughout the principality as a whole, with the coal-mining seats in the industrial south in particular moving to Labour. Some historians like Kenneth O. Morgan have emphasized that by 1922 Liberal Wales had been 'hemmed into the rural fastness like the Men of Harlech in the past'.[12] But the Lloyd George tradition, which gave the former prime minister a regional powerbase in the late 1920s and was represented after his death in 1945 by his daughter Megan Lloyd George, MP for Anglesey, was still an important factor. Even in 1945 the party was still the second force in Wales with seven MPs concentrated in the peripheral Welsh-speaking areas of the north and west.

This means that it is important to apply micro perspectives to the Liberal decline since it is possible that the party might have been able to survive as a more effective force if it had pursued a strategy that reflected its changing electoral base. It is interesting that it was Dingle Foot, the eldest son of Isaac and a future Liberal MP in his own right, who emerged in 1931 as a leading advocate of a change in direction. He claimed that the Liberals could no longer compete against their opponents as a party of government. Foot believed that his party had to copy the examples of the pre-war Labour and Irish Nationalist parties, which had attempted to 'justify their existence, not as potential ministries, but as minority parties'. He described the parliamentary party as almost a gathering of tribal chieftains whose power was based on their ability to command a strong personal vote in their constituencies. One might add that this helps to explain the extent of the internal differences that plagued the party during the inter-war period. But for Foot the critical point was that it meant 'fierce guerilla warfare' was still being conducted in many constituencies regardless of national circumstances. If the party at the next election could 'retain its quota of fifty seats it will have proved that it cannot be driven off the political map'.[13] With a secure parliamentary base the Liberals could then consider the possibility of expansion. In the event, however, the failure in the general election held later that year to focus on locality, combined with the loss of key seats as a result of the creation of the Liberal National group, seriously weakened the party's position. It was only in the decades after the Second World War that locality became a significant factor in Liberal politics, notably in Cornwall through the success of MPs like Peter Bessell, John Pardoe and David Penhaligon.

Foot's electoral successes and failures during the period from 1910 to 1945 should be placed in this broader framework. Despite becoming a prominent figure in the House of Commons during the inter-war period, it is worth noting that he won just four elections, was returned unopposed in the exceptional circumstances of 1931 and was defeated in a further seven contests. Foot's precarious position reflects his failure to obtain, or arguably create, a personal stronghold. Although there is clear evidence of his personal popularity, notably during the early 1920s when he had his greatest victories over the Conservatives in a series of straight fights, Foot's underlying problem was that he only became a parliamentary candidate after the historic landslide of 1906. His sole attempt to win in his native Plymouth ended in a humiliating third place when he stood against Nancy Astor in the Sutton by-election of 1919. Attempts to challenge in rural Devon, notably at Totnes in January 1910 and Tavistock in 1945, ended in failure with him coming 21.2 per cent and 14.2 per cent respectively behind the Conservatives. Only in Bodmin and the Cornish seat of St Ives, where he was just 0.8 per cent behind the winning candidate in a by-election in 1937, was Foot a credible challenger. Yet before the First World War Bodmin can best be described as being on the margins of the Liberal heartland that covered the north and west of the Duchy.[14] It was noted earlier that the party was remarkably successful in the 1920s in some seats that lacked a Liberal tradition. Although Bodmin does not fit into this category, it is still a paradox that this was the Cornish seat most associated with the Liberal mini-revival of the early 1920s and with an 'outsider' who was unsuccessful in his natural homeland of Plymouth and South Devon. In order to understand these developments it is necessary to consider in greater detail the early career of Foot before he was first elected to the House of Commons.

Crossing the Tamar: Contesting Bodmin in the December 1910 General Election

In 1910 the selection of Foot as a parliamentary candidate for a Cornish constituency appeared highly unlikely. He had initially started to play an active role in municipal politics in 1907 when he won a seat on Plymouth City Council. This local government involvement was to continue even when he was a prospective candidate and MP for Bodmin. He served as Deputy Mayor of his beloved Plymouth in 1920 and it was only in 1927 that he stood down as a councillor.[15] Foot's first attempt to enter parliament came in January 1910 when he fought the Totnes constituency in south Devon. The seat had last been won for the Liberals by Francis Bingham Mildmay back in 1885. When Mildmay defected to the Liberal Unionists in the following year his personal popularity as a local landowner, combined with the relative weakness of religious nonconformity and the prevalence of larger farms, meant that the Liberals were in no position to mount a credible challenge.[16] In 1886 Mildmay was the most successful Unionist in Cornwall and Devon with 80.3 per cent of the vote and even in 1906 he had a respectable 63.5 per cent. Significantly, Foot was able to generate sufficient enthusiasm amongst party workers and voters to reduce this figure by 2.9 per cent in 1910 at a time when the average swing away from the Liberals in this election in the South West was 3.9 per cent.[17] Although this result also pointed to the limitations of personal popularity given the fact that Mildmay was still comfortably elected, the election certainly established Foot's reputation as 'a young man of tireless energy and fluent powers of speech' who could make a difference during the course of an election campaign.[18] Foot attempted to build on this momentum and when another election was held just a few months later it was announced at the start of the campaign on 15 November that he would contest the seat again.[19] But the situation had changed dramatically by 21 November when the press reported that Colonel Cecil Grenfell, who had only been elected as Liberal MP for Bodmin in January, was not going to contest the election and that Foot had been selected as the new candidate.[20]

The background to Foot's selection provides useful insight into the nature of Cornish politics during the years leading up to the First World War. In 1906 the Hon. Thomas Agar Robartes, heir to the local Lanhydrock estates, had captured the seat from the formerly dominant Liberal Unionists with a convincing 56.3 per cent of the vote. However, he was subsequently unseated just a few months later following an election petition by his opponents alleging that he had made illegal payments to potential voters including free alcohol.[21] Such a scandalous allegation in a constituency with strong nonconformist tendencies infuriated many Liberal supporters who pointed out that the presiding judge was a Unionist who had rejected similar claims about a Conservative candidate in Great Yarmouth.[22] In the ensuing by-election the economic and political power of the Robartes family came behind Freeman Freeman-Thomas, the new Liberal candidate. The contest was primarily seen as a democratic response by 'the people' to the power of a biased legal system with calls to 'avenge the result of the election petition' by voting Liberal. Moreover, the Robartes were presented as a noble Cornish family that was appealing for the support of the local community against a common foe:

> Speaking on Thursday night at Bodmin close to his home, Lanhydrock House, Mr. Agar-Robartes said he felt justified in asking the electors to sink for once political differences and to help Lanhydrock. He asked them to fight this election on a personal matter. If they returned Mr. Sandys [the Liberal Unionist candidate] they would turn him (Mr. Robartes) out of Cornwall. They had seen his mother, Lady Clifden, standing a butt to the cheap jibes of a Judge; they had seen the Robartes name besmeared. He asked them at Bodmin to preserve the honour of that name and to show practical sympathy by returning Mr. Freeman-Thomas.[23]

The Unionists complained about 'territorial influences' in the by-election and admitted towards the end of the campaign that they had experienced 'a stern uphill fight' with 'a dearth of motor-cars' to take voters to the polling stations. By contrast, the Liberals 'were better supplied with vehicles' and succeeded in generating a sense of 'excitement' in the more populous areas of the constituency.[24] In the event the Liberals were able to claim a moral victory with their vote slipping by just 0.1 per cent. Tommy Robartes, with his personal and family honour restored, could now resume a political career and in February 1908 was returned unopposed in a by-election for the neighbouring seat of St Austell. However, this proved to be the high point for pre-war Bodmin Liberalism. Freeman-Thomas stood down at the subsequent election to be replaced by Grenfell whose share of the vote dropped alarmingly to 50.2 per cent. This was well above the average swing to the Unionists and compared unfavourably to the other Cornish results. A good example was Truro which had been won by George Hay Morgan for the Liberals in 1906 with a lower share of the vote at 53.2 per cent. In January 1910, however, he was able to narrowly increase this figure by an extra 0.1 per cent. As a Baptist preacher he was well placed to attract nonconformist voters and as a Welshman appealed to his Cornish constituents by claiming common Celtic ancestry.[25]

But Freeman-Thomas and Grenfell found it difficult to deploy a local appeal in Bodmin. Freeman-Thomas was a British diplomat who was to eventually become Governor General of Canada and Viceroy of India during the inter-war period. After surprisingly losing his seat at Hastings in the 1906 Liberal landslide he was able to resume a political career by winning Bodmin just a few months later. As an establishment figure he became Asquith's personal secretary and was raised to the peerage in 1910 as Marquess of Willingdon.[26] Grenfell, like Freeman-Thomas, had been educated at Eton and was a member of the London Stock Exchange. Moving in aristocratic circles he was married to the sister of the Duke of Marlborough and the family home was a distant 250 miles away from Bodmin in Buckinghamshire.[27] Despite an urgent need to strengthen a narrow majority of just 50 votes, Grenfell made at least two extensive visits to the USA during the course of the so-called 'short Parliament' of 1910. This gave an advantage to the Unionists who had selected Sir Reginald Pole-Carew, a former Lieutenant General who had served with distinction in the Boer War. Although as an old Etonian, senior army officer and landowner Pole-Carew's social background was similar to his Liberal opponent, he could point to the one crucial difference that he possessed strong Cornish credentials as a member of the Carew family of Antony House.[28] Local deference to the Carews in the Tamarside area, similar to support for the Robartes family in the western part of the constituency, was also a significant political factor in Cornwall in the early twentieth century. Grenfell admitted in September 1910 that local Liberals 'had fought for someone who had only just come down amongst them and who was almost unknown, against a popular resident in the county ... who had been in the field for some time previous'.[29] Earlier in the year Grenfell had apparently announced that he would not be seeking re-election on the grounds that he wanted to focus on his business interests and it appears that when a snap election was called following the collapse of a constitutional convention between the parties over reform of the House of Lords he was still in the USA.[30]

Bodmin Liberal Association was now faced with the dilemma of finding in less than a week a suitable candidate who could match Pole-Carew in terms of local popularity. It appears that beneath the surface morale was low amongst party workers who had become frustrated by the lack of a dedicated champion in the constituency. With a clear threat from the Unionists it was decided that the Bodmin Liberals had to adopt a local candidate who was 'already known to many of the electors'.[31] On the surface at least it appears that Foot was not the only candidate being considered at this time. Indeed, there was speculation that Sir Arthur Quiller-Couch, the famous literary figure from Fowey and chairman of the Bodmin Liberal Association, was going to contest the seat. Other suggestions included Arthur Carkeek, a respected Cornish Methodist and chairman of Camborne Liberal Association, and Dr C. A. Rashleigh, a Liberal activist in south-east Cornwall.[32] However, Foot's relative success in Totnes had impressed the Bodmin Liberals. It was stated at his adoption meeting that he had 'often been mentioned as an ideal candidate' for the seat and it was claimed that he had already addressed meetings at fifty places in the constituency before the election. It is possible that he was already being lined up for Bodmin prior to the election since he had been accompanying Grenfell to party meetings and local activists certainly moved quickly at the start of the campaign to arrange via the Devon and Cornwall Liberal Federation for Foot to stand down from Totnes.[33] Even in 1910 it was clear that Foot had certain advantages in contesting Bodmin. His ability to 'evoke enthusiasm' amongst the party's natural supporters was seen as critical when compared to his predecessors. As Quiller-Couch put it, 'He knew himself by the faces he saw as he went about the constituency that Mr. Foot was their man'.[34] In addition, his nonconformist credentials as a Methodist preacher had developed his skills in oratory and enabled him to pose as the natural champion of Cornish nonconformity. From a local perspective his religious activity, particularly as President of the South Devon and East Cornwall Federation of Free Church Councils, had already created a personal network of local supporters since he had preached at several chapels in south-east Cornwall like Callington and Liskeard.[35]

Moreover, Foot was the ideal leader for the growing spirit of Radicalism in the constituency. In contrast to his predecessors he came from humble origins as the son of a carpenter and had left Grammar School at the age of 14. Although he did not attend university, he trained in Plymouth for five years to become a solicitor and in 1902 had formed a legal partnership with Edgar Bowden.[36] Alongside his social background was a passionate commitment to the so-called New Liberalism of his age. Historians have been divided over the real impact of the party's progressive agenda since the party was failing to adopt working-class candidates and there was still a preference for traditional issues at the provincial level.[37] In December 1910, for example, Liberal candidates appeared to put more emphasis on Free Trade and House of Lords reform.[38] Whilst Foot also raised these issues, it was noticeable that at his adoption meeting he focused on the need for the government 'to attack poverty'. In a speech that must surely have concerned the libertarians in the constituency he stated bluntly that there 'were problems which Free Trade itself would never solve'. He added that 'They might have Free Trade and still have squalor and drunkenness and destitution and land hunger.'[39] This emphasis on the need for social and land reform even led to accusations by his opponents that he was a socialist and a member of the Fabian Society. For Foot's supporters, however, it meant that they could now have confidence in their local parliamentary candidate. Party activists even claimed after his adoption speech that they could not 'remember a more enthusiastic meeting in Bodmin than the one which Mr. Foot addressed, not even when Mr. Robartes was in the field'.[40]

But the new Liberal candidate was still vulnerable to claims that he was an outsider in search of a winnable seat. The opposition stated that Foot was no different from Freeman-Thomas and Grenfell in this respect. They claimed that Bodmin 'has had enough of the political carpet-bagger lately' and the only option was to vote Unionist because 'Sir Reginald is a Cornishman'.[41] Pole-Carew in particular was quite dismissive of Foot at the start of the campaign stating quite bluntly that 'I don't know him. I do know he was not born in this division.'[42] The myth of Isaac Foot as a principled and honourable politician has been sustained by his son Michael who wrote that when he stood in Devon he 'was only narrowly defeated by a few dozen votes. If he had won that Totnes election he would have already started making his mark in the Parliament that he honoured so greatly.'[43] In reality Foot stood no chance of actually winning Totnes since he had been defeated by 1,927 votes so by moving to Bodmin it did appear that he was moving for personal advantage to a Liberal-held seat. Indeed, he clearly felt that he was on the defensive over this issue since in his adoption speech on 24 November he remarked that 'the position he occupied that day was not of his own seeking. He had promised to fight Totnes, and he would rather never get into the House of Commons then do anything which had any suspicion or dishonour (Applause).'[44] Similarly, Foot was forced to admit that his 'worst disadvantage was that he was not a Cornishman'. His wife Eva Mackintosh came from mixed Cornish-Scottish parentage and was secretary of her local Wesleyan Guild at Callington so this provided the basis of his personal connections with the area:

> He was not a Cornishman. But he took the precaution to be born as near Cornwall as he could (laughter). He was born in the greatest city in the British Empire – Plymouth (Applause). And he did what he could to break his birth's invidious bar by coming to Cornwall for his wife (Applause). He felt that he was not coming amongst strangers. He had made there many friends he had known for years. The first speeches he ever made were in that constituency in the great struggle of 1906.[45]

It might have been expected that his Plymouthian background would have at least enabled him to attract support in the Tamarside communities. Yet Pole-Carew's attempts to pose as the Cornish champion, combined with his family interests in the Antony estates on the Rame Peninsula, meant that this area was now moving to the Unionists.[46] During the course of the election campaign Foot had to send a telegram to party workers in Millbrook, Saltash and Torpoint stating that 'West doing magnificently. Rely on Tamarside polling every man to win great victory.'[47] Moreover, there were even limitations to his ability to attract the nonconformist vote. From 1886 to 1900 the Liberal Unionists had been the dominant political force in Cornwall. Their success partly reflected the local hostility of the nonconformists towards Irish Home Rule on the grounds that a separate parliament for Ireland would be dominated by the Roman Catholics. Fear of the 'power of the Pope' even led some Liberal MPs like Robartes to oppose Irish devolution.[48] In 1906 the Home Rule issue had not been such an acute problem since the Liberals had no intention of implementing major constitutional reform, thereby enabling the Liberals to win all seven seats in Cornwall. Yet by December 1910 the Unionists could argue that since the Liberals had lost their overall majority in the previous election they were now dependent on votes from the Irish nationalists to stay in office. Irish nonconformist ministers even spoke at Unionist meetings in Cornwall on the threat to Protestants from any parliament dominated by Roman Catholics. This led Foot to conclude that his eventual defeat in the election was largely as a result of his failure to campaign effectively throughout the constituency and religious fears relating to the Irish issue:

> In spite of complete and most adequate arrangements and an active campaign, I could not cover the district in such a way as to get in touch with the large electorate of South East Cornwall. Also the scare associated with Home Rule and the exploitation of Nonconformist sympathy and the talk about Catholic oppression were against me.[49]

The legacy of 1910

In the event Foot lost to Pole-Carew by just 41 votes. The Unionist share of the vote only increased by 0.4 per cent, which was less than the swing of 1.3 per cent across Cornwall and Devon as a whole but disappointing to many Liberal activists who had genuinely believed that with an excellent candidate they could consolidate their hold on the seat. It certainly appears that whilst Foot was able to rally party activists and their traditional support base in the western parts of the constituency it was losing support in the east because Pole-Carew could play the 'Cornish' card. It is significant that Foot had to wait until changing electoral circumstances, combined with a long period of campaigning at the local level, enabled him to convincingly win the 1922 by-election. The Liberals had to endure a further setback in 1918 when their share of the vote fell further to 41.6 per cent. Admittedly, there were exceptional circumstances since the Liberal split had weakened the party and Sir Charles Hanson, the new Conservative candidate who had been returned unopposed in a by-election in 1916, was endorsed as the official Coalition candidate by Lloyd George in the so-called 'coupon' election. But Hanson was also well placed to compete with Foot for the 'local' vote. Although a wealthy stockbroker and former Lord Mayor of London, he lived in his native Fowey and had been a Methodist minister in Canada in his early adult life.[50] Foot was able to do well in many of the remote rural areas but the towns tended to vote Conservative until circumstances temporarily changed in the early 1920s.[51]

Nonetheless, the election of December 1910 did have long-term significance. In the first place Foot's opponents realized even then that they had to take him seriously. Even Pole-Carew, who had been quite dismissive of the new Liberal champion at the start was forced to admit that he was an effective opponent. He added that 'I only hope he never comes over this side of the Tamar again.'[52] It is interesting that Quiller-Couch remarked after the election that 'although it might seem a paradox, Liberalism in their division was really stronger at that moment than it had been for five years past'.[53] Foot had at least restored a sense of purpose for party activists following the disillusionment generated by his predecessors. There were also indications even before the First World War that he was starting to take on the mantle of the wider leadership of Cornish Liberalism that was so evident during the inter-war period. An interesting example of this can be seen in the so-called 'All Cornwall model election' in 1912. This was apparently one of a number of regional polls organized by the Proportional Representation Society to promote the use of the Single Transferable Vote. Ballot papers were printed in newspapers and also, as Martin Pugh points out, distributed to the public 'through members of the society, who were well represented in each political party'.[54] Although not giving an accurate representation of party support at the time since it ignored the existing franchise restrictions, voters were presented with the names of local parliamentary candidates and other distinguished personalities at the community level. In Cornwall it appears that over seven thousand papers were returned with votes cast for MPs, candidates and other individuals associated with the public life of Cornwall including Quiller-Couch and Silas Hocking.[55] Significantly, it was Foot who topped the poll in terms of first preference votes beating sitting MPs like Robartes and Morgan. Although the poll appears to have attracted more Liberals than Conservatives and was therefore not a true reflection of party support, it does indicate that even at this early stage Foot had emerged as the real champion of Cornish Liberalism.[56] Foot's declaration after the election result that 'I shall stay this side of the Tamar' meant that he could start consolidating his position over time.[57]

Memories of this first contest were to play an important role in sustaining the party's support base in subsequent decades. Some good examples of this process can be seen in a special issue of *Spotlight on Cornwall*, the magazine of the Bodmin Liberal Association, which was produced in 1961 to commemorate Foot's life. It was written by Peter Bessell, then Liberal candidate for the seat who went on to become its MP from 1964–70 and can clearly be seen in general as an attempt on his part to show that he was a worthy inheritor of the Foot tradition. When writing about Foot's initial selection in 1910 Bessell explained that it was 'A shrewd choice not untypical of the Cornishman who combines with his charm and kindliness a hard-headed realism.'[58] Personal reflections in the magazine by individuals alive at the time demonstrated the impact of this first contest on younger activists who were to play a prominent role in future years. Edith Hoskin, chairman of the Liskeard Women's Liberal Association, remarked that she was 'probably one of the few now remaining who was at the first adoption meeting of the "Young Lawyer from Plymouth". What a wise choice it was, and how well he served us!'[59] Similarly, Stuart Roseveare, who arguably played a crucial role in the early 1950s in contesting the seat at a time when Labour came close to pushing the Liberals into third place, wrote that his 'earliest recollection of the late Rt. Hon. Isaac Foot was before the First World War when as a schoolboy without much political knowledge I sat with my father at a meeting watching the faces of the audience, spellbound by the young orator.'[60]

Conclusion

The enthusiasm generated amongst Cornish Liberals by Foot's decision to contest Bodmin in December 1910 can be seen as a prelude to the events of the inter-war period. Memories of this event were to offset the disillusionment of the recent past and to sustain the local party during the difficult years that followed. Foot's reputation as a powerful orator had already been established in the chapel pulpit and at political meetings. Similarly, his progressive views on social reform enabled him to pose, as in the early 1920s, as the effective champion of Cornish Radicalism thereby limiting any meaningful challenge on the part of the Labour Party. Yet local issues made it difficult for Foot to translate his personal popularity into immediate electoral success. The anti-Catholic stance of many Cornish Methodists over the Irish Home Rule issue even limited his ability to attract nonconformist votes. Popular candidates like Pole-Carew and Hanson were also better placed than Foot when it came to posing as the champion of a Cornish constituency. It would therefore take many years of political campaigning before he was in the position to be returned as the Member for Bodmin.

Notes and references:

1. For a recent account of the 1922 Bodmin by-election see J. Ault, 'The Inter-War Cornish By-Elections – Microcosm of "Rebellion"?' in this volume of *Cornish Studies*.
2. S. Koss, *Nonconformity in Modern British Politics* (London, 1975), p. 161.
3. M. Foot and A. Highet, *Isaac Foot: A Westcountry Boy – Apostle of England* (London, 2006), p. 140.
4. *Cornish Guardian*, 3 March 1922.
5. For examples see A. Lee, 'Political Parties and Elections' in P. Payton (ed.), *Cornwall Since the War: The Contemporary History of a European Region* (Redruth, 1993), pp. 253–70. P. Payton, 'Labour Failure and Liberal Tenacity: Radical Politics and Cornish Political Culture, 1880–1939' in P. Payton (ed.), *Cornish Studies: Two* (Exeter, 1994), pp. 83–95. G. Tregidga, 'Socialism and the Old Left: The Labour Party in Cornwall during the Inter-War Period' in P. Payton (ed.), *Cornish Studies: Seven* (Exeter, 1999), pp. 74–93.
6. J. Foot, 'Isaac Foot' in D. Brack et al. (eds), *Dictionary of Liberal Biography* (London, 1998), p. 111.
7. G. Tregidga, '"Bodmin Man": Peter Bessell and Cornish Politics in the 1950s and 1960s' in P. Payton (ed.), *Cornish Studies: Eight* (Exeter, 2000), p. 166.
8. S. Foot, *My Grandfather Isaac Foot* (Bodmin, 1980), p. 4. Foot and Highet, *Isaac Foot*, p. 18.
9. Foot, 'Isaac Foot', pp. 109–12.
10. *Dorset County Chronicle*, 6 June 1929.
11. For a survey of electoral diversity at the local level see M. Kinnear, *The British Voter: An Atlas and Survey since 1885* (Batsford, 1968).
12. K. O'Morgan, *Rebirth of a Nation: A History of Modern Wales* (Oxford, 1981, reprinted 2002), p. 192.
13. D. Foot, 'The Liberal Crisis', *Contemporary Review* 139 (1931), pp. 582–88.

14. H. Pelling, *Social Geography in British Elections 1885–1910* (London, 1967), p. 164.
15. Foot, 'Isaac Foot', p. 110.
16. Pelling, *Social Geography of British Elections*, p. 169.
17. Ibid., p. 164.
18. *Cornish Guardian*, 25 November 1910.
19. *The Times*, 15 November 1910.
20. Ibid., 21 November 1910.
21. Ibid., 19 May 1906.
22. Ibid., 19 June 1906.
23. Ibid., 21 July 1906.
24. Ibid., 21 and 25 July 1906.
25. Pelling, *Social Geography of British Elections*, p. 185. See also G. Tregidga, 'Representing the Duchy: Francis Acland and Cornish politics, 1910–1922' in P. Payton (ed.), *Cornish Studies: Fifteen* (Exeter Press, 2007), p. 175.
26. *The Times*, 13 August 1941.
27. Ibid., 14 August 1924.
28. Ibid., 20 September 1924.
29. *Cornish Guardian*, 23 September 1910.
30. Ibid., 25 November 1910.
31. Ibid.
32. Ibid.
33. Ibid., 23 September and 25 November 1910.
34. Ibid., 25 November 1910.
35. *Royal Cornwall Gazette*, 24 November 1910. Foot and Highet, *Isaac Foot*, p. 52.
36. Ibid., p. 19.
37. For example, see K. Laybourn, *The Rise of Labour: The British Labour Party, 1890–1979* (London, 1988) and K. Laybourn, 'The rise of Labour and the decline of Liberalism: the state of the debate', *History* 80:259 (1995), p. 207.
38. P. Lynch, *The Liberal Party in Rural England, 1885–1910: Radicalism and Community* (Oxford, 2003), p. 207.
39. *Cornish Guardian*, 25 November 1910.
40. Ibid.
41. *Royal Cornwall Gazette*, 1 December 1910.
42. Ibid., 24 November 1910.
43. Foot and Highet, *Isaac Foot*, p. 124.
44. *Royal Cornwall Gazette*, 24 November 1910.
45. *Cornish Guardian*, 25 November 1910. See also *Royal Cornwall Gazette*, 24 November 1910.
46. Pelling, *Social Geography of British Elections*, p. 167.
47. *Royal Cornwall Gazette*, 1 December 1910.
48. *Cornish Guardian*, 31 May 1912 and 23 January 1914.
49. *Royal Cornwall Gazette*, 15 December 1910. See also Acland papers (Devon Record Office), 1148 M/516, Francis Acland to Eleanor Acland, December 1910.
50. *The Times*, 18 January 1922.
51. *Royal Cornwall Gazette*, 18 December 1918.
52. Ibid., 15 December 1910.
53. Ibid.

54. M. Pugh, 'New Light on Edwardian Voters: the Model Elections of 1906–12' in *Historical Research* 51:123 (2007), pp. 103–10.

55. *The Times*, 25 May 1912.

56. Ibid. McDougall Trust, London, 'The All-Cornwall Model Election' in *Representation* (pamphlet of the Proportional Representation Society, 1912), pp. 59–69. My thanks to John Ault in helping to acquire a copy of this pamphlet.

57. *Royal Cornwall Gazette*, 15 December 1910.

58. *Spotlight on Cornwall*, Bodmin Liberal Association, *c*.1961, p. 2. I am grateful to Terry Farmer for a copy of this memorial issue.

59. Ibid., p. 11.

60. Ibid., p. 10.

13

The Inter-War Cornish By-Elections

Microcosm of 'Rebellion'?

John Ault

Introduction

For many years, by-elections have been seen as a barometer of public opinion – giving a local constituency the chance to pass judgment on the government of the day, without generally affecting the government's capacity to continue to govern. As David Butler says 'the main interest in by-elections has undoubtedly lain in what they are thought to reveal about the state of public opinion, both in relation to specific issues and to the likely outcome of the next general election'.[1]

In the period from 1918 to 1945 there were 514 by-elections across the UK,[2] with 103 changing hands between the parties.[3] However, the national significance of by-elections has not always been accepted as taking the nation's blood pressure, Prime Minister Arthur Balfour famously objecting: 'I do not for once instance [*sic*] admit that by-elections are a test, or ought to be regarded as a test, of public feeling. They are of course, a test of the feelings of a particular constituency at the time the by-election takes place. They are not, and they cannot be made, the index and test of what the feeling of the people of the country is as a whole.'[4] However, 'in recent years, by-elections, by producing even more extreme results, have lost much of their power to shock,'[5] argues Butler, as they have become much more the focus of party campaign machines and national media interest. By-elections in the inter-war years were much more frequent than in modern times, partly due to the age of Members of Parliament, the less professional nature of politics, and the multiplicity of reasons for Members to leave, such as ennoblement or other employment (including the judiciary or imperial duties overseas). Because opinion polling did not exist, as it does now, by-elections had even more potential impact than in the post-war period. Indeed, they were the only democratic test of opinion between general elections.

In Cornwall, by-elections followed a similar pattern to others across the rest of the UK. There were five by-elections in the inter-war period, as well as an uncontested by-election in Bodmin in 1941, compared to just one since the Second World War. These by-elections demonstrated a willingness to show, not just opposition to the sitting government, but also opposition to specific government policies, together with a similar willingness to choose between one faction of the government and another, or even between factions within one of the political parties. By looking at the Cornish by-elections during this period it is possible to observe that Cornwall was more than willing to express its reputed 'rebellious' or independent-minded tendencies when given the chance through a parliamentary by-election.

The 1922 Bodmin By-Election: Rejection of the Lloyd George coalition

The Bodmin by-election, held on 23 February 1922, was an important event for the Liberal Party in Cornwall and, arguably, for the United Kingdom as a whole. According to the *Cornish Times*: 'Although everything pointed to a general election in the very near future, the fact of their having a by-election immediately preceding it gave SE Cornwall a prominence and importance almost unique.'[6]

In the 1918 General Election, as *The Times* had reported, in most places: 'The Coalition swept the board, and scored the most overwhelming triumph ever recorded in our political annals ... the Liberal Opposition was swept out of sight.' Indeed, 'Mr Asquith, all his Front Bench lieutenants,[7] and all his whips, were defeated, and where they were engaged in three-cornered contests they were usually to be found at the bottom of the poll.'[8] However, by 1922, the Coalition had run into trouble. The by-election at Bodmin followed a series of electoral setbacks for the Coalition, in which the Labour Party and Asquith's Liberals had scored successes. Interest in, and expectations of, a reversal for the Coalition were high. Importantly, only two candidates were put forward for the Bodmin contest. It was thought that the Coalition candidate, Sir Frederick Poole, might 'benefit by the superiority of the Conservative organization in the division'.[9] Isaac Foot, the 1910 and 1918 Liberal candidate, who had so notably 'drawn the badger'[10] during the historic Plymouth Sutton by-election of 1919, was perceived as being a direct opponent of Lloyd George, not just the Coalition or even the Conservatives – personalising the contest.

As a consequence, the factors that had been identified by *The Times* in 1918 as important in the defeat of so many opposition Liberal candidates (the benefits of the Coupon provided by Lloyd George and the Conservative leadership) were not in place at Bodmin. Neither was this a three-cornered fight, as there was no Labour candidate to draw away radical support from Foot. These factors were to be important, not just in this election, but in future elections in the inter-war period in Cornwall. Additionally, as *The Times* (not a natural supporter) conceded, Foot's campaign in Bodmin had:

> ground for much assurance in the enthusiasm with which [he] has been received throughout the constituency. Some of this may be due to the fact that he is well known, a good speaker, with a gift for humour, and a fighter, as is shown by the fact that this is the third time he has contested the seat. Many have rallied to his support from these causes; many more because of the prevailing discontent with the Coalition.[11]

Yet his style was compared negatively to that of his Coalition Unionist opponent, Major-General Sir Frederick Poole, whose 'freshness, openness and straightforward speeches, devoid of platform tricks and embellishments, are making a great appeal to the average elector, who is showing an increasing dislike to vapid declamation and emotional rhetoric'.[12] Foot seems also to not have had the support of the local press, except, as Dawson has explained, the 'previously pro-coalition *Western Morning News* because his return was seen as more likely to end "the present reckless expenditure" by the Lloyd George government'.[13]

The *Observer* provided additional insight into the campaign that Isaac Foot fought in Bodmin. 'Foot ... travelled nearly seventy miles [on one day]', it reported, 'and spoke at seven meetings inside eight hours'.[14] Nonetheless, the *Cornish Times* considered that Foot was 'lagging behind as far as his election address [was] concerned'.[15] But, having 'the open blessing of the Socialists',[16] as the *Cornish Times* explained, his campaign was helped significantly by 'the formal decision of Labour actively to take part in the contest on the side of Mr Foot'.[17] Yet this local pact was frowned upon by the Labour Party at national level. According to one observer, the 'Bodmin Labour Party was censured for directing its members to vote for the Asquithian Isaac Foot ... though it was supposed that Labour voters, such as there were in Bodmin, would have done so in any case.'[18] Significantly, in backing Foot's campaign, Labour's own members within the constituency had rebelled against the party line expressed by the National Executive.

This support was also criticised by Foot's Coalition opponent, reported by the *Manchester Guardian* as:

> a curious eleventh hour attack on the Liberal candidate because of his supposed league with what is called 'the menace of Socialism'. The decision of the Labour leaders here to assist Mr Foot has given the Coalitionists an opening. Mr Foot is being assailed as if he were an avowed upheavelist of the reddest hue merely because a company of men who worked for and voted for him in two previous contests here have decided to work for and vote for him again.[19]

Not for the last time would right-wing opinion attempt to undermine the potential for Liberal success by linking the party directly with the fortunes of the Labour Party, nor would it be the last time the Liberals would attach themselves to the Labour Party for their own electoral benefit.

Attempting to unite all opposition to the government, Foot and the Liberals 'had to have the motto of that election, "The Coalition must go"', observed the *Cornish Times*, '[arguing that] the Government no longer deserved the confidence of the people'.[20] Foot also received support from another source, one which resonated strongly with Cornish voters: Sir Arthur Quiller-Couch.[21] The *Manchester Guardian* commented: 'Optimism in the Liberal camp is steadily growing. Among letters received by Mr Isaac Foot, the Liberal candidate, is one from Sir Arthur Quiller-Couch.' Echoing Foot, the newspaper added: 'The Government of such a Commonwealth as ours will always need two things far more important even than brains. The first is character and the second is public confidence. This opportunistic Ministry, this obsequious Parliament never had the one, and by consequence they have fatally lost the other.'[22] Indeed, Quiller-Couch's explicit support was a major political coup for Foot. Although a long-standing supporter of the Liberal Party, Quiller-Couch brought colour to the Bodmin campaign, making the election all the more interesting to those national journalists who followed it. He even 'signed Isaac Foot's papers as his principal proposer',[23] lending very public support.

In the Bodmin by-election, 'the size of the Liberal majority[24] was a surprise to everybody, and [was] regarded as a striking anti-government victory'.[25] By defeating a Coalition Unionist, who had been supported by Lloyd George, Isaac Foot was propelled to Westminster, not just as a Cornish champion but also as a direct challenge to the Coalition, the Prime Minister and the authority of both. In this campaign, the Liberals had adopted what was to be their *modus operandi* for the future: they had swallowed up the Labour vote, with, in this case, the co-operation of the local Labour Party. They had emphasised their Cornish credentials by gaining the support of notable Cornish figures, with Foot becoming the *local candidate*. Most importantly, the anti-Coalition Liberals were able to position themselves as the anti-establishment challengers, pitting Cornwall against the Westminster Government. At the declaration, Foot stressed his local allegiances: 'My election,' he said, 'is a reward of twelve years' hard work mainly in the villages ... I am at home among the village people and have learnt to admire them. My keenest workers are frequently my brother Methodists. The village chapel is a rural citadel of democracy.'[26] The Liberals' own victory song cited both the Cornish dimension of Foot's victory and the manner in which they had stood up to the Coalition. 'Tres and Pols and Pens'[27] had all supported Foot, explained the song, and 'The Coalitionists declared [they] should never win.'[28]

Despite the local factors which had contributed to Foot's victory at Bodmin, this by-election, one of a series of setbacks for the Coalition, culminated in the collapse in Coalition Liberal support in the Newport by-election in South Wales a few months later; Lloyd George's own political backyard. The Newport by-election saw the Coalition Liberal candidate move from first to third place, with a Conservative winning the seat. According to Cook and Ramsden, 'Newport was the only by-election which brought down a government – such has been claimed and widely accepted'.[29] It 'helped Conservative MPs to decide at the Carlton Club on the same day to withdraw their support from Lloyd George's Coalition'.[30]

Cornwall, by virtue of the Bodmin by-election and Isaac Foot's victory, had helped spread anti-Coalition feeling throughout the country. Indeed, after Bodmin, Newport, and a series of other by-election reversals, the Coalition fell in October 1922, and a general election was called. It was a disaster for Liberals of all shades, according to Cook and Ramsden, 'because after 19 October 1922 the Liberals were seen [across Great Britain] to be the third party.'[31] Yet this was not to prove true in Cornwall.

The 1928 St Ives By-Election: Reports of the Liberal Party's death had been greatly exaggerated

The mid-1920s saw the rapid switch of support from the Liberal Party to the Labour Party in much of Britain, and with the party reduced to just forty MPs in the 1924 General Election it appeared to be in terminal decline. However, by 1928, the Liberal Party was, to a limited extent, on the road to organisational, if not electoral recovery, following a succession of major electoral setbacks in 1922, 1923 and 1924. The revitalised Liberal Party's improved organisation, once again apparently united under the leadership of Lloyd George, was put to the test in Cornwall in 1928 at the St Ives by-election. Hopes were high that the organisation's improvements would bear fruit, particularly when, the *Manchester Guardian* reported, 'in a scattered region of this sort that organisation counts at its maximum. Mr Lloyd George, [regretted] that in some areas Liberal organisations have fallen to pieces. It [was] not so in St. Ives. The machine [was] all right. Mr Runciman [had] seen to that'.[32]

The by-election was caused by the sitting Conservative member, John Anthony Hawke, being disqualified due to his creation as a High Court judge. This left the Liberal Party with a problem. Their selected candidate, Walter Runciman, was still an MP for Swansea, so his wife, Hilda, 'very much a personality in her own right – stood as a candidate in his place'.[33] It was thought by her Unionist opponents that 'Mrs Runciman was heavily handicapped as she was only a temporary substitute for her husband'.[34] The by-election saw a very brief campaign, arranged well by Government Whips, and designed to prevent an effective Liberal campaign at the potential tail end of the Conservative Government. Other local political associations were mobilised into action to support the candidates. Bodmin Conservatives helped to ensure 'all voters resident in the Division who were entitled to vote at St Ives had been conveyed to the poll thanks to the generous loan of a motor car by supporters in the Division'.[35]

The Runcimans' brand of Liberalism was not popular with the Lloyd George leadership of the time, and a Conservative 'hold' in the seat seemed an entirely likely outcome. Yet Mrs Runciman's campaign worked well with the local audience. As the *Manchester Guardian* explained: 'the geographical detachment of this division has its parallel in a certain detachment in the Liberalism which is being expounded here. If the mainstream of Liberalism to-day is represented by the fruitful research work of the Liberal commissions of inquiry and the Liberal Summer School then the Liberal candidate, admirable as she is in so many ways, is hardly in it'.[36] This 'detachment' also highlighted the continuing bitter squabbles that existed within the Liberal Party. As Wallace says:

> the by-election, held on 6 March 1928 ... had another significance. On 27th February the Liberal Council [led by Walter Runciman] had voted to oppose Lloyd George's Yellow Book [drawn up by one of the aforementioned commissions], which encompassed many of the new interventionist policies, and St. Ives was the first electoral test of this new party division. The by-election was a Liberal Council affair. Hilda openly refused to let Lloyd George speak for her during the campaign.[37]

Despite the infighting, 'the invitation to Sir Herbert Samuel to come and help was one of the most satisfactory features of the contest'.[38] 'It was most praiseworthy as a conciliatory gesture,' according to the *Manchester Guardian*, 'and it was no less valuable tactically in that it permitted of the complementary parts of Liberal policy being presented to the electors of St. Ives.'[39] But, 'Samuel incurred the wrath of Lloyd George when he went down to Cornwall to speak on her [Mrs Runciman's] behalf.'[40] However, 'in West Cornwall the fact that Mr Lloyd George did not send his blessing to Mrs Runciman, "cut no ice"',[41] in the St Ives constituency. Whether because of, or despite, the internal squabbles in the Party, Hilda Runciman, was elected in the by-election of 1928 with 42.6 per cent share of the vote and a majority of 763. Although only acting as the 'warming pan'[42] for her husband, she had become the first ever woman MP for Cornwall, of any party, and the only Liberal MP in Cornwall at that time.

Hilda Runciman's election victory in St Ives was both a personal blow to the authority of Lloyd George's leadership of the Liberal Party – she and her husband Walter still retained their commitment to a less interventionist Liberalism – and a shock to the Conservative Government. It presaged a landslide result for the Liberals in Cornwall only a year later, when the party would win all five seats in Parliament and again show the idiosyncratic tendencies of Cornish constituencies to rebel openly, on this occasion, against more than one opponent.

The 1932 North Cornwall By-Election: Only 'generally speaking' supportive of the National Government

Only months following the General Election of 1931, Sir Donald MacLean, Member of Parliament for North Cornwall, died 'from overwork'.[43] His seat had been the only one in Cornwall that the Liberal Party had been actively required to defend in 1931, as local Conservatives believed 'that they could not accept Sir Donald MacLean to represent them and that they were doubtful as to whether they could trust him to wholeheartedly support a National Party with a programme of tariffs ... he was an unmitigated Free Trader and had voted consistently with the Socialist Party in the late Government'.[44]

Despite a brief career in Cornwall, MacLean was popular locally, and his death prompted regret for the 'Duchy's loss of a great adopted son'.[45] Moreover:

no member of the House of Commons ... is feeling the loss of Sir Donald MacLean so keenly as is Mr Isaac Foot, the Minister for Mines. He speaks of his old friend and found emotion. There have been couples in Parliament who have been called political 'twins', but few companionships have been so sincere and close as that which existed between these two ministers. They had so much in common. Their Liberalism was of an almost identical texture. The 'Nonconformist conscience' was very real in both.[46]

As it was, the local party chose a well-known local candidate for the subsequent by-election in North Cornwall, a man with a national reputation, Sir Francis Acland, the former Member of Parliament for Camborne (from 1910–22) and then Tiverton (from 1923–24). His Asquithian leanings were well known, and he filled the shoes of his predecessor well, being on the traditional, Gladstonian wing of the party. The contest was highly significant politically, as the Liberals were running a by-election campaign from the position of being in government. Indeed, MacLean had been Minister for Education in the National Government at the time of his death.

Although the existence of the National Government might have afforded Acland a fairly untroubled election, the Conservatives decided to contest the seat, claiming 'that the electors of North Cornwall should have an opportunity of assuring the Government's representatives'.[47] Vitally, 'the North Cornwall Labour Party ... decided not to nominate a candidate'.[48] Although the local Liberals claimed 'the one thing we emphasised in considering the selection of a candidate was having one who is a real sincere supporter of the National Government',[49] an interesting aspect of the campaign was that Acland was not entirely supportive of the Government's policies. He was, in many ways, running a traditional Cornish Liberal campaign, and his Conservative opponent was more naturally a supporter of the National Government. Acland admitted himself that he was only 'generally speaking, a supporter of the Government'.[50]

The Conservatives begged to differ however, and launched a negative campaign against Acland's candidature, described in the *Manchester Guardian*:

> In the hope of saving the seat Liberal Organisers in North Cornwall are now appealing to electors in the scattered villages 'to maintain a great tradition' and vote for Sir Francis Acland, the Free Trade candidate. The National Government and Conservative rejoinder points out that the Liberal Free Trade tradition, both in the country and in the House of Commons, is dead, and that, like the potato, the best part of the Liberal Party is now underground.[51]

Indeed, this by-election, and the Conservatives' desire to win the seat from the Liberals, can be seen as part of what might be described as the second stage of the Age of Alignment,[52] to use Christopher Cook's phrase, where the Conservatives tried to completely replace the Liberals as the sole party of the rural parts of Britain.

Renewed in-fighting between Liberal factions also affected the campaign in North Cornwall. As the *Manchester Guardian* observed, 'the Liberal National Executive in the House of Commons passed a resolution declaring that the Liberal Nationals were taking no part in the election against the candidate by the constituency Liberal Association, but expressed its regret that he [Acland] was not a wholehearted supporter of the National Government'.[53] There was subsequently a great deal of open conflict between the two factions, led by Herbert Samuel and John Simon, disputing the status of the National Liberal support for the Government's tariff policies. This was to have an important impact on the by-election, as it allowed Acland to position himself as the anti-Westminster choice, as Liberals had done previously, and have done, for that matter, since. Despite a difficult and often negative campaign, Sir Francis Acland won North Cornwall for the Liberals, with an increased majority. The *Manchester Guardian* noted Acland's speech at the count, identifying 'a strategic mistake of his opponents when they claimed that he ought to give unreserved and unqualified support for the National Government. "'From that moment," he said, "democracy and Liberalism in the division rallied to my side and the wonderful democratic tradition was roused to great enthusiasm.'"[54]

By positioning himself as the candidate opposed to the National Government, leaving his Conservative opponent as its defender, Acland was able to tap into the 'rebellious' and independent-minded nature of the constituency. With no Labour candidate contesting the seat, he was victorious in North Cornwall, as only 'generally speaking'[55] he supported the government.

The 1937 St Ives By-Election: Out of disaster comes hope for the Liberal Party

The elevation of Sir Walter Runciman to the peerage, as Viscount Runciman of Doxford, in 1937, necessitated another by-election for his St Ives constituency, which he had inherited from his wife Hilda at the general election. By selecting Isaac Foot (who had lost Bodmin in 1935) as their by-election candidate in St Ives, the Liberals had chosen a formidable candidate, and he 'accepted the invitation to contest the seat as an independent Liberal'.[56] The National Government candidate, a National Liberal in reality, 'received Lord Runciman's benediction'.[57] Despite Foot essentially being based in East Cornwall, local voters recognised his Cornish Liberal credentials, being 'the inspiration of Liberals in West Cornwall'.[58]

This was a fight that Foot relished. Not only was it a contest for the soul of the party he loved, but it was a specifically Cornish fight and one, by proxy, against one of his bitterest foes: Walter Runciman. Although Foot was more than capable of dropping his antagonism in public, saying, 'whatever may have been our differences in recent years, and those differences have been real and substantial, we yield to none in our recognition of his devotion to public service and his long and distinguished career in the highest offices of the State',[59] this contest was very personal for Foot. It stemmed from Runciman's open support for the Conservative candidate in Foot's Bodmin seat in 1935. Whilst Runciman was elected unopposed in St Ives, being a supporter of the National Government (thus a National Liberal), Foot lost to the 'National' Conservative, John Rathbone, following Runciman's overt support for Foot's opponent. Old political alliances were being broken and re-forged during this second stage of the Age of Alignment.[60] 'Runciman's decision to send a public letter of support to John Rathbone, the Conservative candidate for Bodmin, had confirmed that he was now totally committed to the National government.'[61] In the forthcoming St Ives by-election, allegiances were to be equally complex. Although the National Government candidate, Beechman, was notionally a National Liberal, his campaign was, 'managed by the Conservative's party agent, and Lord Runciman's agent [was] the junior officer'.[62]

In addition to its strong Cornish and Liberal resonance, the St Ives by-election also had an international flavour. The split between Foot and Runciman had a clear basis in policy, as well as personal animosity, with Runciman (hitherto a Free Trade Liberal) now supporting tariffs and becoming a key supporter of the Baldwin government's appeasement strategy towards Italy and Germany. 'Every kind of Conservative scare was mobilised against [Foot]', it was recalled years later: 'He was called a "warmonger".'[63] As the Liberal Party expressed increasing concerns about the threat of Nazi Germany and Fascist Italy, so Foot was identified with anti-appeasement opinion. Labour again threw its support behind Foot, as the *Manchester Guardian* observed: 'the Labour Party may have its differences with Mr Foot, but its discerning local leaders know what his worth would be in the House of Commons at the present time, and they are supporting him'.[64] By contrast, Labour had opposed Hilda in 1928 and Walter in 1929, although as Runciman was part of the National Government they had not opposed his election in 1931 and 1935.

Unlike the 1928 by-election in St Ives, according to the *Manchester Guardian*, 'the Divisional Liberal Association was moribund, and from 1931 there had not been a Liberal meeting in the constituency until Mr Foot went to contest the by-election. Mr Foot's acceptance of the candidature was a tonic.'[65] Foot received a level of by-election support from outside that anticipated late twentieth-century campaigning, with visits from leading Liberals like Sir Archibald Sinclair. 'Richard Acland',[66] it was noted, the 'MP for Barnstaple, tour[ed] the Division with a loud-speaker van'.[67] Foot also received notable defections from the Liberal National camp when, as the *West Briton* put it:

> something in the nature of a bombshell was dropped in the constituency … when it was announced that Mr W. J. White, of Penzance, who [had] been hon. Treasurer of the Liberal National Association for the Division since its formation had resigned and had signed one of Mr Isaac Foot's nomination papers … 'I am a Free Trader pure and simple', stated Mr White. 'I have always been a Liberal and must support Mr Foot. He is a Free Trader; so am I. Mr Beechman has dropped the name Liberal, yet he declares he is a Liberal.'[68]

However, Beechman's campaign was not merely one of defending the National Government's record. It 'struck out on a new line in political campaigning by inviting the wives of neighbouring MPs and candidates to come into the Division and explain the political situation from the view of women, who [were] as keenly interested in politics as the men',[69] this being only the second parliamentary election in which all women in St Ives had been able to vote, the seat having been unopposed in 1931 and 1935. In this way, Beechman sought to mobilise and capture the female vote.

However, other factors may have prevented Foot's eventual victory, as Foot 'returned to the Division … after having been absent for a couple of days on account of being sworn in as a Privy Councillor. In his absence, the Liberal campaign was carried on by Mr Dingle Foot MP and Mr Richard Acland MP.'[70] Foot's absence to attend his investiture as a Privy Councillor must have had an impact on the momentum of his campaign. As the constituency chairman would comment later, 'Mr Foot came to us knowing well the situation. He was under no illusions. The first week of the campaign was heart-breaking.'[71] Perhaps significantly, Sir Francis Acland, the only independent Liberal MP in Cornwall was, 'unable to come to speak for him during the campaign',[72] for which he was deeply apologetic. He 'went down three days early on,' he said, 'was to have gone down again … [but he also] … wanted to speak in the House.'[73] Acland himself attributed the defeat to the fact that the Liberals had:

> too few active members of the party to keep the work going in the House of Commons and to make a good team for by-election work. If the party had been strong enough to make it possible to make speakers like Gwillym Lloyd George and Kingsley Smith and myself

entirely off other work and send them down for the whole course of a by-election the St Ives fight might have been won, but this [was] just what [was] not possible.[74]

Foot failed to regain St Ives for the Liberals, losing by a mere 210 votes. Some of this failure must be put down to the moribund nature of the local Liberal organisation in St Ives at the time, it not having had to contest a general election since 1929. Foot's absence in London for part of the campaign was unhelpful, and likewise the parlous state of the party nationally (it had only twenty-one Members of Parliament) made positive campaigning difficult. With even local supporters like Sir Francis Acland unable to help, the Liberal Party was no longer the major force it had been just a decade earlier. Its capacity to be the vehicle for an independent or 'rebellious' Cornish voice seemed by now to have been much dented.

Yet Foot's campaign in St Ives formed part of the Liberal Party's so-called *General Election in Miniature* strategy,[75] and was hailed by fellow Liberals:

> Foot's large poll – larger than the poll which won the seat for Mr Runciman – in a constituency in which his opponent could plausibly argue that Free Trade would deprive everybody of his work, shows the electoral value of honestly standing by one's principles. Mr Foot made absolutely no compromise on Free Trade or Temperance or anything else, and yet he polled approximately half the votes. With better Organisation, he would have won by 1,000.[76]

Even in defeat, Cornwall showed its support for Liberalism, where, according to the party's own analysis, 'the personality of Mr Foot and local conditions may be held to make an exceptional case'.[77] Indeed, this by-election signalled Cornwall's pre-eminence as part of the Liberal Party's future, as well as its past. Paradoxically, Foot's defeat, being the best result in the *General Election in Miniature* string of by-elections, showed Cornwall's continued adherence to independent behaviour. By backing Foot's unrepentant campaign based on Methodism and Free Trade, Cornwall almost succeeded in propelling him back into Parliament at a point where the party was at an historically low ebb. However, it was still a defeat for Foot and the Liberals, one which was remembered by Hilda Runciman ten years later when writing to Viscount Simon: 'Walter and I have come across [Isaac Foot] in very unpleasant ways and we both warmly dislike him. He behaved extremely badly to Walter in Cornwall and we did so rejoice when Alec Beechman managed to beat him at St Ives!'[78]

The 1939 North Cornwall By-Election: A clear message to Chamberlain on appeasement

The final by-election in Cornwall before the outbreak of the Second World War was caused by the death of Sir Francis Acland. Although he 'had already announced his intention of resigning at the next election on the grounds of ill health',[79] his untimely death caused a by-election that would be a serious test for the Liberal Party, then still at its lowest ever national position, with just twenty-one MPs in Parliament.

Once again the Liberals would benefit from the Labour Party standing aside. The local Labour candidate 'had wanted to stand in the by-election', it was reported, but 'party headquarters in London made the surprising announcement that the party would not be fielding a candidate'.[80] As Tregidga states, 'in the event, both Labour members and dissident Conservatives subsequently signed the nomination papers of Thomas Horabin',[81] the anti-appeasement Liberal candidate in the North Cornwall by-election, the rebellious Tories demonstrating the degree of opposition within their own party against their national leader, Neville Chamberlain. Horabin was thus able to claim that he was 'winning support from all sections'.[82] Winston Churchill, still in the political wilderness, was complicit in supporting Horabin's campaign, exclaiming: 'I think this a fine hour in the life of the Liberal Party because from the moment they realised that rearmament was necessary they have seemed to seek to bring forward the material and moral strength of the country, and I believe that at the moment they represent what is the heart and soul of the British nation.'[83] The Conservative candidate complained that the Liberals, 'were making play, both on the platform and in their literature',[84] of Churchill's implicit support. But this did not stop Horabin campaigning with 'a petition requesting Chamberlain to resign asking the King to entrust to Churchill the formation of a Government of National Defence'.[85] Alongside this Conservative support, the *Manchester Guardian* explained, 'the local supporters of the Labour Party ... do not appear to be violently anti-Liberal. It is estimated that Mr T. L. Horabin, will get 90 per cent of this vote. Some of the [Labour] rank and file are openly supporting him.'[86] Once again, as in the St Ives by-election, the Liberal Party was effectively fighting for its very existence, and, as such, resources were moved in to help the party defend its own seat. Visits were organised for party leader Sir Archibald Sinclair and, perhaps even more significantly, for Lloyd George who 'addressed an open air meeting at Newquay'.[87]

This was a significant by-election for Cornwall, for the Liberal Party and indeed for Britain as a whole, helping to decide the United Kingdom's policy towards the now apparently impending war with Germany. As the *Western Morning News* remarked, 'the people of North Cornwall have an opportunity in the coming by-election of exercising a decisive effect not only upon the affairs of this country and Europe, but those of the whole world'.[88] The Chamberlain government still clung to its policy of appeasement, as Chamberlain himself demonstrated in a letter sent to the Conservative candidate in North Cornwall. Chamberlain, insisting upon the rightness of his policy, explained in his letter that the government 'has always expressed its desire that differences should be settled by discussion and co-operation.'[89] Although Neville Chamberlain had hitherto considered by-elections noteworthy as a 'clear demonstration of the approval of the general policy of the Government by the electors',[90] his attitude seemed to have changed by 1939, leaving the Conservative candidate in North Cornwall in an uncomfortable position.

In his Newquay speech, Lloyd George railed against the ineffective nature of the National Government, exclaiming: 'they are keeping out of the Government the ablest men of their own party, whereas they should be drawing everybody in. It is for you [the voters of North Cornwall] to speak.'[91] The Liberal Party 'criticized the foreign policy of the government as weak and vacillating, bringing Great Britain to the point of war. As ... Lloyd George said at the North Cornwall By-Election ... the country was now the laughing stock of Europe.'[92]

Although a major national political event, the North Cornwall by-election also focused on local issues. As Tregidga has observed:

> Sinclair's advisers recognized the strategic benefits of exploiting rural discontent after tithes emerged as a key issue at the North Cornwall by-election in July 1939. Thomas Horabin, the successful Liberal candidate, adopted a 'clear position' of totally 'removing the burden' thereby enabling him to win the pivotal support of the farming vote. In the adjacent constituency of Bodmin the issue had been regarded as a crucial factor in the Conservative victory in 1935 since Rathbone was the only candidate to promise that he would vote for the total removal of tithes.[93]

Horabin's campaign also tried to focus on old-age pensions. As well as emphasising 'Pride in the part we play in world affairs, Peace that the world and we can be sure of,' he also called for 'Pensions that mean living not merely existing.'[94]

Thomas Horabin was elected in North Cornwall with an increased majority for the Liberals. Commenting at the count, Horabin explained: 'What I have been fighting for is to get a Government which is worthy of the people, a Government to include Mr Churchill, Mr Eden and leaders of the Liberal and Labour parties. We want a government representing the people which will unite the nation. The fact that the majority here has been increased indicates, I think, that the electors support that view.'[95] Neither they, nor he, were to be disappointed. Again, Cornwall had showed its opposition to government policy and the ruling party, again revealing its 'rebellious nature', even to the extent of local Conservatives backing Horabin against their own party leadership. The electorate's support for the Liberal candidate, backed as he was by Lloyd George and tacitly by Churchill, had delivered a warning shot to the government that the policy of appeasement towards Germany and Italy was no longer acceptable.

Conclusion

There are two principal theories as to the significance of by-elections. There is the '"campaign-specific" thesis', described by Norris, which 'sees by-elections as idiosyncratic contests reflecting the strengths and weaknesses of individual candidates and local party organisations in particular constituencies'.[96] However, as Norris adds, 'others suggest that a series of by-elections falls into a systematic pattern which provides an indication of current party strength in the country. As such, by-elections can be treated as equivalent to public opinion polls, perhaps considered more reliable as these contests involve "real" rather than hypothetical votes – the "Referendum" thesis.'[97]

It is possible to place the five Cornish by-elections examined here into either or both categories. The 1922 Bodmin by-election can certainly be placed in both, being a local contest that also had national resonance, acting in part as a 'referendum' against the Lloyd George-led Coalition government. The inherent complexity of Cornish by-elections in this period was exemplified in North Cornwall in 1932 when Liberal 'rebellion' flourished in the sophisticated context of the Liberals being in government. The election of Hilda Runciman in St Ives in 1928 was a sign of departure from the norm, and her gaining the seat was a major fillip for the Liberal Party in Cornwall and for its local prospects in the lead up to the 1929 general election. The narrow failure of Isaac Foot to gain St Ives in 1937 masked the poor state of the Liberal Party at that point, and his close defeat showed, if not the 'rebellious' nature of Cornish voters, then at least that the Liberals (and not the Labour Party) remained the vehicle for electoral 'rebellion' in Cornwall. The by-election also showed Foot's capacity to act as a personal vehicle for Cornish 'opposition'. In contrast to the hostility of the Runcimans, the Labour Party lent its support to Isaac Foot in this election in order to give him the best possible chance to defeat the National Government candidate.

Finally, if one by-election shows the importance of such events, it is

North Cornwall in 1939.[98] By continuing to vote Liberal, the constituency added its voice to the growing clamour against the appeasement policy of the Chamberlain government. But it was a paradoxical result. The constituency returned a Liberal candidate at a time when the party had all but disappeared across the rest of the country, and yet it had also delivered a nationally significant 'referendum' on the Chamberlain government. Taken together, these five by-elections exemplify the 'rebellious' behaviour that voters often allow themselves in by-elections, especially in politically distinct Cornwall in the inter-war period. With the absence of an effective campaigning Labour Party, the contest continued to be a fight between Conservatives and Liberals, or even amongst Liberals themselves, aided and abetted by Labour non-appearance on the ballot paper.

Notes and references

1. C. Cook and J. Ramsden, *By-Elections in British Politics* (London, 1997), p. 5.
2. This figure is slightly inflated due to Ministers, upon appointment, being required to stand for re-election in the period up until 1926.
3. This figure includes by-elections that, by convention, went uncontested during the Second World War.
4. J. K. Pollock, 'British By-Elections Between the Wars', *American Political Science Review* 35 (1941), p. 528.
5. Cook and Ramsden, *By-Elections in British Politics*, p. 5.
6. *Cornish Times*, 10 February 1922.
7. With the exception of Sir Francis Acland, Member of Parliament for Camborne, whose Conservative opponent had failed to return from India in time due to the short notice for the election.
8. *The Times*, 30 December 1918.
9. *The Times*, 24 February 1922.
10. Phrase used by Lord Randolph, 'when the Prime Minister emerged from the crowd of aristocratic and plutocratic mercenaries who surround him to explain his position towards the Liberal cause.' Quoted in M. Foot and A. Highet, *Isaac Foot: A Westcountry Boy – Apostle of England* (London, 2006), p. 130.
11. *The Times*, 24 February 1922.
12. *Cornish Times*, 3 February 1922.
13. M. Dawson, 'Liberalism in Devon and Cornwall, 1910–1931: "The Old-Time Religion"', *Historical Journal* 38:2 (1995), p. 429.
14. *Observer*, 19 February 1922.
15. *Cornish Times*, 10 February 1922.
16. *Cornish Times*, 24 February 1922.
17. *Manchester Guardian*, 23 February 1922.
18. R. McKibbin, *The Evolution of the Labour Party 1910–1924* (Oxford, 1974), p. 120.
19. *Manchester Guardian*, 24 February 1922.
20. *Cornish Times*, 22 January 1922 (Quoting Foot speaking at a public meeting in Liskeard).

21. Distinguished academic and writer who was a leading intellectual and public figure in Cornwall during this period.
22. *Manchester Guardian*, 21 February 1922.
23. Foot and Highet, *Isaac Foot*, p. 138.
24. Foot won by 13,751 votes to 10,610 – a majority of 3,141.
25. *Cornish Times*, 3 March 1922.
26. Ibid.
27. Radcliffe Family of Warleigh Papers (Plymouth and West Devon Records Office) Liberal Victory Song, Bodmin 1922
28. Ibid.
29. Cook and Ramsden, *By-Elections in British Politics*, p. 13.
30. Ibid., pp. 13–14.
31. Ibid., p. 14.
32. *Manchester Guardian*, 18 February 1928, p. 8.
33. R. Douglas, *Liberals – The History of the Liberal and Liberal Democrat Parties* (London, 2005), p. 215.
34. *Cornishman*, 14 March 1928, p. 5.
35. Conservative and Unionist Papers in South East Cornwall (Cornwall Records Office) 385/1 Minutes of a meeting 31 March 1928 – Agent's Report.
36. *Manchester Guardian*, 20 February 1928, p. 9.
37. J. Wallace, 'The Political Career of Walter Runciman, 1st Viscount Runciman of Doxford (1870–1949)', unpublished PhD thesis, University of Newcastle, 1995, p. 294.
38. Former Home Secretary, Former High Commissioner to Palestine and future Leader of the Liberal Party.
39. *Manchester Guardian*, 8 March 1928.
40. Douglas, *Liberals*, p. 215.
41. *Cornishman*, 14 March 1928.
42. E. Vallance, *Women in the House A study of Women Members of Parliament* (London, 1979), p. 28.
43. *Manchester Guardian*, 16 June 1932.
44. North Cornwall Conservative and Unionist Papers (Cornwall Records Office) X382/3 Minutes 29 September 1931.
45. Sir Donald MacLean Papers (Bodleian Library, Oxford) Dep. c.473 Notes by Cornishman, *Western Morning News*, 18 June 1932.
46. Sir Donald MacLean Papers (Bodleian Library, Oxford) Dep. c.473 Political Twins – *Birmingham Daily Mail*, 20 June 1932.
47. *Manchester Guardian*, 28 June 1932.
48. Ibid.
49. *Cornish and Devon Post*, 2 July 1932.
50. *Manchester Guardian*, 7 July 1932.
51. Ibid., 12 July 1932.
52. C. Cook, *The Age of Alignment Electoral Politics in Britain 1922–1929* (London, 1975).
53. *Manchester Guardian*, 31 January 1933.
54. Ibid., 25 July 1932.
55. Ibid., 7 July 1932.
56. Ibid., 31 May 1937.

57. Ibid., 25 June 1937.
58. Foot Family Papers (Plymouth and West Devon Records Office) 2762–68 Letter from Jeanette Peacock to Sarah Foot.
59. *West Briton*, 31 May 1937.
60. Cook, *The Age of Alignment Electoral Politics*.
61. G. Tregidga, 'Turning of the Tide? A Case Study of the Liberal Party in Provincial Britain in the Late 1930s', *Historical Association* (2007), p. 355.
62. *Manchester Guardian*, 25 June 1937.
63. Foot and Highet, *Isaac Foot*, p. 210.
64. *Manchester Guardian*, 25 June 1937.
65. *Manchester Guardian*, 2 July 1937.
66. Eldest son of Sir Francis Acland and future 15th Baronet.
67. *Manchester Guardian*, 7 June 1937.
68. *West Briton*, 14 June 1937.
69. Ibid, 10 June 1937.
70. Ibid.
71. Ibid., 15 July 1937.
72. Foot and Highet, *Isaac Foot*, p. 211.
73. North Cornwall Liberal Papers, *Our Member's Monthly Letter* 5:10 (July 1937).
74. Ibid.
75. The Liberal Party, under Sir Archibald Sinclair, was becoming more organised in terms of contesting by-elections and the party underwent a process of evaluating the numerous by-election results of 1937 which was used to advise future party strategy – it was referred to as The General Election in Miniature.
76. Viscount Thurso Papers (Churchill College, Cambridge University) THRS II 62/4 Political Inferences from the Miniature General Election 1937 (1. Importance of Principles)
77. Ibid., (2. Labour will vote for an Independent Liberal)
78. Viscount Simon Papers (Bodleian Library, Oxford) MS 97 Folios 59–61 Letter from Viscountess Runciman to Viscount Simon 9 December 1947.
79. G. Tregidga, *The Liberal Party in South West Britain since 1918* (Exeter, 2000), p. 92.
80. Ibid., p. 93.
81. Tregidga, 'Turning of the Tide?', p. 355.
82. *Post and Weekly News*, 8 July 1939.
83. Ibid.
84. Ibid.
85. J. Reynolds and I. Hunter, 'Liberal Class Warrior', *Journal of Liberal History* 28 (Autumn 2000), p. 17.
86. *Manchester Guardian*, 11 July 1939.
87. *Manchester Guardian*, 10 July 1939.
88. THRS II 66/10 *Western Morning News*, 19 June 1939.
89. *Observer*, 2 July 1939.
90. E. G. Lewis, *British By-Elections as a Reflection of Public Opinion* (Berkeley [CA], 1943), p. 200.
91. *Manchester Guardian*, 10 July 1939.
92. Lewis (1943), p. 189.
93. Tregidga, 'Turning of the Tide?', p. 357.

94. *Post and Weekly News*, 8 July 1939.
95. *Manchester Guardian*, 15 July 1939.
96. P. Norris, *British By-Elections – The Volatile Electorate* (Oxford, 1990), p. 1.
97. Ibid.
98. It also enjoyed the distinction of being the last successful by-election defence for the Liberal Party in the UK before 1987.

Bernard Deacon: Bibliography

2011

Review of Cathryn Pearce, *Cornish Wrecking 1700–1860* in *Local Population Studies* 87 (2011).

2010

Cornwall and the Cornish, Alison Hodge: Penzance, 2010.

'Mining the Data: what can a quantitative approach tell us about the micro-geography of nineteenth century Cornish mining?' in P. Payton (ed.) *Cornish Studies: Eighteen*, (Exeter, 2010), pp. 15–32.

2009

'Cornishness and Englishness: nested identities or incompatible ideologies?', *International Journal of Regional and Local Studies* 5:2 (2009), pp. 9–29.

2008

Review of John Rule, *Cornish Cases: Essays in Eighteenth and Nineteenth Century Social History*, in *English Historical Review* 123:502 (2008), pp. 769–71.

'*Cornish Cases* and Cornish Social History' in P. Payton (ed.), *Cornish Studies: Sixteen* (Exeter, 2008), pp. 229–43.

2007

Cornwall: A Concise History, University of Wales Press: Cardiff, 2007.

(with Ray Chubb, Michael Everson, Craig Weatherill and Nicholas Williams) *Form and Content in Revived Cornish* (Westport, 2007).

'County, Nation, Ethnic group? The shaping of the Cornish identity', *International Journal of Regional and Local Studies* 3:1 (2007), pp. 5–29.

(with Sharron Schwartz) 'Cornish Identities and Migration: a multi-scalar approach', *Global Networks* 7:3 (2007), pp. 289–306.

'Communities, Families and Migration: some evidence from Cornwall', *Family & Community History* 10:1 (2007), pp. 49–60.

'Reconstructing a Regional Migration System: net migration in Cornwall', *Local Population Studies* 78 (2007), pp. 28–46.

'"We don't travel much, only to South Africa": Reconstructing Nineteenth-century Cornish Migration Patterns', in P. Payton (ed.), *Cornish Studies: Fifteen* (Exeter, 2007), pp. 90–116.

2006

'Cornish or Klingon? The Standardization of the Cornish language', in P. Payton (ed.), *Cornish Studies: Fourteen* (Exeter, 2006), pp. 13–23.

2005

'From "Cornish Studies" to "Critical Cornish Studies": reflections on methodology', in P. Payton (ed.), *Cornish Studies: Twelve* (Exeter, 2005), pp. 13–29.

2004

The Cornish Family (Fowey, 2004).

'Under Construction: culture and regional formation in south-west England', *European Urban and Regional Studies* 11:3 (2004), pp. 213–25.

(with Moira Donald) 'In Search of Community History', *Family & Community History* 7:1 (2004), pp. 13–19.

'The Cornish Identity' in *Heritage Unlocked* (London, 2004), pp. 8–10.

Review of John Titford, *Searching for Surnames*, Countryside Books, 2002, in *Family & Community History* 7 (2004), pp. 81–82.

2003

(with Dick Cole and Garry Tregidga) *MK and the History of Cornish Nationalism* (Cardiff, 2003).

'British National Identity' and 'The Cornish and Manx Languages' in D. Loades (ed.), *Reader's Guide to British History* (London, 2003), pp. 657–59 and 765–66.

'Propaganda and the Tudor State or Propaganda of the Tudor historians?: a review of J. P. D. Cooper's *Propaganda and the Tudor State*, in P. Payton (ed.), *Cornish Studies: Eleven* (Exeter, 2003), pp. 317–28.

2002

'Religion and Community: Frameworks and Issues', *Journal of Family & Community History* 5:1 (2002), pp. 33–44.

'Cornish Studies: new discipline or rhetorical space?', in P. Payton (ed.), *Cornish Studies: Ten* (Exeter, 2002), pp. 24–43.

2001

'Imagining the Fishing: Artists and Fishermen in Late Nineteenth Century Cornwall', *Rural History* 12:2 (2001), pp. 159–78.

2000

The Cornish and the Council of Europe Framework Convention for the Protection of National Minorities, Cornish National Minority Steering Group with the assistance of the Joseph Rowntree Reform Trust (Truro, 2000).

'In search of the missing "turn": the spatial dimension and Cornish Studies', in P. Payton (ed.), *Cornish Studies: Eight* (Exeter, 2000), pp. 213–30.

Foreword to Alan Kent (ed.) *Voices from West Barbary: an anthology of Anglo-Cornish poetry 1549–1928* (London, 2000), pp. 13–14.

Review of John Angarrack, *Breaking the Chains*, Cornish Stannary Publications, Camborne, 1999, in P. Payton (ed.), *Cornish Studies: Eight* (Exeter, 2000), pp. 231–34.

Review of Barry Reay, Microhistories: demography, society and culture in rural England, 1800–1930, 1996, in *Family & Community History* 3 (2000), pp. 161–62.

Review of Edwin Jaggard, *Cornwall Politics in the Age of Reform* (Woodbridge, 1999), in *The Local Historian* 30 (2000), pp. 269–70.

1999

(with Lynne Thompson) 'Back to the land? Service and Self-interest in Adult Education in Rural England 1920–45', in B. Merrill (ed.) *The Final Frontier; Exploring Spaces in the Education of Adults, Proceedings of the 29th Annual SCUTREA Conference* (University of Warwick, 1999), pp. 63–68.

1998

'Proto-regionalisation: the case of Cornwall', *Journal of Regional and Local Studies* 18 (1998), pp. 27–41.

'A forgotten migration stream: the Cornish movement to England Wales in the nineteenth century', in P. Payton (ed.) *Cornish Studies: Six* (Exeter, 1998), pp. 96–117.

(with Ella Westland) 'Centering a Degree on the Periphery: curriculum design in Cornwall and the politics of space' in R. Benn (ed.), *Research, teaching, learning: making connections in the education of adults. Proceedings of the 28th Annual SCUTREA Conference*, University of Exeter, 1998, pp. 47–51.

Review of J. D. Marshall, *The Tyranny of the Discrete. A discussion of the problems of local history in England* (Aldershot, 1997), in *Family & Community History* 1 (1998), pp. 86–87.

1997

'"The hollow jarring of the distant steam engines": images of Cornwall between West Barbary and Delectable Duchy' in E. Westland (ed.), *Cornwall: The cultural construction of place* (Penzance, 1997), pp. 7–24.

'Proto-industrialization and Potatoes: a revised narrative for nineteenth century Cornwall', in P. Payton (ed.) *Cornish Studies: Five* (Exeter, 1997), pp. 60–84.

1996

'Language Revival and Language Debate: modernity and postmodernity', in P. Payton
(ed.) *Cornish Studies: Four* (Exeter, 1996), pp. 88–106.
Review of Marilyn Palmer and Peter Neaveson, *Industry in the Landscape 1700–1900*,
(London, 1994), in *The Local Historian* 26 (1996), p. 120.

1995

Review of Norman Pounds, *The Culture of the English People: Iron Age to the Industrial
Revolution* (Cambridge, 1994), in *The Local Historian* 25 (1995), p. 116.

1993

'And shall Trelawny Die? the Cornish identity' in P. Payton (ed.) *Cornwall Since the
War: The Contemporary History of a European Region* (Redruth, 1993), pp. 200–23.
(with Philip Payton) 'The Ideology of Language Revival' in P. Payton (ed.) *Cornwall
Since the War: The Contemporary History of a European Region* (Redruth, 1993),
pp. 271–90.
(with Philip Payton) 'Re-inventing Cornwall: culture change on the European
periphery' in P. Payton (ed.) *Cornish Studies: One* (Exeter, 1993), pp. 60–84.

1992

(with Colin Robins) *Merlin's Diner* (Tiverton, 1992).
'Conybeare for Ever' in T. Knight (ed.), *Old Redruth: Original Studies of the Town's
History* (Redruth, 1992), pp. 37–43.

1989

Liskeard and its People in the Nineteenth Century (Redruth, 1989).
'The smile on the face of the Cornish cat', *Planet: The Welsh Internationalist* 72
(1988–89), pp. 3–8.

1988

(with Andrew George and Ronald Perry) *Cornwall at the Crossroads* (Redruth, 1988).
'"A race apart": the fishing communities of the west in the nineteenth century', *Old
Cornwall* 10 (1988), pp. 268–71.

1987

'Migration and the Mining Industry in East Cornwall in the mid-Nineteenth
Century', *Journal of the Royal Institution of Cornwall* 10 (1986–87), pp. 84–104.

1986

'How many went? The size of the Great Cornish Emigration of the nineteenth
century', *Devon and Cornwall Notes and Queries* (1986), pp. 7–8.

'Heroic Individualists? The Cornish miners and the five-week month 1872–74', *Cornish Studies* 14 (1986), pp. 39–52.

1983

'The Electoral Impact of Cornish Nationalism' in C. O. Luain (ed.) *For a Celtic Future: A Tribute to Alan Heusaff* (Dublin, 1983), pp. 243–52.

'Is Cornwall an Internal Colony?, in C. O. Luain (ed.) *For a Celtic Future: A Tribute to Alan Heusaff* (Dublin, 1983), pp. 259–72.

1982

'Attempts at Unionism by Cornish Metal Miners in 1866', *Cornish Studies* 10 (1982), pp. 27–36.

Forthcoming

'D'une Ethnie à Une Nation? Les trois moments de l'identité cornouaillaise moderne', *Le Bulletin d'Histoire Politique*

'Regional Identity and Regionalism in late Nineteenth-century England; discursive terrains and rhetorical strategies', *Journal of Historical Sociology*

'Cornwall, an Inside-out Industrial Region', in P. Payton, H. Doe and A. Kennerley (eds), *The Maritime History of Cornwall* (Exeter).

'Chameleon Celts: the Cornish in the Americas' in M. Newton (ed), *Celts in the Americas* (Cape Breton).